NIGREDO

PART ONE OF A COURSE IN MODERN ALCHEMY

Dr Simon Robinson

NIGREDO — Revised Edition (2025)
Part One of A Course in Modern Alchemy
© 2025 Dr. Simon Robinson. All rights reserved.

No part of this publication may be reproduced, stored in a retrieval system, or transmitted in any form or by any means—electronic, mechanical, photocopying, recording, or otherwise—without prior written permission of the copyright holder.

First published in the United Kingdom by Dr. Simon Robinson

ISBN: 978-1-0684310-0-5
Printed and distributed by IngramSpark

Book design and typography by the author.
Text set in Crimson Text.
Headings set in IM Fell English.
Cover and interior images created by the author with AI assistance.

Some editorial assistance and study guide formatting provided with the support of AI tools (ChatGPT, Perplexity, Ideogram). All core content and insights remain the author's own.

This is a work of nonfiction rooted in spiritual practice. The information contained herein is intended for educational and contemplative purposes only. The author assumes no responsibility for any outcomes resulting from the use or interpretation of this material.

A catalogue record for this book is available from the British Library.

This book is printed on acid-free paper that meets the ANSI Z39.48 standard for permanence.

contact@drsimonrobinson.com

Introduction

*"When you see your matter going black, rejoice:
for that is the beginning of the work."*

- *Rosarium Philosophorum* (ca. 1550), as cited in Johannes Fabricius, *Alchemy: The Medieval Alchemists and Their Royal Art*, p. 159.

Nigredo

The Emerald Tablet

Tis true without lying, certain and most true.
That which is below is like that which is above and that which is above is like that which is below
To do the miracle of one only thing
And as all things have been and arose from one by the mediation of one:
so all things have their birth from this one thing by adaptation.
The Sun is its father, the moon its mother,
the wind hath carried it in its belly, the earth is its nurse.
The father of all perfection in the whole world is here.
Its force or power is entire if it be converted into earth.
Separate thou the earth from the fire,
the subtle from the gross
sweetly with great industry.
It ascends from the earth to the heaven and again it descends to the earth
and receives the force of things superior and inferior.
By this means you shall have the glory of the whole world
and thereby all obscurity shall fly from you.
Its force is above all force,
for it vanquishes every subtle thing and penetrates every solid thing.
So was the world created.
From this are and do come admirable adaptations where of the means is here in this.
Hence I am called Hermes Trismegist,
having the three parts of the philosophy of the whole world.
That which I have said of the operation of the Sun is accomplished and ended.[1]

---

[1] Newton, Isaac. "Keynes MS. 28," *The Chymistry of Isaac Newton*, ed. William R. Newman, June 2010.

INTRODUCTION

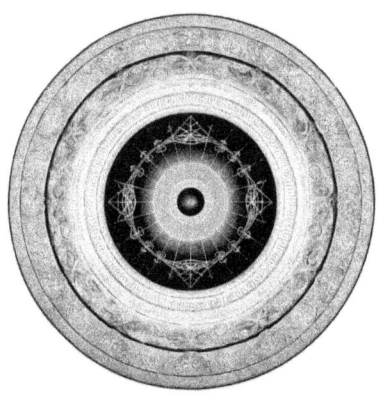

Preface

"No matter how isolated you are and how lonely you feel, if you do your work truly and conscientiously, unknown friends will come and seek you."[2]

Alchemy is not for the faint of heart. It is not a hobby, nor a passing interest, but a transformation— one that strips away every illusion, every false certainty, and leaves only the raw material of what you truly are. This book does not seek to convince —it is a guide, and only those already walking the path will find its meaning.

I began writing *Nigredo* as a collection of notes — fragments of insight that helped me navigate my own journey. I had spent years immersed in different traditions, first studying Kabbalah and Gnostic Christianity before finding my way to Buddhist philosophy. Unlike the cryptic and often inaccessible texts of Western esotericism, Buddhism provided clear, structured teachings, freely available to anyone willing to look. It was there that I found the same themes that had drawn me to alchemy: the dissolution of the self, the refining of consciousness, and the slow, deliberate work of transformation.

---

[2] Jung, C. G. (1976). *Letters of C. G. Jung: Volume II, 1951—1961* (G. Adler & A. Jaffé, Eds.) (R. F. C. Hull, Trans.). Princeton University Press, p. 595

Nigredo

This book is the first in a four-part course in spiritual alchemy, mirroring the classical process of transmutation: *Nigredo* (blackness), *Albedo* (whiteness), *Citrinitas* (yellowness), and *Rubedo* (redness). The stages of colour reflect the changing nature of the philosopher's stone, which, in my definition, is the *Subjective Reality* of the alchemist. In the beginning, this stone — our mind, our being — is wild and chaotic, shaped by conditioning and blind reaction. In the *Nigredo* stage, we confront this darkness. We stop rejecting the *Shadow*, instead choosing to work with it, to dissolve the *dross* of our habitual patterns. As our understanding deepens, the stone lightens, progressing through the phases of purification until it becomes gold.

But none of this is easy.

Alchemy, at its core, is a destructive process. It does not build upon the existing self but demands its dissolution. This is not a practice for those seeking comfort. It is for those who have already glimpsed the truth that something is deeply wrong—not with the world, but with their own perception of it. If you have ever felt the deep, gnawing sense that there is something more—that beneath the distractions, the addictions, the endless loops of suffering—lies a hidden structure, a way through the maze, then this book may be of use to you.

But be warned: the price of knowledge is everything you think you are.

To those who choose to step forward, I offer no promises, only this—what follows is not theory, nor philosophy in the conventional sense, but the result of direct experience. It is my map, drawn from my own journey. It may not align perfectly with yours, but given that all true paths lead to the same destination, perhaps it will help you navigate the impossible.

Take your time. Be patient. This work is slow and often brutal. You will lose things along the way—beliefs, attachments, even the comforting certainty of who you think you are. But you will also gain something greater: a glimpse of reality as it is, unfiltered, unmediated. A moment of clarity in the darkness.

And that is where the real journey begins...

INTRODUCTION

CONTENTS

The Emerald Tablet	4
Preface	5
Illustrations & Tables	10
Introduction	11

STUDY GUIDE

How to Use This Book	14
Useful Resources	41
Youtube Resources	44
Essential Definitions	45

MYTHOS

1. *The Landscape*	51
2. *The Alchemist*	57
3. *Evolution of Adulthood*	63
4. *The Symbols and their Meanings*	67
5. *The Fable of Alchemy*	73
6. *Enlightenment*	79
7. *The Call to Adventure*	87
8. *The Fisher-King Wound*	93
9. *The Rebis & Rejection of Identity*	99
10. *The Shadow & The Lost Infant*	103
11. *The Dark Night of the Soul*	109
12. *The Seed of Nirvāṇa*	113

Dharma

13.	*The Realities*	121
14.	*The Matrix of Conditioned Reality*	125
15.	*The 72 Types of Entities*	131
16.	*Consciousness*	137
17.	*The Mental Factors*	147
18.	*Materiality*	165
19.	*The Forces that Drive The Matrix*	177
20.	*Saṃsāra*	185
21.	*The Four Noble Truths*	191
22.	*The Cycle of Becoming*	201
23.	*The Fetters that Bind*	211
24.	*The Eightfold Noble Path*	219

Object

25.	*The Great Work*	229
26.	*The Trees of Consciousness*	239
27.	*The Golden Middle Path*	249
28.	*The Four Grades of Realisation*	259
29.	*Realms of Existence*	265
30.	*Different Worlds and Jhāna*	273
31.	*Path Consciousness*	281
32.	*Sotāpanna*	287
33.	*Sakadāgāmī*	295
34.	*Anāgāmī*	301
35.	*The Subtle Fetters*	305
36.	*Arahant*	313

INTRODUCTION

SUBJECT

Introduction to Subject	321
37. *What Went Before*	323
38. *The Fall*	329
39. *Exile*	335
40. *Wandering*	341
41. *The Night*	347
42. *Confusion*	353
43. *Commitment*	357
44. *Spiritual Orientation*	361
45. *No Self*	367
46. *First Steps*	371
47. *Establishing the Way*	375
48. *The Key to the Gate*	381

GLOSSARY & INDEX

Alchemic Terms	388
Buddhist Terms	390
States of Consciousness	396
Metaphors	397
Psychological Concepts	397
Kabbalistic Terms	398
Practices & Techniques	399
States & Attainments	400
Index	401
Part Two – Albedo	403

Illustrations & Tables

The Emerald Tablet	4
The Retort	46
The Early Alchemic Path	47
The Three Realities	78
Aspects of 'The Calling'	91
The Fisher-King Wound	92
Aspects of Healing the Lost Infant	107
Aspects of The Dark Night	111
The Dark Night of the Soul	117
Aspects of the Nature of Reality	120
Components of Conditioned Reality	120
Four Great Elements	120
The Five Skandhas	130
The 72 Types of Entities	136
Consciousness root types	136
Sensory Sphere Citta	141
Form-sphere Citta	141
Formless Sphere Citta	142
Path and Fruit Citta	142
The 8 Consciousnesses & Elements	145
Realms of Consciousness	145
Mundane Citta (81 types)	146
Supramundane Citta (40 types)	146
Universal Mental Factors	148
Occasional Mental Factors	149
Categories of Mental Factors	150
Universal Mental Factors	152
Occasional Mental Factors	153
Unwholesome Mental Factors	156
Universal Beautiful Mental Factors	157
Occasional Beautiful Mental Factors	161
A candle metaphor	164
Material Categories	172
Material Categories by Type	172
The 28 Categories of Matter	173
Characteristics of Matter	175
The 4 Realms of Consciousness	176
Conditioned Reality	183
Noble Eightfold Path Factors	184
Aspects and Manifest. of Saṃsāra.	190
Stages of Alchemical Development	195
The 12 Links of Dependent Origination	198
The Noble Eightfold Path Components	199
The 12 Links of Dependent Arising	200
The Causes of Suffering	209
The Ten Fetters	210
The Gross Fetters	218
The 4 Stages of the Hinayana Vehicle	218
'Grades' of Enlightenment	228
The Great Work	228
The Ten Sephirot and Their Attributes	237
3-D Tree Of Life	238
Layers of Consciousness	241
Stages of Enlightenment	263
The Realms of Six Classes of Being	264
Life-continuum of different beings	267
Roots of Consciousness	269
Formless Realm (Arūpa Loka)	271
Form Realm (Rūpa Loka)	272
Sensual Realm (Kama Loka)	272
Jhanic Realms	279
The Rebis	285
Enlightenment by Fetters	291
Citta involved in Enlightenment	291
First Three Gross Fetters	292
The Three Marks of Existence	298
The Subtle Fetters	311
What Went Before	328
The Fall	328
The Transformation of Sub. Awareness	334
Symbology of Genesis	338
Wandering	344
Types of Suffering	344
The Long Dark Night of the Soul	352
Confusion	352
Commitment	359
Spiritual Orientation	365
Progression	365
Progress Indicators	365

Introduction

"The real nature of matter was unknown to the alchemist: he knew it only in hints. In seeking to explore it he projected the unconscious into the darkness of matter in order to illuminate it." [3]

Welcome to the first stage of an extraordinary journey into spiritual alchemy. This book represents the initial phase of a four-part course exploring the ancient art of inner transformation — a practice that predates and transcends religious boundaries while remaining deeply relevant to modern spiritual seekers.

Nigredo, meaning *blackness* or *darkness*, marks our entry point into genuine spiritual work. It is here, in the depths of our own *Shadow*, that we begin the process of transforming our consciousness through what I call spiritual alchemy — a systematic approach to hacking your own reality.

This isn't just another book about meditation or mysticism. Rather, it's a practical guide to understanding how religions initially form around the seed of enlightenment, though they often become preoccupied with the flower it grows into. By combining alchemical wisdom with Buddhist insights, we'll explore how to navigate the challenging terrain of spiritual awakening.

---

[3] Jung, C.G. (1968). *Psychology and Alchemy (Collected Works of C.G. Jung Vol. 12).* Princeton University Press, p. 244.

NIGREDO

The alchemists of old deliberately obscured their teachings, partly to avoid persecution from the church, but also because the very nature of their work defied simple explanation. They left us a cryptic map to transformation — one that becomes clearer only through dedicated study and practice.

While this book stands alone as a guide to the *Dark Night* of spiritual work, it is part of a larger system. The complete course follows the four classical stages of alchemical transformation: *Nigredo* (blackness), *Albedo* (whiteness), *Citrinitas* (yellowness), and *Rubedo* (redness). Each stage builds upon the previous, creating a comprehensive path to inner transformation.

I've structured this work to be both profound and accessible, weaving together practical exercises with deeper philosophical insights. Throughout the text, you'll find references to Buddhist teachings, particularly the *Abhidhamma*, which provides a sophisticated framework for understanding consciousness and its transformation.

A word of caution: this is serious spiritual work. While I maintain a lighthearted tone, the practices and insights contained here can profoundly impact your understanding of reality. This isn't about adopting new beliefs or following doctrine — it's about discovering the truth of your own nature through direct experience.

What follows is my understanding of alchemy, drawn from years of study and practice. Take what resonates, question everything, and remember that this is a guide, not gospel. The real work happens in your own consciousness.

May this book serve as a reliable companion on your journey through the darkness of transformation.

Good luck

INTRODUCTION

Overview &
Study Guide

How to Use This Book

This book represents the first stage of a comprehensive journey into spiritual alchemy. While you can read it cover-to-cover like a traditional text, you'll get the most benefit by approaching it as an interactive workbook for inner transformation.

Structure and Organisation

The book is divided into four main sections:

- **Mythos**: Exploring foundational concepts through myth and symbol
- **Dharma**: Examining the mechanics of consciousness and reality
- **Object**: Understanding the practical aspects of transformation
- **Subject**: Working with personal experience and integration

Study Guides

At the end of each chapter, you'll find detailed study guides that include:

- New terminology and concepts introduced
- Core themes to contemplate
- Practical exercises and reflection points
- Connections to other chapters and ideas

Working with the Material

Take your time with each chapter. The concepts build upon each other, and rushing through won't serve your development. Feel free to:

- Read chapters multiple times
- Make personal notes and observations
- Spend time with the reflection points
- Practice the exercises until they feel natural

A Note on Difficulty

Some concepts may initially seem abstract or challenging. This is normal and expected. The material is designed to stretch your understanding gradually. If you encounter a particularly difficult section:

- Review the prerequisite chapters
- Consult the glossary
- Focus on what resonates personally
- Remember that confusion often precedes breakthrough

Personal Practice

While this book provides a theoretical framework, the real work happens in your own consciousness. Set aside regular time for:

- Quiet contemplation
- Working with the exercises
- Journaling your insights
- Observing changes in your perception

Introduction

Technical Aspects

I. INTRODUCTION TO SPIRITUAL ALCHEMY

A. The Great Work

- Personal transformation through inner alchemy
- Synthesis of Western and Eastern wisdom traditions
- The four stages: Nigredo, Albedo, Citrinitas, Rubedo

B. Alchemical Symbolism

- The Emerald Tablet and its significance
- Metaphorical language of transformation
- Importance of personal interpretation

II. FOUNDATIONS OF CONSCIOUSNESS

A. The Nature of Mind

- Citta: Fundamental units of awareness
- Cetasikas: Mental factors accompanying consciousness
- Nāma and Rūpa: Mental and physical aspects of reality

B. Levels of Consciousness

- Sense-sphere Realm (Kāmāvacara)
- Form Realm (Rūpa-loka)
- Formless Realm (Arūpa-loka)
- Transcendental Consciousness

C. The Life Continuum (Bhavaṅga)

- Underlying stream of consciousness
- Karmic influence on rebirth

III. REALITY AND PERCEPTION

A. The Illusion of Stability

- Impermanence of all phenomena
- Arbitrary nature of labels and concepts

B. Space and Movement

- Space as a mental construct
- Illusion of movement through air element

C. Intrinsic vs. Dependent Nature

- Self-defining vs. relational phenomena
- Implications for understanding reality

IV. THE PATH OF TRANSFORMATION

A. Karmic Mechanics

- Karma as a force shaping future moments
- Wholesome vs. unwholesome actions
- Skilled vs. unskilled karma

B. The Ten Fetters (Saṃyojana)

- Gross fetters: Attachments to worldly phenomena
- Subtle fetters: Internal conceptual barriers

C. Stages of Enlightenment

- 1. Sotāpanna (Stream-enterer)
- 2. Sakadāgāmī (Once-returner)
- 3. Anāgāmī (Non-returner)
- 4. Arahant (Fully liberated)

D. The Buddha and Beyond

- Distinction between Arahant and Buddha
- Nirvāṇa with and without residue

Nigredo

V. PRACTICAL ASPECTS OF THE GREAT WORK

A. Meditation and Jhāna

- Samatha: Tranquility meditation
- Vipassanā: Insight meditation
- Jhanic states and their role in transformation

B. Ethical Development

- Importance of moral conduct
- Cultivation of wholesome mental factors

C. The Middle Way

- Balancing extremes in practice and understanding
- Application of the Diamond Sūtra's teachings

VI. INTEGRATION OF OPPOSITES

A. The Rebis

- Symbol of unified duality
- Transcendence of gender and conceptual opposites

B. Shadow Work

- Confronting the Fisher-King Wound
- Integration of rejected aspects of self

C. Non-Self (Anatta)

- Challenging the illusion of a permanent self
- Liberation through understanding emptiness

VII. ADVANCED CONCEPTS

A. The Heart Base

- Physical anchor for consciousness
- Electromagnetic field theories

B. Psychic Abilities

- Development of siddhis through practice
- Cautions and ethical considerations

C. Buddhahood and Beyond

- The alchemical "Rubedo" state
- Compassion and the bodhisattva path

This outline provides a comprehensive overview of the main themes and learning path presented in Nigredo. As the aspiring alchemist progresses through these topics, they will develop a deeper understanding of consciousness, reality, and the transformative journey of spiritual alchemy. The integration of Buddhist philosophy, particularly Abhidhamma, with Western alchemical traditions offers a unique framework for self-discovery and ultimate liberation.

Introduction

Chapter Overview

1. The Landscape

Spiritual alchemy begins with an unflinching look at reality, not as we assume it to be, but as it is experienced. This chapter explores the subjective nature of existence, showing how our perception shapes not only our external world but also the internal landscape we must navigate in the work of transformation. The alchemical journey is not a comfortable one —it demands that we question the foundation of our beliefs, our sense of self, and the nature of suffering itself. Here, we examine why suffering is not simply an affliction to be avoided but a necessary element in the refinement of consciousness. Just as a flame tempers metal, discomfort and inner conflict create the conditions for true change. The chapter also introduces the idea that reality is not fixed, but a fluid construct shaped by our conditioning, habits, and mental formations. This realisation is the first step in developing the awareness required for deep inner work.

2. The Alchemist

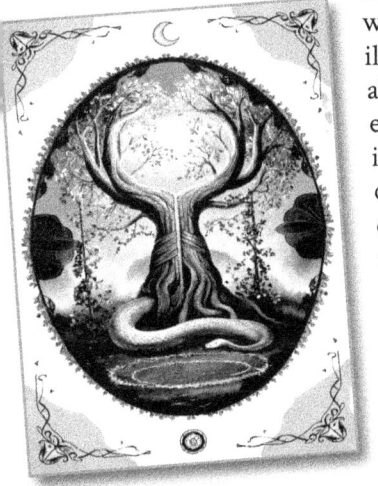

An alchemist is not simply someone who studies transformation but one who embodies it. This chapter explores the qualities and mindset that define an alchemist, moving beyond the historical figure of the medieval philosopher to the psychological and spiritual seeker of today. The process of alchemy does not begin with external experiments, but with an internal shift —a willingness to deconstruct the illusions that have built up over a lifetime. The alchemist must learn to observe their thoughts and emotions without attachment, recognising that the self is not a fixed entity but an evolving process. The chapter also discusses the importance of retracing developmental steps, returning to a state of innocence not through ignorance, but through deep wisdom. Using the metaphor of the Garden of Eden, we see how the work of the alchemist is not to acquire new knowledge but to strip away the conditioning that has obscured their original nature.

NIGREDO

3. Evolution of 'Adulthood'

Adulthood is often seen as a stage of completion —a point at which we have accumulated knowledge, skills, and stability. Yet, from an alchemical perspective, adulthood is not an achievement but a form of imprisonment. This chapter explores how the process of growing up often distances us from direct experience, replacing the immediacy of childhood perception with a rigid framework of language, expectations, and conditioned responses. We no longer see reality as it is, but through a filter constructed by society, education, and personal experience. The chapter delves into how the mind creates conceptual frameworks to simplify and categorise reality, and how these frameworks, while useful, also limit us. To move forward in alchemy, one must first unlearn —dismantling the unconscious structures that dictate how we perceive the world. This does not mean rejecting knowledge, but refining it, learning to balance wisdom with direct experience.

4. The Symbols and Their Meanings

Alchemy speaks in symbols, using metaphor and allegory to convey truths that cannot be grasped by logic alone. This chapter introduces the key symbols of alchemy, from the philosopher's stone to the prima materia, and explores their deeper meanings. More than mere representations, these symbols act as catalysts, shifting the consciousness of those who engage with them. The chapter examines the historical use of symbolism in esoteric traditions, showing how alchemists deliberately encoded their teachings to protect them from misuse and misunderstanding. However, understanding alchemical symbols requires more than intellectual study; it demands inner reflection and personal experience. Just as a single symbol can have multiple meanings depending on the stage of one's journey, the chapter explores how the interpretation of symbols evolves as one progresses in the Great Work.

INTRODUCTION

5. The Fable of Alchemy

Alchemy has long been shrouded in mystery, with tales of turning lead into gold capturing the imagination of those outside the tradition. However, this chapter reveals that these stories are not about physical transformation, but the transmutation of the self. The great secret of alchemy is not found in laboratories but in the depths of one's own consciousness. This chapter explores how medieval alchemists used coded language and metaphor to describe a process that takes place within the mind and spirit. By understanding the fable of alchemy —how the base elements of human experience are refined into something luminous —we begin to see that the search for the philosopher's stone is, in truth, the search for ultimate self-realisation.

6. Enlightenment

The concept of enlightenment is often misunderstood as an achievement, a final state of wisdom or bliss. This chapter dismantles the myths surrounding enlightenment, revealing it as an ongoing process rather than a destination. The irony of spiritual seeking is that the very desire for understanding can become an obstacle —grasping for enlightenment is, itself, a form of attachment. The chapter explores how enlightenment cannot be acquired, but only recognised, and why it often eludes those who seek it too aggressively. Drawing from Buddhist philosophy and alchemical principles, we examine why direct descriptions of enlightenment fail, and why the realisation of non-duality cannot be forced through effort alone.

NIGREDO

7. The Call to Adventure

The path of transformation is not for everyone, and those who embark upon it often do so reluctantly. This chapter explores how certain individuals feel a pull toward spiritual work, even before they fully understand what that entails. The call to adventure may come in the form of dissatisfaction with the world, an unexplained longing for deeper meaning, or a sudden crisis that forces one to reexamine their assumptions. This chapter also discusses the unique challenges of answering the call —how it can disrupt one's sense of stability, alienate one from familiar relationships, and demand sacrifices that not everyone is prepared to make. However, the chapter  also emphasises that ignoring the call does not make it disappear; it only delays the inevitable confrontation with the deeper truths of existence.

8. The Fisher-King Wound

 At the heart of the alchemical journey lies a wound —one that shapes our entire experience of life. This chapter explores the myth of the Fisher-King, a wounded ruler whose suffering extends to the entire land, turning it barren. This wound is not physical, but existential; it represents the deep psychic scars inflicted by cultural conditioning, emotional suppression, and the unspoken pain carried by all individuals. The chapter examines how spiritual work requires not the avoidance of pain, but its conscious engagement. By turning toward the wound rather than away from it, we begin to understand its origins and ultimately transform it. In doing so, the barren wasteland of our inner world begins to heal, allowing new growth and insight to emerge.

Introduction

9. The Rebis and Rejection of Identity

One of the greatest challenges on the alchemical path is the dissolution of identity. This chapter explores the Rebis, the alchemical symbol of unity, which represents the reconciliation of opposites — male and female, light and dark, conscious and unconscious. The self, as we commonly understand it, is a construction held together by social conditioning, memory, and personal narrative. However, the alchemist must recognise that this identity is not fixed; it is a temporary structure that can be deconstructed and reassembled. This process is not without difficulty, as it requires stepping beyond the familiar and embracing the unknown. The chapter discusses the psychological resistance that arises when one begins to question the reality of the self, and the liberation that comes when this resistance is finally overcome.

10. The Shadow & The Lost Infant

Alchemy is not about escaping from the darker aspects of the self but fully integrating them. This chapter introduces two key elements of psychological transformation: the Shadow and the lost infant. The Shadow consists of the aspects

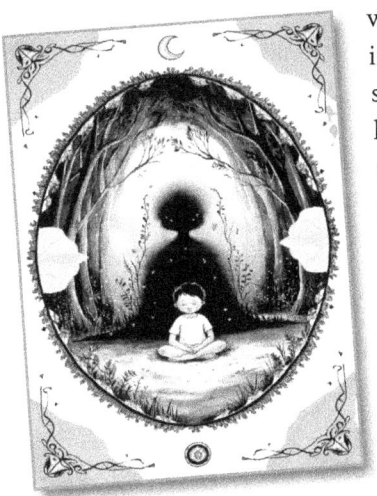

of ourselves we have repressed or denied, hidden deep within the unconscious. These parts often manifest in irrational fears, compulsions, or aversions, subtly shaping our interactions and self-perception. The lost infant represents our original, unconditioned self —the state of being before societal norms and personal experiences shaped our identity. The work of the alchemist involves recognising, accepting, and ultimately reintegrating these two aspects. The chapter explores practical techniques for Shadow work, showing how confronting our buried fears and vulnerabilities leads to wholeness and deeper self-awareness.

Nigredo

11. The Dark Night of the Soul

A moment comes in the alchemical journey when everything falls apart. The structures of the self, once seen as stable, begin to dissolve, leading to profound existential crisis. This chapter explores the phenomenon known as the Dark Night of the Soul —a period of intense inner turmoil where meaning itself seems to collapse. The mind confronts its own illusions, and the alchemist is left with nothing but raw, unfiltered experience. While this stage is deeply painful, it is also essential. It marks the breaking down of ego structures and conditioned patterns, making way for authentic transformation. The chapter discusses how to navigate this period, the role of faith and doubt, and how even the deepest despair can become the soil from which enlightenment grows.

12. The Seed of Nirvāṇa

The darkest point in the journey is also the place where the first glimpse of liberation appears. This chapter examines how the initial stages of alchemical transformation contain within them the seed of ultimate realisation. The moment when everything seems to dissolve is also the moment when the mind becomes open to something entirely new. The chapter explores the paradoxical nature of suffering —that deep within it lies the key to its own transcendence. The experience of this shift, even if momentary, permanently alters consciousness, setting in motion a gradual but irreversible process of awakening. This chapter also marks the transition from *Nigredo* (the blackening phase) to *Albedo* (the purification phase), preparing the alchemist for the next stage of the journey.

INTRODUCTION

13. The Realities

Reality is not a single, fixed entity but a multi-layered experience shaped by perception. This chapter introduces the distinction between Apparent Reality, conditioned reality, and ultimate reality. Drawing from Buddhist philosophy, it explores how our understanding of what is 'real' is often shaped by habitual thought patterns rather than direct experience. By dismantling these illusions, the alchemist begins to perceive reality with greater clarity. The chapter also examines how different spiritual traditions define reality and why breaking free from conditioned perception is a key aspect of inner transformation.

14. The Matrix of Conditioned Reality

Much like the digital simulation in *The Matrix*, our everyday experience is structured by invisible forces that shape how we perceive and interact with the world. This chapter breaks down the fundamental components of conditioned reality — how thoughts, emotions, and sensory experiences arise and are sustained by mental and physical processes. By understanding this framework, the alchemist gains the ability to work directly with the forces that construct their reality, learning how to reshape their experience rather than being unconsciously shaped by it.

NIGREDO

15. The 72 Types of Entities

This chapter presents a systematic breakdown of the elements that compose experience, from the subtlest mental factors to the more tangible physical components. Drawing from the Buddhist Abhidhamma tradition, it categorises these entities into a framework that allows the alchemist to understand the mechanics of perception. Rather than viewing reality as a single entity, we begin to see it as a composite of many interacting forces. This insight allows for deeper self-awareness and greater control over the forces that shape consciousness.

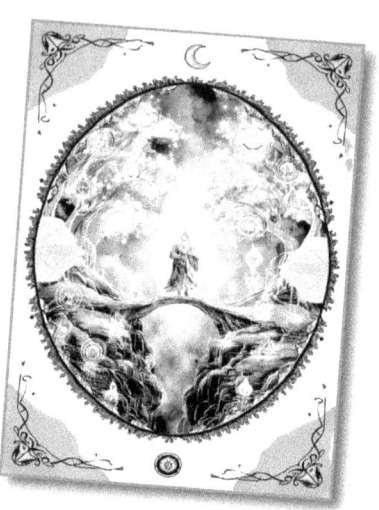

16. Consciousness

Consciousness is not a monolithic entity but a constantly shifting process. This chapter explores the different levels of consciousness, from ordinary waking states to altered and transcendental experiences. The discussion includes how consciousness functions in different realms of existence, its role in spiritual awakening, and how practices such as meditation can alter its nature. The alchemist must come to understand consciousness as both the tool and the field of their work, learning how to refine and direct it toward transformation.

Introduction

17. The Mental Factors

Every moment of experience is shaped by a constellation of mental factors —qualities of mind that determine how we perceive and respond to the world. This chapter maps out these factors in detail, exploring their influence on thoughts, emotions, and actions. Some mental factors bind us to suffering, while others lead to liberation. By understanding and cultivating wholesome mental states, the alchemist gains the ability to shift their experience in profound ways.

18. Materiality

What is the nature of physical reality? This chapter examines the relationship between consciousness and materiality, exploring how form and mind interact to create our experience of the world. It also introduces the idea that matter, like the self, is not a fixed entity but a process in constant flux. The chapter draws from both scientific and esoteric perspectives, revealing the deeper implications of understanding material existence.

Nigredo

19. The Forces that Drive the Matrix

Beyond mental and physical elements, hidden forces sustain the illusion of an independent self. This chapter explores the primary forces —karma, craving, aversion, and ignorance —that keep beings trapped in cyclic existence. Understanding these forces is the key to unraveling them and stepping beyond conditioned reality.

20. Saṃsāra

The cycle of birth, death, and rebirth is not just a metaphysical concept but a psychological reality. This chapter examines how our habitual patterns of thinking and reacting create endless loops of experience. Whether viewed through a literal or symbolic lens, *saṃsāra* represents the repetitive nature of conditioned existence, and this chapter provides insight into how to begin breaking free.

Introduction

21. The Four Noble Truths

Buddhism presents a simple yet profound formula for liberation: understanding suffering, its cause, its cessation, and the path leading to that cessation. This chapter explores these Four Noble Truths through an alchemical lens, showing how they provide a blueprint for transformation.

22. The Cycle of Becoming

Existence unfolds through a process known as dependent origination —a chain of causes and effects that perpetuate suffering. This chapter deconstructs this process, revealing how ignorance leads to craving, attachment, and rebirth. By understanding this cycle, the alchemist gains the ability to disrupt it, opening the way to liberation.

NIGREDO

23. The Fetters that Bind

What keeps us trapped in suffering, preventing deeper realisation? In Buddhist thought, the process of awakening is marked by progressively breaking ten mental fetters —deep-seated patterns that bind consciousness to cyclic existence (saṃsāra). This chapter explores these fetters, beginning with the most fundamental obstacles —self-identity, doubt, and attachment to rituals —and continuing through subtler impediments like restlessness and craving for existence itself. Understanding these bonds is crucial because they shape not only how we experience the world but how we react to suffering. The chapter provides practical ways to recognise and loosen these fetters, allowing for greater freedom and clarity of mind.

24. The Eightfold Noble Path

If suffering arises from attachment and ignorance, then what is the path to liberation? This chapter presents the Buddha's Eightfold Noble Path —a structured approach that integrates ethical living, mental discipline, and deep wisdom. Far from being a rigid doctrine, this path offers a practical guide for navigating the challenges of spiritual work. The chapter explores the threefold division of the path —wisdom (prajna), ethical conduct (sīla), and meditative absorption (samadhi) —showing how they complement and reinforce each other. By cultivating right view, right intention, right speech, right action, right livelihood, right effort, right mindfulness, and right concentration, the alchemist systematically reshapes their perception and behaviour, leading toward transformation.

INTRODUCTION

25. The Great Work

The essence of alchemy lies in what is known as the Great Work —an intensive process of purification and refinement that transforms base consciousness into something luminous. This chapter explores how the Great Work is not a single step but a lifelong undertaking that unfolds in stages, each requiring deeper levels of honesty, effort, and surrender. Unlike conventional self-improvement, which seeks to build a better version of the self, the Great Work is about dissolution —breaking down everything that is false to reveal what is real. The chapter introduces the key alchemical operations — calcination (burning away ego), dissolution (breaking down mental structures), separation (distinguishing truth from illusion), conjunction (integration of opposites), and ultimately, the creation of the Philosopher's Stone —a mind purified of delusion and attachment.

26. The Trees of Consciousness

Just as a tree has roots, trunk, and branches, consciousness also develops through distinct stages. This chapter presents a model of spiritual growth that parallels the structure of a tree, exploring how awareness expands from basic perception to profound realisation. By examining how consciousness develops and matures, the alchemist can gain insight into their own spiritual progression. The chapter also draws comparisons to the Kabbalistic Tree Of Life, showing how different traditions have mapped the ascent from ignorance to enlightenment.

27. The Golden Middle Path

The alchemical journey requires balance. Too much attachment to pleasure leads to stagnation; too much asceticism leads to self-destruction. The Middle Path, as taught by the Buddha, represents the perfect equilibrium between indulgence and denial. This chapter explores how the Middle Path applies not only to spiritual practice but to everyday life, showing how wisdom emerges from maintaining a delicate harmony between effort and surrender.

28. The Four Grades of Realisation

The path of enlightenment unfolds in stages, each marked by profound shifts in perception. This chapter explores the four grades of realisation recognised in Buddhist thought: **Sotāpanna** (Stream-Enterer), **Sakadāgāmī** (Once-Returner), **Anāgāmī** (Non-Returner), and **Arahant** (Fully Liberated Being). Each stage represents a point of no return -once an individual reaches a certain level of understanding, they can no longer fall back into ignorance. The chapter examines how these realisations change one's relationship with suffering, desire, and self-identity.

Introduction

29. Realms of Existence

Beyond human experience, different realms of consciousness exist, each shaped by karma and mental development. This chapter explores the Buddhist cosmology of existence, from the lower realms of suffering (*hell-beings, hungry ghosts, and animals*) to the higher realms of refinement (*heavenly beings and formless states*). While these realms are traditionally seen as external realities, they also function as metaphorical states of mind -places we inhabit based on our habitual thought patterns. Understanding them allows the alchemist to recognise and transcend the limitations of conditioned existence.

30. Different Worlds and Jhāna

The mind has the capacity to enter radically different states of being, known as *jhānas*. These deep meditative absorptions alter perception so completely that they can feel like stepping into entirely different worlds. This chapter explores the nature of *jhāna*, how it relates to the realms of existence, and how these states can be cultivated as part of the spiritual path.

Nigredo

31. Path Consciousness

Enlightenment is not a gradual accumulation of knowledge but a moment of direct realisation —an instant where the mind sees reality as it truly is. This chapter explores the nature of **path consciousness** —the sudden, transformative shift that occurs at key points along the spiritual journey. It examines how these insights occur, what conditions make them possible, and how they change one's perception forever.

32. Sotāpanna

The first stage of enlightenment, **Sotāpanna** (Stream-Enterer), is where the alchemist takes their first irrevocable step toward liberation. This chapter explores what it means to reach this stage, how self-view is fundamentally altered, and how the first three fetters —self-illusion, doubt, and attachment to rituals —are permanently broken.

Introduction

33. Sakadāgāmī

Building upon the insights of Sotāpanna, **Sakadāgāmī** (Once-Returner) represents a further purification of consciousness, where craving and aversion weaken significantly. This chapter explores how this second stage shifts one's emotional and psychological landscape, leading to a profound sense of equanimity.

34. Anāgāmī

The **Anāgāmī** (Non-Returner) stage represents a radical departure from ordinary human concerns. Here, all attachment to sensual pleasures is transcended, and only the subtlest mental fetters remain. This chapter explores how an Anāgāmī experiences the world, why they no longer feel drawn to material existence, and how their consciousness operates at a profoundly refined level.

35. The Subtle Fetters

Even at advanced stages of realisation, subtle attachments remain. This chapter explores the final five fetters —desire for existence, pride, restlessness, attachment to formless states, and fundamental ignorance —that keep even highly realised beings from full enlightenment. These fetters are the most difficult to perceive because they operate at the deepest levels of identity.

36. Arahant

The journey culminates with the **Arahant**, the one who has reached full enlightenment. This chapter explores the characteristics of the fully liberated being, how they live, and why their perception of reality is fundamentally different from that of ordinary individuals. It also addresses the distinction between an Arahant and a Buddha, and what it truly means to reach the end of the path.

INTRODUCTION

37. What Went Before

The alchemical journey does not begin at the moment of conscious recognition —it has been unfolding long before that. This chapter explores how past experiences, conditioning, and even previous spiritual explorations set the foundation for the path ahead. Often, individuals who find themselves drawn to deep transformation have spent years, even lifetimes, accumulating the necessary insight and curiosity. The longing for truth, the dissatisfaction with surface—level existence, and the intuitive sense that there is something beyond ordinary perception are not random occurrences but signposts that the journey has already begun. This chapter helps the alchemist reflect on their own path, recognising the moments of preparation that led them to this point.

38. The Fall

One of the most crucial moments in spiritual development is *The Fall* —the point at which an individual rejects inherited belief systems and begins seeking their own truth. Traditionally seen as a tragic event, this chapter reinterprets the Fall as a necessary step toward enlightenment. Just as Adam and Eve's departure from Eden symbolised the birth of self-awareness, so too does every spiritual seeker undergo a moment where they realise that the world they have been given does not fully align with their inner knowing. This chapter examines how breaking from conventional paradigms — whether religious, philosophical, or personal — sets the stage for profound transformation.

NIGREDO

39. Exile

After the Fall comes Exile —the difficult period of separation from past identities, communities, and ways of being. This chapter explores the psychological and emotional toll of leaving behind old belief systems, relationships, and even entire ways of life. The seeker often finds themselves caught between two worlds — no longer able to return to the comfort of ignorance, yet not fully established in a new way of being. Drawing from mythological narratives such as Cain and Abel, this chapter reveals how exile is not merely an individual experience but a universal stage in transformation. It offers insight into how to navigate this challenging phase, finding stability amid uncertainty.

40. Wandering

Exile often leads to a period of wandering —both physically and mentally. Many seekers find themselves drifting between different spiritual traditions, searching for a framework that resonates with their evolving understanding. This chapter explores the nature of this phase, emphasising that while it may feel aimless, it is actually an essential process of refinement. By exposing oneself to different philosophies, perspectives, and practices, the alchemist gathers the necessary tools for their own path. However, the danger of this phase is becoming lost in endless seeking —mistaking the journey for the destination. This chapter provides guidance on recognising when wandering has served its purpose and when it is time to commit.

INTRODUCTION

41. The Night

The Night is the deep descent into the unknown —the phase where the seeker must confront their inner darkness. Unlike the earlier Dark Night of the Soul, which is characterised by existential crisis, *The Night* is an active confrontation with the hidden aspects of the self. This chapter explores how consciousness fragments, creating inner conflicts that manifest as fears, doubts, and unresolved wounds. It examines how the mind projects these internal struggles onto the external world, leading to experiences of suffering and confusion. However, by turning inward and facing these aspects head-on, the alchemist can begin the process of true integration.

42. Confusion

The moment of breakthrough often brings with it an unexpected consequence: deep confusion. This chapter explores the paradox of enlightenment —how profound realisations often dismantle previous structures of understanding, leaving the seeker in a state of cognitive disorientation. As conditioned reality begins to unravel, the mind struggles to comprehend its new experience. This chapter provides insight into navigating this phase, emphasising the importance of patience, trust, and grounding. It also examines how traditional spiritual paths provide structures for managing this confusion, and how the alchemist can develop their own framework for integrating insight.

Nigredo

43. Commitment

After periods of exile, wandering, and confusion, a moment arrives when the seeker must make a choice: continue half-heartedly, or fully commit to the path. This chapter explores the necessity of commitment —not to a belief system or doctrine, but to the process of transformation itself. Commitment requires a willingness to let go of all safety nets, trusting that what lies ahead is worth more than what is left behind. This chapter also examines the fears that arise at this stage—fear of failure, losing oneself, or the unknown. By acknowledging these fears and moving forward despite them, the alchemist solidifies their path.

44. Spiritual Orientation

At a certain point, the path becomes clearer, though not necessarily easier. This chapter explores the shift from external seeking to internal knowing —where the alchemist begins to orient themselves naturally toward spiritual development without the need for external validation. This phase is marked by a deepening of wisdom, a greater sense of stability, and an increased ability to navigate challenges with equanimity. However, it also presents its own obstacles, such as spiritual complacency or the temptation to retreat into isolation. The chapter provides practical guidance on maintaining momentum while allowing natural growth to unfold.

INTRODUCTION

45. No Self

One of the most challenging realisations in spiritual work is *Anatta* —the concept of No-Self. This chapter explores how identity is constructed, maintained, and ultimately dissolved. Unlike earlier stages of letting go, which focus on individual aspects of conditioning, this realisation strikes at the very core of existence. The alchemist begins to see that the self is not a fixed entity but an ever-changing process, and that clinging to any aspect of identity —whether positive or negative —perpetuates suffering. The chapter also examines the psychological challenges of this realisation—particularly the fear of non-existence—and how one can transcend these fears to reach genuine liberation.

46. First Steps

After deep insight, the real work begins. This chapter explores the delicate period following initial enlightenment experiences, when the alchemist must learn to integrate their newfound understanding into daily life. While the temptation may be to retreat into solitude or abandon conventional responsibilities, the true test is bringing wisdom into every moment. This chapter examines how to navigate relationships, work, and society while maintaining an awakened perspective. It also discusses the phenomenon of "spiritual amnesia" —how insights can fade if not actively cultivated —and how to prevent this from happening.

47. Establishing the Way

At this stage, the path is no longer theoretical —it has become a lived reality. This chapter explores how the alchemist develops a natural rhythm of practice, where spiritual insight becomes the foundation of daily existence. While external challenges still arise, they are no longer seen as obstacles but as opportunities for refinement. This chapter examines how this stage differs from earlier ones, focusing on the deeper sense of trust and surrender that develops over time. It also explores the concept of *Bodhicitta* —the desire not just for personal enlightenment, but for the awakening of all beings.

48. The Key to the Gate

The final chapter of *Nigredo* marks the threshold between the darkness of transformation and the emergence of something new. This chapter explores how, after a long process of dissolution and purification, the alchemist reaches a point where they are ready to step into a new way of being. However, this is not an endpoint but a beginning —the transition from *Nigredo* to *Albedo*, from death to rebirth. The chapter reflects on the entire journey, preparing the reader for the next stages of the Great Work. It also emphasises that while the work continues, the one who began the journey is no longer the one who stands at its gate.

INTRODUCTION

Useful Resources

This can only be a guide — at this stage of learning, it is important to develop one's curiosity by exploring whatever 'spiritual text' appeals to you.

These are some of the main resources I found helpful;

- **The Comprehensive Manual of Abhidhamma** is a wonderful book; it will take some time for you to get familiar with its main points. I recommend watching Bhikkhu Bodhi's YouTube lectures where he goes through the main parts, explaining the foundational points. Keep at it; it takes time to gain a comfortable familiarity with its content.

- **The Path of Purification** is also an excellent resource, but rather than reading this cover to cover, I found it better as an encyclopaedia to deepen my knowledge and understanding about any particular topic. It can be an expensive book to purchase, so remember it is available fully online.

- **The Buddhist Cosmos** is an easy book to read and can be a helpful adjunct to listening to Ajahn Punnadhammo's YouTube lectures, which are excellent despite occasional audio issues. It can be purchased from Amazon and is also available as a free PDF download from his website.

- **The Manuals of Buddhism** are available for free download, and at this stage, you can use them like the Path of Purification — as encyclopaedias to increase your understanding of any particular topic. They are not the sort of book one generally reads from cover to cover. Enlightenment is not about 'knowing everything,' and it can be a distraction later on if you cling to the idea of needing to know everything. You need a certain confidence in your understanding, but don't try to learn everything.

- **A Critical Analysis of Jhāna** is recommended as an overview of the *jhanic* states. Meditation can be a valuable tool, but it is not essential. One must have some *jhanic* experience, but only some paths require expertise in meditative tranquility. If you are a meditator, this is excellent, but don't despair if you find deep meditation difficult.

- **The Occult Anatomy of Man** is a short, fascinating read and is freely available for download. It is an excellent introduction to the subtle body from Western occult practice.
- Lastly, for excellent discussion about Western Hermetic practice, I highly recommend The **Secret History of Western Esotericism Podcast (SHWEP)** with Earl Fontainelle. (Spotify).

NIGREDO

Comprehensive Manual of Abhidhamma (Abhidhammattha Sangaha)
- Bhikkhu Bodhi

https://tinyurl.com/3hhrskny

This is the main resource text for this course.
A free PDF version appears to be available online.

The Path of Purification (Visuddhimagga)
- Bhadantácariya Buddhaghosa

https://tinyurl.com/2s3aphsb

One of Buddhism's foundational texts, the "Visuddhimagga" is a systematic examination and condensation of Buddhist doctrine and meditation technique. The various teachings of the Buddha found throughout the Pāli canon are organised in a clear, comprehensive path leading to the final goal of nibbāna, the state of complete purification.

The Buddhist Cosmos — Ajahn Punnadhammo

https://tinyurl.com/4urur5yy

An encyclopaedic survey of Buddhist cosmology and mythology according to the Pāli canon and commentaries. Covers the nature of the universe, of time and of the various classes of beings inhabiting the various realms and levels of the cosmos.

The Manuals of Buddhism — Ledi Sayadaw

https://tinyurl.com/mnnkstbe

In depth analysis of insight approaches to enlightenment.

A Critical Analysis of Jhāna
— Henepola Gunaratana

https://tinyurl.com/3rm3dvk2

Detailed exploration of Jhāna.

INTRODUCTION

The Occult Anatomy of Man — Manly P. Hall
https://tinyurl.com/4udvm9u6

Great introduction to Occult Anatomy.

The Secret Teachings of all Ages — Manly P. Hall
https://tinyurl.com/45tjxvbm

Excellent resource for occult teachings.

Psychology & Alchemy (Collected Works Vol. 12) — C.G. Jung
https://tinyurl.com/46jbf2pc

Jung's landmark account of the connections between alchemy, its symbolism, the collective unconscious, and modern psychology. Psychology and Alchemy is one of Jung's most influential works.

He: Understanding Masculine Psychology— Robert A. Johnson
https://tinyurl.com/2by4etw4

As timely today as when it was first published, He provides a fascinating look into male identity and how female dynamics influence men.

Iron John: A Book About Men — Robert Bly
https://tinyurl.com/ew6345a4

Iron John searches for a new vision of what a man is or could be, drawing on psychology, anthropology, mythology, folklore and legend.

A Little Book on the Human Shadow — Robert Bly
https://tinyurl.com/3w529dyf

Excellent introduction to Jungian Shadow work

NIGREDO

Youtube Resources

Abbas the Alchemist
www.youtube.com/@abbasalchemist
Excellent channel about Alchemy (advanced).

Ajahn Punnadhammo
www.youtube.com/@AjahnPunnadhammo
Really good introduction to Buddhist Philosophy.

Altrusian Grace Media
www.youtube.com/@AltrusianGraceMedia
Excellent resource for Hermetic texts and other mystical scriptures.

BAUS Chuang Yen Monastery
www.youtube.com/@BAUSChuangYenMonastery
Home channel of Bhikkhu Bodhi — Excellent lectures about Abhidhamma and Buddhism.

Let's Talk Religion
www.youtube.com/@LetsTalkReligion
Excellent lectures on religion.

ReligionForBreakfast
www.youtube.com/@ReligionForBreakfast
Excellent lectures on religion.

Samaneri Jayasāra — Wisdom of the Masters
www.youtube.com/@SamaneriJayasara
Wonderful channel with lots of valuable resources.

Introduction

Essential Definitions

Alchemy—A process, not a metaphor. It is the disciplined transformation of consciousness, refining raw, reactive being into something sharp, clear, and unshakeable.

Anāgāmī (Non-Returner)—One who has severed attachment to sensual craving and aversion. Rebirth will not occur in lower states.

Anatta—No-self. The understanding that nothing within can be possessed or controlled as 'me' or 'mine'. The central shock of awakening.

Arahant—One who has finished. The final liberation, where all traces of delusion, clinging, and becoming are extinguished.

Dark Night—A brutal but clarifying passage, where all spiritual illusions are burned away. What survives is real. What doesn't, never was.

Dependent Origination (Paṭiccasamuppāda)—The mechanism behind suffering. We arise not from a self, but from an intricate, self-perpetuating chain of mental processes. What we call 'self' is just the momentum of past choices.

Fetters (Saṃyojana)—The illusions that bind. Ten in total. Cutting the first three makes one a 'stream-enterer'—destined to completion.

Fruit Consciousness—The aftershock of seeing clearly. The mind stabilising around its new perception, integrating the irreversible.

Gnosis—Direct knowledge, not belief. A shift in awareness so fundamental that once seen, the world is never perceived the same way again.

Karma—Not cosmic justice, not punishment. Merely the inescapable echo of past volition, continuing until seen clearly. It binds until it doesn't.

Jhāna—Absorption, the deep stabilisation of mind into refined states of concentration. Powerful, seductive, but ultimately a tool—not the goal.

Nigredo—The blackening, the first stage of alchemy. A necessary disintegration of self-concept, forcing confrontation with all that was previously ignored or excused.

Path Consciousness—The precise mind-moment where fundamental insight shifts from intellectual to undeniable. Rare, irreversible.

Sakadāgāmī (Once-Returner)—One who has weakened desire and ill-will to such an extent that only one more birth remains.

Saṃsāra—The unending cycle of conditioned existence, where suffering is self-created and self-perpetuated. One does not 'escape' Saṃsāra—it collapses when seen for what it is.

Solve et Coagula—To dissolve and to recombine. The core of all inner work—destruction of illusions followed by integration of what remains. It is painful, it is necessary.

Sotāpanna (Stream-Enterer)—One who has seen through the first illusions and cannot return to blind ignorance. The process is now irreversible.

Śūnyatā—Emptiness. Not void, but the absence of inherent existence. All things arise conditionally, including the illusion of separation.

Vipassanā—Insight, pure seeing. A practice of stripping perception down to its raw, immediate nature. The seeing itself is the liberation.

NIGREDO

The Early Alchemic Path

The bastion of Ego and Personality crumbles with increasing knowledge. The alchemist starts with dissatisfaction about life. This dark material is the Prima Materia or raw substance from which the stone arises. Once personality view and the rights and ritual fetters are abandoned AND one finds faith in the path, one undergoes the Dark Night of the Soul before the first path moment and the achievement of Sotāpanna (Nigredo). This is a confusing time and one initially tries to return to conditional existence.

However, the Sotāpanna process is irreversible and one eventually commits to the spiritual path towards Albedo, which involves the 'sacrifice' of all prior conditionality.

The Retort

HERMETIC VESSEL

The vessel is symbolic of the Great Work. It is sealed to represent that this work is inner—meaning it requires introspection, contemplation, and meditation. Rather than seeking remedies elsewhere, the alchemist begins to recognize that the problem is subjective awareness and not necessarily external reality. The seal prevents external influences from disrupting the process, ensuring that the transformation occurs entirely within. Just as the alchemist must resist seeking external solutions, the vessel remains closed so that all impurities can be worked through rather than expelled prematurely.

DROSS

The dross represents the conditional responses that arise in reaction to a reality that is perceived as unsatisfactory. The alchemist recognizes the dissatisfaction inherent in conditional experience. This stage is often confusing and painful at first. Only through the sustained presence of heat can the dross begin to break down. Without this pressure, the impurities remain dormant, and no refinement can take place.

HEAT

Initially, the drive to transform arises through pain, despair, and suffering. This acts as a catalyst, bringing the alchemist toward Nigredo—the blackening of one's subjective experience. Once the dark night has been experienced, faith arises in the path, along with a curiosity that draws the seeker back, again and again, to the Great Work. Over time, what once felt like destruction reveals itself as refinement, as the raw and chaotic elements give way to something clearer, lighter, and more stable—preparing the way for the next stage of transformation.

"Open your mind"

Part One
MYTHOS

The first part of Nigredo explores the rich tapestry of myths, symbols, and stories that form the foundation of spiritual alchemy. Here we examine how different traditions have encoded profound truths about consciousness transformation through metaphor and allegory. From the Fisher-King's wound to the mysterious Rebis, these ancient symbols serve as guideposts for understanding our own journey through the darkness of spiritual transformation.

While modern science has debunked literal interpretations of alchemical transmutation, the symbolic language of alchemy points to something far more significant — a sophisticated system for transforming consciousness itself. Through exploring these myths and their meanings, we begin to understand how religions initially form around the seed of enlightenment, though they often become preoccupied with the flower it grows into.

The chapters in this section provide essential context for understanding both the universal patterns of spiritual development and the specific challenges of the Nigredo phase. We'll examine how cultural conditioning shapes our experience, explore the nature of psychological wounds that must be healed, and investigate the profound symbolism that points toward liberation. This mythological framework, while seemingly abstract, provides crucial orientation for the practical work that follows.

Remember that these myths and symbols are tools for understanding, not the understanding itself. Like signposts on a journey, they guide us but are not the destination. As we proceed through this section, maintain both intellectual curiosity and spiritual discernment, recognising that the map is not the territory, but a useful guide nonetheless.

Nigredo

What is Reality?

MYTHOS

1. The Landscape

'Do not embark on a quest for enlightenment... unless you have the same amount of desire as a drowning man has to breathe air.'

In this opening chapter, we explore the fundamental terrain of spiritual alchemy — the inner landscape where transformation occurs. Here we examine the nature of Subjective Reality, the requirements for inner work, and the relationship between suffering and spiritual awakening. This chapter lays the groundwork for understanding how our perceived reality shapes our experience and introduces the alchemical approach to transformation.

The Landscape, from here, is pretty bleak. I won't lie to you, this isn't for everybody. But yet here you are. So let us start...

Alchemy is a process of inner transformation, kind of the *science* of sainthood, but not quite. Unfortunately, this will have to do for the moment, but it will suffer redefinition as we progress through necessary types of understanding.

The *power* of the Alchemist outlined in this course is personal. If you are interested in *bettering* yourself, whatever that means, this is for you. This *power* is always subtle and tends to liberate one from things that used to cause suffering. Through an understanding of our true nature, the alchemist loses fear of death, and through this, most other fears.

Nigredo

The path of the Alchemist is not unique. Rather, it is a system that points towards a way of unravelling the complexities of being that plague a normal person. This way is a function of the system, a kind of back door, that those who find can access and free themselves from their mental prison of being.

The alchemists, along with Buddhists, Gnostics, Sufis and all other types of mystics learn to hack into the very system that creates being, and uncouple the natural but painful attachment to it.

In contemporary film, this is explored almost explicitly in *The Matrix* series. I highly recommend watching these as they present a reasonable metaphor on the nature of becoming a prisoner in one's own mind.

Rather than reinventing the wheel, I will introduce terms from the mystery religions such as Kabbalah, Buddhism and Gnostic Christianity as interested readers will then find deeper research easier.

There needs to be a bit (or a lot) of suffering to make you into an Alchemist. You can still progress so far, but there reaches a point where you have to let go of everything that defines you. Unless you are willing to risk everything, you simply can't get the leap of faith to achieve what is known as *I will know the unknown.*

However, there is no rush. And even if you find yourself *stuck* on a stage, read on, but just be aware it might get more difficult to understand.

The work is inner and generally can be done along with most modern lifestyles. Here, what I am saying is you don't need to be a solitary monk. It is, however, also a spiritual path and progression will result in a certain disinterest in more mundane concerns. The *darker* — i.e. more difficult parts of the path don't have to be terrible, although if we experience them *naturally* they often are. But by all means, don't go out of your way to make things harder for yourself.

The only real quality you need is curiosity and a willingness to expand your capacity of belief.

What do I mean by 'reality?'

Reality is *subjective*. What does this mean?

MYTHOS

Reality is how you experience your existence. It is experienced only by you, with your distinct take on it, based on your conditioning. We all have our own subjective realities that, through primarily the use of language or numbers, we build into a kind of mutually-agreed *objective reality.*

Most of science works very hard to exclude differences between our subjective realities which we call subjective bias. Science generally strives to observe an objective reality and uses standards of measurement to base its objectivity.

Yet, this *objective* and seemingly real reality is one of convention. It is simply a consensus on agreement. And if individuals have a very unconventional or *problematic* experience it is based on this consensual *normality* that their abnormality is judged.

So, each of us has a personal experience that, to a degree, matches others when we communicate through the symbols of words and number. Yet what *blue* means to you and what it means to me are both unexplainable and generally unconscious.

We come into our awareness of ourselves without ever really knowing how or what has happened. We are a process that thinks it is a thing. This confuses us, and generally, we are unlikely to work out what has happened, as we become obsessed with a thing, that's really a process.

Our true *Subjective Reality* is chaotic and ever-shifting, but our constructed reality of things and beings is stable and makes *sense*. We fear the dissolution when we see process and not thing, so habitually always *thing* and *people* our experience. This is a habit that takes us not just through this life of becoming, but subsequent lives of becoming, an inexhaustible drive that takes us through countless numbers of existences.

This thing is once we *become* we fear unbecoming without ever realising both are illusions.

Throughout our existence we form memories of experiences but some of these memories haunt us. It's easy to blame psychological trauma on *bad* memories, yet even *good* memories will eventually become problematic. We can become just as miserable grasping at a once-pleasant but now distant past as easily as we can suffer from a traumatic one.

Nigredo

The Alchemist progresses through distinct stages which represent a change in their fundamental mechanism of being. Although there is a definite risk of what would be perceived as mental illness, I think it is more likely that those already suffering from generally a degree of depressive illness are already attracted toward alchemy, once they understand what it is about.

On the whole, the transmutations (changes in the substance) are beneficial and only troublesome if unrecognised. They are, however, one-way — once you break through and know a deeper truth you can never un-know it.

At any certain stage, curiosity will mix with faith and find wisdom. This manifests as a confidence in one's progress and understanding and the ignition of an inner type of fire. This fire creates an internal obsession with finding the truth and manifests as a restless obsession in completing the process. Again, this is not incompatible with many lifestyles but might represent a changing of priorities.

Take your time, learn to ponder and use whatever resources you have available to deepen your understanding. These processes take time and developing patience is a natural *side-effect* of learning. There will always be plenty to satisfy your curiosity.

> *"You must be ready to burn yourself in your own flame;*
> *how could you rise anew if you have not first become ashes!"* [4]

---

[4] *Nietzsche, Friedrich. Thus Spoke Zarathustra. Translated by Adrian Del Caro, Cambridge University Press, 2006. Originally published 1883–1885.*

Mythos

Study Guide: The Landscape

This opening chapter establishes the foundational framework for understanding spiritual alchemy as a transformative path. It introduces key concepts about the nature of reality, consciousness, and the requirements for inner transformation, while setting expectations for the journey ahead.

CORE CONCEPTS

- Prerequisites for the path
- Deep dissatisfaction with conventional existence
- Willingness to question fundamental beliefs
- Capacity for sustained curiosity
- Readiness to face personal suffering
- Ability to maintain ordinary life while pursuing transformation

NEW TERMINOLOGY

Abhidhamma: A sophisticated Buddhist framework for understanding consciousness

Albedo: The whitening stage of alchemical transformation

Alchemist: One who practices spiritual alchemy, seeking inner transformation

Alchemy: A process of inner **transformation**, described as the 'science' of sainthood

Citrinitas: The yellowing stage of alchemical transformation

Nigredo: The blackening or darkness stage of spiritual alchemy, marking the entry point into spiritual work

Objective reality: Consensual agreement about reality based on mutual understanding

Prima Materia: The primary raw material or starting substance in alchemy

Rubedo: The reddening stage of alchemical transformation

Spiritual Alchemy: A systematic approach to transforming consciousness through ancient alchemical principles

Subjective Reality: Personal experience of existence unique to each individual

Transmutation: Changes in the fundamental substance or nature of being

MAIN THEMES

- The paradox of seeking enlightenment through structured methods
- Relationship between suffering and spiritual awakening
- Nature of subjective versus consensual reality
- Process-based view of existence versus object-based perception
- Connection between various mystical traditions

TECHNICAL FRAMEWORK

- Understanding reality
- The Matrix metaphor
- Stages of transformation

PRACTICAL APPLICATIONS

- Initial curiosity and questioning
- Recognition of Subjective Reality
- Encounter with suffering
- Development of faith
- Irreversible insights

INTEGRATION POINTS

- Links to Chapter 3 (Evolution of Adulthood)
- Links to The Fisher-King Wound (Chapter 8)
- Preparation for understanding The Shadow (Chapter 10)
- Foundation for working with The Rebis (Chapter 9)

NIGREDO

COMMON MISCONCEPTIONS

- *Mental imprisonment through conditioning*
- *Systemic nature of perceived reality*
- *Liberation through understanding*
- *Role of faith and doubt*

REFLECTION QUESTIONS

- *How do you experience your own Subjective Reality differently from others?*
- *What aspects of your existence feel most "real" to you, and why?*
- *In what ways do you notice yourself creating a "mutually-agreed reality" with others?*
- *How does your understanding of reality change when you're alone versus with others?*

PROGRESS INDICATORS

- *The drowning man metaphor — examining true motivation*
- *The relationship between suffering and transformation*
- *The nature of irreversible insight*
- *The balance between ordinary life and spiritual pursuit*
- *The role of faith versus understanding*

2. The Alchemist

'This is not your first rodeo.'

This chapter explores the unique characteristics and mindset of those drawn to the alchemical path. We examine how previous spiritual development creates the conditions for alchemical work, while investigating the fundamental nature of existence and consciousness. Through understanding the alchemist's perspective on reality, we gain insight into both the challenges and rewards of this transformative journey.

To develop an interest deep enough to reach this point, you are standing on the shoulders of giants. We will learn much more about this later, but you only have an interest in this material because of the hard work of previous existences.

Be inspired, even when things get tough. You are the current incarnation of a long line of seekers of truth.

What is existence?

Existence is the subjective nature of being. It is the concept of a semi-permanent observer and participant in the sensory and mental process of life.

There is a sense of persistence in existence. What falls asleep at night awakens to a new day. Something, or someone is falling asleep; something or someone awakens the next day.

Nigredo

Yet, this sense of being extends beyond the physical. We can observe another fall asleep, and then awaken, yet when this happens to ourselves, it is more than our body that settles into rest. Subjectively, we get a sense of withdrawing into our body as our senses darken and we lose consciousness. There is a kind of extinguishing of awareness when we fall asleep as we can never quite remember the point at which we fall asleep.

Existence is therefore more than just our physical environment. We experience dreams, fantasies, thoughts and ideas. We experience feelings about both our physical well-being and our mental state of affairs. The same picture or sound can soothe one individual and instil unknown terror in another. Defining experience on a purely objective basis is nothing like actual subjective experience which includes feelings, perceptions, thoughts and consciousness.

When we ignore our subjective existence and get fully involved in an objective, but imaginary world, we can suffer. If we reduce ourselves to a thing, we then develop anxiety as we learn what might happen to us. Even the most princely of upbringings only delays the inevitable discovery that as living beings we must surely die, and before this, suffer maybe illness, poverty or both.

The aspiring alchemist must learn to pull themselves away from this objective but mutually suffered delusion and find the reality from which it springs. One only does this if one has suffered disenchantment or disappointment with the ultimate conclusion of being a *living* being.

The *method* of the alchemist is to put *subjective* experience into the *retort* of analysis and synthesis. With some difficulty at first, but then with obsessive ease, the alchemist constantly breaks down experience into its most primitive elements (analysis) and then rebuilds a mental (and therefore subjectively real) model through which to further examine existence.

The process is stepwise. One struggles, sometimes for long periods of time, with a difficult concept that once grasped, unlocks many other problems. It is regressive, in that we are learning to retrace our own evolutionary steps, trying to resist primitive drives and tendencies.

The first step is the most difficult. It is oblique, subtle and elusive. The more one seeks it, the more elusive it becomes. This is the *white rabbit* of Alice in Wonderland and later *The Matrix* fame, a tendency for consciousness to be fleeting, elusive and oddly reflective.

Our problem is that our minds are most receptive to catching hold of this elusive viewpoint when we are infants. Once we learn language and particularly once we learn to write, we reduce our capacity to grasp new concepts and have an overarching tendency to think rather than experience the raw impression of the senses. By the time we realise we are prisoners, we can no longer remember how it happened.

So, the first part of our quest involves a certain *reduction* or *regression* as we attempt to return to the experience of childhood. We must identify and heal certain mental wounds and bring our experience of being back towards a more innocent time. However, we cannot simply retrace our steps. Our past innocence was due to ignorance, but now we know. Our path back towards that simpler perspective must be a new one.

We call this simple and innocent, pre-adult viewpoint, the *Garden of Eden*. We will explore what we mean by this in much more depth later, but for the moment, this will do. The *Garden of Eden* is the name of a concept, a *place of being* or *state of being*, that we all experienced, but cannot quite remember. It was a time of development when the words or symbols of existence lacked meaning and we existed without thinking about things. At that stage we had not learned we are a separate piece of reality, this *separation*, which gives us the sense of individuality soon forms, but prior to this we exist in a blissful and unworried state.

As alchemists we don't seek this blissful state for its sublime experience. In fact, it can be a trap for some seekers who can get lost for many incarnations in pursuing heavenly bliss. We seek this state for its detached tranquility. Here we can find a place of stability with which we can *study* reality. This state of mind is like an island on which the alchemist can observe inner and outer experience, relatively uninvolved.

For the alchemist this is only the first stage, and a preliminary one. Through a deepening understanding of consciousness one finds stability in the simpler forms, until through this stability a breakthrough occurs. With this breakthrough the aspiring alchemist's mind experiences *Nirvāṇa* or unconditioned reality. This only happens for a fraction of a second but through this experience, the alchemist changes their perspective of being. Further stages refine this experience until the tendency to become is eliminated, and one learns to *dwell* in unconditioned reality.

Much of this may be difficult to contemplate, and we will expand on these topics as needed. At this stage I feel it's important to impart a sense of direction, as alchemy is confusing enough.

So, the initial work of the alchemist is finding a way back to a state of being associated with a more simple view of reality. There is a sense of working with the *dross* that one has accumulated since childhood. This *dross* is not discarded or rejected, but is a substance that can be refined or purified.

This *dross* is the very substance of the alchemist's being. It is a conditioned experience, and memories of it. Simplistically, it is a lifetime of meaning plus many lifetimes of cultural programming, that act like an unconscious filter over the simpler, reality of subjective experience.

The process of refining this '*dross*' is known as *Nigredo*, or *darkness*. The aspiring alchemist must develop a passion and desire to seek out their own inner darkness and through understanding, transmute it. But this is neither pleasant nor easy. This *darkness* often manifests as depressive or psychotic illness, and is associated with really challenging states like despair, hopelessness and helplessness. Few alchemists realise they are on a path at this stage. Many may be severely unwell, experiencing intellectual despair and deep despondency. It can be a very dangerous time.

The only real difference between an alchemist and another suffering with mental illness is a curiosity towards their symptoms. The alchemist always has a deep, often unspoken or unthought suspicion towards experience, that can only really come from a deep level of insight associated with a previous existence.

In the next lesson we will examine the evolution of a typical human consciousness which will act like a map that we can build on as we progress.

Mythos

Study Guide: The Alchemist

This chapter explores existence and consciousness through alchemical metaphor, revealing how subjective experience shapes reality's foundation. It introduces key concepts of being, spiritual transformation, and the early stages of alchemical work.

CORE CONCEPTS
- The subjective nature of being
- The alchemical process of analysis and synthesis
- The relationship between physical and mental existence
- The role of consciousness in transformation

NEW TERMINOLOGY

Dross: Accumulated mental and emotional material requiring refinement

Garden of Eden: Concept representing pre-verbal state of consciousness

Nirvāṇa: Unconditioned reality beyond normal perception

MAIN THEMES
- Existence and consciousness
- The alchemical process
- Transformative journey
- States of consciousness

TECHNICAL FRAMEWORK
- The nature of existence
- The alchemical method
- The Garden of Eden state
- The Nigredo phase

PRACTICAL APPLICATIONS
- Working with inner darkness
- The assumed persistence of consciousness
- Transformation of suffering
- Development of detached observation

INTEGRATION POINTS
- Breaking down experience through analysis
- Rebuilding understanding through synthesis
- Working with mental substance
- Understanding the observer/observed relationship

COMMON MISCONCEPTIONS
- The trap of blissful states
- The illusion of objective reality
- The nature of breakthrough experiences
- The persistence of consciousness

REFLECTION QUESTIONS
- What drives your curiosity about deeper truths beyond everyday existence?
- How do you experience the difference between your physical and mental existence?
- When do you feel most aware of your consciousness as a process rather than a fixed thing?
- What aspects of your existence feel most persistent and which feel most transient?

PROGRESS INDICATORS
- Development of detached observation skills
- Understanding of subjective experience as primary reality
- Ability to work with mental dross
- Recognition of pre-verbal consciousness states

NIGREDO

"*He who fights with monsters should be careful lest he thereby become a monster. And if you gaze long into an abyss, the abyss also gazes into you.*"

– Friedrich Nietzsche, Beyond Good and Evil, Aphorism 146 (1886), translated by Helen Zimmern (1909)

3. Evolution of Adulthood

"In every real man a child is hidden that wants to play." [5]

In this chapter, we explore the fundamental transition from childlike to adult consciousness, examining how language and perceptual frameworks create a filter between pure sensory experience and conceptual understanding. We'll investigate how the development of language and meaning changes our experience of reality, and why understanding this process is crucial for the aspiring alchemist. The journey from child to adult consciousness represents a key alchemical transformation that must be understood to begin the Great Work.

We all arrive at *adulthood* in a variety of different states. Still, there is a consensus that adults are not children, but when we try to examine what exactly are the differences between adult and child, it gets tricky once we go beyond the obvious physical.

Hormones certainly play a role, but they are not a primary concern for us as alchemists. We will cover gender later on, but our interest lies deeper — we are interested in *being* not what sort of body this being is associated with. I can find no reason beyond obvious misogyny to exclude the female aspiring alchemist, and in truth, the only barrier is that in accessing education that I think explains a relative lack of reported female alchemists.

---

[5] *Nietzsche, F. (1883—1885). Thus Spoke Zarathustra. Translation by Walter Kaufmann (1954).*

NIGREDO

Here, we are interested in the changes to state of being that arises from transforming a childish awareness to that of an adult. This is complicated as I have to introduce terms and ideas that might be entirely new, but take your time and try to familiarise yourself with each stage by reflecting on your own experience. The early stages will be very abstract at the moment, which is okay, and something you are going to have to get very used to!

Our state of being is shaped by awareness—not just of the sensory world, but of the meaning we assign to things. This awareness *of what things mean* is called perception. Perception is a kind of awareness that clings to basic awareness and tells us what things are. We look at a cup — but only see shape and colour. Our mind then tells us, often by referring to the word *cup*, either visually or as an inner voice, what this shape and colour means. This happens almost instantly, so while we do see the shape and colour, our minds immediately attach meaning, and all we consciously perceive is *a cup*.

Perceptions shape our experience. If we have suffered abuse or psychological trauma we might develop phobic reactions, where we have a panic attack at the mere thought or sight of a sensitive object.

The *pre-verbal* child lacks words which are a perception. They cannot understand language and experience a world without these perceptions acting as a filter. You ask a *pre-verbal* child to pass you the cup, and it is meaningless. So, when you look and see a cup, and when a *pre-verbal* child does, we are not experiencing the same thing.

For adults to experience the child's reality, they either must be a dedicated meditator or take, particularly LSD. LSD seems to inhibit this perceptual overlay and the world becomes brighter, indistinct and distracting.

So, the difference between an adult and *pre-verbal* childish awareness is that the child experiences only what they sense. They can get caught up with their environment and are fascinated and play with it. The Adult can no longer experience this pure sensory awareness as they have learned to automatically categorise it into things and beings. These are a subtle form of awareness that attaches itself to what we sense and gives it meaning. As an adult, we are primarily interested in what things mean and so our reality moves from a blissful and connected, purely sensory one into a reality where we just observe our own perceptions.

If our interpretations are unpleasant, we become prisoners of our own perceptions, trapped within a mental cell. This is the *Matrix*. A layer of subtle awareness that manifests as we learn and cuts us off from the life-giving pure sensory experience. This is why the intellectual tends to suffer alienation and feelings of disconnection. Unless they find ways of *switching off* they remain like a prisoner in their own thoughts.

Are You Still with Me?

The main difference between the adult and *pre-verbal* child is how they experience the senses. In the child their experience is unfettered. They gain a kind of vitality from just being, yet, once they learn the words to describe this experience, they then tend to lose access to it.

The Alchemist learns to ponder this problem. They recognise that one cannot understand reality this way. As *understanding* in truth is illusory, and tends to just create a poor imitation of the original, that somehow blocks one from fully experiencing it.

The Bible contains deep alchemical symbolism, which we will explore in depth later. In the first book we learn about the *Garden of Eden*. This is our *pre-verbal* state of being, something we all once experienced however transiently. In this Garden are two *Trees*, these *Trees* are analogies for consciousness.

We are warned not to eat from the *Tree of Knowledge* as this will cause suffering and death. Yet, we all learned to speak and name the objects in our world. This creates the perceptions that now coats sensory experience and cut us off from the naturally life-giving properties. We will examine these *Trees* in much more detail later.

I hope this explanation was clear. To summarise, the difference between *adult* awareness and the innocent state of awareness we call the *Garden of Eden* is the presence of a layer of perception that coats our pure sensory experience. This pure sensory experience is blissful and energising yet as adults, particularly those who like to learn, one can become increasingly cut off or alienated through perceptions *blocking* this experience.

So as aspiring alchemists we must find a way of stopping this layer of perception forming and interrupting pure sense experience.

Nigredo

Study Guide: Evolution of Adulthood

This chapter explores the transition from childlike to adult consciousness, examining how language and perception create a filter between pure sensory experience and conceptual understanding, examining how adults lose direct experiential awareness as linguistic and conceptual frameworks take over.

CORE CONCEPTS

- *Pure sensory awareness versus perceptual awareness*
- *The role of language in shaping consciousness*
- *Loss of direct experience through conceptualisation*

NEW TERMINOLOGY

Matrix: *Layer of perception that filters pure sensory experience*

Perception: *Awareness that includes interpretation of meaning*

Pre-verbal: *State before language acquisition*

MAIN THEMES

- *Consciousness development*
- *Perceptual transformation*
- *Alchemical perspective*
- *Biblical symbolism*

INTEGRATION POINTS

- *Connection to The Shadow (Chapter 10)*
- *Foundation for Enlightenment (Chapter 6)*
- *Preparation for working with Symbols (Chapter 4)*

PRACTICAL APPLICATIONS

- *Meditation practices for accessing pure consciousness*
- *Integration of direct and conceptual experience*
- *Balancing immediate and abstract awareness*

COMMON MISCONCEPTIONS

- *Pure experience versus conceptual understanding*
- *Relationship between language and consciousness*
- *Role of pre-verbal experience in spiritual development*

REFLECTION QUESTIONS

- *How has your perception of reality changed since childhood?*
- *Can you recall moments when you first began attaching meanings to pure sensory experiences?*
- *In what ways do you notice language filtering your direct experience of reality?*
- *How does your adult consciousness differ from your memories of childhood consciousness?*

4. The Symbols and their Meanings

*"The excellence of the soul is understanding;
for the man who understands is conscious,
devoted, and already godlike."* [6]

This chapter explores how alchemical symbolism serves as a specialised language for understanding spiritual transformation. We'll examine how symbols evolved as tools to convey complex spiritual concepts while safeguarding esoteric knowledge, exploring their role in personal development and consciousness evolution. Understanding these symbols provides a foundation for working with the transformative processes described in later chapters.

Words are perceptual symbols. Each word is a perception that the mind learns to recognise and associate with a certain set of meanings. These meanings are not fixed but evolve through our experience and understanding, much like the alchemical process itself.

Alchemy employs symbols to communicate complex or abstract ideas. There was a need to keep the lessons secret during times of possible misinterpretation or persecution. The downside of using obscure symbols is there often has to be an oral tradition of masters, teaching students, the precise meaning of these symbols. This tradition ensures the authentic transmission of knowledge while protecting its deeper significance.

---

[6] *Hermes Trismegistus, Corpus Hermeticum*

Nigredo

The Bible is a book on alchemy.

What does this mean?

The Bible is a book that details the evolution of human consciousness. The concepts we use are necessarily abstract, so we used symbolic language. This is why as an adult reading the bible it doesn't make sense until you understand that terms and names are symbolic. For instance, the *Garden of Eden* represents a state of original consciousness, while the serpent symbolises the awakening of discriminative wisdom.

During this course we will touch on some of the symbols we find in alchemy. However, I won't tend to depend on them, for a number of reasons. Firstly, unless anybody knows any better, we can only guess at what these symbols mean. We can spend and waste time arguing about this. My premise is that there is a process that is common to all mystery schools. Different religions have differing approaches. Often, these symbols are highly personal, and you will learn to develop your own understanding.

These symbols represent what can often not be described adequately. They are labels of types of experience that is deeply personal. Consciousness needs to be dissected, and its constituent parts analysed. These symbols represent markers or labels that help us do this. Like signposts on a journey, they guide us but are not the destination themselves.

Ultimately, one must learn to transcend symbols—yet they remain necessary when discussing or expressing these experiences. You will need to gain a certain fluency in a pretty obscure type of language. This language speaks to the soul rather than the intellect.

Practically this is a problem for the aspiring alchemist. Often there are no shortages of clues or inspiration, the answers really are sitting there for all to see. But we habitually look past them, into the world of things and people and fail to see the nose on our faces. Our conditioning blinds us to the obvious.

On my journey I found that as a non-classically educated, native English speaker, that Buddhism offers the most complete access to a system of spiritual enlightenment. However, for a Hebrew speaker or Mandarin speaker, other systems might be more accessible. There is no point re-inventing the wheel, so the backbone of this course will use Buddhist terminology, which is generally pretty accessible for those who wish to deepen their understanding.

We begin by examining a few key symbols in alchemy.

The *Retort*.

This is the apparatus in which we place the raw material for transformation. It is a sealed, refluxing device, upon which we apply a carefully controlled and very prolonged *heat*. The alchemical process during which the alchemist transmutes their substance of being (*the raw material*) is called the Great Work, or work for short. This *retort* or vessel is a metaphor for the alchemist themselves. They take their current experience of being, and through a certain separation or hermitage, focus inwards with the aim of understanding. The raw substance is subjected to an increasing level of observation and analysis, and through this *heat* (Wisdom or insight) breaks down into its elemental parts. The *retort's* sealed nature symbolises the focused containment of energy required for transformation.

The Raw Substance.

This is the conditionality that the alchemist suffers. It is an accumulation of perceptions that the alchemist, on some level, is aware of and wishes to purify. This Raw Substance is the starting ingredient of what will become the stone of the philosophers — a metaphysical ground of being that is transmuted through a number of steps to a substance of increasing refined purity. It encompasses all our psychological material: our thoughts, emotions, memories, and habitual patterns of behaviour.

The Secret Alchemist's Fire.

This intellectual curiosity begins as a faint spark but strengthens with faith and later wisdom. It manifests initially as curiosity and doubt, with doubt eventually turning inwards and corroding inner (delusional) structures of self. This doubt is transformed into faith and hope, which later transforms into a certain confidence and deep sense of knowing (*Gnosis*). This fire is the transformative power of awareness itself, burning away illusion to reveal truth.

The Crow or any dark bird.

This represents Nigredo or darkness, the *dross* that is part of the raw substance that one must initially work with. It symbolises the *Dark Night of the Soul*, the period of confusion and despair that precedes spiritual awakening. The blackness signifies both the decay of old patterns and the fertile ground for new understanding.

Planetary figures.

Each planet was associated with a metal, with different metals representing various aspects of consciousness or temperament. Mercury represents fluidity of mind, Mars represents will and determination, Venus represents harmony and beauty, Jupiter represents expansion and wisdom, Saturn represents discipline and limitation, while the Sun and Moon represent consciousness and unconsciousness respectively.

The *Rebis*.

This represents unified duality, the reconsolidating of opposites. In order to reach the awareness we associate with the Garden, the path is a narrowly balanced one. It points to the transcendence of apparent contradictions and the discovery of underlying unity. The *Rebis* is often depicted as a composite symbol uniting multiple elements into a single harmonious form.

The Lion (or sun).

Generally this represents the self, or purified self. We will explore this much deeper later on. The lion symbolises both the raw power of the ego and, when tamed, the noble strength of the transformed consciousness. Its golden colour connects it to solar consciousness and spiritual illumination.

The Moon.

The moon has no light of its own, but is reflective. It appears to change in a cyclical manner and represents natural rhythms such as seasons especially with regards to fertility. It symbolises the unconscious mind, intuition, and the feminine principle of receptivity. Its phases represent the cycles of spiritual transformation.

This is certainly enough to start with. Don't focus too much on this archaic symbology — it is interesting but also tends to confuse. I'll point out any correspondences between systems, or at least those that I think correspond. Remember that these symbols are tools for understanding, not the understanding itself.

Mythos

Study Guide: The Symbols and their Meanings

This chapter explores alchemical symbolism as a language for understanding spiritual transformation, examining symbols as tools for conveying complex spiritual concepts, their role in personal development, and their impact on consciousness evolution.

CORE CONCEPTS
- *Transformative vessel*
- *Raw material transformation*
- *Symbolic language*

NEW TERMINOLOGY

Anima Mundi: *Soul of the universe*
Raw Substance: *The conditionality the alchemist works to purify*
Rebis: *Symbol of unified duality*
Retort: *Symbolic vessel for transformation*
Secret Alchemist's Fire: *Intellectual curiosity that transforms into wisdom*

MAIN THEMES
- *Nature of symbols*
- *Evolution of meaning through personal experience*
- *Limitations of symbolic communication*
- *Role of symbols in protecting esoteric knowledge*
- *Words and perceptions as symbolic constructs*

SPIRITUAL FRAMEWORKS
- *The Bible as an alchemical text*
- *Buddhist terminology for English speakers*
- *Personal interpretation and meaning*
- *Universal process across mystery schools*

PRACTICAL APPLICATIONS
- *Connection to Nigredo phase*
- *Links to meditation practice*
- *Progressive refinement of consciousness*
- *Working with conditioned existence*

INTEGRATION POINTS
- *Connection to enlightenment*
- *Links to meditation practice*
- *Relationship to Fisher-King Wound*

REFLECTION QUESTIONS
- *How do you experience the interplay between solar and lunar consciousness in your life*
- *How do you see the retort symbol manifesting in your own inner work*
- *What does the concept of the raw substance mean in terms of your own psychological material*
- *Which alchemical symbols resonate most strongly with your personal experience*

PROGRESS INDICATORS
- *Evolution of meaning through practice*
- *Personal interpretation*
- *Universal process across traditions*

With serpents entwined, the winged caduceus stands,
Placed upright between the horns of Amalthea.
Thus, it signifies men strong in mind and skilled in wisdom,
Indicating that abundant wealth blesses the earth.

The sacred caduceus of Mercury stands upright, crowned with a cap,
With two serpents entwined —one mild, the other fierce —
Which, through their entwining, form the Herculean knot.
It signifies that those who are unknown may be loved,
And those who are separated may be united.
What Alciatus has insightfully inferred from this
May be easily understood by those who recognise his
Sharp intellect and eloquence, through which he excelled above others.
For such knowledge and skill bring great honour
And wealth earned through true prudence. [7]

---

[7] *Andrea Alciato, Emblemata, Padua: Pietro Paolo Tozzi, 1621.*

5. The Fable of Alchemy

> *"The opus magnum had two aims:*
> *the rescue of the human soul and the salvation of the cosmos."* [8]

In this chapter, we explore the deeper meaning behind alchemical mythology and its true spiritual significance. While modern science has debunked the literal interpretation of physical transmutation, the rich symbolism of alchemy points to a profound system of inner transformation. We'll examine how the alchemist's work with metals and materials serves as a sophisticated metaphor for spiritual development, revealing the true nature of the philosopher's stone as a path to liberation from suffering

We cannot ignore the findings of modern science when it comes to the primary mythos of alchemy. If we take it literally, that is. Most modern readers will know that the atomic transmutation of, say, lead into gold is possible, but not without a particle collider or supernova at hand. To achieve this using some other means is the textbook definition of magic.

It is far more likely that actual witnessed events of physical transmutation were part of a confidence or, at least, *magical trick*. Plating the base metal with gold might fool untrained observers, and the scope to use any chemical or physical sleight of hand lends itself to use as part of a confidence trick.

---

[8] *Jung, C.G. (1952 Interview at Eranos)*

Nigredo

Even if physical transformation were possible, surely the focus should be much more on the actual practitioners, rather than an interest in their recipes.

Those few wise folk that were labelled *alchemist* were more than metallurgists or primitive chemists. Many either seemed to have other miraculous powers or were mystically spiritual. They talked of reincarnation, past lives and other realms of existence.

Such mystical folk often spoke in metaphor and riddle, frequently suffering persecution and censorship. The idea of a personal union with the divine didn't go down too well with those intent on taxing faith. So it is hardly a stretch of the imagination to consider that the transmutation is of the self, and not the contents of a crucible.

It would be easy to dismiss *physical* alchemy altogether, if it wasn't completely possible to reach spiritual enlightenment through sitting and staring at a motionless *retort*. Yet, this is very similar to a Buddhist (and other religions') meditative practice where a *kasina* or simple visual disk is selected for prolonged consideration. So, it is entirely possible that alchemists achieved *jhanic* (a special form of awareness) consciousness, that then permitted insights and transmutations (of self).

The basic premise for the main alchemical process is the alchemist takes some common substance, maybe even excreta like urine, and seals it within a vessel that allows the refluxing of escaped vapours to return to the main chamber. It would be analogous to modern distilling equipment.

Then, through the careful application of a mild, but increasing heat, a certain series of processes occur that, through stages, transform the raw substance into a living one.

The process, called the *Great Work*, is and would be laborious. Like the *retort*, this process is hermetic—sealed off from outside influence. The alchemist must carefully attend to the process which must be observed continuously — for weeks and even months. Subtle changes in colour, or nature indicate important stages which if missed, ruin the whole process. Vapours and fluids are collected to be remixed at a later stage. It is important we consider the concept of analysis and synthesis (*solve et coagula*) — the alchemist *breaks down* the raw material into its elemental constituents and then remixes or synthesises something more pure (divinely pure) with these parts.

The resulting *substance* is described as both waxy and powdery. It is said to be reddish in colour, and when mixed—even in a tiny amount—with a base metal and heated, it catalyses a reaction, transforming the whole into gold. This same substance can be made into a tincture and consumed; here it heals or even confers immortality.

So, while the *myth* largely focuses on a *process*, the alchemist's commitment and dedication are unmistakable. Such individuals were often successful in their own lives and more than wise enough to find unlimited wealth less attractive than loftier matters. Sure, we could all do with a bit more coin, but these individuals are unlikely to commit to such a dedicated task for just a bit more wealth.

We must therefore consider, more closely, the other claims of this manufactured substance. Firstly, it is healing. And, secondly, it confers immortality, whatever that means.

The great alchemists were deeply spiritual and mystical, often serving as natural healers who employed both herbal remedies and esoteric methods. Some were Christians and most followed a Platonic or Aristotelian model of the cosmos. Themes of healing and immortality form the backbone of these ideologies and here we find correspondences between the goals and rewards of spiritual enlightenment in these mystery religions and the goals of alchemy.

What would the ability to make gold give us? We would no longer fear material poverty. I accept that in all probability it would cause more problems than it solves, but if this is a riddle we must think laterally. Unlimited wealth could almost equate to a perfect satisfaction with the now, an elimination of mundane worries. But what about other worries, such as sickness or death?

Well, funny enough, our special substance also addresses these concerns.

So our goal through this process is a substance that, in a primitive way, eliminates suffering. Once we get access to this substance we no longer need to worry about poverty, sickness, old age or death.

Those familiar with the beginning of Gautama Buddha's life will recall that his father sought to shield him from these very conditions. These are the things that once the Buddha experienced caused him to turn away from a royal life in search of the truth.

Now this makes much more sense. These spiritual and wise people are trying to convey an elusive and possibly heretical secret that transforms suffering, rather than a get-rich-quick scheme.

However, this secret need not be concealed, for it is hidden in plain sight. Teaching another person to perceive it is no simple task. There are many methods which all seem nonsensical to those who cannot see it, and therefore to even pursue it, one needs faith.

After studying alchemy for a reasonable period of time I am more and more convinced that *hermetic western alchemy* is nothing more or less than another system of spiritual enlightenment. This viewpoint is supported through a subsequent, and equally reasonable assessment of Buddhism, where there is significant correspondence. These correspondences are likewise reflected in Greek and Kabbalistic traditions.

So, with that premise we shall continue exploring my synthesis of these systems or what I'm calling modern alchemy.

Study Guide: The Fable Of Alchemy

This chapter explores alchemy as a spiritual transformation system, comparing Western hermetic traditions with Eastern practices, moving beyond material pursuits to inner development.

CORE CONCEPTS

- Transformation through alchemical processes
- Integration of physical and spiritual practices
- Universal principles of spiritual development
- Relationship between observation and spiritual growth

NEW TERMINOLOGY

Great Work: The main alchemical process of transformation

Jhāna: Special form of awareness in meditation

Philosopher's Stone: The ultimate goal of alchemical transformation

MAIN THEMES

1. Myth vs Reality
- Physical transmutation as metaphor
- Historical context of alchemical practice
- The role of symbolism and esoteric knowledge
- Connection to spiritual enlightenment

2. The Great Work
- Nature of spiritual transformation
- Importance of dedicated observation
- Analysis and synthesis principles
- Stages of inner development

3. Spiritual Dimensions
- Links to Buddhist meditation practices
- Universal aspects of transformation
- Role of faith and understanding
- Connection to enlightenment

4. The Philosopher's Stone
- Symbolic meaning of transmutation
- Freedom from suffering
- Relationship to Buddhist teachings
- Links to later alchemical symbols

PRACTICAL APPLICATIONS

- Nature of true transformation versus superficial change
- Relationship between dedication and spiritual growth
- Possibility of liberation from suffering
- Role of faith in spiritual development
- The role of patience in spiritual and alchemical transformation

REFLECTION QUESTIONS

- What aspects of your own spiritual journey mirror the alchemical process?
- How do you understand the relationship between physical and spiritual transformation?
- What does the philosopher's stone represent in your personal development?
- How do you relate to the concept of inner transmutation?

INTEGRATION POINTS

- Connection to enlightenment (Chapter 6)
- Links to later alchemical symbols (Chapter 4)

NIGREDO

The Three Realities

APPARENT REALITY

"The world of things, beings, and concepts—where perception constructs identity."

- Apparent Reality is the mundane, everyday world we navigate, governed by objects, labels, and structured experiences.
- This is the reality of form, where we categorise and define things: "This is an apple," "This is me," "This is time."
- It is shaped by sensory input and conditioned thought, meaning that what we perceive is a filtered interpretation rather than truth.
- Mistaken as absolute reality, it creates attachment, suffering, and illusion when taken at face value.

"The world of name—where objects, identities, and perceptions define existence."

CONDITIONAL REALITY

"A deeper framework that governs perception—where conditioned forces shape experience."

- Conditional Reality reveals the underlying forces that determine experience:
- Karma and mental formations shape how events unfold.
- The mind operates through conceptual models, language, and cause-effect relationships.
- Everything experienced here is still conditioned—subject to patterns of cause and effect, bound by mind's interpretations.
- This reality can be studied and understood, allowing one to gradually dismantle the illusion of self and form.

"The unseen forces shaping perception—where karma, mind, and interpretation create experience."

UNCONDITIONAL REALITY (NIRVANA)

"Beyond perception, beyond concept—only pure awareness remains."

- Unconditional Reality (Nirvana) is not a "thing" or a state, but rather the absence of conditioned perception.
- It is not merely the absence of suffering, but the absence of the self-construct that experiences suffering.
- It cannot be grasped conceptually, because concepts themselves belong to conditional reality.
- The closest metaphors include:
- A candle flame ceasing, but not being destroyed.
- The moon reflected in water—it appears real, but is only an illusion of form.
- Only through direct realisation does one step beyond the veil of conditioned perception.

6. Enlightenment

*"Enlightenment is a destructive process.
It has nothing to do with becoming better or being happier.
Enlightenment is the crumbling away of untruth.
It's seeing through the facade of pretence."* [9]

In this chapter, we explore the paradoxical nature of enlightenment — a state that defies conventional understanding yet represents the ultimate goal of spiritual alchemy. We examine why direct descriptions fail, how understanding itself can become an obstacle, and what enlightenment means in practical terms. Understanding itself can become an obstacle; we will also examine what enlightenment means in practical terms. By carefully analysing different types of reality and the nature of consciousness, we develop a framework for approaching this ineffable state while embracing its fundamental mystery.

It might be useful at this stage to offer you a working *understanding* of enlightenment, sadly, with the following premise.

Understanding is a mental process in which we construct a working mental model that closely applies to some reality. If we think we understand something, yet it acts contrary to our expectations, then we must conclude we don't understand everything about it.

---

[9] *Adyashanti*

Nigredo

Understanding is a mental construct that depends on a conceptualised model of reality—this is its limit. It itself is constructed from conditioned reality, which is our main problem. If I asked you what exactly is gold, and in reply, you simply showed me different pieces of gold jewellery, you would be missing the point. No matter how many shapes or forms of gold you show me, they still do not answer my question.

Trying to *understand* enlightenment is like this. Understanding draws on elements from conditioned reality, which themselves are of conditioned reality, to try to explain what is unconditioned. It's like trying to describe Beethoven's Fifth Symphony using only scent.

Rather than explaining what it is, which is impossible, one has to rely on metaphor. We then say *it is like...*

Even this is problematic; it is often compared to the Zen metaphor of a *finger pointing at the moon*.

If I try to describe something, say a tiger, I might say it's like a cat. This is accurate and offers some information, yet, if I have only ever known cats it could lead to some interesting mistakes. If I am trying to get your attention, and I point towards the moon as I say *moon*, the bright student looks to where the finger points, and sees the moon and understands.

But if instead you mistake my finger for *moon* then you miss both the moon and the finger (which you think is *moon*).

To help counter this one must remember that one's current understanding is not the truth. Hopefully, if your guidance is worthy, it will progressively approximate a truth, but it is never the truth. For the truth *about* enlightenment is beyond the clumsy grasp of words.

In order to find where exactly one *looks* for enlightenment, one must come to understand *conditioned reality*.

Three types of reality:

- 1. **Apparent Reality** — this is normal adult existence. A world of things, beings and concepts. This is the mundane world of normal concerns.
- 2. **Conditional Reality** — this is a model for the true nature of reality. Remember, it is still only a model, an understanding, but it is one that offers an accurate picture for one purpose only, and that is, to understand so that one might transcend (escape) conditioned existence.
- 3. *Nirvāṇa*, or unconditioned existence, is difficult to conceptualise, but attaining it requires mastering the ability of becoming.

Nirvāṇa is the unconditioned element. There is very little more we can say about it. It isn't a thing, for that is conditioned. Neither can it be any concept about it, although accurate concepts point at it, like a finger points towards the moon.

Nirvāṇa is not simply the absence of conditionality—for that, too, is a conditioned thing. Rather, it encompasses the absence of conditionality.

To illustrate the difficulty of conceptualising conditionality, consider the Mississippi River. Now I can ask you *where* is this river, and if you know, you might point it out on a map, or tell me which part of the world it exists in, or, if I am close enough, you might say *over the next hill*. We all know what we are talking about.

But if I asked you for a *piece* of this river, would you bring me a bucket of water?

Could I say that this bucket of water *belongs* to the Mississippi?

And is this water still part of the river, here in a bucket? If it is, then the river is likely to eventually be everywhere. If it isn't then the Mississippi river has nothing to do with this water.

A river is the name of a process. This is the same for any label — we are trying to pin the illusion of sameness on something that is never the same, it is a process.

When we name things we attribute labels that give an illusion of stability. Our choice of which parts of the world to *thing* is arbitrary, where does a tree end or a forest start?

Nigredo

Attempting to define reality is like trying to nail smoke.

In our attempt to understand enlightenment we make it more elusive.

Thankfully, and relatively recently, there was at least one person who worked it all out. If we cannot understand the destination then maybe we can understand the path towards this destination. We cannot grasp it, for grasping itself prevents us from attaining it. So, one must follow a series of steps, all which might be considered preliminary to the ultimate goal.

One cannot seek or force enlightenment. One can only work towards providing the ideal conditions for it to happen. It occurs in distinct stages. Misunderstood, partial enlightenment often leads to confusion, sometimes mistaken for mental illness.

So, if we can't exactly describe enlightenment, because it escapes definition, why would we want to seek it?

Enlightenment is a state of non-being where one has managed to develop a fearless but benevolent approach to life. The enlightened non-being is desire-less, totally desire-less. They lack subtle clinging which non-enlightened individuals suffer. They have total disregard towards a self.

This fearlessness arises from a deep shift in perspective, one that trivialises life from an expanded view. We will, in a much later lesson get into the technicalities, but for now, a process occurs which grants the *Arahant* (fully enlightened being) complete access to all their memories. But, it doesn't stop there. When the filter of *self* is removed they gain complete access to any memory in any past life.

Again, words fail to express the magnitude of the vision that befalls the *Arahant* on full realisation. It isn't like hypnotic past life regression where one might get glimpses into a dreamlike, half fantasy existence.

Upon realisation the *Arahant* becomes aware of all the memories, including their experience of death, of thousands and thousands of past lives.

With the vivid recall of thousands of deaths, what concern could remain for the *Arahant*?

Enlightenment is the cessation of suffering. To a chronic sufferer, this may seem magical or unbelievable, but it is simply a process that shifts one's mental perspective.

Another way to consider it is as a hidden pathway within the mechanisms that condition life and existence—gradually uncoupling mental experience from suffering.

The path to enlightenment unfolds in stages. Whilst I cannot truthfully endorse the more wild claims of enlightenment I can say that until now nothing has deterred me from believing their validity. The *dharma* that has got me thus far has been both uncanny and accurate.

The term *enlightenment* can be misleading—nothing is gained. It is simply the awakening to delusion. One simply sees the delusion. One might suggest that one gains freedom, emancipation, which means a liberation from suffering. But this is not really a gain, as one doesn't revel in this liberation.

If one thinks a close friend has stolen something precious, but then finds it was simply misplaced, one doesn't continue to be angry at that friend. It was our mistake and at least in this instance our friend was innocent of what we feared.

Suddenly mundane concerns are no longer any worry. The automatic *involvement* and identification with one's problems ceases, and the meaning we attribute changes. Without attachment to things, being or concepts the *Arahant* floats through life. They can still be subject to *karma* they made prior to their realisation but this doesn't bother them as they no longer cling to existence.

They have no enemies or adversaries, for they cling neither to concepts nor to time. Each experience is new, without prejudice of prior ones. Insight penetrates completely and one cannot see any self. One is free from choice or decision as this requires a self to decide about. They act with *wholesome* actions simply because this is their only possible action, although they are indifferent to any reward for such behaviour.

Without any inner concept of self there can be no clinging. They eat when hungry, sleep when tired and move through the world, almost invisible without creating any ripples in the social fabric, and this is before we consider any psychic abilities they may develop.

Furthermore, whilst they tend to enjoy good health through the avoidance of intoxicants or unhealthy living, they are healers. They naturally dampen *karma*, mean gestures towards them are not reflected, nor are kind gestures. They affect others effortlessly and slowly transform their moral qualities by being merely present.

Lastly, they become free of volition—ceasing to create *karma* and severing themselves from *Saṃsāra*, the great cycle of becoming. In this way, they become deathless.

Desirelessness, the inductive transmutation of moral qualities, and deathlessness are all features of the philosopher's stone—our purified raw substance and the very essence of the alchemist.

With our groundwork laid, let us now explore the preliminary stages an alchemist must consider before embarking on the *Great Work*.

The Realities

Apparent: *This is the reality of normal existence. Here the focus is on the dynamics common to life such as interpersonal, professional, family, political relationships. It is the reality of things, people, concepts, ideas. This reality is governed by deeper rules that are seldom appreciated, instead, one attributes misfortune to fate or external factors rather than appreciating any personal causation.*

Conditional: *A conceptual reality based on observation of Apparent Reality. Here is a recognition that Subjective Reality is governed by largely unseen mental forces, such as karma, that condition our experience. This reality was discovered and described by the Buddha most recently — the understanding of which allows progression along a spiritual path out of the inherent suffering (unsatisfactoriness).*

The alchemist, through either personal observation or study, learns of a deeper set of rules that govern life. They then undergo personal transmutations associated with relinquishing attachments to Apparent Reality by recognising the illusion of this superficial existence.

Mythos

Unconditional: This reality is difficult to describe—perhaps even to believe—yet it is the experience of pure awareness, free from all conceptual definition. Awareness, lacking any specific object is limitless and omniscient. This reality is called Nirvāṇa, yet in truth, it is the same reality—simply perceived from a different side.

The primary task of an aspiring alchemist is to study conditioned reality to comprehend the finer aspects of the mind. It is not purely academic and in truth an accurate model is less important than a model one has faith in.

The main purpose of studying conditioned reality is to develop a kind of map of subjective experience. Armed with this understanding, one learns how to cultivate non-conceptual experience and cross the final Veil.

Study Guide: Enlightenment

The chapter explores enlightenment through Buddhist and alchemical lenses, examining the paradoxical nature of understanding, three levels of reality, and characteristics of the enlightened state.

CORE CONCEPTS

- *Understanding through mental models and their limitations*
- *Three distinct levels of reality: apparent, conditional, and unconditional*
- *Enlightenment as freedom from desire and transcendence of self*

NEW TERMINOLOGY

Arahant: *Fully enlightened being*
Dharma: *Natural law or truth*
Saṃsāra: *Cycle of becoming and rebirth*

MAIN THEMES

1. *Understanding Paradox*
- *Understanding as mental modelling*
- *Limitations of conceptual frameworks*
- *Finger pointing at moon metaphor*
- *Descriptions versus reality trap*

2. *Reality Levels*
- *Apparent Reality (everyday experience)*
- *Conditional Reality (causation framework)*
- *Unconditional reality/Nirvāṇa*

3. *Enlightenment Nature*
- *Freedom from desire and clinging*
- *Transcendence of self-concept*
- *Complete memory access*
- *Liberation from suffering*
- *Philosopher's stone connection*

4. *Description Challenges*
- *Direct description limitations*
- *Metaphor role*
- *Language limits*
- *Symbols and meanings connection*

5. *Process Reality*
- *River metaphor*
- *Phenomena impermanence*
- *Stable identity illusion*
- *Rebis connection*

6. *Enlightened State*

Nigredo

- *Freedom from karmic cycles*
- *Natural healing presence*
- *Spontaneous moral transformation*
- *Connection to the Call to Adventure*

Reflection Questions

- *How do you experience conceptual thinking limitations?*
- *What experiences point beyond conditioned reality?*
- *How do you relate to the three reality types?*
- *What does unconditioned existence mean personally?*

Progress Indicators

- *Understanding conceptual limitations*
- *Recognition of multiple levels of reality*
- *Reduced attachment to self-concept*
- *Increased awareness of impermanence*

Integration Points

- *Connection to Symbols and Meanings (Chapter 4)*
- *Link to The Rebis (Chapter 9)*
- *Relationship to The Call to Adventure (Chapter 7)*

Common Misconceptions

- *Confusing descriptions with direct experience*
- *Misinterpreting Unconditioned Reality*
- *Oversimplifying the characteristics of enlightenment*

7. The Call to Adventure

"The unexamined life is not worth living." — *Socrates* [10]

The spiritual path begins with an inexplicable calling—a profound restlessness that worldly success alone cannot satisfy. This chapter explores how certain individuals are drawn to the alchemical journey through a combination of intellectual capacity, moral inclination, and an innate dissatisfaction with conventional existence. We explore the prerequisites for spiritual seeking and how the genuine call to transformation is both a blessing and a burden.

It seems very likely that only certain individuals can foster an interest in alchemy. Not only is there a certain intellectual requirement, but one must have a certain insight into suffering for one to have the motivation to turn away from conditionality.

Whether it truly is a manifestation of *karma* or something else, one probably needs to be born in relative comfort. The perspectives necessary to *question* the authority of conditioned reality means that one must be relatively distanced from mere survival. A mind shaped solely by adversity is more prone to ill-will or greed, which perpetuates its restlessness.

---

[10] Plato. (399 BCE/1997). Apology, 38a. In J.M. Cooper (Ed.), Complete Works. Hackett Publishing.

There needs to be a certain level of dissatisfaction with the current status quo. To seek deeper understanding, one must first recognise life's inherent dissatisfaction through experience and wisdom.

It is likely, if one accepts reincarnation, that once one becomes human, one remains human for several rebirths. I love the idea that domesticated animals are the lucky few that get *taught* how to be human, and as such have a chance of being blessed with human rebirth subsequently.

Buddhism teaches that humans can be reborn into ten different states of being, shaped by the composition of their *life continuum* consciousness. Whilst all humans have to be born with one of eight types, it is possible, say through addiction or brutalisation, that one becomes animal and utterly obsessed with one's immediate needs.

So, it is likely that naturally intelligent humans have simply had more human incarnations. It is also possible that they have descended to become humans from a heavenly or formless realm, but we will cover this later.

This will manifest as a deep but often hard to explain fascination with the unknown. Such individuals find being *good* relatively easy; it just makes sense. They might excel relatively, but then suffer boredom with any success. They will be fascinated with science or religion, but dissatisfied with any limitations in scope.

The drive that infects certain individuals cannot make sense but manifests as a vague calling towards the unknown. This is like a silent *call* that disturbs the peace and tranquillity (and normal and often successful life). Like the Buddha, who, despite being a prince and newly married, could no longer rest in ignorance—no matter how comfortable his life seemed.

This *Call* doesn't need to be dramatic. Ideally it isn't, but frequently it isn't understood and manifests as a restlessness that isn't sated with normal success.

Ultimately, a genuine interest in alchemy is likely the only true prerequisite for success. I could warn you that it might become consuming and obsessive but for the interested this wouldn't deter them. There are lots of differing routes, and one doesn't necessarily have to sell all and go and live in a cave.

The path is both moral and spiritual. *What do I mean by this?*

Mythos

In order to reach the tranquillity of mind that allows the breakthrough to transcendental awareness, one has to make every effort to settle it. Acts of anger, greed or delusional pursuits keep the mind restless and preoccupied with mundane things. One may sit in meditation for hours, yet with a restless mind, it remains mere thinking.

Improving one's moral outlook for the alchemist is therefore largely practical. One needs a relatively low profile and time alone. Creating adversity is likely to be counterproductive, as is stealing, sexual misconduct and violence. So one learns to be morally fluent so as to circumnavigate mundane problems that are bound to distract.

The alchemist must consider strange concepts, worlds and beings. Ultimately, these cancel each other out, yet one must embrace the mysterious and *impossible* to leave the reassuring shores of normality.

It is wise to foster a certain respect for beings, whether one believes in their existence or not. A deepened respect for *life* or the soul of the universe, the *anima mundi*, is important which manifests as the developing qualities of kindness, compassion, appreciative joy and fairness. There is a natural development to a more *wholesome* state of being, that accelerates once confidence (faith) appears.

At this stage however, we are preparing the raw substance. I guess normally one must learn to navigate the pitfalls of this process by oneself, and in truth I have no idea about the transferability of this process.

Still, I will endeavour. In the next lesson, we will explore the first challenge for the aspiring alchemist: the *Fisher-King Wound*.

> "And, when you want something,
> all the universe conspires in helping you achieve it." [11]

---

[11] Coelho, P. (2009). *The Alchemist*

Nigredo

Study Guide: The Call To Adventure

This chapter explores the relationship between material comfort, intellectual capacity, and spiritual seeking, examining how these conditions enable yet must be transcended. It explores the traits of those drawn to alchemy—dissatisfaction with conventional existence, a natural moral inclination, and an evolving consciousness—while examining karma and spiritual maturity across lifetimes.

CORE CONCEPTS

- *Material comfort as foundation for spiritual inquiry*
- *Intellectual capacity and moral development*
- *Spiritual calling as culmination of multiple lifetimes*
- *Harmonising solitude with worldly engagement*

NEW TERMINOLOGY

Gnosis: *Deep spiritual knowing*

Karma: *Law of cause and effect*

MAIN THEMES

1. Nature of the Calling
- *Origins in intellectual capacity*
- *Relationship to material comfort*
- *Connection between dissatisfaction and awakening*
- *Links to enlightenment*

2. Prerequisites for the Path
- *Distance from survival concerns*
- *Capacity for spiritual questioning*
- *Natural moral inclination*
- *Connection to evolution of adulthood*

3. Signs of Readiness
- *Fascination with the unknown*
- *Ease with moral behaviour*
- *Excellence with dissatisfaction*
- *Interest in scientific and spiritual realms*
- *Links to symbols and meanings*

PRACTICAL APPLICATIONS

- *Balancing material comfort with spiritual growth*
- *Developing moral character*
- *Cultivating intellectual understanding*
- *Balancing spiritual pursuit with worldly engagement*

INTEGRATION POINTS

- *Connection to enlightenment concepts*
- *Links to evolution of adulthood*
- *Relationship to symbols and meanings*

COMMON MISCONCEPTIONS

- *Material comfort as obstacle rather than foundation*
- *Necessity of dramatic lifestyle changes*
- *Separation of intellectual and spiritual development*

REFLECTION QUESTIONS

- *What form has the call to adventure taken in your life*
- *How has dissatisfaction with conventional existence manifested for you*
- *How does morality influence your spiritual development?*
- *How do you experience the connection between suffering and spiritual awakening?*

Progress Indicators

- *Growing ease with moral behaviour*
- *Natural questioning of conventional existence*
- *Balance of worldly excellence and spiritual seeking*
- *Integration of intellectual and spiritual understanding*

Aspects of The Calling

Aspect	Characteristics	Manifestation
Calling	Inner restlessness	Dissatisfaction with conventional success
Prerequisites	Material comfort	Freedom to pursue spiritual questions
Readiness	Natural morality	Ease with ethical behaviour
Development	Gradual growth	Progressive spiritual awakening

Nigredo

The Fisher-King Wound

1. Pre-Verbal Awareness (The Infant)

At birth, the infant exists in a state of pure being. There is no concept of self and other, no rejection, no separation— only undifferentiated awareness. The world is whole because no distinctions exist yet.

2. Conditional Awareness (The Child)

As the child develops, so does self-awareness. They begin to recognise themselves as separate, yet they do not yet fully reject parts of themselves. The early self-image is curious and fluid, reflecting the world without deep projection or distortion.

3. Brutalised Awareness (The Adolescent)

The adolescent experiences cultural conditioning, social pressures, and survival mechanisms. They reject any qualities perceived as weak, reinforcing an identity that values power, control, and detachment. They become a half-being—capable of compassion, fairness, and kindness, but only when rationalised through ego (strength, status, or achievement).

4. The Wounded King (The Isolated Self)

The final stage is emotional desolation. The Fisher King, though powerful, is wounded and unable to heal. Their inner world becomes barren, their capacity to feel is severed. Encased in armor and status, they lose their ability to connect—with others or themselves. Only confronting the wound directly can restore wholeness.

The Fisher-King's wound is not a life sentence but a call to integration. The path to healing is not in rejecting the wound, but in understanding it, facing it, and reclaiming the lost self. In the Grail myth, only a seeker who asks the right question can heal the wounded king. Likewise, self-inquiry and awareness are the keys to restoring inner wholeness.

8. The Fisher-King Wound

"The wound is the place where the Light enters you." [12]

The Fisher-King Wound represents a fundamental psychological pattern that emerges from societal conditioning and emotional numbing. This chapter explores how cultural demands for toughness, particularly but not exclusively in males, create deep psychological scarring that manifests as emotional disconnection and hidden suffering. Through understanding this wound, we begin to recognise how early conditioning shapes our current experience and learn paths toward healing and integration.

The *Fisher-King Wound* refers to a pattern of conditioning that brutalises the individual, leading to a fundamental shift in experience. Whilst traditionally in many cultures it has been the males who were deliberately *toughened up*, this wound or pattern of conditionality can and is present to some degree in all conditioned beings.

The name of this *wound* is taken from the myth of Sir Percival and The *Fisher-King*.

There are several versions of this deeply elaborate and symbolic story. It involves concepts of healing, redemption and a wounded *Fisher-King*. And what is a *Fisher-King* — this is the highest position of fisherman, or one who seeks, especially the teachings of Christ (or equivalent saviour figure).

---

[12] *Rumi, J. Mathnawi, I, 3150—3175*

Nigredo

The *Fisher-King* was a valiant and dangerous man in his prime, but he sustains a wound, in his groin (genitals) that leaves him in great pain. This pain keeps him in perpetual misery, yet, he lives in a castle where everybody around him seems to be having a continuous party.

Percival is a young and successful knight, who lives with his mother, and basically spends all his time training to be a better fighter. He first comes across the castle of the *Fisher -King* in his early manhood, and he is instructed how he needs to proceed. Basically, he gets a chance to remove the curse and heal the *Fisher-King*, but it is dependent on him asking the King a very specific question: *Whom does the grail serve?* The grail is a magic cup, that heals if one drinks from it.

However, our young knight gets drunk and too involved in the party, and forgets to ask the question. When he awakens, he is alone and the castle is gone.

Now this is deeply mysterious and brings together important themes.

Our protagonist, Percival, has issues. He is in an *Oedipal* relationship with his mother, and he spends all his time squaring up to whoever will fight him, winning and killing every opponent. Despite this he is dissatisfied and eventually succumbs to a depressive despair despite his now considerable wealth.

It seems he has two chances to change things, the first when he first visits the castle, but then gets drunk and forgets to ask the question. He has a second chance, kind of when his mid-life crisis strikes, and this time it is inferred that he succeeds. But the tale is one of mystery and deliberately leaves things hanging, perhaps to implore the reader to dig deeply when trying to understand.

The *Fisher-King* could be a forewarning for Percival—like Percival, the king was a valiant and deadly warrior. Through this fighting he sustains a wound. This wound is more than physical, it injures the very source of life, the reproductive organs. This wound is also painful and disabling, and keeps the king in painful isolation despite being in the very centre of a party.

The myth examines masculine duty. This arises through an expectation that we largely, but by no means only, place on boys. It varies from culture to culture and within each culture, but there is some form of obligation that at some time boys become men. In our still far from civilised society, we habitually and deliberately encourage boys to develop dispassionate cruelty, pretty much on a whim. This cycle of habitual brutalisation persists across generations, often unquestioned.

When this brutalisation is supported by the mother, it creates a dependence which becomes a poor quality and conditional love. The individual becomes bound by duty or even a code of how to behave, often as chronic but necessary disassociation makes *feeling* impossible.

So, our *Fisher-King* myth is about a kind of depression that arises through following a perverted sense of duty, which numbs and isolates one from feeling. Like most boys Percival has the chance to separate from his mother and define his own path, yet he succumbs to indulgence, drifting into midlife as a heartless warrior.

The Grail is our feminine symbol, but also the symbol of healing associated with the *Christ Consciousness*. (The *Christ Consciousness* is the pure consciousness of the *sephirot* (light or number on the *Tree Of Life*) of *Chesed* — we'll come to this later.)

Our hero has the chance to question his motives, which currently arise through an *Oedipal* love of his mother, but he forgets to ask the question. (He never thinks to question the dodgy relationship he has with his mother.)

The *Fisher-King* is a vision of things to come. His wound is synonymous with the depressive and Hellish existence of one who is habitually violent. The King cannot ask the question himself; he too forgot, consumed by the riches of his success. Now, he reaches back to Percival, urging him to take a hard look at himself.

Well, are you still with me? Do you see how fantastically complex the hidden message is? This brutalisation, which manifests as prejudice and the justification of terrible behaviour leaves the individual dependent on a very poor type of love. They must feel dutiful, and should they fail to maintain this, they are totally cut off, depressed, isolated and in a living hell. This is the very picture of PTSD.

As an alchemist my sole focus is healing. One must learn to undo this in oneself and others.

The first sign of true male maturity is called *learning to shudder*. This is where a man becomes aware of the true horror of his own capacity to disassociate. From this point on the man *gentles*. They have seen enough horror and from that point on strive for peace and harmony. Notice the *Christ Consciousness*, the grail here.

Whilst in this talk I have tended to say this is a male or masculine problem, I do so as traditionally, the deliberate brutalisation of men is more prevalent than that of women. Furthermore, it helps in describing and getting these ideas across. However, the mechanism of this brutalisation has nothing to do with gender. Girls do suffer brutalisation both individually and culturally, but they learn to disassociate to other things. So I encourage all readers irrespective of gender to consider how they might have suffered some form of *toughening up* that now, might, in some way be problematic.

One of the features of the *Fisher-King Wound* is called resentment of the innocent. This is an anger or irritation to innocence or the vulnerable. It manifests as an anger towards *stupid questions* as the learning experience of the aggressor was overtly or subtly traumatic, maybe even they were shamed into thinking the innocent state is inferior.

The primary stages of Alchemy involve an examination of the dark sides of one's personal journey. Like Percival, we are encouraged to question our deeper motives and either we are wise enough to drop things right away and embark on a spiritual path, or we delay, and then through painful spiritual symptoms our quest becomes necessary.

Ideas about who we should be, the mother figure here is symbolic from tradition and duty, are not truly ours. We are rewarded by society for being dutiful yet how many veterans end up discarded once they start to falter. We can become confused about how we identify without ever asking why we need to identify.

Recognition of this wound, a dutiful but karmically unskilled set of habitual conditioning is necessary as one must learn to work with it. A good exercise is to sit in meditation and ask yourself *Who am I?* One must persist as initially there will be many definitions. Each must be examined for emptiness — i.e. a lack of selfness. One continues until the mind lapses into a kind of sulky silence. But do not be perturbed. Sit, and ask yourself every once in a while, *who am I?* The idea is to listen for the slightest response, and then to examine that response. The answer arises once you cease getting any response.

MYTHOS

I hope that was clear enough. In truth one could easily write a whole book about this. Robert Bly's *Iron John* is a worthwhile read on this topic.

As we will be following a largely Buddhist approach, this *wound* is addressed once one understands how *karma* works. Yet, it is definitely worth contemplating early in one's journey and its mysteries are liberating, to a degree, themselves.

*"Every man has a wound,
and the wound is always in the same place —
where love should be."* [13]

[13] Johnson, R.A. *He: Understanding Masculine Psychology*

Nigredo

Study Guide: The Fisher-King Wound

This chapter explores the psychological wound from societal conditioning and emotional numbing, using the Fisher-King myth as a framework, examining how cultural demands for toughness create psychological scarring manifesting as emotional disconnection, isolation, and hidden suffering.

CORE CONCEPTS

- Psychological scarring from emotional numbing
- Loss of connection to authentic self
- Manifestation of trauma and PTSD
- Systematic brutalisation and conditioning
- Development of conditional love patterns
- Resentment of vulnerability
- Hidden suffering beneath social masks

NEW TERMINOLOGY

Fisher-King Wound: Pattern of conditioning from societal brutalisation

PTSD: Post-traumatic stress disorder

MAIN THEMES

- Fisher-King as wounded healer archetype
- Grail quest as path to wholeness
- Role of Percival as seeker
- Connection to Christ consciousness

INTEGRATION POINTS

- Links to Shadow Work (Chapter 10)
- Foundation for Understanding Rebis (Chapter 9)
- Preparation for Enlightenment (Chapter 6)
- Connection to Raw Substance (Chapter 4)

REFLECTION QUESTIONS

- How have you experienced the effects of emotional numbing in your life?
- What aspects of your conditioning have created disconnection from feeling?
- How do you relate to the concept of "learning to shudder"?
- What forms of brutalisation have you experienced or witnessed?
- What aspects of your experience point beyond conditioned existence?

PROGRESS INDICATORS

- Growing comfort with vulnerability
- Reduced emotional numbing
- Natural expression of feeling
- Integration of wounded aspects
- Development of authentic connection

9. The Rebis & Rejection of Identity

"The stone which the builders rejected has become the head of the corner." [14]

The Rebis represents the unity of opposites —the hermaphroditic figure symbolising spiritual completion. In this chapter, we examine how identity must dissolve to achieve this state. The unified being emerges when opposites are reconciled. The aspiring alchemist learns that their sense of self is largely constructed from cultural conditioning and personal history. Through understanding the nature of duality and moving beyond rigid self-definitions, one begins the process of inner unification that characterises true alchemical transformation. This stage marks a critical decision point where one must choose between the comfort of familiar identity and the unknown territory beyond it.

The Alchemist learns that how they define themselves is based only on culture and personal history. They realise that *true self* must be something beyond mere conditioning. The scope of their insight turns inward, looking for patterns within the chaos of existence, searching and hoping for a satisfactory meaning or answer.

Initially, their task is difficult. They can see that the problems of existence stem not from existence itself, but from a tendency towards selfishness, which creates problems for the individual and environment. The alchemist with insight

---

[14] *Ps. 118:22 New International Version*

recognises that they themselves suffer from a condition of selfness, and it can be a troubling time as one hones in on the truths of one's own personal suffering.

Nigredo, the first stage of alchemy, is an utter recognition that any answers must lie beyond the individual concept of self, and now a dynamic of increasing hopelessness develops as the self realises answers lie beyond it. One becomes merciless to one's own indiscretions, and one firmly engages in tackling the *dross* of one's reactions and habits.

In Buddhism, this process is outlined in what is called the noble eightfold path. This is a set of eight attributes or qualities that, if developed, foster the tranquillity of mind necessary for the breakthrough (or development) of transcendental awareness.

The alchemist finds themselves increasingly dissatisfied with the babble and drama of *Apparent Reality* and retreats into a more solitary practice. The examination of *Subjective Reality* is continued, and one learns to question the very labels we give ourselves or others.

The alchemic *Rebis* is a figure with two heads — often opposites, male or female, sun or moon. It represents a more complete being when one has accepted one cannot be one thing without a recognition of its opposite.

This is a little tricky, so I will elaborate.

Could we have a world inhabited by only rich people? Is it possible?

No. As to understand what *rich* means, we must have *poor*.

Could you describe what *up* is without ever referring to *down*?

These are dualities — and the basis of the mental evaluation of phenomena. It is a fundamental flaw in how we communicate reality. The path of the alchemist is one of increasing unification.

The alchemist has a burning curiosity that allows them to pull their attention away from worldly pursuits. They have the ability to be very successful materially, but this doesn't interest them. If it did, they may take pride in any worldly achievements, but it simply doesn't interest them beyond the immediate challenge.

This means there is a gradual challenge of concepts of identity. With a critical mind, they analyse their own motivations and, finding these conditioned, gradually reduce the tendency to identify with anything.

The *Rebis* reminds us of this. Here we have a unified being. Or, a being that is in the process of unification. Between the two heads, we have the diversity of experience. This is symbolised by the male/female duality.

In Buddhism, there is a heuristic that arises in the diamond *sūtra*. It epitomises the approach of the *middle way*. When one contemplates any being, one must consider they exist as both a being and they don't exist, being a being. One must find the middle mental path of belief, balancing the possibility of existence with an absolutely perfectly balanced possibility of non-existence. Here, the mind finds a middle way where possibilities are balanced, and most importantly, no longer pondered unnecessarily and ultimately, with futility.

The *Rebis* is a stage—one where both the dichotomy and interdependency of duality are clearly identified. The hermetic principle of gender is clearly laid out, so as to clear the mind of the alchemist of lowly ideas of perfection as a gender, or any aspect of reality.

Contemplating the *Rebis* is the natural antidote to the *Fisher-King Wound*. It is a unification of self that relies on a turning away from stereotype, and embracing one's *Shadow*. One seeks completeness, not differentiation, and this stage, when complete, resonates with the penultimate stage of multiplication, where the radiant effect of *karma*-less activity induces changes in others.

We will cover other aspects of this unification as we walk through *Nigredo*; however, for now, as an aspiring alchemist, one must recognise that we have reached an important decision point. To be successful, we will eventually face the choice of returning to the comfort of conditionality or sacrificing this all for what has to be unknown. This is the a pivotal choice between comfort and the unknown, and in truth, is rarely a fair choice. Nevertheless, at this stage, digging deeper, we approach a kind of door, one that can only really be knocked on, but never opened, from this side. With skill, sincerity, and dedication, this door will eventually open for most—but once opened, it can never be closed again.

Study Guide: The Rebis And Rejection Of Identity

This chapter explores how the Rebis symbolises the integration of opposing forces within consciousness, examining the alchemist's journey from conditioned identity to transcendent awareness. It details how recognising duality leads to spiritual transformation by integrating seemingly opposing aspects of the self.

CORE CONCEPTS

- Integration of opposing forces
- Journey from conditioned to transcendent awareness
- Recognition and transformation through duality

NEW TERMINOLOGY

Diamond Sūtra: Buddhist text discussing non-attachment

Middle Way: Buddhist concept of balanced approach

MAIN THEMES

1. The nature of identity

- Conditioning through culture and personal history
- Connection to Chapter 3 (Evolution of Adulthood)
- Recognition of the self beyond conditioning
- The role of selfishness in suffering

2. The process of transformation

- Links to Chapter 10 (The Shadow)
- Nigredo as initial dark phase
- Role of the Noble Eightfold Path
- Withdrawal from mundane concerns

3. Understanding duality

- Connection to Chapter 4 (Symbols and Meanings)
- The interdependence of opposites
- The middle way approach
- Transcendence through integration

REFLECTION QUESTIONS

- How do you experience the interplay of opposites in your life?
- How do you relate to the concept of transcending duality?
- What aspects of your identity feel most constructed or conditional?
- What parts of your identity feel most difficult to question or release?

INTEGRATION POINTS

- Connection to Chapter 3 (Evolution of Adulthood)
- Connection to Chapter 4 (Symbols and Meanings)
- Links to Chapter 10 (The Shadow)

10. The Shadow & The Lost Infant

"One does not become enlightened by imagining figures of light, but by making the darkness conscious." [15]

In this chapter, we explore the critical process of psychological integration that every alchemist must undertake. The Shadow represents those aspects of ourselves we have rejected or denied, while the lost infant symbolises our original, unconditioned nature. Through accepting and reintegrating these elements, the alchemist begins the essential work of gathering together the fragmented aspects of consciousness. This process, though potentially challenging, is fundamental to the Great Work and marks a crucial stage in the Nigredo phase of transformation.

The alchemist must gather in all the parts of their experience that have become fragmented and lost through normal psychological processes. This is painful unless one knows what one is doing, which is almost never.

With doubt eroding the concept of personality, the alchemist questions their motivations and drives. These learned folk had knowledge and access to poisons and intoxicants and invariably would have explored altered states of consciousness. It is likely they therefore suffer addiction and with this a fragmentation of identity.

This broken being continues to be driven for a truth, a model of experience that, in making sense, unifies the deep mental disquiet that these individuals suffer. Mental

---

[15] *Jung, C.G. Psychology and Alchemy, Page 99*

illness is likely common, as the hyper-critical mind relentlessly analyses every motive and intent.

Thankfully, a reasonable understanding about projection and the *Shadow* can really help clear things up. For those new to this, I recommend you deepen your understanding as this is important.

It all comes back to duality. Remember, this is the idea that you cannot know what up is without defining down. For there to be rich, there must be poor.

The most intimate duality is that between subjective experience and the perspective of *me*, and that of objective reality *other*.

Our sense of self is created during childhood and adolescence, and we tend to attach labels to it. We might think we are smart, in certain ways, or kind, or generous. Unfortunately, we have a filter that tends to remember examples that support our beliefs and dismiss those that don't.

We may be accurate in our self-assessment, yet, if bias is going to happen it will, and it is far easier to convince ourselves we have certain qualities due to this filter of remembering examples that support it whilst dismissing (forgetting) those that challenge it.

This means as we attach more qualities to our sense of being, if they are erroneous, which often they are, at least in part, we must forget all experience that challenges this.

If we are relatively happy and fortunate, we might have a loving family that accepts our occasional digressions, even when we later deny them. However, in positions of power, misbehaviour that is later denied is often tolerated.

The alchemist's priority is the truth, even if this is painful. Recognising that all attributes—good or bad—are simply labels, often with a diverse range of personal meaning, the alchemist rejects the deeply ingrained habit of self-definition, seeing all labels as ultimately empty.

The *Shadow*.

The *Shadow* is a concept of an alter-ego that can form and seem to explain paradoxical behaviour in the mentally unwell. Basically, if one clings to self-definition, there is a habit of rejecting opposite qualities. An individual might have a strong desire to be known as generous, and then get angry when the times they were driven by greed are highlighted. The need to be associated with one pole of a duality prohibits the contemplation of the very real possibilities that one also displayed other, opposite behaviours.

If one becomes particularly fixed on *goodness* one might, through this mechanism only relish in a few examples when one behaved well, and literally dismiss any prior example that contradicts this. Consciousness is an *aggregate* — this means what we think of as a single awareness, is more analogous to a cloud of many, smaller awarenesses. If the awareness we associate with dominance literally blinds itself to its own awareness, it weakens. Now this is where things get interesting. Those qualities dismissed from self appear in *other*. In most forms this manifests as irritation, hatred and projection. In severe forms it manifests as hallucinatory and threatening figures or voices.

Projection is the phenomenon of seeing these rejected qualities, projected upon others. A hatred towards a particular *type* means that upon meeting anybody who qualifies as this *type* we see not the unique individual, but a set of hateful speculations we take as truth. The Alchemist learns to foster curiosity towards anything that upsets them, for here they are learning about their *Shadow*.

The *Shadow* is neither Evil nor really a being. However, with severe cases of projection, it distorts reality even more. These rejected qualities almost become living and can torment the suffering individual.

The *Shadow* is tackled by remembering that any definition of self can only ever really come from within and labels are useless. One recognises that within the scope of experience, both self and other, the most holy and most wicked dwell within. Any attempt to grade oneself according to other is simply narcissistic delusion and pointless. Only when one recognises that it is only ourselves that are both the most holy and most wicked.

Our journey begins by going inwards and down. The Alchemist recognises they are in the Hellish reality of thought, but recognising the illusion of conditionality begins to rattle their chains. These chains are normally invisible as we chase goals and flee problems. But once, with curiosity, the alchemist turns towards what irritates or distresses with a question of why, they feel, for the first time the chains of conditionality.

By embracing and accepting one's shameful faults, we cease to empower the *Shadow*. Gradually we turn inwards and challenge our prejudices, starting off big but getting ever smaller. Recognising both darkness and light come from within, and are projected onto reality, we cease reacting to both imaginary and real conflicts.

Nigredo

This process will be easier to understand once one has a basic understanding of *karma*. Through persistence the alchemist transforms habits that are selfish and as they clear, their *Shadow*, become less reactive towards any conflict. The darkness of the stone, Nigredo is lightening, and this paves the way for the second stage, *Albedo*.

Still, we have some way to go, for this in itself is significant work. It can often take until middle age to iron out some of the harsher tendencies we thought were normal, and one might often be troubled with symptomatic mental illness. It's hardly reassuring, but maybe a little reassuring to recognise this as a process.

The preparation that the alchemist undertakes is an attempt to return to the simpler awareness of childhood. In order to do this, they track back and deeper through their developed personality and slowly strip off the labels they have acquired.

The concept of *lost child* embodies both the principles of projection and the *Shadow*, and also the *Fisher-King Wound*. This *lost child* is a part of us that we reject when we take on the mantle of adulthood. For some, acting like an adult occurs very early as it arises commonly through a betrayal of trust — one grows up when one can no longer depend on another for *wholesome* development.

Generally these concepts are pretty complex, yet, as the alchemist develops deeper insights they become less significant. If you are suffering depression, despair or some of the more severe mental illnesses then this suggests closer attention is needed. However, it does seem to be a process, so if you are struggling the most powerful thing to remember is that it is probably temporary and hopelessness and despair are symptoms rather than a true evaluation of things.

Embracing the *Shadow* or *lost child* seems to be a metaphorical tool that we use to explain the mess of experience, yet, it is not uncommon for one to have very meaningful dreams or experiences when one is working in this area. I hope that covered enough to illustrate the importance of this stage. Success is very unlikely until one learns to recognise and master one's own projections based on fear, greed or ignorance.

Study Guide: The Shadow & The Lost Infant

This chapter explores psychological fragmentation through development, examining how alchemists must reintegrate lost aspects of self, focusing on Shadow work, projection mechanisms, and the path to psychological wholeness.

Core Concepts
- Psychological fragmentation and identity formation
- Shadow mechanics and projection
- Integration process toward wholeness

New Terminology
Lost Child: Rejected innocent aspects of self
Projection: Seeing rejected qualities in others
Shadow: Rejected aspects of self that become unconscious

Main Themes
1. Psychological Fragmentation
- Process of identity formation and loss
- Role of addiction and altered states
- Impact of hyper-critical analysis
- Connection to Fisher-King Wound

2. Shadow Mechanics
- Nature of psychological projection
- Formation of the Shadow self
- Role of duality in consciousness
- Links to Rebis

3. Integration Process
- Recognition of rejected qualities
- Working with projections
- Path to wholeness
- Connection to Enlightenment

Reflection Questions
- What aspects of yourself do you tend to reject or deny?
- How do you experience projection in your relationships with others?
- What qualities in others trigger strong emotional reactions in you?
- How do you relate to your own lost child?

Integration Points
- Connection to Fisher-King Wound (Chapter 8)
- Links to Rebis (Chapter 9)
- Connection to Enlightenment (Chapter 6)

Aspects of Healing the Lost Infant

Aspect	Manifestation	Integration Path
Shadow	Rejected qualities	Conscious acceptance
Projection	External blame	Internal recognition
Lost Child	Abandoned innocence	Psychological reunion
Duality	Split consciousness	Unity through awareness

NIGREDO

"In the middle of the journey of our life, I found myself within a dark woods where the straight way was lost." – Dante Alighieri, Inferno, Canto I, lines 1-3.
Translated by Henry Wadsworth Longfellow.

MYTHOS

11. The Dark Night of the Soul

*"In a dark night, with anxious love inflamed,
forth unobserved I went, my house being now at rest."* [16]

The Dark Night of the Soul represents a profound spiritual crisis that marks a critical phase in the alchemist's journey. During this stage, one experiences deep despair and isolation as the ego confronts its own dissolution. Yet this darkness holds transformative potential — it is the blackening phase (Nigredo) where old patterns must die before rebirth becomes possible. This chapter explores the nature of this spiritual crisis and how to navigate its challenges.

This is the point where the trainee alchemist realises that their personality and sense of self is nothing more than a construct of circumstance. Deep down, they are developing something called *The Faculty of I Will Know the Unknown*, which represents a growing distrust of conditioned reality. This faculty has yet to mature, and until it does, there is a tendency to fall into fits of despair and hopelessness.

Silently, a growing faith in the inauthenticity of reality allows one to question all of one's beliefs, and doubt cuts away at the inner structures of conditioned being.

When the alchemist discovers a way, either through personal observation or through learning of a system (of enlightenment), their faith in this way is essential. It doesn't need to be overwhelming, just that there is a possibility of escape.

---

[16] *Cross, St. John of the. (1908). The Dark Night of the Soul. (D. Lewis, Trans.). Thomas Baker.*

There approaches a level of understanding that is only hampered by the tendency of the personality, which is being eroded by doubt to cause distressing and distracting symptoms.

It can be a dangerous time for the alchemist. It is arduous and often results in the utter loss of all material security. Yet, in truth, it is nothing more than the death shudders of the dying personality, which, lacking the necessary faith, the alchemist clings to and suffers with.

Yet, despite the personality's worst fears, it is simply not necessary to live with definitions of oneself. And eventually, the alchemist overcomes the tendency to try. Suddenly there is an opening within which floods a kind of hopeful acceptance into the being. There seems to arise an arena in which life begins to make sense. One no longer focuses on the dissatisfactory elements but sees them as parts of a whole.

This *breakthrough* occurs with a loss of attachment to identity or personality, along with a doubt that mere rituals or customs are meaningful when it comes to morality. This breakthrough is only possible when doubt in the authenticity of conditioned reality is significant enough to permit faith to develop. When this faith peaks, and it doesn't have to be tremendous as doubt has weakened self-view, the *faculty of I Will Know the Unknown* matures, which propels normal awareness into the transcendental, but only for the briefest of moments.

The *Dark Night* is generally only recognisable retrospectively. The mind is often so troubled that guidance is limited by focus, yet, I am sure the more we recognise this process, the more we can offer support for those facing this and probably, the most gruelling spiritual stage.

The pain comes from clinging to ideas and concepts of self that are dear to us. It remains painful until our faith in there being a deeper truth gives us the confidence to let go of the remaining fragments of self and pursue a deeper, but unknown goal.

The *Dark Night of the Soul* is the part when the alchemist experiences a kind of union of self. Through the helplessness of recognising the limit of personality, there is a kind of surrender in the need to label oneself. With this, a huge wave of pressure lifts and the sun rises differently that day.

This is where the stone of the philosophers first arises, the blackness of *Nigredo* unifying into a mass of darkness; somehow, now unified, it is not as painful.

The Alchemist, learning that rules and customs are largely meaningless, is invigorated by this brief glimpse of unconditioned reality, no longer troubled by ideas of personality, they renew their attempts at understanding.

Through a deeper understanding of *karma*, they gradually learn to use it with skill, which gradually transforms the honest darkness into honest purity, which is the process of *Albedo*.

The Dark Night represents both crisis and opportunity — a necessary phase of spiritual development where the aspirant must face their deepest fears and attachments. While intensely challenging, this stage prepares the ground for transformation through the acceptance and integration of Shadow aspects.

> "There can be no rebirth without a Dark Night of the Soul, a total annihilation of all that you believed in and thought that you were." [17]

Aspects of The Dark Night

Aspect	Manifestation	Transformation
Doubt	Erosion of beliefs	Liberation from conditioning
Darkness	Depression/despair	Integration and unity
Faith	Trust in the path	Enables breakthrough
Identity	Fragmentation	Union and release

---

[17] Khan, Pir Vilayat Inayat. (2025). *Thinking Like the Universe: The Sufi Path of Awakening.*

Nigredo

Study Guide: The Dark Night Of The Soul

This chapter explores the critical phase where the alchemist confronts the illusory nature of personality and experiences profound spiritual crisis. It examines how doubt erodes conditioned structures while faith facilitates breakthroughs into transcendental awareness.

CORE CONCEPTS

- *Recognition of self as construct*
- *Erosion of conditioning through doubt*
- *Integration of darkness and despair*
- *Balance of faith and doubt*

NEW TERMINOLOGY

Dark Night: *Period of spiritual crisis and transformation*

Faculty of I Will Know the Unknown: *Growing distrust of conditioned reality*

MAIN THEMES

- *Death of personality*
- *Development of transcendental faculty*
- *Transformative process*
- *Release of identification*
- *Breakthrough to unconditioned reality*
- *Union of fragmented self*

INTEGRATION POINTS

- *Connection to Chapter 10 (The Shadow)*
- *Links to Chapter 6 (Enlightenment)*
- *Connection to Chapter 9 (The Rebis)*

REFLECTION QUESTIONS

- *How have you experienced periods of spiritual crisis or despair?*
- *What role has doubt played in your spiritual development?*
- *How do you relate to the concept of surrendering personal identity?*
- *What gives you faith during times of darkness?*

PROGRESS INDICATORS

- *Growing distrust of conditioned reality*
- *Integration of darkness*
- *Release of identification*
- *Balance of faith and doubt*

12. The Seed of Nirvāṇa

"The Dark Night of the Soul comes just before revelation." [18]

In this chapter, we explore how the initial stages of alchemical transformation contain within them the seed of ultimate realisation. Like a lotus growing from muddy waters, the darkest aspects of our spiritual work Like a lotus growing from muddy waters, the darkest aspects of spiritual work paradoxically hold the potential for enlightenment. We'll examine how the Nigredo phase, though characterised by difficulty and confusion, plants the essential seed that will eventually blossom into transcendent awareness. Understanding this relationship between darkness and light is crucial for the aspiring alchemist.

The alchemist only really becomes an alchemist when they find the stone of the philosophers. Once they *discover* it, they must *refine* it. This seed starts off as raw material. What does this mean?

The raw material is the subjective awareness of the trainee alchemist, which in many ways, is beyond control and often comprehension. This becomes the material with which the alchemist works.

This is an important concept to grasp.

---

[18] *Campbell, Joseph. (1991). Reflections on the Art of Living: A Joseph Campbell Companion.*

What is reality?

Reality is the experience one has that appears real. All reality is subjective, objective reality is a myth of science. No one reality can be the same, but, thinking reality is really objective, nobody challenges this.

So every reality is *solipsistic* — absolutely created around and for the awareness it serves. Of course, in a manic state, people kind of get this but miss the point, thinking existence itself is solipsistic.

There can be no normal, and recognising this, the alchemist starts playing with the edges of reality.

There reaches a point of awareness, either reached through tranquillity practices like *samatha* (focused) meditation, or through either brilliant insight or terrifying experience when consciousness finds an absolute neutral point, and for two or three moments, a breakthrough to world-transcending awareness is possible.

To find this point oneself is reasonably tricky, but a genuine guru with skill can bring those who are ready close enough to allow for a breakthrough. Typically, unless the alchemist is learning from a Master, this breakthrough is achieved only through the exhaustive process of the *Dark Night of the Soul*.

Reality is a dynamic between how the world reacts to us, and what we think this means. The alchemist learns that through modifying meaning, one's experience of reality changes. Whilst early in their career the alchemist may not realise this, once they experience the breakthrough to transcendental awareness, this experience, even though it literally lasts only a single moment of realisation, and then two or three experiences of the consequences of this realisation, forever changes their perspectives.

This breakthrough experience is so profound it cannot be forgotten. In fact, it forever changes the individual. This experience acts like a new position of internal observer. But this observer is transcendental, and can always offer a viewpoint detached from personal need. One tends to become naturally moralistic and one's wisdom increases through this truly impartial guidance.

Whilst the experience of this breakthrough is never subtle, it is momentary, and often it can be some weeks or months until the alchemist experiences both a lightening of mood and the benefit of changing one's moral outlook.

It can also be sometimes confusing. This breakthrough reduces the attachment to material gains and prestige. Previous goals and aspirations can become meaningless. Sometimes this breakthrough occurred as part of an intoxicating high — drugs can give a temporary but unstable access to *jhāna*, a kind of super-normal awareness. Achieving *jhāna* and then a breakthrough to transcendental awareness can result in big changes of personality that get caught up in addiction.

This seed of transcendental awareness slowly transforms the morality of the alchemist, gradually allowing the *fetters* of self that bind awareness to conditioned existence to be sequentially challenged. We will cover these later.

This *Breakthrough* is the start of *Albedo* or whiteness. At this moment the raw material is largely normal, yet, somewhere deep within is the seed of the deathless, or *Nirvāṇa*. The transcendental experience, although it happens only for the briefest of moments, is beyond time and therefore always available. This godly and neutral position tends to reduce self-interest and the need for volition. This naturally decreases karmic influence and whilst the moral character of the alchemist is now destined to improve, they become more and more indifferent to the world at large.

I hope, as ever, that was interesting.

This is the end of the first part of *Nigredo*. I'll flesh out the experience from another three viewpoints, before we then move into exploring *Albedo*.

Nigredo

Study Guide: The Seed Of Nirvāṇa

This chapter explores how the initial breakthrough to transcendental awareness Marks the foundational stage of alchemical transformation. It examines the nature of Subjective Reality, the conditions for breakthrough experiences, and their lasting effects on consciousness and behaviour.

CORE CONCEPTS
- *Subjective experience as primary reality*
- *Breakthrough to transcendental awareness*
- *Transformative effects on consciousness*

NEW TERMINOLOGY

Fetters: Bonds that tie consciousness to conditioned existence

Samatha: Focused meditation practice

Solipsistic: Relating to self-centred reality

MAIN THEMES

1. Nature of Reality
- *Creation of meaning*
- *Illusion of objective reality*
- *Subjective experience as primary reality*

2. The Breakthrough Experience
- *Conditions for transcendental awareness*
- *Importance of qualified guidance*
- *Role of meditation and insight*

3. Transformative Effects
- *Changes in moral perspective*
- *Creation of transcendental observer*
- *Reduction of worldly attachment*

INTEGRATION POINTS
- *Albedo phase foundation*
- *Connection to Path Consciousness (Chapter 31)*
- *Foundation for working with Fetters (Chapter 23)*
- *Links to Chapter 4 (Symbols and Meanings)*
- *Links to Chapter 6 (Enlightenment)*
- *Links to Dark Night (Chapter 11)*

REFLECTION QUESTIONS
- *How do you experience the relationship between darkness and enlightenment?*
- *How has your understanding of reality shifted through spiritual practice?*
- *What glimpses of transcendental awareness have you experienced?*

The Dark Night of the Soul
by St John of the Cross. (Translated By David Lewis)

In a dark night,
With anxious love inflamed,
O, happy lot!
Forth unobserved I went,
My house being now at rest.

In darkness and in safety,
By the secret ladder, disguised,
O, happy lot!
In darkness and concealment,
My house being now at rest.

In that happy night,
In secret, seen of none,
Seeing nought myself,
Without other light or guide
Save that which in my heart was burning.

That light guided me
More surely than the noonday sun
To the place where He was waiting for me,
Whom I knew well,
And where none appeared.

O, guiding night;
O, night more lovely than the dawn;
O, night that hast united
The lover with His beloved,
And changed her into her love.

On my flowery bosom,
Kept whole for Him alone,
There He reposed and slept;
And I cherished Him, and the waving
Of the cedars fanned Him.

As His hair floated in the breeze
That from the turret blew,
He struck me on the neck
With His gentle hand,
And all sensation left me.

I continued in oblivion lost,
My head was resting on my love;
Lost to all things and myself,
And, amid the lilies forgotten,
Threw all my cares away.

*"The source of this suffering is attachment.
When attachments exist, old age and death come to be."*

— *Samyutta Nikaya (SN 12.66)*

Part Two
DHARMA

In this second part of Nigredo, we delve into the core teachings and concepts that form the theoretical foundation of spiritual alchemy. Dharma, a Pāli word meaning "natural law" or "truth," represents the systematic understanding of consciousness and reality that makes transformation possible. Here we examine the detailed maps of mind and matter that both Buddhist masters and alchemical adepts have used to navigate the territory of inner transformation.

While the mythological section provided context through story and symbol, Dharma offers precise technical knowledge about the nature of consciousness, reality, and the mechanisms of spiritual development. We'll explore how different levels of consciousness arise and interact, examine the matrix-like structure of conditioned existence, and investigate the forces that keep us bound to cycles of suffering. This might seem daunting at first, but remember — we're building a practical framework for understanding your own experience, not just accumulating abstract knowledge.

The chapters in this section systematically unpack the Buddhist Abhidhamma teachings alongside their alchemical correspondences. We'll examine the 72 types of entities that comprise conscious experience, explore the nature of mind and mental factors, and investigate how materiality interacts with consciousness. While some of this material is necessarily technical, I've aimed to present it in accessible language that connects directly to your own experience of being.

Don't worry if you don't grasp everything immediately—this section provides reference material. Think of it as gradually building a map that will help you navigate the territory of consciousness transformation. The concepts introduced here lay the groundwork for the practical techniques and experiences described in later sections. As always, maintain both intellectual rigour and experiential curiosity as we explore these deeper waters of understanding.

Nigredo

Aspects of the Nature of Reality

Aspect	Manifestation	Purpose
Apparent Reality	Things, beings, concepts	Normal experience
Conditioned Reality	Underlying patterns	Path to liberation
Consciousness Spheres	Sensory, form, formless	Levels of awareness
The Unconditioned	Transformed consciousness	Path of liberation

Components of Conditioned Reality

Aspect	Components	Function
Matter	Four Great elements	Forms physical reality
Consciousness	Eight types	Creates knowing
Citta	89 (or 121) types	Moments of consciousness
Mental factors	52 types	Conditions experience

Four Great Elements

Element	Property	Function
Earth	Tangibility	Solidity
Water	Cohesion	Binding
Air	Movement	Motion
Fire	Entropy	Transformation

Dharma

13. The Realities

"The map is not the territory." [19]

In this chapter, we explore the fundamental nature of reality and consciousness from both alchemical and Buddhist perspectives. We'll examine how our perception shapes what we consider real, the different levels of conscious experience, and why understanding these distinctions is crucial for spiritual transformation. Through careful analysis of apparent and conditioned reality, we begin to map the territory that the aspiring alchemist must navigate to transcend ordinary consciousness.

The first myth the alchemist approaches is the myth of objective reality. Reality is a function of realness that arises between a perception and the awareness that perceives it. Reality is always firsthand and subjective, but we all grow up to believe that in truth, there is a more real reality, the one we all agree on and which science venerates, objective reality.

Objective reality is what both the scientist and priest seek, a comprehensive and unifying vision encompassing all things. Now, whilst I think this possible, as being an alchemist I am kind of both scientist and priest, this ultimate vision has to transcend the stuff it governs.

The alchemist must at first contain themselves, for they are not looking necessarily for a unified theory that explains all, they are focused on finding the path that leads

---

[19] *Korzybski, Alfred. (1931). A Non-Aristotelian System and Its Necessity for Rigour in Mathematics and Physics.*

out of conditioned reality. As they leave conditioned reality they may look back and see how things work, but there is a certain risk in looking back, especially if one is now furnished with the knowledge to change things.

The Names and Divisions of Reality.

First, we must remember what a *reality* is. A reality is simply the perception and awareness of this perception. Subjective experience can never be wrong or unreal; it can, however, be frightening or unpleasant, or the evaluation of an experience that later leads to concern and further worry. For the psychotic, their hallucinatory experiences are real enough for them to not know if they are real. Yet, their experiences, even if hallucinatory, seem valid experiences; they just don't make sense.

Normal human experiences occur in what is called *Apparent Reality* and largely within the sense-sphere plane of consciousness. What does this mean?

Apparent Reality is populated with things, people, beings, concepts and ideas. Here we learn to evaluate experience based on the things we fear or desire. Here we recognise an apple without ever really knowing that there is no apple. As illustrated in the previous sentence, it is not easy to leave *Apparent Reality*, for there is an inherent paradox that one must fully understand to appreciate just how unsatisfactory it is. We will explore this later when we come to emptiness — it's the riddle behind *The Matrix* (film): *There is no spoon.*

Consciousness will occur in any plane where the mind perceives. The very act of perception creates an awareness. Normally, humans generally preoccupy themselves with what is called the sensory-sphere plane. This is the world of the five senses and mind. Although *mind* here is abstract, in underdeveloped and in very materially oriented beings, the mind will largely preoccupy itself with material objectives.

Thinkers and meditators can train themselves to think about abstract concepts. If they become completely absorbed in an idea or meditative focus, they can lose track of their surroundings and time. Unless they are very skilled or focused, it is unlikely they totally lose contact with their senses, but it is possible. Once they completely lose contact with bodily sense and become fully absorbed into the mind, they enter what is called the *form-sphere* or *fine-material sphere* of awareness. We will cover this much more later, but we need to introduce the idea that awareness can arise in any place where the mind can perceive.

Underneath Apparent Reality is what is called conditioned reality.

Now we must remember that our model (understanding) of conditioned reality is simply a more accurate version of *objective* reality with the purpose of escaping it. Remember, if we are escaping a prison, we only really need to know the path out, and not the whole layout of the prison, no matter how interesting this might be. If our path is well researched and suitable, we need not bother with anything else.

The Buddha gave us a model of conditioned reality for this very purpose. There are close approximations to any other system that materialises as a *Mystery Religion*, but for myself, Buddhism is the most accessible. I love the synergy between systems, and so I'll introduce relevant concepts and explain their context.

The *Map* of conditioned reality is outlined in a very technical set of books called the *Abhidhamma*, or higher teachings of the Buddha. We will outline the parameters and features of this map in later discussions.

To summarise:

The Alchemist learns to manipulate reality through the philosopher's stone. This *stone* is the *Subjective Reality* of the alchemist themselves.

The Alchemist learns that *Apparent Reality* is illusory as it is empty of actual objects, just sensory patterns in which the object is inferred.

So, to probe *reality* the Alchemist seeks a grand and unifying theory of existence.

The *traditional* system is archaic and difficult to reliably access, so, in reflection of my path, I will use Buddhism as the chassis of the system we need to build to examine and understand *conditioned reality*.

We will introduce a model of underlying reality that has the purpose of illuminating a path, a path which leads us, and our experience out of conditionality.

Of course, we cannot describe the destination, but that is some way off for now, and we will, in time, have a much greater grasp of the process.

NIGREDO

Study Guide: The Realities

This chapter explores the fundamental nature of reality through alchemical and Buddhist perspectives, examining how different levels of consciousness shape our experience and understanding. It introduces key concepts about the relationship between perception and awareness while establishing a framework for transcending conditioned existence.

CORE CONCEPTS

- The relationship between perception and reality
- Different levels of consciousness and their characteristics
- Framework for transcending conditioned existence

NEW TERMINOLOGY

Apparent Reality: The world of everyday experience populated with things, people, and concepts

Conditioned Reality: The underlying reality beneath Apparent Reality

Fine-material (Form) sphere: A more refined plane of consciousness accessed through meditation

Formless-sphere: The most subtle realm of consciousness

Sense-sphere: The world of the five senses and mind

MAIN THEMES

1. Nature of Reality
- Subjective versus objective experience
- Role of perception in creating reality
- Relationship between awareness and experience
- Links to Chapter 4 (Symbols and Meanings)

2. Levels of Consciousness
- Sense-sphere awareness
- Form-sphere consciousness
- Fine-material sphere experience
- Connection to Chapter 6 (Enlightenment)

3. Framework of Understanding
- Buddhist Abhidhamma system
- Alchemical transformation process
- Path beyond conditioning
- Links to Chapter 9 (The Rebis)

REFLECTION QUESTIONS

- How does your perception of 'objective reality' differ from your direct subjective experience?
- In what ways do you notice the difference between Apparent Reality and conditioned reality in your daily life?
- How might understanding the different levels of reality impact your spiritual practice?

INTEGRATION POINTS

- Links to Chapter 4 (Symbols and Meanings)
- Connection to Chapter 6 (Enlightenment)
- Links to Chapter 9 (The Rebis)

Dharma

14. The Matrix of Conditioned Reality

*"The Matrix is everywhere. It is all around us.
Even now, in this very room.
You can see it when you look out your window
or when you turn on your television.
You can feel it when you go to work...
when you go to church...
when you pay your taxes."* [20]

The Matrix represents the fundamental structure that gives rise to and sustains our experienced reality. This chapter explores how consciousness, matter, and mental factors interweave to create the fabric of conditioned existence. Through understanding this matrix-like structure, we gain insight into both the nature of our current experience and potential paths beyond it. Like the alchemist's understanding of base materials, this knowledge forms an essential foundation for the Great Work of transformation.

What do we mean by *Matrix*? A *matrix* is a structure upon which things can propagate — the word *matrix* is derived from roots that include mother and illusion. It is the name we give for our world of senses and ideas, but with an emphasis on a nurturing element. The *Matrix* out of which we come, those structures that support and permit both life and the propagation of life.

In Gnostic terms we have the *Pleroma*, from which all creatures arise, the living beings, *creatura*, driven by a need to differentiate. *Go forth and multiply.*

---

[20] *The Matrix.* (1999). Written by The Wachowskis.

A model of this *Matrix* (out of which being arises) is the subject of the *Abhidhamma*.
The *Abhidhamma* begins by outlining four types of absolute reality. Three of these types are *conditioned* — which means they are part of the reality of conditioned beings — pretty much all of us. A fourth type of reality is unconditioned, or *Nirvāṇa*, and is the experience of full enlightenment.

Conditioned reality is the experience of being a being within the physical world of matter and mental worlds of awareness and the mental factors that accompany this awareness. Don't worry about trying to understand what unconditioned *experience* is like for just now. It will be easy to have an idea about what the unconditioned is like once you fully understand conditionality.

So, conditioned reality has three main groups:
1. Matter
2. Consciousness
3. Mental factors

Matter represents all phenomena that arise from what is called the four great essential elements: *earth* (tangibility), *water* (attractive forces, cohesion), *air* (movement or vibration) and *fire* (entropy). A further 24 *types* of matter are constructed from these four essentials.

Consciousness arises when a specialised class of matter (called *sensitive matter*) detects a respective sense object which enters its field of activity. For example, the retinal cells detect photons of differing wavelengths and convert this into electrical activity. Patterns in the current are interpreted by the mind as visual consciousness.

Whilst *consciousness* appears to be both continuous and singular, it is neither. There are different ways of classifying consciousness, but to start with we will refer to the less technical, *sūtra* model, which divides consciousness into eight types. Although these types are distinct, to the untrained subject, consciousnesses all blend into one.

Eight different types of consciousness:

1—5 are the sense consciousnesses. Sight, sound, smell, taste and touch. These arise when the sensitive matter in a special organ or, in the case of touch, distributed across the body, interacts with a sense object, which is called *near* in the case of touch, smell and taste, and *far* in the case of seeing and hearing. Although in truth these consciousnesses are all the same type, to the novice and worldling these appear as distinct awarenesses. Furthermore, each sense can develop attachments to its own sense objects, and then craving. This adds to the confusion of conditioned existence as each sense can chase after objects creating internal conflicts.

6 is what the layman calls the mind. As alchemists we learn to understand this is just an aspect of mind, and a particularly problematic one. We call this *discriminative mind* and it is an aspect of self that arises through duality, and habitually and incessantly divides and compares.

7 is what forms subjective awareness, i.e., the position of being a physical being in a physical world. This consciousness arises deep within the process and when created is initially empty. This emptiness allows reality to function without the distortion of self, it is an ideal position, like the *Tree Of Life*, which is a perfect ideal. Once we *incarnate*—start operating as an independent being, often around age 7 (but this varies), we fill this consciousness with self concepts, that if we idolise, corrupt the *Tree Of Life* and bring in Qliphotic (*demonic* influences based on distortions through excesses of self) qualities transforming our existence from heavenly to hellish.

8 is difficult to understand initially. It is kind of *atomic* consciousness out of which all the other awareness are *built*. It is called *Ālaya*. We will cover this largely in *Citrinitas* and *Rubedo*, parts three and four of the series.

In the *Abhidhamma*, the higher teaching of the Buddha, we classify things more precisely, and we will come to this. I just wanted to make you aware of this differing classification. Note, the *sūtra* classification we have just discussed follows an elemental correspondence, with sensory consciousness each matching an element, touch—*earth*, sight—*fire*, hearing—*space*, smell—*air*, taste—*water*. The discriminative mind—the mental factor of volition. The sense of self — the mental factor of perception. *Ālaya* is pure consciousness, which can become its own object, and propagates through a mixing of perception and consciousness through a process called *papañca* — or *mental proliferation*.

Conditioned reality is therefore made of *stuff* and an awareness of this *stuff*. The physical *stuff* is called *rūpa* which means *deformable matter*, but includes all four inseparable great elements. It is important to remember *rūpa* is insensate. Even our bodies are just matter and as much as we think otherwise, they cannot be hurt or feel anything. All matter is simply elemental — stuff that is always changing according to conditions, but, never capable of feeling, thought or awareness.

The part of conditioned reality that can feel, or get worried, or get excited, is the mind. We call this *Nāma*. *Nāma* means all the bits of conditioned reality that aren't matter, i.e. our feelings, thoughts, ideas and awarenesses. Even *contact* between our sensitive matter and a sense object is mental. When you think you *touch* something, this experience occurs in the mind. The finger, or whatever it touches, is physical and so cannot have any opinion on the matter.

Nāma is divided into two: Consciousness and mental factors. The mental factors support and condition the quality of the consciousness. In the *Abhidhamma* there are 52 mental factors which include things like feeling, perception, wisdom or anger.

So, the initial aim for the alchemist is to update their *objective* reality with a model that is crafted to understand experience with the goal of eventually escaping conditioned existence. Once we have an understanding this will guide the mind towards a breakthrough point which allows the alchemist to experience the unconditioned. Once this is achieved, this reinvigorates the work and strengthens one's resolve.

To summarise:

Conditioned Reality is divided into *Nāma* (consciousness and mental factors) and *Rūpa* (physical matter created from the four great elements). Consciousness, although it appears both singular and continuous is neither. It can be divided simply into eight different types, five based on the *four great elements* and the *element of space,* which we call physical senses, the *discriminative mind* which is based on *volition* (choice), the self, which is based on perceptions and a subtle and complex kind of awareness, called *Ālaya*. *Mental factors* are fifty-two conditioning factors that influence the type and process of consciousness.

"*The universe is not only queerer than we suppose, but queerer than we can suppose.*"
21

Study Guide: The Matrix Of Conditioned Reality

This chapter explores how consciousness, matter, and mental factors create our experienced reality, examining the Buddhist model of existence through an alchemical lens. It details the structure of conditioned existence while establishing foundations for understanding transcendental awareness.

---

[21] Haldane, J.B.S. (1927). *Possible Worlds and Other Essays,* p. 286.

Dharma

Core Concepts
- *Structure of reality through matrix foundation*
- *Eight types of consciousness and their manifestation*
- *Mental factors and their conditioning elements*
- *Relationship between physical and mental reality*

New Terminology
Ālaya: *Fundamental or store consciousness*
Cetasika: *Mental factors that condition consciousness*
Creatura: *Created living beings, driven by a need to differentiate*
Matrix: *A structure upon which things propagate, derived from roots meaning mother and illusion*
Nāma: *Mental aspects of reality including consciousness and mental factors*
Papanca: *Mental proliferation or conceptual elaboration*
Pleroma: *In Gnostic terms, the source from which all creatures arise*
Rūpa: *Physical matter or "deformable matter"*

Main Themes
1. Structure of Reality
- *Matrix as foundation of experience*
- *Three aspects of conditioned existence*
- *Relationship between physical and mental reality*
- *Connection to Chapter 4 (Symbols and Meanings)*

2. Nature of Consciousness
- *Eight types of consciousness*
- *Role of sensitive matter*
- *Emergence of awareness*
- *Links to Chapter 6 (Enlightenment)*

3. Mental Factors
- *52 conditioning mental elements*
- *Relationship to consciousness*
- *Role in experience*
- *Connection to Chapter 9 (The Rebis)*

Reflection Questions
- *How do the eight types of consciousness manifest in your own experience?*
- *What role does discriminative mind play in your daily perceptions?*
- *How do you experience the relationship between your sensory consciousness and mental consciousness?*

Integration Points
- *Connection to Chapter 4 (Symbols and Meanings)*
- *Links to Chapter 6 (Enlightenment)*
- *Connection to Chapter 9 (The Rebis)*

NIGREDO
The Five Skandhas

CONSCIOUSNESS

(Viññāṇa) - The awareness of experience, arising in dependence on sense contact and conditioned by past karma.

PERCEPTION

(Saññā) - Recognition and labeling of experiences, forming the basis of memory and conceptual understanding.

FEELINGS

(Vedanā) - The experience of sensation categorized as pleasant, unpleasant, or neutral, shaping emotional responses.

MENTAL FORMATIONS

(Saṅkhāra) - Volitional constructs, including thoughts, intentions, and habitual patterns that shape behavior.

MATERIALITY

(Rūpa) - The physical form, including the body and external matter, subject to decay and impermanence.

In the Abhidhamma, Perception and Feelings are Cestasikas (total 52), along with the citta, the eighteen types of materiality and Nirvāṇa totals 72 types of entities.

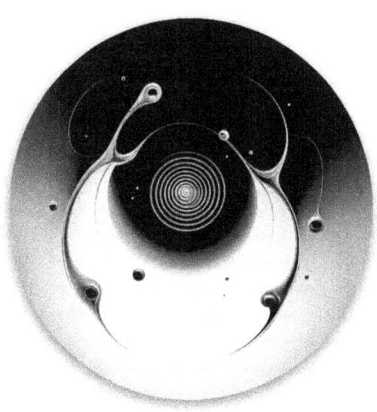

15. The 72 Types of Entities

*"That which is Below corresponds to that which is Above,
and that which is Above corresponds to that which is Below,
to accomplish the miracle of the One Thing."* [22]

In this chapter, we explore the fundamental building blocks of conditioned reality — the 72 distinct entities that form the basis of all experience. We'll examine how consciousness, mental factors, and material elements combine to create our perceived reality, while understanding how this knowledge serves as a bridge toward liberation. This systematic breakdown of existence provides the alchemist with a practical framework for understanding the nature of conditioning and its transcendence.

An entity is a phenomenon with its own intrinsic nature — e.g. tangibility, a resistance to any attempt to put two material objects in the same place and time, is not dependent on any other single factor for its ongoing manifestation. Delimiting space is a mental *dharma* that creates the illusion of space between different objects. This *space* is a mental projection and important for conscious processing yet it doesn't have intrinsic nature.

---

[22] *Hermes Trismegistus, The Emerald Tablet, translated in multiple versions including Fulcanelli's translation (1964).*

These 72 types are the absolute range of our palette that we need to create our model of conditioned reality. Remember, we are not aiming to create an exhaustive model of reality — just one that will grant us the tools to escape conditionality.

To help with getting this stuff into memory, we'll build on our previous model.

Normal, everyday experience involves *Apparent Reality* — this is the world of things, beings, self and ideas about this. The alchemist learns to abandon this reality in search of a deeper, more truthful one. The reality the alchemist looks for is inaccessible from where they start, so initially they must build a bridge from which they then can access their true goal.

This *bridge* is a mental model or map of reality that whilst no different really from any other deluded ideas about life, i.e., it's made of the same stuff, this model in particular is tailored to permit a breakthrough to what is called The Unconditioned or *Nirvāṇa* — the end of suffering. It is impossible to understand how or even if this is possible initially, and this is why faith is necessary.

Our previous model therefore explored this underlying reality based on causes and conditions — *conditioned* reality.

Conditioned reality is made of three types of stuff: physical matter or *rūpa*, and mind, *nāma*, made of consciousness and the mental factors that condition this consciousness.

Nirvāṇa itself is considered an entity with intrinsic nature, and when added to the 71 entities of conditioned reality make up our 72.

So, *Conditioned* reality is *made* of 71 distinct entities:

- **Consciousness**, which in its most basic form is called the '*citta*'

- 52 **mental factors**

- 18 types of **matter**

And that's all. We will explore each of these in some depth, but for now, it's not hard to remember that all we have is consciousness, 52 supporting mental factors and 18 types of physical phenomena. Add in *Nirvāṇa* and that is 72.

In the next chapter we will explore the different types of consciousness, but for this part, consciousness is considered a single entity.

The 52 mental factors are factors that always accompany the *citta* (point instance of awareness). Consciousness always must have an *object*, which can be a sensory object like a visual object, a sound, a taste, etc., or it can take mental phenomena and past *cittas* as objects. At this level, the level of the *citta*, consciousness only has a single function, where many *citta* operating in sequence are needed to *run* mental processing.

Every *citta* always has at least seven mental factors, which are called *cetasika*, which arise and perish with it. These mental factors are called *the universals* and they are essential in stabilising the *citta* and allowing it to work. Other mental factors are additionally present and affect the nature of consciousness, sometimes unpleasantly, other times pleasantly. In our exploration of conditioned reality we will cover all 52 mental factors and how they shape awareness.

Although the *Abhidhamma* delineates 28 distinct types of matter, 10 of these categories lack intrinsic nature. *Space* is a mental quality that imparts separateness; it requires the presence of other qualities to exist. We will explore matter in greater depth, but at this stage, the most important thing to grasp is that all categories of matter depend on the four great essentials (*earth, air, fire* and *water*) as bases.

The 18 material elements are therefore:

- **4 great essentials** (*earth, air, fire* and *water*);

- **5 material bases** (special *sensitive matter* such as the retina, cochlea, etc., that interacts with a sense object and creates, if conditions are right, sensory awareness);

- **4 sense objects** (qualities of matter that impinge on sensitive matter such as colour in a visual object, taste in an olfactory object, etc.) — note, touch is represented by three of the great essentials — earth, air, fire;

- **1 heart base** — an electromagnetic vortex associated with a current of iron-rich blood — the heart base is the physical base for the mind. For the mind to interact within the sensory sphere it needs this vortex;

- **2 physical sex bases** — These are the polarities of gender, note there are two, not a single polarity — this means the qualities of masculinity and femininity can vary in expressional intensity;

- **1 life faculty** — this is equivalent to *prāṇa* or the physical and energetic process of maintaining a very balanced internal environment to sustain life;

- **1 nutritional factor or *oja***, this is the factor that requires external elements for growth and repair of living organisms.

At this stage don't concern yourself too much trying to understand what these terms mean. We will revisit them all.

So, that's it. 72 entities with intrinsic existence build everything. 71 of these qualities build our *Matrix* of *Conditional Reality*, and one entity is the goal of the alchemist, *Nirvāṇa* or liberation from *Conditional Reality* and therefore suffering.

I hope this makes sense.

> *"Number is the ruler of forms and ideas, and the cause of gods and daemons."* [23]

Study Guide: The 72 Types Of Entities

This chapter introduces fundamental building blocks of conditioned reality, presenting a framework for understanding how consciousness, mental factors, and physical matter combine to create experience,

---

[23] Iamblichus, "Life of Pythagoras," translated by Thomas Taylor (1818)

Dharma

establishing foundation for later exploration of consciousness and spiritual transformation.

CORE CONCEPTS
- Reality comprises 72 fundamental dhammas with one representing unconditioned state
- System includes consciousness (citta), mental factors (cetasikas), and material elements (rūpa)
- Bridge between conventional and ultimate reality
- Three categories of reality: Rūpa, Nāma, Nibbāna

NEW TERMINOLOGY

Asankhata: The unconditioned

Bhava-rūpa: Sex bases

Dharma: Fundamental entity with intrinsic nature

Hadaya-vatthu: Heart base

Jivita-rūpa: Life faculty

Mahabhuta: The four great elements

Oja: Nutritive essence

Pannatti: Mental projection or concept

Paramattha-sacca: Ultimate reality

Pasada-rūpa: Sensitive material bases

Sabbacitta-sadharana: Universal mental factors

Sammuti-sacca: Conventional reality

Sankhata dharma: Conditioned reality

MAIN THEMES

1. Structure of Reality
- Basic building blocks of experience
- Relationship between consciousness and matter
- Role of mental factors in shaping awareness

2. Components of Existence
- Nature of consciousness (citta)
- Mental factors (cetasika)
- Material elements (rūpa)

3. Bridge to Transformation
- Model for understanding experience
- Path from apparent to conditional reality
- Role of faith in practice

TECHNICAL FRAMEWORK
- Components of Experience
- Consciousness: Momentary awareness, requires object, functions sequentially
- Mental Factors: 52 types, minimum 7 universal factors, colour consciousness with qualities
- Material Elements: 18 types with intrinsic nature

PRACTICAL APPLICATIONS
- Understanding basic building blocks of reality
- Categorising reality into distinct entities
- Observing interaction of consciousness, mental factors, and matter

INTEGRATION POINTS
- Connection to Chapter 14 (Matrix of Conditioned Reality)
- Links to Chapter 16 (Consciousness)
- Connection to Chapter 6 (Enlightenment)

COMMON MISCONCEPTIONS
- Dharma vs Pannatti distinction
- Understanding Conventional vs Ultimate reality
- Nature of consciousness and its requirements

REFLECTION QUESTIONS
- How does understanding basic building blocks of reality change your perspective on experience?
- In what ways do you notice consciousness, mental factors, and matter interacting in your experience?
- How might categorising reality into distinct entities help with spiritual development?

NIGREDO

PROGRESS INDICATORS
- *Recognition of fundamental dhammas in experience*
- *Understanding interaction between consciousness and matter*
- *Ability to distinguish between conventional and ultimate reality*

The 72 Types of Entities

COMPONENT	NUMBER	FUNCTION	NATURE
Consciousness	1	Basic awareness	Fundamental
Mental Factors	52	Shape experience	Conditional
Material Elements	18	Physical basis	Structural
Nirvāṇa	1	Liberation	Unconditioned

Consciousness Root types

ROOT TYPE	COMPONENTS	EFFECT
Unwholesome	Greed, hatred, delusion	Creates negative karma
Wholesome	Non-greed, non-hatred, wisdom	Creates positive karma
Transcendent	Beyond wholesome/unwholesome	Breaks karmic cycle

DHARMA

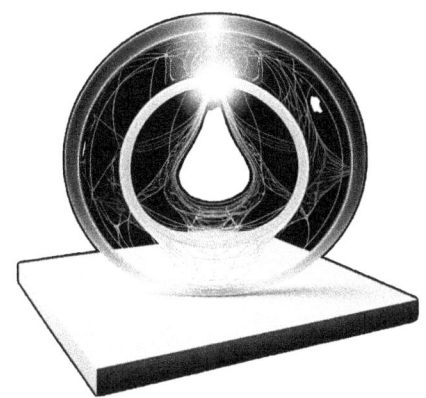

16. Consciousness

*"The spirit of man is the candle of the Lord,
searching all the inward parts of the belly"* [24]

Consciousness lies at the heart of alchemical transformation. This chapter explores the intricate nature of awareness through both Western alchemical and Eastern Buddhist frameworks. We examine how consciousness manifests across different realms of existence, from ordinary sensory experience to the most subtle spiritual states. Understanding these classifications provides the aspiring alchemist with a detailed map for navigating inner transformation while revealing how different states of consciousness relate to spiritual development.

Traditionally, in alchemy, subjective experience is made of three parts: *salt*, *sulphur* and *mercury*. Due to my limited familiarity with traditional approaches, I cannot definitively say but it is not too hard to suggest that salt is matter, sulphur the mental factors and mercury, consciousness. I will leave it up to those who have a deeper understanding to rate the accuracy of this. The vast majority of our model of consciousness I have gleaned from Buddhism.

The *Sūtra* classifications.

The *sūtras* divide consciousness into eight types. Five are the respective sense consciousnesses, then the sixth is called *discriminative mind* and it's what most of us

---

[24] *Prov. 20:27 KJV*

regard as *our mind*. The seventh is a space within our subjective experience that we come to know as *self*. This *self* arises as a subjective space as a reaction to the process of objectifying reality through perception. The eighth type is called *Ālaya*, and is a kind of atomic consciousness out of which the others are created.

For some, those who follow the meditative path of tranquillity, this level of detail might be sufficient. But for the alchemist, who follows a middle path that balances intellect and faith, a greater detailed understanding allows a more accurate evaluation of experience which, through insight permits breakthrough. So, without delay, let us introduce ourselves to how the *Abhidhamma* describes consciousness.

Spheres or *Planes* of Consciousness.

Consciousness can exist in two other *realms* that are more subtle than normal awareness. When one dreams, the reality in which this takes place is a mental world that is in some ways based on reality, but in other ways very different. There is an even more abstract realm beyond the dream realm, that is only accessible by advanced meditators.

The sphere or plane of normal experience is called the *sense-sphere realm*. This is the world of the five senses and a mind that is largely preoccupied with sense objects. This is a normal type of consciousness that through its attachment to certain aspects of life, creates craving and eventually suffering.

The two realms that are increasingly subtle forms of awareness are only accessible through fairly dedicated meditative practice. Here the consciousness is called *jhanic* consciousness and is more subtle than normal awareness. The first realm is called the *form* or *fine-material realm*. It starts off with the dream realm, but goes much deeper until one reaches the realm where ideas and concepts arise through entities like creator Gods. Beyond this lies an even subtler state of consciousness—the *formless realm*—where, apart from its threshold, space ceases to exist, leaving only pure mind.

These three spheres of consciousness represent our normal experience. Most of it is focused on our sensory-orientated goals, but if we are a thinker, we habitually spend time in the form realm as we consider concepts and ideas. Although our normal experience does include the formless realm, unless we are established in meditation or occult practice we cannot be aware of this part of experience.

There is a fourth realm of consciousness, although it is difficult to say whether it really should be called consciousness, as it is markedly different from the other realms. This is when consciousness takes *Nirvāṇa* as its object. When this happens, a breakthrough occurs, allowing one to see through some—and eventually all—of the mental conditions that bind us to suffering, known as *fetters*. This breakthrough can occur in increasing depth of insight, each corresponds to the *colour* of the stone of the philosophers. This realm is called transcendental consciousness and the *cittas* (point moments of consciousness) that arise are called *path* consciousnesses as they are points along the path towards liberation (the eightfold noble path). So, consciousness occurs in four distinct spheres or planes of activity:

- **sensory sphere realm** — where most normal awareness occurs,
- **form** or **fine-material realm** — where thinking, dreams, imagination occurs — normally only deliberately accessible to meditators and those with psychic powers,
- **formless realm** — very subtle, alien and abstract aspect of mind where extension and all manner of form are absent and
- **transcendental awareness** or **Nirvāṇa** — the goal or destiny of the alchemist, is reached in four distinct stages each corresponding with a stage in the 'creation' of the philosophers stone.

The *citta*.

The *citta* is the point instance of awareness. If consciousness is like a beam of light that comes from a light source, the *citta* is like a photon. It is a single moment of awareness that arises and then fades away, never to happen again. It arises always with seven mental factors that support it, and sometimes many more that arise and influence it.

Now, most importantly, there is only ever one *citta* at a time. Rather like an old film reel, each moment of awareness is a single frame, arising briefly before passing away, only to be immediately replaced by the next *citta*.

This happens really fast, like unbelievably fast. As you start to understand this stuff you might ask, how can we know this? Just put any doubt aside and feed your mind and in time your doubts will be answered. Anyway, back to the *citta*.

The *citta* is a single moment of awareness, that is followed by a succession of ongoing moments of awareness. Now although in truth the *cittas* are only experienced one at a time, they happen so fast that the experiencer of this consciousness seems to have multiple simultaneous experiences.

We start by learning the *atomic* construction of the *Matrix* of conditioned reality which in time will make sense as your depth of insight progresses.

The *citta* and its required seven mental factors arise and perish together. A *citta* cannot manifest without these essential mental factors. The *qualities* and types of mental factors condition the *citta* so that it can be of 121 different types (89 in some classifications).

So the *citta* can exist in 121 different states according to what mental factors accompany its arising. When, for example, we experience greed, this is because in addition to the seven necessary mental factors there are additional, *unwholesome* mental factors such as ignorance and desire.

Karma is the name of the force that causes subsequent *citta* to arise. It is produced by all *citta* to a small degree, but in some *citta*, they produce most of the *karma*. These are the *citta* where we make a choice or decision about something. In this choice we condition reality to be a certain way, which gives it meaning.

There are two *phases* to normal experience, although, because we cannot remember one of the phases, we only think we experience one.

The background phase of awareness is like a river carrying millions of sense impressions toward and through our sense of being. This is the awareness of being asleep. We cannot remember it because we don't register the experience.

During *waking* consciousness we have thoughts, ideas, feelings and sensations, which we react to. Each active and conscious experience is a distinct set of *citta* that emerge and go through a sequence, after which our mind lapses back into this background phase. Every thought, sensation, experience that we are aware of is like a brief halting in the background phase, and using the stream analogy, it's like we suspend this flow, and look back, upstream to see what we have just experienced.

It is only this active period that we can remember, and during waking experience our mind is jumping between active processing and this background, passive one.

Consciousness can therefore be of two main types, an active type when decisions are made that creates *karma* that will eventually cause the other type, called *resultant consciousness* to manifest. The passive and background awareness is just a stream of a certain type of *resultant consciousness* that shapes how we experience life.

We can categorise the 121 types of consciousness based on whether they generate *karma* or manifest as the result of past *karmic* forces. Those *citta* that produce *karma* can be divided into the *wholesome*, if they produce fortunate *karma* or *unwholesome* if they produce unpleasant *karma*.

Dharma

Sensory Sphere Citta

Type of Citta	Number	Notes
Unwholesome	12	8 Greed, 2 Hate and 2 Ignorance rooted.
Wholesome	8	Two or three rooted karmically wholesome consciousness.
Resultant	23	7 unwholesome and 8 wholesome, unrooted resultant citta, plus 8 rooted wholesome resultants.
Functional	11	8 Functional (wholesome) citta of the Arahant and 3 Functional rootless citta.

Within the sensory sphere realm, there are 54 types of *citta* 12 of these *citta* are considered *unwholesome* in that they, through *karma*, condition painful or unpleasant future consciousnesses. These 12 *unwholesome citta* condition a further 7 *resultant consciousnesses* which are also called rootless, which means they are weaker. There are 24 *wholesome citta* which can condition two types of resultant awareness. 8 of these are rootless but another 8 are *resultant consciousness* with *roots*. This explains why some of the results of good deeds lead to ongoing and stable future pleasant states. There are also three neutral types of consciousness in relation to *karma*, involved in mental processing.

Form Sphere Citta

Type of Citta	Number	Notes
Wholesome	5	One wholesome citta for each grade of jhāna — which in the Abhidhamma is five.
Resultant	5	Each jhanic wholesome citta has a corresponding resultant citta that acts as a rebirth linking consciousness.
Functional	5	Arahants who operate in the form realm produce functional cittas.

Within the form or fine-material realm there are 15 distinct types of *citta*. There are five *levels* of subtlety (*jhāna*) — and for each realm there is a *wholesome* consciousness, a *resultant consciousness* and a karmically neutral *citta* called functional. In this realm it is not possible to have *unwholesome* consciousness, in fact, it is said that jealousy is lethal, to beings who dwell in this realm. So, five levels, each with a single *wholesome citta*, and then a resultant *citta*. In *Arahants*, the fully enlightened being, karmic actions cease, so there is a karmic-less version of *citta* called *functional*. This only applies to *Arahants* who experience this *jhanic* level of awareness.

Formless Sphere Citta

Type of Citta	Number	Notes
Wholesome	4	One citta for each grade of formless jhāna with each karmically active wholesome citta creating a formless resultant than permits formless rebirth. Arahants don't produce karma and therefore their cittas are functional.
Resultant	4	
Functional	4	

Within the formless realm there are four levels, and it follows the 3 *citta* per level as the fine material. So each level has a *wholesome citta* with a resultant *citta*, plus a *functional citta* which lacks karmic potential which is experienced only by *Arahants*.

We use the metaphor of a path, with four stages to describe transcendental *citta*.

There are four paths, with a disciple achieving the *path* when, through insight, they realise (see through) the mental delusions called the *fetters*. A disciple works towards providing the conditions for the *citta* to *break through* to a transcendental *citta*.

Path and Fruit Citta

Type of Citta	Number	Notes
Path Consciousness	4	Four stages of realisation with a wholesome karmically active 'path' consciousness occurring only a single time in any series of existences. Each path moment is followed by two or three fruit consciousness that are resultants and can reoccur.
Fruit Consciousness	4	

There is only ever a single moment of *path consciousness*—it happens for a single moment, and then is followed by two or three *citta*, which we call *fruit* consciousnesses. These brief two or three moments are the mind realising the implications of the realisation of the path consciousness. This moment might be brief, but it shakes the very foundation of being.

So, when we start to categorise transcendental consciousness, we do so by the way of four paths, the four stages of enlightenment, each with a path and fruit consciousness, which means 8. However, to reach transcendental awareness one must gain at least the first *jhāna*. The *jhānas* are the subtle forms of awareness that permit access to the fine material and formless realms. So each path and fruit can be achieved based on five different *grades* of *jhāna*. We then multiply the 8 by 5 levels of *jhāna* to come to 40 types of transcendental awareness.

We will explore this in greater depth as we go.

To summarise.

There are 121 distinct types of *citta* (point awareness).

Consciousness is found in four types of realm. Three are conditioned and the fourth is where the *citta* takes *Nirvāṇa* as its object and approaches *Nirvāṇa*.

In the sensory sphere there are 54 types, which include the *active* types, which can be *unwholesome* or *wholesome*, and the resultant types. There are also *functional* types, which are either neutral because they help with mental function or because they are experienced by an *Arahant* who no longer produces *karma*.

In the fine material there are 15 types, three for each level of *jhāna*. One is the active *wholesome* type, one is the result of this, and one is functional and exclusive to *Arahants*.

In the formless there are only four levels, with three for each level, for a total of 12.

And lastly there are 40 types of transcendental *citta* that take *Nirvāṇa* as an object, with four paths at five levels of jhāna and a path and fruit *citta* for each. Note, the fruit *citta* is the resultant of the path *citta*.

I recommend Bhikkhu Bodhi's book — *A Comprehensive Manual of Abhidhamma* — plenty of good charts and detail in this book — which seems to be available as a downloadable PDF. Also check out his YouTube lectures.

Study Guide: Consciousness

This chapter explores consciousness classification through alchemical and Buddhist frameworks, examining how point-moments of awareness (cittas) create experience across existence realms, detailing karma-consciousness relationships and providing practical spiritual transformation foundations.

CORE CONCEPTS

- Three alchemical principles (salt, sulphur, mercury)
- Eight types of Buddhist consciousness
- Momentary points of awareness (cittas)
- Relationship between karma and consciousness

NEW TERMINOLOGY

Ahetuka: Consciousness without wholesome or unwholesome roots

Akusala: Morally harmful mental states rooted in greed, hatred, or delusion

Cittas: Point-moments of awareness

Kiriya: Functional consciousness producing no karmic results

Kusala: Morally beneficial mental states

Sobhana: Consciousness associated with wholesome factors

Vipāka: Results of past wholesome or unwholesome kamma

MAIN THEMES

- Structure of consciousness
- Realms of consciousness
- Karmic aspects

TECHNICAL FRAMEWORK

Types of Consciousness:

- Functional (Kiriya)
- Wholesome (Kusala)
- Unwholesome (Akusala)
- Resultant (Vipāka)
- Rootless (Ahetuka)
- Beautiful (Sobhana)

PRACTICAL APPLICATIONS

- Understanding different spheres of consciousness
- Recognising karmic influences on consciousness
- Distinguishing between active cognition and background awareness

INTEGRATION POINTS

- Connection to Chapter 4 (Symbols and Meanings)
- Links to Chapter 6 (Enlightenment)
- Connection to Chapter 7 (The Call to Adventure)

COMMON MISCONCEPTIONS

- Clarification of active vs resultant consciousness
- Understanding wholesome and unwholesome states
- Role of consciousness in spiritual transformation

REFLECTION QUESTIONS

- How do you experience different spheres of consciousness in daily life?
- What is your understanding of how karma influences consciousness?
- How do you notice the difference between active cognition and background awareness?

PROGRESS INDICATORS

- Recognition of different consciousness types
- Understanding of karmic relationships
- Development of awareness across different realms

The Eight Consciousnesses and Their Elements

Element	Manifestation	Consciousness
Earth	tangibility	touching
Water	cohesion	tasting
Fire	maturation	seeing
Air	movement	smelling
Space	limiting nature	hearing
Mind	choice	thinking
Being	realness	perceiving
Ālaya	existence	ground of Being

Realms of Consciousness

Realm	Types	Characteristics	Purpose
Sensory	54 cittas	Normal awareness	Daily experience
Form	15 cittas	Subtle awareness	Meditation states
Formless	12 cittas	Abstract awareness	Deep meditation
Path	40 cittas	Path consciousness	Liberation

Mundane Citta (81 types)

SENSE-SPHERE CONSCIOUSNESS (54)	
Unwholesome Cittas (12)	
Greed-rooted	8 types
Hatred-rooted	2 types
Delusion-rooted	2 types
Rootless Cittas (18)	
Unwholesome-resultant	7 types
Wholesome-resultant	8 types
Rootless functional	3 types
Beautiful Cittas (24)	
Wholesome	8 types
Resultant	8 types
Functional	8 types
FINE-MATERIAL-SPHERE CONSCIOUSNESS (15)	
Wholesome	5 types
Resultant	5 types
Functional	5 types
IMMATERIAL-SPHERE CONSCIOUSNESS (12)	
Wholesome	4 types
Resultant	4 types
Functional	4 types

Supramundane Citta (40 types)

PATH CONSCIOUSNESS (20)	
Stream-entry	5 types
Once-returning	5 types
Non-returning	5 types
Arahantship	5 types
FRUITION CONSCIOUSNESS (20)	
Stream-entry	5 types
Once-returning	5 types
Non-returning	5 types
Arahantship	5 types

The point of realisation of each of the stages of Sotāpanna, sakadāgāmī, Anāgāmī and Arahant is the arising of a single citta called the Path Consciousness. This is followed immediately by 2 or 3 fruition citta. The type of path and fruit citta depends on the prior maximum depth of jhanic experience.

17. The Mental Factors

*"As a goldsmith removes impurities from silver,
so the wise remove the defilements of the mind one by one,
gradually, from moment to moment."* [25]

In this chapter, we explore the intricate landscape of mental factors (cetasikas) that shape our consciousness and experience. These 52 distinct mental qualities work together with consciousness and physical matter to create our Subjective Reality. Understanding these factors provides a detailed map of how different mental states arise and interact, offering practical insights for spiritual transformation. Like an alchemist carefully analysing the components of their work, we'll examine how these mental factors combine to create both unwholesome states that bind us and beautiful states that lead to liberation.

In exploring our model of *conditioned reality*, we learn it has three groups of stuff:

- **consciousness**.
- **physical matter**, which is both the object of the senses and, as *sensitive matter*, detects these sense objects.
- **mental factors**, which support and condition the interactions between consciousness and its objects.

We have learned that consciousness can exist in three *mundane* planes, and a *transcendental* type. The *point-instance* of consciousness is the *citta*, which can exist in

---

[25] *Dhammapada, verse 239*

Universal Mental Factors

Wholesome

Faith
Mindfulness
Shame
Morality
Non-greed
Non-hatred
Neutrality of Mind
Tranquility of Mental Body
Tranquility of Consciousness
Lightness of Mental Body
Lightness of Consciousness
Malleability of Mental Body
Malleability of Consciousness
Wieldiness of Mental Body
Wieldiness of Consciousness
Proficiency of Mental Body
Proficiency of Consciousness
Rectitude of Mental Body
Rectitude of Consciousness

Ethically Neutral

Contact
Feeling
Perception
Volition
One-pointedness
Life faculty
Attention

Unwholesome

Delusion
Shamelessness
Fearlessness of Morality
Restlessness

Occasional Mental Factors

Unwholesome Occasionals

Greed
Wrong View
Conceit
Hatred
Envy
Avarice
Worry
Sloth
Torpor
Doubt

Ethically Neutral Occasionals

Initial Application
Sustained Application
Decision
Energy
Zest
Desire

Wholesome Occasionals

Right Speech
Right Action
Right Livelihood
Compassion
Appreciative Joy
Wisdom

121 different types.

All physical matter is dependent on the *four great essentials*. These are 'qualities' often known as *earth, air, water* and *fire*. It is perhaps more accurate to consider these as tangibility, movement, cohesion and entropy to a modern scholar. A further 24 groups of derived matter are categorised in the *Abhidhamma*, yet 10 of these groups lack *intrinsic* nature and so are excluded from our list of 72 entities.

There are 52 different mental factors and they represent a diverse group of factors that influence the type of *citta* that arise and perish with them. We will, in time, examine most of these factors individually but at this stage we are only after an overview.

Categories of Mental Factors

Category	N.	Nature	Examples
Universal	7	Present in all consciousness	Contact, feeling, perception
Occasional	6	Sometimes present	Initial application, energy, zest
Unwholesome	14	Create suffering	Greed, hatred, delusion
Beautiful	25	Support enlightenment	Faith, mindfulness, wisdom

The *Cetasika*.

Cetasika is the name for *mental factor*. In the *Abhidhamma* there are 52 *cetasikas*, which are categorised as following.

Ethically Variable Factors (13)

- **7 *universal* cetasikas** — these are the minimum seven factors that must accompany every *citta*. They are ethically neutral, being present in *wholesome, unwholesome* and functional *citta*. They each have a function that supports or directs the consciousness onto the object.

- **6 *occasional*** *cetasikas* — these six factors are sometimes present, but not always, and present in both *wholesome, unwholesome* and functional *citta*.

Unwholesome factors (14)

- **4 *universal unwholesome*** *cetasikas* — these four factors are present in all types of *unwholesome* consciousness.

- **10 *occasional unwholesome*** *cetasikas* — these mental factors are sometimes, but not always present in *unwholesome citta*.

Wholesome (beautiful) Factors (25)

- **19 *beautiful*** (*wholesome*) universal *cetasikas* — these mental factors are always present in *wholesome citta*.

- **3** *cetasikas* are called **abstinences** — the presence of these mental factors is important for right speech, right action and right thought.

- **2 *illimitables*** — there are in truth 4 illimitables — but kindness and neutrality of mind are covered in the 19 beautiful universals — leaving compassion and appreciative joy.

- **1 *Non-delusion (wisdom)*** — which like the two groups above are occasionally present in *wholesome citta*.

So, how does all this work and why learn it?

Developing an understanding of this model allows one to follow one's own experience by recognising how certain states of consciousness lead to others. There are only a limited number of patterns, which initially might seem overwhelming. Yet, with persistence any learning is rewarded with insights as one contemplates subjective experience.

Let us start by examining a simple operation and how the first group of cetasikas work.

Universal Mental Factors (Sabbacitta-sādharāna)

Factor	Function	Effect
Phassa (Contact)	Connects mind with object	Foundation for experience
Vedanā (Feeling)	Experiences object's quality	Pleasant/unpleasant/neutral sensation
Saññā (Perception)	Recognises object's marks	Memory and recognition
Cetanā (Volition)	Organises mental factors	Karmic accumulation
Ekaggatā (One-pointedness)	Focuses on single object	Mental stability
Jīvitindriya (Mental life)	Maintains mental factors	Continuity of consciousness
Manasikāra (Attention)	Directs mind to object	Mental engagement

The seven universals.

- 1. **Contact** is the process when a sense object impinges on sensitive matter and if the right conditions are present, sense consciousness arises, which in this example is the *citta*.

- 2. **Feeling** arises through contact and is analogous to the *citta tasting* or evaluating the nature of this contact. Every moment of consciousness has a certain feel — either positive, negative or neutral.

- 3. **Perception**. This is like the *citta* marking or noting the experience from previous or for future familiarity.

- 4. **Volition**. This is evaluation of worth of the object experienced. Remember at this level this is very simple.

- 5. **One-pointedness** — This is a factor that keeps the *citta* on the object — it unifies the *citta* with its object.

- 6. **Life faculty** — This is a factor that supports the other *cetasika* and makes them happen.

- 7. **Attention** — This has a function of attaching the other *cetasika* together towards the object.

There is a sense that each of these factors build and support one another. Contact conditions feeling, which itself conditions perception. However, there is no suggestion of a temporal sequence, more each factor influences the arising of other factors according to the conditions present.

If we now examine the next group, the *occasionals* we'll see how the complexity of the *citta* can develop from the more basic forms of awareness to a form more analogous to thinking or thought.

The first two *occasionals* are called *initial application* and *sustained application*. These factors hold and steady the object, and allow a discursive element.

Occasional Mental Factors (Pakiṇṇaka)

Factor	Function	Effect
Vitakka (Initial Application)	Directs mind to object	Thought formation
Vicāra (Sustained Application)	Maintains mind on object	Continued examination
Adhimokkha (Decision)	Conviction about object	Mental determination
Viriya (Energy)	Supports mental activity	Effort and persistence
Pīti (Interest)	Refreshes mind and body	Rapture and zest
Chanda (Desire)	Wants to obtain object	Motivation to act

The six *occasionals*.

- 8. **Initial application** — this focuses the mental factors firmly onto the object.

- 9. **Sustained application** — the maintained focus on the object.

- 10. **Decision** — this *releases* the mind onto the object— it is a factor that seems to permit a certain commitment to the process.

- 11. **Energy** — This supports the other *cetasikas* and prevents them from collapsing.

- 12. **Zest** — This has a function of refreshing the mind and body.

- 13. **Desire** — This represents the mental factor of the drive to complete the process and not necessarily greed (attachment) — i.e. this factor will be present in both the materialistic pursuit of wealth and the spiritual pursuit of knowledge.

Don't (unless you are very keen) try to remember these just yet. We will return to them, the idea is to just give you an overview so you can start to see how this all works.

The four *universal unwholesome cetasikas*.

Four *cetasikas* are always present in all *unwholesome citta*. These are important and understanding them will be useful in learning to control your own unhelpful states of mind.

- 14. **Delusion** — This is a huge concept that we will explore. For now, we'll keep it simple. Delusion here simply means not knowing about *Nirvāṇa*, and the path to *Nirvāṇa*. This, of course represents pretty much everybody not on a spiritual path. And, delusion remains present right until the last stage. Delusion is therefore simply not knowing a profound truth, which is the same truth the alchemist seeks.

- 15. **Shamelessness** — the *unwholesome citta* are all universally selfish, they require a distortion where we prioritise ourselves over the welfare of another. If we fully accepted this, we wouldn't be able to be greedy or cruel. But, in order to have greedy or hateful thoughts we must also think this is ok, or justified. Later, we might recognise this and feel shame.

- 16. **Fearlessness of consequence** — this is closely related to shamelessness and is a denial of adverse outcomes due to *unwholesome* actions. Remorselessness or recklessness might be another word.

- 17. **Restlessness** — all *unwholesome citta* are restless. Even when experiencing greed's contentment, deep down, one remains aware of its selfish nature.

The ten *unwholesome occasionals*.

- 18. **Greed** — this forms all sorts of selfish desire or attachment. Greed, along with delusion and ill-will can form roots which stabilise and strengthen the *unwholesome citta*.

- 19. **Wrong view** — this is holding ideas or viewpoints that justify *unwholesome* actions that are based in delusion.

- 20. **Conceit** — this is a function of the valuation of self, and can refer not only to a haughty elevation of self-worth, but any sort of attempt to equate self with others.

- 21. **Hatred** or **ill-will** — this is aversion towards the sensory or mental object that manifests in thoughts of harm or rejection.

- 22. **Envy** — this is dissatisfaction with another's success.

- 23. **Avarice** — this is concealing one's success or gains so as not to share it with others.

- 24. **Worry** — this is remorse about doing wrong without any attempt to right it.

- 25. **Sloth**—always present alongside torpor, manifests as dullness in the *citta*, hindering its actions.

- 26. **Torpor** represents difficulty applying or holding the *cetasikas* to the *citta*, so there is a dullness in mental processing.

- 27. **Doubt** — this is particular and represents hindrances that arise through sceptical doubt about the process.

In later talks we'll see how various states of consciousness arise and their combinations of the *cetasikas*. Again, just initially try to get a flavour of this list.

The *beautiful (wholesome) citta* are always accompanied by the nineteen *universal beautiful* factors. In some states some factors are more prominent.

Unwholesome Mental Factors (Akusala)

UNIVERSALS		
FACTOR	FUNCTION	EFFECT
Moha (Delusion)	Mental blindness	Confusion
Ahirika (Shamelessness)	Lack of moral shame	Ethical transgression
Anottappa (Fearlessness)	No dread of wrong	Moral recklessness
Uddhacca (Restlessness)	Mental agitation	Distraction
OCCASIONALS		
Lobha (Greed)	Clinging to objects	Attachment
Dosa (Hatred)	Aversion to objects	Ill-will
Diṭṭhi (Wrong view)	Misapprehension	False understanding
Māna (Conceit)	Inflated self-worth	Pride
Issā (Envy)	Resentment of others' success	Jealousy
Macchariya (Avarice)	Concealing one's success	Stinginess
Kukkucca (Worry)	Remorse over past actions	Mental unease
Thina (Sloth)	Mental sluggishness	Laziness
Middha (Torpor)	Unwieldiness of mind	Drowsiness

The *beautiful (wholesome) universal cetasikas.*

- 28. **Faith** — this is the function of trusting and necessary for the establishment of *wholesome* consciousness. Note, this faith is not *having faith*, it's more basic and closer to trust.

- 29. **Mindfulness** — this is the process of attending to the mental process and is an active kind of remembering.

- 30. **Shame** — this might initially seem strange as shame being a beautiful factor, yet often it is badly processed shame that causes problems. Shame is essential for moral development and is the recognition of one's *unwholesome* views or decisions.

- 31. **Fear of moral wrongdoing** — whilst shame is a personal uncomfortable feeling with the realisation of *unwholesome* consciousness, fear of moral wrongdoing is an apprehension towards the consequences (to others) of one's mistakes. Clearly the development of this supports mindfulness in one's present and future states to avoid harmful consequences to another.

- 32. **Non-greed** — perhaps this *cetasika* is termed this way as it's kind of a development of the *unwholesome root* of greed. Here it manifests as generosity, which is necessary in *wholesome* consciousness.

- 33. **Non-hatred** — again, perhaps through development, a more natural and instinctive hatred is tamed and becomes its opposite, which manifests as kindness.

- 34. **Neutrality of mind** — this manifests as a desire towards fairness and balance.

- 35. & 36. **Tranquillity** — these factors occur in pairs, one extends to tranquillity of the *citta*, the other the mental factors. This is a factor that promotes stillness and peaceful harmony.

- 37. & 38. **Lightness** — again, paired factors relating to the buoyancy or lightness of the *citta* and *cetasika*. These factors oppose sloth and torpor.

- 39. & 40. **Malleability** — these paired factors subdue rigidity within the *citta* and *cetasika*, it is manifested as non-resistance.

- 41. & 42. **Wieldiness** — again, paired *cetasika*, one that pertains to the *citta*, the other the *cetasika*. Wieldiness pertains to the ability of the *citta* to successfully grasp its object.

- 43. & 44. **Proficiency** — again, paired, and these factors pertain to the *health* of the *citta* and *cetasika* in performing their functions. It ensures the smooth operation

Universal Beautiful Mental Factors (Sobhana)

Factor	Function	Effect
Saddhā (Faith)	Confidence in wholesome action	Mental clarity
Sati (Mindfulness)	Non-forgetfulness	Clear awareness
Hiri (Moral shame)	Shrinking from evil	Inner restraint
Ottappa (Fear of wrong)	Fear of consequences	Moral caution
Alobha (Non-greed)	Non-attachment	Generosity
Adosa (Non-hatred)	Non-aversion	Loving-kindness
Tatramajjhattatā (Mental balance)	Equilibrium of mind	Equanimity
Kāya-passaddhi (Tranquility of factors)	Calming mental factors	Mental peace
Citta-passaddhi (Tranquility of mind)	Calming consciousness	Mental peace
Kāya-lahutā (Lightness of factors)	Removing heaviness	Mental agility
Citta-lahutā (Lightness of mind)	Removing heaviness	Mental agility
Kāya-mudutā (Malleability of factors)	Removing rigidity	Adaptability
Citta-mudutā (Malleability of mind)	Removing rigidity	Adaptability
Kāya-kammaññatā (Wieldiness of factors)	Removing unwieldiness	Fitness for work
Citta-kammaññatā (Wieldiness of mind)	Removing unwieldiness	Fitness for work
Kāya-pāguññatā (Proficiency of factors)	Removing sickness	Competence
Citta-pāguññatā (Proficiency of mind)	Removing sickness	Competence

| Kāyujukatā (Rectitude of factors) | Removing crookedness | Uprightness |
| Cittujukatā (Rectitude of mind) | Removing crookedness | Uprightness |

of the whole process by opposing disability or dysfunction.

- 45. & 46. **Rectitude** — the last paired factors — again one sustains the *citta*, the other the accompanying *cetasika*. This pertains to moral straightness or simple truth. It opposes deviance and convolutedness.

The Abstinences.

The next three mental factors are also factors on the eightfold noble path. They pertain to *wholesome* attitudes towards creating *karma*.

- 47. **Right Speech** — is a mental factor that when present prevents slanderous speech, lying, and gossip.

- 48. **Right Action** — is a mental factor that when present prevents *unwholesome* actions such as stealing, killing or sexual misconduct.

- 49. **Right Livelihood** — is a mental factor that is present when one's daily actions are *wholesome* and one isn't involved in harmful pursuits such as selling weapons, poisons or being involved in killing.

The illimitables.

There are four illimitables — these are qualities that can be developed without limit.

— **Kindness**, also called *mettā* is considered to be the same cetasika as non-hatred.

— **Equanimity**, or fairness, is considered to be the same cetasika as neutrality of mind.

— **Compassion**, which is a recognition of another's suffering and a desire for them not to suffer.

— **Appreciative joy** is sharing the joy of another's success or happiness.

- 50. **Compassion** is a mental quality that manifests as the desire to remove the suffering of another. It manifests as non-cruelty.

- 51. **Appreciative joy** is the gladness at the success of others.

The last *cetasika*, wisdom, like the *abstinences* and *illimitables* is only occasionally present in *wholesome* consciousness.

Wisdom.

52. **Wisdom**. This is seeing things as they really are — i.e. without the delusions that arise through gross or subtle attachments. Its function is to *illuminate the field of knowledge like a lamp.*

Now, I know this seems a diverse and complex list. But once you gain some familiarity with the terms it starts to make sense.

Remember that all 52 *cetasikas* are included in the 72 entities with intrinsic nature, so working through one list complements the other.

The thing to grasp is that *citta* and *cetasika* arise and perish together. The *citta* understands and comprehends its object through the *cetasikas*, and depending on whether they are *wholesome* or *unwholesome cetasikas* the *citta* takes on different *flavours*.

Those *citta* that arise with the *unwholesome cetasikas* will become consciousnesses that feel greed, envy, anger, hatred and often provoke reactions that themselves will create future unfortunate karmic states. Whilst those *citta* that arise with the nineteen beautiful factors with variations in the presence of other mental factors will be kind, generous or forgiving.

In time, this insightful knowledge provides one with a *map* of one's own experience, granting control, mindfulness and eventually wisdom in one's actions.

Occasional Beautiful Mental Factors (Pakiṇṇaka Sobhana)

Factor	Function	Effect
Sammāvācā (Right Speech)	Abstaining from false speech, harsh speech, slander and idle talk	Verbal restraint
Sammākammanto (Right Action)	Abstaining from killing, stealing, and sexual misconduct	Physical restraint
Sammā-ājīva (Right Livelihood)	Avoiding wrong means of livelihood	Purification of conduct
Karuṇā (Compassion)	Desire to remove others' suffering	Elimination of cruelty
Muditā (Appreciative Joy)	Rejoicing in others' success and prosperity	Elimination of envy
Pañña (Wisdom)	Understanding things as they really are	Penetration of truth

Nigredo

Study Guide: The Mental Factors

This chapter examines the 52 mental factors (cetasikas) and their interaction with consciousness and physical matter in creating experiential reality, providing a framework for understanding mental states and spiritual transformation.

CORE CONCEPTS

- Three components of experience: consciousness, physical matter, mental factors
- 52 distinct mental factors that shape consciousness
- Relationship between wholesome and unwholesome states
- Integration of mental factors with consciousness

NEW TERMINOLOGY

Cetasika: Mental factors that influence consciousness

Citta: Point-instance of consciousness

Four Great Essentials: Earth, air, water, fire (tangibility, movement, cohesion, entropy)

Illimitables: Qualities with no limit, such as kindness, compassion, appreciative joy, and equanimity.

MAIN THEMES

1. Structure of Experience
2. Categories of Mental Factors
3. Practical Applications of Understanding Mental States
4. Transformation of Consciousness

TECHNICAL FRAMEWORK

- **Universal Cetasikas**: Contact, feeling, perception, volition, one-pointedness, life faculty, attention
- **Occasional Cestasikas**: Initial application, sustained application, decision, energy, zest, desire
- **Unwholesome Universal Factors**: Delusion, shamelessness, fearlessness of morality, restlessness
- **Unwholesome Occasional Factors**: Greed, hatred, wrong view, conceit, envy, avarice, worry, sloth, torpor
- **Beautiful Universal Factors**: Faith, mindfulness, shame, moral fear, non-greed, non-hatred, neutrality, tranquility, lightness, malleability, wieildiness, proficiency, rectitude.
- Beautiful Occasional Factors: Right speech, right action, right thought, compassion, appreciative joy, wisdom

PRACTICAL APPLICATIONS

- Recognition of mental states
- Development of wholesome factors
- Transformation of consciousness
- Application to spiritual practice

INTEGRATION POINTS

- Links to consciousness (Chapter 16)
- Connection to forces driving the matrix (Chapter 19)
- Relationship to Eightfold Noble Path (Chapter 24)

Dharma

Common Misconceptions
- Shame as wholesome versus unwholesome processing
- Distinction between faith and trust
- Nature of delusion in spiritual development

Reflection Questions
- How do universal mental factors operate in your experience?
- How do wholesome and unwholesome factors affect your mind?
- How can understanding mental factors enhance mindfulness?

Progress Indicators
- Development of wholesome mental states
- Reduction in unwholesome mental factors
- Increased awareness of mental processes
- Growth in wisdom and understanding

Nigredo

A Candle:Flame::Cestasika:Citta Analogy

Smoke
Volition - (Pāli: Cetanā) The mental factor that drives intention and action, shaping future karma.

Air
Attention - (Pāli: Manasikāra) The directing of awareness toward an object, initiating mental engagement.

Shape & Edge
Perception - (Pāli: Saññā) The mental process of recognizing and labeling objects, sensations, and experiences.

Wick
Contact - (Pāli: Phassa) The point where the senses meet an object, creating awareness of an experience.

Heat
Feeling - (Pāli: Vedanā) The response to contact, experienced as pleasant, unpleasant, or neutral sensations.

Wax
Life Faculty - (Pāli: Jīvitindriya) The sustaining force that maintains mental and physical vitality.

Candlestick
One-Pointedness - (Pāli: Ekaggatā) The ability of the mind to remain focused and undistracted on a single object.

The seven ethically neutral universal mental factors (cestasika) that arise and perish with every moment of consciousness (the citta) -the light it produces.
The light—the citta or single moment of consciousness—121 distinct types
The conditions that support and arise with this 'light', the cestasika or mental factors—52 distinct types.

Dharma

18. Materiality

"Form is emptiness and the very emptiness is form;
emptiness does not differ from form,
form does not differ from emptiness,
whatever is emptiness, that is form" [26]

In this chapter, we explore the Buddhist analysis of materiality and its relationship to consciousness. We'll examine how matter exists as both tangible and intangible phenomena, understanding its dynamic, impermanent nature through the lens of the four great elements and their derivatives. This framework is essential for grasping how material reality interfaces with mind and consciousness, providing crucial insights for the alchemical transformation of experience. While the categorisation may seem technical, each aspect serves to illuminate the true nature of physical existence and its role in spiritual development.

Before we examine the categories of materiality, let us get to grips with exactly what we mean. The *material* is that part of experience that isn't mind. Mind and matter are different in one clear way, and that is awareness. All matter is insensate. Furthermore, we can only really concern ourselves with matter that we can sense. If there is matter (most likely) that we cannot sense it is irrelevant to our goal.

---

[26] *Heart Sūtra, translated by. Edward Conze*

Matter is more than the solid and tangible. Matter is all phenomena that can be sensed and taken as a sense or mind object. So, light, sound, colour, taste are matter in this model.

Some types of matter are *sensitive*. This is material present in the organs of sight, hearing, taste, smell and distributed over the body as touch.

When we sense something, this sensitive matter, being matter cannot take part in consciousness. Instead, one material phenomena interacts with another, and in this interaction patterns in electrical circuits are *read* by the mind, which creates a sense object that is taken by consciousness and processed.

We might think our back aches, yet in truth our material body is insensate. It is our mind that creates but mixes the pain (which is as *body*).

The Four Great Essential Material Elements.

All categories of matter depend on the four great essentials, *earth, air, water* and *fire*.

In the smallest unit of matter there always has to be these four present. They arise together and each support and condition each other's presence. In truth, the smallest unit has to have eight qualities, *earth, air, fire, water, colour, taste, smell* and *nutritive essence*.

It is important that as we examine the qualities of the great essentials that you get rid of concepts of *fire, air, earth* and *water*. As an alchemist we are interested in the most elemental (has no parts) aspect of analysis, so imagining *earth* that has tangibility is wrong. There is no *earth*, just the quality of tangibility, which is a resistance to co-occupation of identical temporal-spatial coordinates by a body with tangibility. When we talk about the *water element* there is no water, just the principle of cohesion.

The four great essentials support each other. *Earth* acts as a physical base upon which the others are physically supported. *Water* holds the elements together. *Air* permits translocation which is interpreted as movement, or microscopically vibration. And *fire* creates time through changes in recurring material groups taken as entropy.

If we are to understand the elements, then grasping *air* and *fire* are particularly important. *Earth* and *Water* are simple enough. But to consider the last two we must introduce how things really are.

Dharma

Although matter appears stable and solid, we know this is not truly the case. Matter decays, rusts, falls apart, changes. Often, unless it is ice cream on a warm day this is not obvious.

On a microscopic level, physical matter arises and ceases continuously, each time being replaced by a nearly identical copy, which arises and then ceases. The Buddhists postulated this over 2000 years ago, and recently science can prove that what we think is *solid* is really oscillating fields of energy, that manifests in locations that approximate an atom.

The reason why this isn't apparent is whilst matter has groups that phase in and out, these are not synchronised, so matter appears largely stable. Furthermore, this happens really quickly. However, consciousness is 17 times faster in its cycles of oscillating between arising and ceasing, so when consciousness takes material phenomena as its object, or at least the pattern that arises between a sense object and its sense base (the sensitive matter of that sense), it persists for 17 moments of *citta*, giving a sense of permanence.

Don't worry about the numbers and complexity just now.

The important thing is to remember that any object is not stable. It is constantly being replaced by a near identical version. Now, it is important that it is *near-identical*. If we set a camera onto anything material, and could record for that period of time, we would see everything slowly changes. A block of ice melts in a warm room.

Consider our block of ice. Each moment a near identical copy replaces it. But, through warmth (*fire*) each new arising is manifestly different. The actual substance changes, through time, directly corresponding with temperature, which is the very definition of entropy and gives us time.

Now, consider something stable, like a diamond. Every moment all of the diamond is replaced with a near copy. Can I move the diamond?

The answer is no. All movement is illusory. Through the air element, which manifests as pressure on the tangible earth element, subsequent groups of matter are conditioned to appear in a location that is slightly different from the one which the previous conditioning groups ceased. The air element enables objects to appear as though they move through spatial dimensions, yet in reality, this process is more akin to teleportation.

I hope that has set the scene for how we categorise matter.

28 Categories of Matter.

Matter is categorised into 28 types, 18 of which possess intrinsic nature, meaning they exist as self-defining entities. Some of these categories are a little oblique to understand initially, but in time it makes sense.

4 Great Essential Elements.

The four great essentials—*earth, air, fire,* and *water*—form the foundation from which the other 24 categories are derived.

5 Material Sense Bases.

There are 5 sense bases—*sensitive matter* present in the retina, etc, that interacts when healthy, with sense phenomena that enter its respective field of activity.

4 Types of Sense Phenomena.

There are 4 sense phenomena that are detected by these sense bases. These are colour with respect to sight, the sound object to hearing, the smell object to smell and the taste object to taste. Note there is no touch object, touch is the direct sensing of three of the four great essentials, tangibility, pressure, temperature. *Water's* defining property, cohesion, is not directly perceivable through physical senses but may be understood by those who develop heightened awareness.

2 Faculties of Gender.

There are two material faculties (expressions) of gender. This represents a dual polarity where degrees of masculinity and degrees of femininity are present.

The Heart Base.

There is the material *heart base*. The *heart base* is a standing electromagnetic field that is created through the movement of metallic atoms (mainly iron, but copper and magnesium in some species), which are present in circulating blood. This field is most intense at the centre of our bodies, and it is this field that acts as physical tether to the mind. This is why sense aware consciousness ceases the moment blood flow stops, but note not all consciousness. *Jhanic* consciousness is possible in those who have developed it, even incidentally if they were thinkers. If circulation is re-established fairly promptly then these *jhanic* awarenesses are remembered as a near death experience.

The Material Life Faculty.

There is the material life faculty. These are all the physical processes that support and sustain life. *Prāṇa* might be something similar.

The Nutrient Element.

The last group of materiality is that matter that is nutrient and supports growth and maintenance of the physical body.

10 Types of Non-concretely Produced Matter.

There are ten groups of more abstract material factors, called *non-concretely produced matter*. These factors help us understand how matter *works* in Conditional Reality.

The Space Element.

The first of this group is called the *space* element. This can be a little tricky, as one must consider *space* as a potential element that arises when it is necessary to comprehend phenomena. *Space* is what appears when we make a hole or it is what surrounds discrete objects. It is not air, either modern understanding nor the element of *air*. We can have *space* even in a vacuum.

The next two types of material phenomena are how the mind, and *karma* directly produce matter.

Bodily intimation.

This is how the body moves. The mind, through intention causes muscles to contract and the body changes shape, or breathes, or walks. Here the mind creates the *air* element, which gives the appearance of movement.

Verbal intimation.

This is how we verbally communicate. This is the mind manifesting *earth* element, tension in the body and vocal cords causing vibrations as air is expelled through the mouth.

The next three groups are called *mutable phenomena*, and pertain to living physical matter, i.e, the physical body of the meditator.

Lightness.

Lightness is the ease with which the mind can move the body.

Malleability.

Malleability is the flexibility and subtleness of the body and lack of resistiveness.

Wieldiness.

Wieldiness is the skill, ease and efficiency of physical processes.

The last four groups are even more abstract, and are called the *Characteristics of Matter*. Remember that matter only appears stable because it has a presence of 17 moments of consciousness.

Production.

Production is the factor that, given suitable conditions causes material phenomena to arise.

Continuity.

Continuity is the factor that causes groups of matter to continue, from one arising to the next.

Decay.

Decay is the factor that causes matter to age and tarnish and tend towards dissolution.

Impermanence.

Impermanence is the factor that causes the ultimate dissolution of material phenomena.

These last four factors are all always present, but in differing amounts. Production is like growing, continuity is necessary for ongoing presence. Decay is present, even at the beginning, but becomes more prevalent as production declines.

Now, these 28 groups may seem overly complex and inconsistent—an intellectual discomfort—until one remembers our goal. We are not trying to understand everything about matter, we are taking what is relevant for our goal. The Abhidhamma is like the technicalities behind the *sūtras*, and like the *sūtra* therefore its focus is exclusively on spiritual liberation.

Later we will learn how matter is conditioned by various factors like the *citta* (consciousness) and *karma* which influence our physical environment. Other factors outside the being can clearly influence matter, and the abhidhamma simply classifies these as those originating from temperature — which if we regard this as modern entropy is incredibly insightful. Plants, for example, lacking volition are treated the same as rocks and minerals in the *Abhidhamma* not because in truth it really is that simple, but as understanding these aspects of reality is unnecessary for our main goal.

It's helpful now that we have some concepts to return to our model of conditioned reality. Remember our model is tailored for a specific purpose of understanding that puts us in the position to experience the breakthrough to transcendental awareness.

Our model is built of three kinds of structures —

> 1. **Consciousness**, which is aware of sensory and mental objects.
>
> 2. The **Material** world, analysed in a way that identified 28 groups of material types, 18 of which are concretely produced (have intrinsic nature), 10 are *abstract* qualities of matter.
>
> 3. The 52 **mental factors** that provide a functional framework and sustain the *citta* in its processes.

Next, I'll introduce the laws and forces that *animate* this model, and drive the experience of self toward patterns that perpetuate suffering. These laws are complicated, so at this stage, we'll simply introduce some of the more important concepts.

> *"All conditioned things are impermanent — when one sees this with wisdom, one turns away from suffering."* [27]

---

[27] *Dhammapada, verse 277*

Material Categories

Category	Number	Examples
Great Essential Elements	4	Earth, Air, Fire, Water
Material Sense Bases	5	Eye, Ear, Nose, Tongue, Body
Sense Phenomena	4	Colour, Sound, Smell, Taste
Gender Faculties	2	Masculine, Feminine
Heart Base	1	Electromagnetic field
Life Faculty	1	Life-sustaining processes
Nutrient Element	1	Growth-supporting matter
Non-concrete Matter	10	Space, Intimation, etc.

Material Categories by Type

Category	Properties	Function
Essential Elements	Tangibility, cohesion, movement, temperature	Foundation of all matter
Sense Bases	Sensitivity to stimuli	Interface with consciousness
Abstract Matter	Space, intimation, characteristics	Support material processes
Life Faculties	Sustenance, nutrition, gender	Maintain physical existence

The 28 Categories of Matter

Concretely Produced Matter		Non-concretely Produced Matter	
Earth — tangibility	The four great essentials upon which all concretely produced matter is based.	Space Element	Space here delineates physical objects and is the elemental base out of which the great essentials arise.
Water — cohesion			
Fire — maturation			
Air — movement			
Eye Sensitivity	Sensitive matter that interacts with phenomena. If the right conditions are met, it triggers the arising of sense consciousness.	Bodily Intimation	This is how the mind influences materiality through volition activities and speech. The matter arises through the arising of air or earth element.
Ear Sensitivity			
Nose Sensitivity		Vocal Intimation	
Tongue Sensitivity			
Body Sensitivity			
Visible Form	The phenomena that sensitive matter detects. *Tangibility is a combination of three of the four great elements excluding water.	Lightness	Mutable phenomena — qualities of the physical body depending on mental faculties and health.
Sound			
Smell		Malleability	
Taste			
*Tangibility		Wieldiness	
Feminity	The Faculty of Sex	Production	Characteristics of Matter.
Masculinity			
Heart Base	The base of mind.	Continuity	
Life Faculty		Decay	
Nutrient		Impermanence	

Study Guide: Materiality

This chapter examines Buddhist analysis of materiality and its relationship to consciousness, focusing on matter's dynamic nature through four great elements and their derivatives.

CORE CONCEPTS

- Matter differs from mind through lack of awareness
- Four Great Essential Elements form the foundation of material existence
- Matter exists in 28 distinct categories
- Material phenomena are impermanent and constantly changing
- Matter interfaces with consciousness through sense bases

NEW TERMINOLOGY

Bodily intimation: Mind-driven physical movement through muscle contraction

Continuity: Factor causing material groups to persist

Decay: Factor causing matter to age

Four Great Essential Elements: Earth (tangibility), Water (cohesion), Air (movement), Fire (entropy)

Heart Base: Electromagnetic field from blood movement acting as mind's physical tether

Impermanence: Factor causing material dissolution

Life Faculty: Physical processes supporting life

Malleability: Body's flexibility and lack of resistance

Production: Factor causing material phenomena to arise

Sensitive Matter: Material in sense organs interacting with sense objects

Space Element: Potential element necessary for the comprehension of phenomena

Verbal intimation: Physical process of speech production

Wieldiness: Efficiency of physical processes

MAIN THEMES

1. Nature of Matter
- Fundamental difference from mind
- Dynamic and impermanent nature
- Relationship with consciousness

2. Four Great Elements
- Earth as tangibility
- Water as cohesion
- Air as movement
- Fire as temperature/entropy

3. Material Categories
- 18 intrinsic categories
- 10 derived categories
- Sense bases and phenomena
- Gender faculties

PRACTICAL APPLICATIONS

- Understanding material impermanence
- Observing sensory processes
- Recognising matter-consciousness interaction

INTEGRATION POINTS

- Links to Forces that Drive the Matrix

Dharma

- Foundation for understanding Saṃsāra
- Connection to Path Consciousness
- Relationship to Different Worlds and Jhāna

REFLECTION QUESTIONS

1. How do you experience the four great elements daily?
2. How do you observe matter's impermanent nature?
3. How does understanding matter affect your view of physical existence?

PROGRESS INDICATORS

- Recognition of matter's impermanent nature
- Understanding of sense—consciousness interaction
- Insight into material phenomena's true nature

Characteristics of Matter

Type	Function	Manifestation
Production	Causes arising	Beginning phase
Continuity	Maintains presence	Middle phase
Decay	Creates aging	Later phase
Impermanence	Causes dissolution	Final phase

NIGREDO

The Four Realms of Consciousness

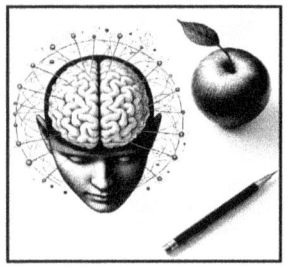

1. Sense-Sphere Consciousness

Consciousness engaged with the sensory world and habitual thought patterns.
- *Arises in relation to objects of sight, sound, smell, taste, touch, and mental formations.*
- *Can be unwholesome, wholesome (beautiful), or functional (karmically neutral).*

2. Form-Sphere Consciousness

Consciousness refined through meditative absorption, focused and unified.
- *Arises when one of the other consciousnesses is taken as an object in deep meditation.*
- *Has five progressive stages of increasing stillness and depth.*
- *Can only be wholesome or resultant—never unwholesome.*

3. Formless-Sphere Consciousness

Consciousness transcending the realm of form, dissolving into vastness.
- *Arises through meditation when the limitations of form-realm absorption are abandoned.*
- *Has four increasingly subtle stages:*
- *Limitless Space*
- *Limitless Consciousness*
- *Nothingness*
- *Neither perception nor non-perception*

4. Transcendental Consciousness

Consciousness taking Nirvana as its object—beyond all conditioned experience.
- *Occurs in two ways:*
- *Path Consciousness: The singular breakthrough moment of awakening.*
- *Fruit Consciousness: The stabilisation of awakening, occurring immediately after the path moment.*

Consciousness unfolds through four distinct realms, progressing from sensory engagement to transcendence beyond conditioned experience. As perception refines, awareness moves from reactivity to stillness, from form to formlessness, culminating in the direct realisation of Nirvāṇa.

19. The Forces that Drive The Matrix

*"Every Cause has its Effect; every Effect has its Cause;
everything happens according to Law;
Chance is but a name for Law not recognised;
there are many planes of causation, but nothing escapes the Law."* [28]

In this chapter, we delve into the fundamental forces that shape and animate our perceived reality. We examine how consciousness, matter, and mental factors interweave to create the matrix of existence, with particular focus on karma as a primary driving force. Through understanding these mechanisms, the aspiring alchemist gains crucial insights into how their own consciousness simultaneously creates and navigates reality, setting the foundation for eventual transformation. While the concepts may seem complex, they provide essential tools for understanding the nature of existence and the path toward alchemical transformation.

The early task of the alchemist is to recognise that *objective* reality is a myth and construct based only on individual experience. They may not *realise* this explicitly; indeed, it often starts with a a distrust or paranoia regarding reality itself.

Through exploration, they either explicitly or gradually replace this consensual objective reality with a more accurate version that includes subjectiveness. This is

---

[28] Three Initiates. (1908). *The Kybalion: A Study of the Hermetic Philosophy of Ancient Egypt and Greece.* Chicago: The Yogi Publication Society

the mystical path, where the sensory experience is felt to be closer to truth than ideas and concepts about reality.

I have started to outline *a* model of *Conditional Reality* that was brought to us by Gautama Buddha, which I find useful and thus wish to share.

In this model, reality is *conditioned* with the exception of a place/destination/state called *Nirvāṇa*, which has something to do with our goal.

The three parts of this model are:

1. consciousness
2. matter
3. mental factors that support consciousness.

Now, we must introduce the forces that drive and animate these systems, ultimately creating a reality which we experience.

Firstly, to set the tone, we are well into Advanced Buddhism. The Abhidhamma is already considered pretty lofty, and the bit which describes these conditions is probably the most complex bit.

Don't worry, if you have got this far with me, you'll get there!

There are 24 different types of condition that shape how mind and matter interact (some are exclusively mind-mind or matter-matter). These 24 conditions describe the relationships between elements in our model, and how one causes another to happen.

At this stage we will just focus on one of these *forces* — *karma* — as this is important to understand how most of the operations work. But remember *karma* is just part of a larger group of conditional relations that give stability, direction and animate reality.

An Introduction to *Karma*.

Firstly, unless you have studied it, you probably have a completely wrong idea about what *karma* is. Rather than dismissing this model, let us adopt a specific Abhidhamma definition of *karma*.

Karma is the name of the *force* that causes a later moment of awareness to arise, in relation to the current one. Remember, at the atomic level, consciousness is a point-instance of awareness, called the *citta*. Although we cannot be aware of this, unless we develop very high meditative skills, consciousness is like a strobe light. It is a single *citta* that arises and perishes, followed by another, in a sequence that continues until death.

Karma arises in every moment of awareness but in most *citta* it is so weak as to be discarded. In certain *citta*, that occur during cognition, most (practically all) of the *karma* is generated. These *citta* are ones where a decision or choice is made. If the choice is predominantly selfish, this is called unskilled use and leads to future awarenesses that are dissatisfactory. The *citta* that condition are therefore labelled *unwholesome*.

If one makes a choice that is predominantly selfless, this is called skilled use (of *karma*) and this leads to future *citta* being accompanied by satisfactory states of being.

There are two *phases* of normal awareness.

1. An active stage of cognition. This is a series of exactly 17 *citta* that result from either a sense object entering the respective field of a sense, or an object coming to mind. This is the briefest of moments, and thousands of these processes make up *thought*. Since we remember parts of this process, we perceive it as normal awareness. We are unaware that this phase is transient, and arises out of a background awareness that the psychologists call *The Unconscious*.

2. The Background awareness or unconscious. Firstly, whilst this is totally unconscious we must remember MOST of active cognition is also unconscious. This is a deeper awareness, the awareness of a completely relaxed individual in deep dreamless sleep. In truth, the awareness pervades all the other awarenesses, which arise and fall, leaving what is called the *life continuum*. This *life continuum*, which we will explore more deeply later on, is a single type of *citta* that always has the same object, and repeats from the start of life to the last moment of life. Like a flickering light, always there, but too subtle for most to notice. This *life continuum* is what illuminates our dreams and distracts the meditator and is also known as the mind-door, through which objects *enter* the mind.

Karma is primarily generated during active cognition when choices are made. These choices are often habitual and occur at an atomic level of awareness.

In order to understand how *karma* conditions the *citta* I have to introduce a more advanced topic and take it as proven. This is the concept of self. The concept of self exists in most multicellular beings to some extent. While it is crucial for physical survival, it acts like a cancer to consciousness, generating suffering.

Once the concept of self has developed it taints every choice the mind makes. Very basically it makes the mind ask *what's in it for me?* for every single decision. Struggles with greed or anger arise because the mind expands its criteria for attachment and rejection.

If the mind is expected to *always be on the lookout* for pretty objects or terrifying threats it ceases to function effectively. And the root cause of both desire and anger is illusion — the illusion that you are either your physical body or have an inner *soul* we call self.

This can be confusing—if we discard the concept of soul, what then is it that reincarnates?

We answer this through a proper understanding of *karma*. *Karma* is the conditioning force that causes subsequent moments of awareness to arise.

To illustrate this, consider we found a bag of cash.

Now, this bag of cash, mostly, will preoccupy our thoughts. It's not our cash, but, maybe if nobody finds out, we might keep it. Most of us know what the *right* thing is to do, but do we do it?

The *right* choice, of course, is to either leave it, or hand it into a trusted authority. We (mostly) know stealing is wrong. But our sense of self makes what is really not a choice, into one. We might hesitate in handing in the cash, especially if we could really do with it.

And what if nobody really notices? Nobody comes looking for it, so we take it and spend it. From the very moment we made this choice, we have conditioned ourselves through *karma* to unpleasant states of mind. Once we have spent the cash, anything that reminds us of it will create unpleasant states of mind.

However, if we thought about it and recognised that whoever lost the cash might be equally in need of it—after all, it's their money! So, even maybe regretfully, we hand it in. Even if we never hear about it again, we do not develop worry or guilt. We handed it in, no longer our problem. We might even feel that we are decent and if reminded are conditioned to feel good about ourselves.

Now this doesn't even include any recognition or reward. And even without these this might help us continue to act selflessly.

Why is a knowledge of the skilful use of *karma* necessary for the alchemist?

Firstly for practical reasons. Our work requires solitude and peace. Being in trouble with authorities, neighbours and others will not give one physical peace in pursuing the work.

Secondly, and most importantly, the *breakthrough* from mundane awareness into transcendental needs the mind to be tranquil. One must develop what is called *samatha* — which is a tranquillity where the mind settles upon, and then becomes fascinated with a single object. This awareness is called *jhāna* and is a bridge towards the transcendental.

It is not merely sufficient to learn to *jhāna*. One must transmute the entirety of one's subjective experience through skilful use of *karma*, and when this *jhanic* consciousness arises at the very centre of a *balanced* being, the breakthrough arises. The transmutation of the raw substance of being is called *Albedo*, which means to whiten, the next stage of the *Great Work*. For now, we will remain focused on defining this raw substance, *Nigredo*.

In the next lesson we move from the atomic level to the grand level and explore how this karmic force conditions rebirth, and how this forms a part of a great cycle of rebirths we call *saṃsāra*.

Nigredo

Study Guide: The Forces That Drive The Matrix

This chapter explores reality construction through individual experience and consciousness, focusing on karma as a primary driving force within conditioned existence, examining Buddhist models and their connection to alchemical transformation.

CORE CONCEPTS
- Karma as a driving force behind subsequent awareness
- Life Continuum as the repeated arising of resultant consciousness
- Reality understood as subjective experience rather than fixed objective existence
- Relationship between consciousness, matter, and mental factors

NEW TERMINOLOGY

Citta: Point-instance awareness in moment-to-moment consciousness

Jhāna: Refined states of meditative consciousness

Karma: Force causing subsequent moments of awareness to arise

Life Continuum: Repeating process of resultant consciousness throughout existence

Samatha: Tranquility meditation leading to jhāna

MAIN THEMES
- Reality Construction
- Consciousness Structure
- Karmic Mechanics
- Preparation for achieving transcendental breakthrough

TECHNICAL FRAMEWORK
- Consciousness Components
- Mental Factor Elements
- Physical Form Support
- Karmic Conditioning Processes

PRACTICAL APPLICATIONS
- Development of tranquility meditation (samatha)
- Understanding karmic mechanics in daily choices
- Observation of consciousness structures
- Recognition of Subjective Reality

INTEGRATION POINTS
- Connection to Saṃsāra (Chapter 20)
- Foundation for Albedo understanding
- Links to Garden of Eden state (Chapter 3)
- Relationship to Fisher-King Wound (Chapter 8)
- Preparation for transcendental breakthrough
- Connection to Great Work (Chapter 25)

COMMON MISCONCEPTIONS
- Objective reality is an absolute truth
- Karma is a simplistic cause-and-effect process
- Nature of consciousness as continuous rather than point-instance
- The role of self-concept in karmic mechanics

REFLECTION QUESTIONS
- In what ways do you observe karma operating in your life?
- What role does choice play in your understanding of karmic forces?
- How might understanding these forces change your approach to spiritual practice?

PROGRESS INDICATORS
- Development of tranquility in meditation
- Recognition of Subjective Reality nature

- Understanding of karmic mechanics in daily life
- Capacity to observe the structures of consciousness

Conditioned Reality

Aspect	Component	Function	Relationship to Great Work
Consciousness	Citta	Moment-to-moment awareness	Raw material
Matter	Physical form	Support for consciousness	Vehicle for transformation
Mental factors	Conditioning elements	Shape experience	Target for transmutation

Nigredo

Noble Eightfold Path Factors

Factor	Focus	Transformation
Right View (Samma Ditthi)	**Perspective/Faith** — Initial faith and trust in the process — Progressive deepening of insight and understanding — Transcendence of ordinary perspective	Foundation for practice
Right Intention (Samma Sankappa)	**Commitment** — Complete commitment to the path — Balance of worldly duties — Commitment to sustained practice	Direction of effort
Right Speech (Samma Vaca)	**Verbal Karma** — Verbal karma awareness — Abstention from harmful speech — Impact of speech on inner tranquility	Communication purification
Right Action (Samma Kammanta)	**Physical Karma** — Importance of virtue — Control of habitual patterns — Recognition of harmful actions	Behaviour refinement
Right Livelihood (Samma Ajiva)	**Professional ethics** — Alignment of profession with values — Karmic implications of work — Sustainable ethical practice	Environmental harmony
Right Effort (Samma Vayama)	**Continuous practice** — Cultivation of wholesome states while reducing unwholesome tendencies — Maintenance of steady progress	Energy management
Right Mindfulness (Samma Sati)	**Present awareness** — Present—moment awareness — Development of detached viewpoint — Focus on understanding the dharma	Consciousness development
Right Samadhi (Samma Samadhi)	**Mental stability** — Development of mental tranquility — Understanding of jhanic states — Alternative paths through dry insight	Transcendental access

20. Saṃsāra

*"The wheel of becoming revolves like the wheel of a cart.
The being goes from birth to death and from death again to birth,
revolving like a wheel."* [29]

Saṃsāra is the endless cycle of existence through which all unenlightened beings must wander. In this chapter, we explore the profound Buddhist concept of cyclical existence, examining how consciousness perpetuates itself through death and rebirth, driven by karma and ignorance. We'll investigate the intricate mechanics of the death process, rebirth linking, and the nature of the life continuum that maintains our sense of existence. Understanding these processes is crucial for the aspiring alchemist seeking liberation from this perpetual wandering.

Saṃsāra means *to wander*, which is chillingly apt. It is the name of a great cycle of becomings, where each life conditions the arising of the subsequent. With *karma* as the driving force, each being is born into ignorance and, not knowing, clings to sensory objects—either grasping at *becoming* or *unbecoming* (annihilation).

It is easier to consider reincarnation when one considers that every life starts with a *learning how to use this body* phase. All complex living beings first develop a physical body; only later does a sense of self incarnate, often unaware of its own nature or purpose.

---

[29] *Buddhaghosa, Visuddhimagga (The Path of Purification), Chapter XVII, verse 298*

We will examine the chain of conditions that start with a fundamental *lack of knowing* and eventually condition a sense of being that must suffer disease, poverty and death. This chain is called *The Law of Dependent Arising* — but one must be significantly more familiar with the model before we tackle this.

Before we consider *Saṃsāra*, we must more closely examine what happens at the start, and end, of a single existence.

The life continuum.

The *life continuum* isn't really a thing. It is the name we give to a process.

This process is the arising of a single type of *resultant consciousness*, that repeats itself, then ceases, and then arises like a single light, flicking on and off for the whole existence.

So, at the heart of every one of us is this *life continuum*. It is a resultant *citta*, which means it arises through the karmic force of an active cognitive process. Yet, if *we* have had this resultant *citta* from the beginning of existence, when and where did the cognitive process first arise?

Detailed in the *Abhidhamma* are the processes the mind goes through on dying. This is the last cognitive moment before death. At some stage, perhaps in a kind of ghostly in-between zone (*The Bardo of Death*) if death was sudden, the mind *realises* it has died. Note, this doesn't have to be an active thing, it is more likely that the energy that sustains the mental structures falters, and they kind of untangle through a natural tendency to return to separateness. Here, what tangles are the five sense impressions and the mind, which in life, habitually cluster into things and beings.

Nevertheless, there arises a moment where the mind goes through the *death process*. This is the last cognitive moment, and not a full one.

The *object* taken by the *citta* of this last cognitive series is special. Often, there is a review of the whole life, and then, the most karmically significant experience is taken as an object. Note this can be *wholesome* as well as *unwholesome karma*.

Sometimes, rather than taking a significant event as this object, a symbol called *a symbol of karma* arises. This is often when there isn't just a single event, but more habitual occurrence of what becomes significant *karma*. A butcher might imagine their bloody knife or simply hear the screams of animals. A doctor might see a stethoscope, etc.

The third type of object taken by this death process is called a *sign of destiny*. This is a symbol that represents their destined rebirth — might be flames for Hell or harps for Heaven...

Interestingly, this death experience is apparently vividly real; if it's a sound, image, smell, etc., it feels real. It takes this object and runs almost the 17 *cittas* but falters before it can finish.

After the death process, the *life continuum* of the last life continues but will falter with any more cognitive processes.

During the death process which takes this object, symbol or sign, and the *karma* from this process conditions the resultant *citta* that will eventually become the *life continuum* of the next life. There is debate over whether this occurs immediately or if a period of time must pass before conditions favour the arising of the next life. What is interesting is that for the individual awareness, there is no temporal delay. Indeed, it is said that when the first flicker of consciousness arises in the developing embryo, it still has the object from its death process in the prior existence, as the process is shorter than the usual 17 *citta*, and given the object can last 17 moments it is still present to be taken by this first flicker of awareness. This object (or symbol or sign) then is taken by the very next *citta* that arises, which is identical to the first one in type.

The first *citta* of an existence is called the *rebirth-linking citta*, and it is a resultant of the death process in the prior life. This *citta* arises and perishes whilst the original object is still present, despite there being a possible time between death and rebirth.

When the *rebirth linking consciousness* ceases it is replaced by an identical *citta*, but this is the first *citta* of the new *life continuum*. This now perishes, but also conditions the next *citta* to arise, which is also of the same type, which then forms the new *life continuum*.

We will examine the different types of *life continuum* later, but at this stage it is enough to simply know what it is.

Active cognition, in a human, won't occur for some time. The *life continuum* becomes the mind of the future existence and arises and is dependent on blood flow, and therefore the heart. Through karmic conditioning the five senses arise and their respective consciousnesses develop, along with, and are later picked up by the mind.

As we are learning, *karma* conditions how we view the world — if we treat life badly, we will tend to think life deserves it, because it treats us badly. We fail to recognise that *karma* is about meaning. When we introduce justifications for bad behaviour, these rationalisations tend to shape reality.

Beings are generally born with ignorance, and for many cycles of existence one develops one's understanding in a harsh, animal existence. Here, it is very hard to ever have the experience to know better, and it is only the very few animals that get to experience domestication and few of these are treated kindly enough for them to develop the insights necessary for human rebirth.

Tragically, it seems easier to fall into an animal existence than rise to a human one!

Saṃsāra is a great cycle. It is without end or beginning. We might well begin as a spark of the divine, eager to learn, and thrown off some distant star find ourselves as basic life in the froth on an ocean's surface. We might progress through hundreds of thousands of existences before developing piety and *wholesomeness*, and enjoy rewards for an equally massive period of time in Godly contemplation.

Yet, until we learn the secret that drives our habitual beginning we must experience a never-ending cycle of becoming. Even the most blissful contentment eventually subsides, and one must experience grim existence again.

Escaping *Saṃsāra* is the quest and goal of the alchemist and Buddhist. *Saṃsāra* is viewed as eternal non-consensual suffering, where even the best parts must eventually return to times of suffering.

The *Arahant*, the fully enlightened being, learns to eliminate the concept of self from the mind, and with this eliminates the creation of *karma*. Once this is realised they no longer produce karmically active cognition and upon physical death, they lack any clinging to any future existence (as well as any clinging to non-existence), so whilst they have a process similar to the death process, the *cittas* here are a special type that only *Arahants* can have called *functional*, which don't produce *karma*. This means there are no resultant *cittas* produced, cutting off future rebirths.

The Buddha was one of a number of very rare beings who personally developed the insights necessary to understand how existence occurs through a chain of events which inevitably lead to suffering and death. Initially, he recognised this was just too hard to explain, but thankfully he was persuaded to explain it.

Nirvāṇa is the unconditioned element. Through certain practices the student can bring together the conditions where the mind can leap from what it understands and *knows* into something different. This *something different* is so profound that, when experienced for even a single moment, it shakes the very foundations of being. If it occurs within the first three steps, one attains partial enlightenment; at the final stage, full enlightenment is realised.

Study Guide: Saṃsāra

The chapter explores Saṃsāra, examining consciousness through cycles of birth, death, and rebirth, focusing on karma, consciousness continuity, and liberation possibilities.

CORE CONCEPTS

- Cyclical nature of existence through Saṃsāra
- Life continuum as consciousness stream
- Death and rebirth mechanics
- Liberation through cessation of attachment
- Role of karma in perpetuating cycles

NEW TERMINOLOGY

Bardo: Intermediate state between death and rebirth

Death Process: Final cognitive moments before death

Life Continuum: Stream of consciousness maintaining existence

Rebirth-linking Consciousness: First moment of consciousness in new existence

Saṃsāra: Endless cycle of existence and rebirth

MAIN THEMES

1 Cycle of Existence
- Nature of wandering through lives
- Role of karma in perpetuation
- Relationship between ignorance and rebirth
- Connection to enlightenment

2 Life Continuum Process
- Stream of resultant consciousness
- Development of awareness
- Role of cognitive processes
- Links to consciousness studies

3 Death and Rebirth Mechanics
- Final cognitive moments
- Objects taken at death
- Rebirth-linking consciousness
- Connection to becoming cycles

PRACTICAL APPLICATIONS

NIGREDO

- *Understanding karma's influence on rebirth*
- *Recognising consciousness continuity*
- *Developing awareness of life continuum*
- *Working toward liberation*

INTEGRATION POINTS
- *Connection to enlightenment concepts*
- *Relationship to consciousness studies*
- *Links to becoming cycles*
- *Understanding karmic mechanics*

COMMON MISCONCEPTIONS
- *Life continuum as static entity*
- *Immediate rebirth necessity*
- *Simplistic karma interpretation*
- *Liberation process complexity*

REFLECTION QUESTIONS
- *How do you understand life continuum in relation to existence?*
- *What is your perspective on death and rebirth relationship?*
- *How does understanding saṃsāra affect your view of spiritual liberation?*

PROGRESS INDICATORS
- *Development of awareness understanding*
- *Recognition of karmic cycles and patterns*
- *Insight into consciousness continuity*
- *Understanding of liberation path*

Aspects and Manifestations of Samsara

Aspect	Manifestation	Function
Life Continuum	Stream of consciousness	Maintains concept of existence
Death Process	Final cognition	Conditions rebirth
Rebirth Linking	First new consciousness	Establishes new existence
Liberation	Cessation of attachment	Ends the cycle

21. The Four Noble Truths

"As a physician prescribes medicine according to the illness, so the Buddha taught according to the suffering of beings." [30]

The Four Noble Truths represent Buddhism's core teaching about the nature and cessation of suffering. Using a medical diagnostic model, this chapter examines how the Buddha identified existence's inherent unsatisfactoriness (dukkha), traced its origins to craving and attachment, and prescribed a systematic path to liberation. Through understanding these truths, we gain insight into how spiritual transformation occurs and how the alchemical work parallels this ancient wisdom.

Gautama Buddha came up with this succinct definition and solution to the problem facing living creatures. At that time, Indian medical systems had a four-fold approach to sickness:

— ***definition***
— ***cause***
— ***remedy***
— ***treatment***

The four noble truths follow this pattern.

---

[30] Nāgārjuna: Mūlamadhyamakakārikā (The Fundamental Wisdom of the Middle Way). c. 150 CE.

To begin we must consider the Pāli term *dukkha*. This loosely means *suffering*, but it is all-pervasive and exists both in overt and subtle forms.

Dukkha can mean suffering, as in physical and mental pain and anguish that arises due to poverty, persecution and disease.

The Buddhists argue that *dukkha* is present even when we are happy or enjoying ourselves. The reason for this is that everything eventually must end, as with the ending of happiness arises suffering. They argue that even those destined for blissful heavenly births will eventually fall and once again be born among the less fortunate beings.

Dukkha can also mean the general unsatisfactoriness of existence.

Dukkha is seen to be inevitable and arises along with existence.

The First Noble Truth

All is Dukkha

The first noble truth is a recognition that existence as we know it is inevitably caught up with *dukkha*.

Dukkha arises because we crave. We fall in love with sense objects, people, places and concepts. And in craving these things, which are all temporal, we inevitably suffer.

Craving arises through a chain of conditions called *Dependent Arising*. *Craving* arises because we mentally cling to objects that make us happy. We feel our very identity is dependent on them, they bring us some sort of completeness, and the fear of losing this causes us to *crave* harder for them.

Craving arising because of *feeling*. Some things make us feel good, and these we cherish. In truth, we cherish feeling good and so habitually seek what makes us feel good.

Feeling arises through (mental) *contact* between a sense object, sense base (sensitive matter) and the sense consciousness.

Contact arises because of the five senses and mind.

Five senses and mind arise through the mind/body duality, itself which arises through choice.

Mind and Body (*Name* and *Form*) arise through *choice*. It is the very act of *choosing* that creates awareness of a self, the viewpoint of the *decision*.

Choice arises through *delusion*. This *delusion* is deep and closely bound up with consciousness.

The Second Noble Truth
Dukkha arises through craving

It is when the mind *craves* sense objects and concepts, which being temporary and bound to cease or change, that suffering occurs.

Gautama Buddha manages to deeply penetrate through insight into this chain of conditionality which through primary *delusion* creates beings that are bound to cycles of *Saṃsāra*. The Buddha realised that suffering is dependent on mental attachments. Once the mind ceases to become attached all suffering ceases. Furthermore, these attachments can extend from this life, and condition an ongoing cycle of existences called *Saṃsāra*.

The Third Noble Truth
Liberation (from suffering) is possible once the mind ceases to crave

Initially, although Gautama realised this personally, he recognised that teaching others would be challenging. Thankfully, he embarked on teaching others how to realise the depth of insight that permanently eradicates suffering.

The Fourth Noble Truth

The path to the liberation of suffering is the Eightfold Noble Path

The fourth noble truth does all the heavy lifting once the problem is identified and solution explained. The *eight-fold noble path* are eight qualities that must be perfected. The qualities are meditative; initially, the focus is to bring tranquillity and calmness to the mind, which permits *breakthrough* into positions of greater and greater insight.

We will explore the *eightfold noble path* that leads us out of suffering in more detail later. At this point let me introduce you to the eight factors:

1. *Right Intention* — in pursuing enlightenment one must have absolute resolve. There are many challenges and without absolute intention success is unlikely.

2. *Right Speech* — one cannot achieve mental tranquillity with deceit. Slander, gossip and *harsh* speech (swearing) is counterproductive to mental tranquillity.

3. *Right Action* — one must conduct oneself appropriately. Killing, stealing, sexual misconduct all leads to worldly and karmic repercussions and is counterproductive for inner tranquillity.

4. *Right Livelihood* — one must refrain from occupations that involve killing, the sale of weapons or poisons. Again for the same reasons as 2 and 3.

5. *Right Effort* — one must develop *wholesome* states of mind and learn to refrain from states of anger, greed or ignorance.

6. *Right Mindfulness* — one must be careful on what and how one pays attention. This is the birth of insight as one learns to examine experience as it happens.

7. *Right Concentration* — one must develop one's meditative skills — not to a very high level — although this is always helpful. It is not essential that one masters *jhāna* (refined consciousness) — progress can be possible with pure insight, but the Buddha recommends that some degree of tranquillity is achieved initially.

8. *Right View* — View is very important, and means perspective. Gaining this perspective is hard, and often one must work diligently slowly unpicking each challenge. View can be guided by another, and this is how the presence of a skilled guide can accelerate one's progress.

The *Noble Eightfold Path* could be seen as a method, that if followed brings the mind of the practitioner close to a point where transcendental awareness arises. A single moment of the *Nirvanic* awareness is enough to shatter deeply held concepts that bind the individual to cycles of rebirth.

The disciple, if they progress, can only have four of these breakthrough moments, the last one is complete, and cuts off all mental attachments, and with this, all suffering and all rebirths. Each breakthrough is called a *path* consciousness, and is a realisation into the *ten fetters*—illusory mental chains that bind one to *Saṃsāra*.

Each *path* consciousness, is associated with a breaking or loosening of these *fetters*, which partially liberate and then with the final path consciousness, completely liberate the *being*. In truth, there is never any being that is liberated, more the tendency to create one.

Stages of Alchemical Development

Stage	Mental State	Manifestation	Outcome
Initial Interest	Curiosity	Questioning reality	Beginning of path
Nigredo	Dark Night	Depression, isolation	Recognition of conditioning
Albedo — Analysis	Critical mind	Self-examination	Breaking down identity
Citrinitas — Synthesis	Integration	Acceptance of opposites	Unification of dualities
Rubedo — conclusion	Transcendence	Beyond identification	Liberation from self

Study Guide: The Four Noble Truths

The chapter explores Buddhism's Four Noble Truths, examining suffering (dukkha), its causes, and the path to liberation through a medical diagnostic model.

CORE CONCEPTS

- Nature and universality of dukkha
- Causal framework of suffering through craving and attachment
- Path to liberation via Noble Eightfold Path
- Progressive stages of enlightenment

NEW TERMINOLOGY

Anicca: Impermanence of all phenomena

Dukkha: Suffering or unsatisfactoriness inherent in existence

Magga: Path leading to end of suffering

Nirodha: Cessation of suffering

Pāli: Ancient Indian language of early Buddhist texts

Paññā: Wisdom or understanding

Samadhi: Mental concentration or meditation

Samudaya: Cause of suffering rooted in craving and ignorance

Sīla: Ethical conduct

Taṇhā: Craving or thirst leading to suffering

MAIN THEMES

1. Four Noble Truths
- Universal nature of dukkha
- Origin in craving
- Possibility of cessation
- Path to liberation

2. Noble Eightfold Path Components
- Right View
- Right Intention
- Right Speech
- Right Action
- Right Livelihood
- Right Effort
- Right Mindfulness
- Right Concentration

3. Stages of Enlightenment
- Stream-entry
- Once-returner
- Non-returner
- Full Awakening

TECHNICAL FRAMEWORK

1. Three Types of Dukkha
- Physical and mental suffering
- Suffering of change
- Existential unsatisfactoriness

2. Chain of Dependent Origination
   1. **Ignorance**
   2. **Formations**
   3. **Consciousness**
   4. **Name-and-Form**
   5. **Six Sense Sources**
   6. **Contact**
   7. **Feeling**
   8. **Craving**
   9. **Grasping**
   10. **Becoming**
   11. **Birth**
   12. **Aging and Death**

Dharma

PRACTICAL APPLICATIONS
- *Regular meditation practice*
- *Ethical conduct development*
- *Mindfulness in daily life*
- *Development of wisdom through study and practice*

INTEGRATION POINTS
- *Links to Fisher-King Wound*
- *Connection to Matrix of Reality*
- *Relationship to Enlightenment concepts*

COMMON MISCONCEPTIONS
- *Dukkha extends beyond mere suffering*
- *Path develops simultaneously not sequentially*
- *Nirvāṇa is a state not a place*
- *Buddhism acknowledges pleasure while recognising impermanence*
- *Path transforms rather than eliminates desire*

REFLECTION QUESTIONS
- *How do you experience dukkha in daily life?*
- *How does craving create suffering in your experience?*
- *How might the Noble Eightfold Path guide your practice?*

PROGRESS INDICATORS
- *Development of mental tranquility*
- *Breakthrough moments of insight*
- *Loosening of mental fetters*
- *Progressive liberation from suffering*

The Twelve Links of Dependent Origination

Link	Sanskrit/Pāli	Description	Results In
Ignorance	Avijjā	Fundamental delusion about reality	Volition/Mental formations
Volition	Saṅkhāra	Mental formations and choices	Consciousness
Consciousness	Viññāṇa	Awareness arising through choice	Name and Form
Name and Form	Nāma-rūpa	Mental and physical phenomena	Six Sense Bases
Six Sense Bases	Saḷāyatana	The six ways of experiencing	Contact
Contact	Phassa	Meeting of sense organ and object	Feeling
Feeling	Vedanā	Pleasant, unpleasant, neutral evaluation	Craving
Craving	Taṇhā	Desire for pleasant experiences	Clinging
Clinging	Upādāna	Attachment to desired experiences	Becoming
Becoming	Bhava	Process of existence taking form	Birth
Birth	Jāti	Beginning of new existence	Aging and Death
Aging and Death	Jarā-maraṇa	Decay and end of existence	Ignorance (the cycle begins anew)

The Noble Eightfold Path Components

Factor	Purpose	Relationship to Alchemy
Right View	Understanding reality	Seeing through delusion
Right Intention	Commitment to truth	Dedication to transformation
Right Speech	Ethical communication	Breaking social conditioning
Right Action	Moral conduct	Working with raw substance
Right Livelihood	Ethical living	Creating proper conditions
Right Effort	Energy management	Maintaining the work
Right Mindfulness	Clear awareness	Observing transformations
Right Concentration	Mental stability	Containing the process

NIGREDO

The Twelve Links of Dependent Arising

1. *(Ignorance - Avijjā)*
Lack of true understanding obscures reality, leading to delusion and mistaken views.

2. *(Formations - Saṅkhāra)*
Mental and volitional formations condition future experiences through habitual actions.

3. *(Consciousness - Viññāṇa)*
Awareness arises based on past conditioning, forming the seed of personal existence.

4. *(Name & Form - Nāmarūpa)*
The mind and body take shape as identity emerges, reinforcing a sense of self.

5. *(Six Senses - Saḷāyatana)*
The faculties of sight, sound, smell, taste, touch, and mind engage with the world.

6. *(Contact - Phassa)*
Sensory contact arises when the senses meet objects, creating new experiences.

7. *(Feeling - Vedanā)*
Sensory experiences produce pleasure, pain, or neutrality, conditioning reaction.

8. *(Craving - Taṇhā)*
Attachment to pleasure and aversion to pain intensify the cycle of grasping.

9. *(Clinging - Upādāna)*
Desire hardens into attachment, reinforcing identity and further karmic entanglement.

10. *(Becoming - Bhava)*
Mental and volitional momentum crystallizes future experiences and rebirth.

11. *(Birth - Jāti)*
A new conditioned existence arises, setting the stage for suffering.

12. *(Old Age & Death - Jarāmaraṇa)*
The inevitable decline of all conditioned things results in suffering and renewal.

The Twelve Links of Dependent Arising illustrate the cyclical nature of conditioned existence, perpetuated by ignorance and craving. Each link represents a stage in the continuous process of becoming, binding beings to the cycle of birth, suffering, and death. The Buddha at the centre symbolises liberation—awakening breaks this cycle, leading to the cessation of suffering. Through insight and practice, one transcends the conditioned chain, moving toward true freedom.

Dharma

22. The Cycle of Becoming

*"He who sees dependent origination sees the Dharma;
he who sees the Dharma sees dependent origination."* [31]

The cycle of becoming (saṃsāra) represents one of Buddhism's most profound teachings on how beings perpetuate their existence through mental processes. This chapter examines the intricate chain of dependent origination (paṭiccasamuppāda) that explains how our sense of self and suffering arise from fundamental delusion through consciousness, feeling, and craving. Understanding this cycle is essential for those seeking liberation, as it reveals how our very existence is self-created and how we might break free from this pattern of becoming.

In order to fully comprehend these concepts, it is important that we remember clearly.

By the time we are mature enough to seek spiritual wisdom, we are often fully caught up with conditioned existence (*saṃsāra*).

Breaking free is not easy. The Buddha learned that progression wasn't possible through extreme attitudes. Extreme piety tended to lead to fortunate and blissful rebirths, with minimal suffering, which removed the impetus to develop wisdom.

---

[31] *The Buddha, Majjhima Nikāya i.28*

Extreme selfishness leads to animal or hellish rebirths, where suffering is frequent and counterproductive to the mental tranquillity necessary for progress.

So, Gautama Buddha developed a *middle approach* (*majjhimā paṭipadā*), one where duality is balanced, permitting a *narrow* middle path of balance. Once awareness is balanced and the mind still, then realisation can occur as *path* moments (*magga-phala*).

The Buddha developed insight into the chain of causes and conditions that cause the arising of beings. He realised that *being* is a mental concept, and the cause of a pervasive delusion that is bound to cause suffering (*dukkha*). Recognising that suffering is related to craving (*taṇhā*), he closely examined the mental conditions that cause craving to occur. He recognised that beings oriented themselves towards things and beings who make them feel good, and that they become attached to these good feelings which manifest as craving.

He worked backwards through each cause and condition until he arrived at the fundamental delusion (*avijjā*), that arises with, and is mistaken for the mind. True mind is there, but masked by a very close *Shadow*, that we mistake for true awareness.

Recognising that it is this fundamental delusion and not knowing that causes all living creatures to evolve into beings that then, through craving are bound to suffer. This is an important point. Here *beings* are mental concepts. We might think that the being is the body, yet if a limb is lost, the being remains. *Being* is a mental concept that arises through the clinging or grasping (*upādāna*) to concepts and things. We define our sense of being by that which is important. Once *being* is established as a concept, then this gives us an inner sense of self. It is this sense of self that fears death, disease and loss, and ultimately becomes *the sufferer.*

With this understanding, we now turn to the core of the problem: fundamental delusion.

Delusion.

Fundamental delusion. Sorry, pretty much need to leave the best to last. At this stage (*Nigredo*) any attempt to explain it will confuse rather than explain. We'll tackle this in the last part of the course. At this stage, this is something that *infects* the *citta* (mind-heart), and taints experience. This taint stops beings from realising the truth.

Volition.

Decision (*cetanā*) arises from our tendency to regard things and beings as concrete and ongoing occurrences. To explain this, consider a vortex of water in a river. The vortex appears to be a lasting *thing*, yet in truth, the vortex is merely the current shape of the water. There is no lasting or separate thing called the vortex, just an amorphous shape of fluid following the laws of hydrodynamics. All *beings* and *things* are like this. Whilst we regard ourselves and others as beings, we must consider them in a world where they really only exist in the imagination. Choice arises as we must consider these concepts.

When we make a decision, over a thing or being, we mark the experience, which is a perception (*saññā*). A perception is how we remember, and we only remember that which has meaning. By making a decision we impart meaning to the experience. To make a choice is to be aware of this choice. And it is this awareness that we know as *consciousness* (*viññāṇa*).

Some types of consciousness are the simple recognition of previous learning (perceptions) that echo back as *resultant consciousness* (*vipāka-viññāṇa*). For example, when you grasp what *blue* means, then any examples of *blue* become noticeable.

Even our inner dialogue is a careful construction of resultant awareness of the words and even letters, that we once learned to recognise in both visual and auditory ways.

At this stage we have an opportunity to scale the *citta* to *normal* awareness.

The *citta* is the point instance of awareness. It is aware only of a single object, which can be sensory or mental. Many millions of point awareness recognise the most basic bits of sense objects, and these arise as sense consciousness. In normal sense awareness this is *resultant consciousness*, arising because at some time prior we had decided (made a perception) on the original object.

The *mind* arises in relation to the heart and can directly perceive the sense consciousnesses, along with *mental senses* where it can take previously experienced *citta* as objects.

So, choice is the mechanism by which consciousness arises.

Consciousness.

Consciousness arises through decision, and through consciousness the concepts of mind and body arise. This is an important step, and imparts a sense of separation between mind and body.

Through this illusory separation, the five senses and mind each seem to have separate objects, and can develop craving in six competing ways.

Through this separation the illusion of contact arises, which creates feeling.

Contact.

Contact (*phassa*) is the phenomenon when a sense object interacts with a sense base (*āyatana*) with the right conditions and attention. This creates the sense consciousness which takes the sense object and processes it through the mind. Contact is the point where if conditions are suitable, a sense consciousness arises.

Every contact is mental. And every contact, even visual or auditory, elicits a feeling, which is very simple, either positive, negative or neutral.

Feeling.

Feelings (*vedanā*) arise as any sense or mental experience is necessarily evaluated, into positive, neutral or negative. When contact arises, feeling follows as a necessary evaluation of its nature.

Remember this is at the *atomic* level of consciousness, all we are generally aware of is the sum of all feelings. If these are overwhelmingly positive and attached to another being or thing, then we can develop craving as we seek more of these positive feelings.

It is a terrible tragedy when you think of it. We automatically seek out what makes us feel good, and avoid what doesn't. Yet, in doing so we develop attachments to those things that make us feel good, and when they are absent or change we miss this and develop a craving for it.

Craving.

In life, we can become attached to others, or things. We can become attached to our health, our youth, our prestige or victories. Yet, in truth, we just want to feel good. It is hard to see this when you are caught in cycles of craving and wanting.

If we crave something it is on our minds. In fact, we will crave it if we think it will make us feel better. We are distracted and cannot concentrate.

Now, let's examine this. When we can normally concentrate on things we can give them our full attention. Yet, when we crave, we are constantly reminded of an unhappy version of ourselves. It is important that you grasp that we only become aware of ourselves when it truly matters. If we have no concerns we tend to forget about ourselves and get involved with life. But when we crave, we are constantly reminded there is a sufferer.

Our focus in this work is purely on liberation. So the chain of conditionality is focused on the side of suffering. This means that when we crave, we create a sense of being that also suffers. There are other ways of creating a sense of being, but that is not our focus. We are interested in the sense of being that is created on craving.

Craving is not limited to sense phenomena, we crave existence. Once craving is established it creates a sense of being who lacks whatever is craved. To understand this we must regard when and how we create a sense of being. This craving, when reinforced, solidifies into attachment, which in turn leads to the process of becoming.

Clinging leading to Becoming.

If we don't feel good, we might remember times, people or things that we associate with feeling good, and how we might try to get this. All the time we are projecting a concept of self into our futures.

Once we habitually crave we habitually create a concept of future self.

Generally things aren't too bad for the first half of our lives, but as we decline physically we face illnesses and maybe poverty. Our craving moves then for health or even to be pain free. All the time we are projecting the mental image of self into the future.

At the end of our lives all these attachments to things, places, states of mind and states of being are experiences along our *life continuum*, and when the forces that support our living consciousness fail, then these attachments drive the creation of our *rebirth-linking consciousness* (*paṭisandhi-viññāṇa*), which, depending on *karma* will be bound to manifest, beginning our next existence.

Remember, *karma* is the force that causes subsequent moments of consciousness to arise. Only by mastering *karma* at the deepest level does the *Arahant* prevent this sense of being from manifesting.

The key to understanding dependent arising is that our true arena of experience is the mind. The mind forms and creates structures which then shape it.

Dependent arising starts with a fundamental lack of knowing. We are programmable but cannot realise this. We then habitually mistake our fundamental ground of being as the program, rather than the mind that manifests the program.

The program is the instinctive but erroneous progress of a mind that is born in delusion.

We could never be aware of this, but consciousness arises through choice, and choice arises through the introduction of the concept of being. Consciousness then goes on, through the chain of dependent arising, and leads to the creation of being. Being is nothing more than the sense of becoming that arises through our attachments and future desires.

Once our sense of being is established, then so is our apprehension about threats to the ongoing welfare of this being, and existential anxiety is created.

The important thing to take home from this process is that it is intrinsic—i.e. starting with a fundamental lack of knowing, ignorance, the system *creates* beings without any need for any external, divine intervention. The Buddhists don't dismiss either Gods or God but they simply describe a way where such external agencies are not necessary.

I hope that was clear — this is one of the more complex topics so feel free to research it further — we will return to Dependent Origination towards the end of the course.

Understanding the cycle of becoming is crucial for anyone seeking liberation from suffering. This intricate process of dependent origination (*paṭiccasamuppāda*) reveals how our very existence and suffering are self-created through ignorance and craving. By understanding this process, we can begin to see the possibility of breaking free from this cycle. Through mindful observation of these processes as they occur in our own experience, we can gradually weaken the links in this chain, ultimately leading to the cessation of suffering and the realisation of *Nibbāna*.

Study Guide: The Cycle Of Becoming

The chapter explores Buddhist teachings on Dependent Origination (paṭiccasamuppāda), explaining how suffering arises through mental conditions and how beings perpetuate cycles of existence through mental processes.

CORE CONCEPTS

1. Dependent Origination explains how suffering arises through mental conditions

2. The Middle Path balances extreme approaches

3. Being is fundamentally a mental concept rather than physical

4. Understanding mental processes is key to liberation

5. Consciousness arises through choice and decision-making

NEW TERMINOLOGY

Avijjā: Fundamental delusion about reality

Bhava: Process of existence taking form

Bhavachakra: Wheel of Life depicting realms of existence

Citta: Point instance of awareness

Paṭiccasamuppāda: Dependent origination chain of causation

Phassa: Contact between sense organ and object

Saṃsāra: Cycle of birth death and rebirth

Taṇhā: Craving or desire for pleasant experiences

Three Fires: Greed hatred and delusion at existence's centre

Upādāna: Attachment to desired experiences

Vedanā: Feeling evaluation (pleasant unpleasant neutral)

Viññāṇa: Consciousness arising through choice

Yama: Lord of Death holding the wheel of existence

MAIN THEMES

Nigredo

1. Nature of Becoming
- Mental processes creating self
- Role of delusion
- Relationship between craving and suffering
- Connection to enlightenment

2. Chain of Causation
    I. **Ignorance** (Avidyā) — fundamental misunderstanding of reality
    II. **Formations** (Saṃskāra) — mental conditioning and karmic activities
    III. **Consciousness** (Vijñāna) — awareness and mental cognition
    IV. **Name-and-Form** (Nāma-rūpa) — mental and physical phenomena
    V. **Six Sense Sources** (Ṣaḍāyatana) — the six sense bases including mind
    VI. **Contact** (Phassa) — meeting of sense organs with their objects
    VII. **Feeling** (Vedanā) — pleasant, unpleasant, or neutral sensations
    VIII. **Craving** (Tṛṣṇā) — desire and attachment to sensations
    IX. **Grasping** (Upādāna) — intensified craving and clinging
    X. **Becoming** (Bhava) — process leading to renewed existence
    XI. **Birth** (Jāti) — manifestation in a particular form
    XII. **Aging and Death** (Jarā-maraṇa) — decay and cessation of aggregates
- Role of consciousness in perception
- Creation of mental structures
- Breaking the cycle

3. Liberation Process
- Understanding dependent origination
- Middle path approach
- Role of mindful observation
- Breaking free from conditioning

PRACTICAL APPLICATIONS
- Understanding mental processes
- Observing chain of causation
- Developing non-attachment
- Breaking cycles through wisdom

INTEGRATION POINTS
- Connection to enlightenment concepts
- Links to mental transformation
- Relationship to broader Buddhist teachings
- Integration with alchemical processes

COMMON MISCONCEPTIONS
- Being is not physical but mental
- Suffering arises from mental processes not external circumstances
- Liberation requires understanding not extreme practices

REFLECTION QUESTIONS
- How do you observe dependent origination in your experience?
- What role does delusion play in perpetuating existence?
- How might understanding this cycle help break free from conditioning?

PROGRESS INDICATORS
- Decreased attachment to self-concept
- Greater awareness of mental processes
- Understanding of causal relationships
- Reduced reactivity to conditions

The Causes of Suffering

Link	Function	Result
Delusion	Creates misperception	Volition arises
Consciousness	Divides experience	Subject-object split
Contact	Enables sensing	Feeling arises
Craving	Drives attachment	Being manifests

The Ten Fetters

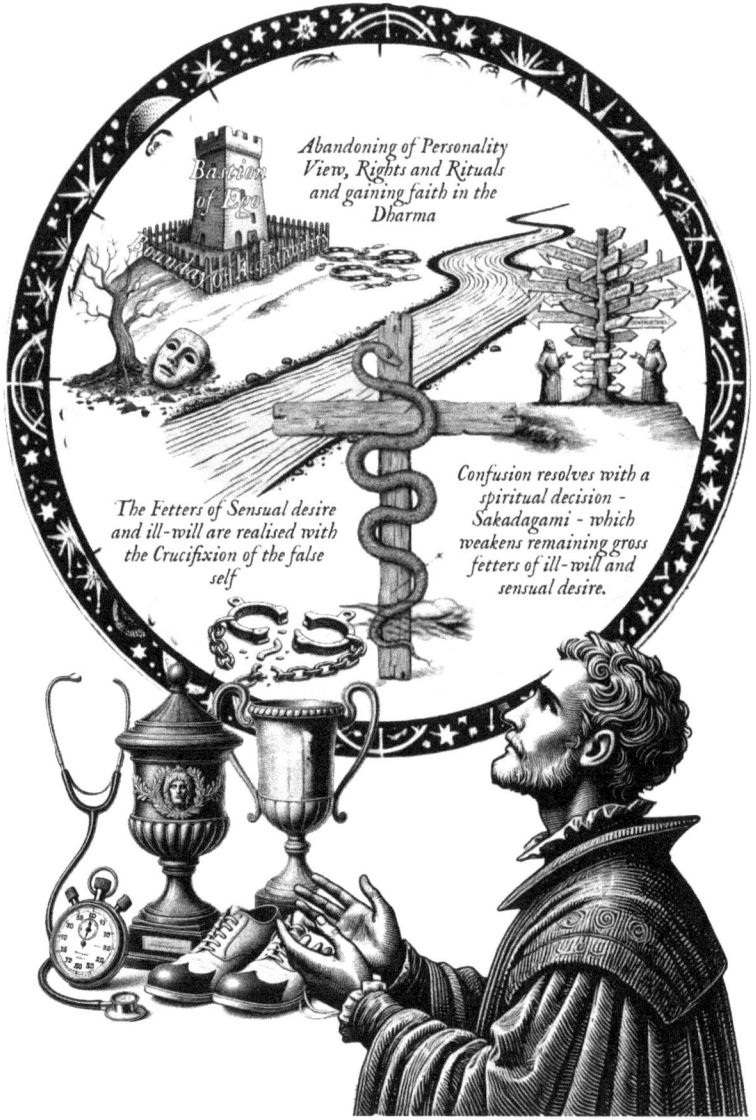

The ten fetters that bind awareness to conditional existence. The gross fetters (upper circle) bind one to material existence with the first three realised by the Sotāpanna with the first path moment. The last two gross fetters are weakened at the Sakadāgāmī stage and realised by the Anāgāmī. The subtle fetters bind one to heavenly existence and are realised by the Arahant.

Dharma

23. The Fetters that Bind

"We are travellers on a cosmic journey, stardust, swirling and dancing in the eddies and whirlpools of infinity. Life is eternal. We have stopped for a moment to encounter each other, to meet, to love, to share. This is a precious moment. It is a little parenthesis in eternity." [32]

The ten fetters (saṃyojana) represent the fundamental mental bonds that keep beings trapped in cycles of conditioned existence. This chapter explores how these deep-seated concepts shape our experience and their relationship to the stages of alchemical transformation. Understanding these fetters is crucial for the aspiring alchemist, as their progressive dissolution corresponds directly to the changing colours of the philosopher's stone and the four degrees of enlightenment.

The *fetters* (saṃyojana in Pāli) are mental concepts that we take to be true, yet, upon closer examination they are found to be false. These are deep mental concepts that shape our experience that we inherit from others as we grow and develop.

There are ten *fetters*, grouped into two groups of five. The first five are called the *gross fetters* as these are largely related to worldly, external experience. The remaining five are called *subtle fetters,* and they pertain to inner aspects of self.

---

[32] *Chopra, D. The Seven Spiritual Laws of Success*

Nigredo

The *fetters* are important to the alchemist, because they directly relate to the *colour* of the stone of the philosophers. There are four stages to the stone, and four grades or degrees of enlightenment.

Nigredo

The first stage (or path consciousness) is called *Nigredo*, or darkness, and it is the stage of initially awakening one's spiritual faculties. The first path consciousness is called the path of *Sotāpanna*, which means stream-enterer (they have entered a stream that inevitably leads to full realisation). This is achieved when the first three *fetters* are cut (seen as illusory) and occurs at the darkest part of the path. Unless one is in a dedicated holy order there is often a period of confusion following this breakthrough.

Once the *Sotāpanna*, the being who has achieved the first grade of enlightenment, has adjusted they will inevitably return to the *path* invigorated and motivated as a *Sakadāgāmī*, which is the path towards *Albedo*.

Albedo

The second alchemical stage is called *Albedo*, or whiteness, and it is a stage of purification and karmic mastery that has a healing effect through restoring balance. The path to *Albedo* starts once the *Sotāpanna* makes the personal resolve to go further.

The path to *Albedo* involves the mastery of *karma*, which, when internalised purifies the mind of sensory attachments and ill-will.

Albedo peaks with the realisation of the first five, *gross fetters*. This is a painful ordeal called *The Dark Night of the Spirit* and involves letting go entirely of being defined by the *skandhas*, or aggregates of conditioned reality.

Once *Albedo* is achieved the disciple is now *Anāgāmī* which means non-returner and is the third stage of Buddhist enlightenment. Through realising the *gross fetters* the individual is liberated from the fear of death as well as sensory temptations.

The disciple must now attend to the *subtle fetters*—inner attachments of the mind to *being, non-being, conceit*, and the deepest attachment to *delusion*, along with the *restlessness* it causes.

Up until this stage one is freeing oneself from external definitions and identifications. Now one must tackle the mind's fundamental nature.

Citrinitas

The third stage is called *Citrinitas* or yellowing, and it is the stage where all *fetters* are realised and the individual has achieved full liberation. Now the disciple is called *Arahant* and they have fully cut away any mental attachments. As such they remove the final subtle veil that distorts reality and perceive objects differently — Now, phenomena glow!

For the *Arahant* this is often the end of the path — their search is over and they can *enjoy* the fruits of their labour. They are kind of magical, but also elusive and secretive.

For the alchemist who has embarked on their quest for the genuine betterment of others, they cannot (or decide not to) achieve arahantship, for they have compassion for others that they refuse to relinquish. These individuals are called *Bodhisattvas*, which means *enlightened beings*.

The *Bodhisattva* therefore cannot achieve total detachment but they can realise the fetters. They progress along 5 more paths, with 10 to 16 stages called *Bhumis*, depending on source.

Rubedo

The final stage of the philosopher's stone is associated with a redness that appears called *Rubedo*. I cannot speak from experience, but I suspect this is related to what is called meditative warmth. This is a physiological reaction to the cessation of thought, which has a twofold effect: a loss of *flight or fight* sympathetic nervous tone — which results in a flushing and reddening of the skin, and a decreased respiratory rate that gives a purplish discolouration, sometimes represented in particularly Hindu art as bluish skin tones.

Meditative warmth arises once the Bodhisattva has mastery over refraining from allowing the mind to reach out to objects, which creates subjective awareness. It's a bit complicated at this stage — we'll cover it towards the end.

The Gross Fetters

The first five *fetters* are called gross (*oḷārika*). They bind beings to sensory sphere rebirth, which includes human, animal and more exotic varieties like *ghost, demon, angel* or some of the older gods. The likely reason for this is that only the more developed forms of consciousness can be self-sustaining. Lower, more mundane awareness is transient and chases after external objects, and there needs a material base, the heart base. This idea is supported by the fact that *unwholesome citta*, i.e. those *rooted* in greed (*lobha*), hatred (*dosa*) but not delusion (*moha*) are toxically lethal to *angelic consciousness* that has a *life continuum* rooted on pure consciousness.

Let's look at these *fetters*. In this introduction we are only aiming to familiarise ourselves with the layout of conditioned reality. Through the series we will return to these concepts, with the aim of helping you personally realise them.

First Fetter (Sakkāya-diṭṭhi)

The first delusion is that we have *personality*. In truth, we only have many different experiences that happened to many different aspects of self, which we cobble together mentally and call a *person*. Generally, unless one meditates or has experienced the struggles of addiction, this is hard to see. An addict, who is reduced to uncomfortable sober self and cunning self, finds it easier to realise that there never was a person, even if this is somewhat to avoid shame or responsibility.

Second Fetter (Sīlabbata-parāmāsa)

The second delusion is that *acting* being *good* is the same as being *good*. Many of us delude ourselves into thinking we must be good because of *blah blah blah*. You know you are good because you have fully accepted all your terrible parts. Only when we recognise we must be the darkest part of our world can we embrace and work with our darkness. Believing you are worthy because you have medals, awards or recognition is delusional. Spiritual worth arises through sacrifice and humility and for the true seeker even worthy recognition of one's quality is a needless distraction.

Spiritual progress is generally impossible whilst one still identifies with society. This is why a mental and physical hermitage is necessary.

Third Fetter (Vicikicchā)

The third delusion is *scepticism*. This is a really challenging one for the thinker, for it is faith in that which cannot be known. By embracing the very comforting intellectual side of Buddhism progress is possible through pure intellect —often referred to as *dry insight*. In Buddhism faith is never expected to be blind, and one must diligently wade through the scriptures, and satisfy one's need to understand.

Sceptical doubt is eliminated at the point you develop respect for the process. Personally, reading the *Abhidhamma* I am awestruck with the sheer elegance and detail of this model. Find something or someone to believe in, as this will help cultivate the necessary leap of faith.

This *fetter* is the one that can torment the individual who is primarily intelligent. They can want to have faith, but simply can't let go of the need to understand, before one can fully embrace it as belief.

This creates what is called the *Dark Night of the Soul*, which tends to tear the person apart to a state of necessary vulnerability they literally cry out to what they cannot believe.

Fourth Fetter (Kāma-rāga)

This is the delusion of *sensory craving*. Remember, craving arises through feeling, and feeling through contact. Whilst this and the subsequent *fetters* are cut by the third stage of enlightenment, it is weakened by a sense of commitment that is experienced during the second stage.

Fifth Fetter (Vyāpāda)

This is the delusion of *ill-will*. Hatred, anger, jealousy and hoarding are all features of *unwholesome citta* and there reaches a stage where the disciple thoroughly recognises the dissatisfaction of *ill-will* and adverse effect it has in personal tranquility.

The *gross fetters* are cut at the third stage of enlightenment. Whilst anger is still possible, it is always reactive and never spontaneous. The remaining fetters are called the *subtle fetters* and pertain to concepts of self.

Nigredo

The Subtle Fetters

We will explore these more in the third book of this course, *Citrinitas*. Briefly these are:

Sixth Fetter (Rūpa-rāga)

This is the delusion of future existence and attachment to being. It is the mental speculation and desire for future (pleasant) experience.

Seventh Fetter (Arūpa-rāga)

This is the delusion and attachment to future non-being, or annihilation.

Eighth Fetter (Māna)

This is the remaining shreds of self that manifest as reactionary conceit.

Ninth Fetter (Uddhacca)

At this stage only a *restlessness* is present, which is a manifestation of entanglement between the *citta* and primal delusion. Delusion here is a beguiling brightness that must be distinguished from the *citta*.

Tenth Fetter (Avijjā)

This is the primal delusion which, once cut, fully enlightens the *individual*.

Do not be concerned if some of this seems unclear. At this stage (*Nigredo*) we are outlining the structures that ultimately become the substance that *transmutes* into the philosopher's stone.

We'll finish this part of *Nigredo* with the practical steps that are necessary to *prepare* the mind for the breakthrough we seek. This is beautifully illustrated in the eightfold noble path which we will next examine

---

Study Guide: The Fetters That Bind

This chapter explores the ten mental fetters binding beings to conditioned existence, their relationship to alchemical transformation stages, and the path to spiritual liberation through their dissolution.

CORE CONCEPTS

Dharma

- *The nature and division of ten mental fetters (saṃyojana)*
- *Four stages of alchemical transformation*
- *Progressive stages of Buddhist enlightenment*
- *Integration of Eastern and Western spiritual traditions*

NEW TERMINOLOGY

Arahant: *One who has cut all ten fetters*
Bhūmi: *Stages of Bodhisattva development*
Citrinitas: *Yellow stage of transformation*
Gross Fetters: *First five fetters related to worldly experience*
Nigredo: *Dark stage of transformation*
Non-returner (Anāgāmī): *One who has eliminated first five fetters*
Once-returner (Sakadāgāmī): *One who has weakened fourth and fifth fetters*
Rubedo: *Red stage of transformation*
Saṃyojana: *Ten fetters binding beings to saṃsāra*
Skandhas: *Aggregates of conditioned existence*
Stream-enterer (Sotāpanna): *One who has cut first three fetters*
Subtle Fetters: *Last five fetters relating to inner attachments*

MAIN THEMES

1. Nature and Structure of Fetters

FIRST FIVE (GROSS) FETTERS

- *Personality view (Sakkāya-diṭṭhi)*
- *Ritual attachment (Sīlabbata-parāmāsa)*
- *Skeptical doubt (Vicikicchā)*
- *Sensual craving (Kāma-rāga)*
- *Ill-will (Vyāpāda)*

LAST FIVE (SUBTLE) FETTERS

- *Attachment to form (Rūpa-rāga)*
- *Attachment to formlessness (Arūpa-rāga)*
- *Conceit (Māna)*
- *Restlessness (Uddhacca)*
- *Ignorance (Avijjā)*

2. Alchemical Stages

Nigredo: *Initial awakening and stream-entry*
Albedo: *Purification and karmic mastery*
Citrinitas: *Full liberation (Arahant state)*
Rubedo: *Final transformation through Bodhisattva path*

PRACTICAL APPLICATIONS

- *Self-examination of personal fetters*
- *Understanding transformation stages*
- *Recognition of progress markers*
- *Integration of meditation practice*
- *Application of alchemical principles*

INTEGRATION POINTS

- *Connection between Buddhist enlightenment and alchemical stages*
- *Relationship between mental fetters and spiritual freedom*
- *Integration of meditation and transformation*

REFLECTION QUESTIONS

- *How do self-identity views manifest in daily experience?*
- *What role does skepticism play in spiritual practice?*
- *How does attachment to rules affect practice?*
- *What is the relationship between sensual desire and suffering?*
- *How do you experience the higher fetters like craving for form and formlessness?*
- *In what ways do you notice conceit operating in your spiritual journey?*
- *How might understanding the fetters help in breaking free from them?*

PROGRESS INDICATORS

- *Breaking of the first three fetters*
- *Weakening of the sensory attachments*
- *Dissolution of self-concept*

The Gross Fetters

Fetter	Nature	Effect
Personality view	False self	Identity attachment
Ritual attachment	False virtue	Spiritual materialism
Skeptical doubt	Lack of faith	Blocked progress
Sensual craving	Desire	External seeking
Ill-will	Aversion	Mental disturbance

The Four Stages of the Hinayana Vehicle

Stage	Mental State	Key Changes
Worldling	Unenlightened	All fetters intact
Stream-winner	Initial breakthrough	First three fetters realised
Once-returner	Partial liberation	Weakening of sensual desire and ill-will
Non-returner	Advanced liberation	Free from gross fetters
Arahant	Full liberation	All fetters realised

Dharma

24. The Eightfold Noble Path

"The path is like an ancient road leading to a long-lost city. One does not create the path — one discovers it." [33]

The Eightfold Noble Path represents the Buddha's systematic approach to spiritual transformation, offering a comprehensive framework for moving from fundamental ignorance to enlightened awareness. This chapter explores each aspect of the path, showing how these eight interconnected factors work together to create the conditions necessary for spiritual breakthrough. While rooted in Buddhist tradition, these principles align perfectly with the alchemical Great Work, providing practical guidance for the aspiring alchemist seeking to transmute their consciousness.

Fundamental ignorance means we are born spiritually blind. With the exception of very few individuals, we all succumb and fall into materiality. We learn that we are a body that lives in a hostile, dangerous and ultimately lethal world.

Opening the *dharma eye* requires pulling away the mind from the distractions of the five senses (*pañcandriya*) and mind (*manas*). This requires the development of a mental faculty named *I will know the unknown* (*abhiññā*). A certain leap of

---

[33] *The Buddha, Samyutta Nikaya*

consciousness occurs where normal awareness is momentarily replaced with transcendental awareness. This moment and viewpoint completely transcends *normal* concerns and, if misunderstood, creates confusion that manifests as mental illness.

The initiate or trainee alchemist cannot know the transcendental personally, or they would no longer be a trainee. They can only prepare the raw material and stick diligently to this task until the breakthrough occurs. It cannot be made to happen, yet when the conditions are right, it is inevitable.

So, the first part of the work is preparatory.

I couldn't write a more succinct approach than that outlined by the Buddha, and *why reinvent the wheel?* So, as with most of this course, Buddhism will provide the backbone of both practical and theory, with a sprinkling of deliciousness from other sources when relevant to the contemporary alchemist.

Approaching the Path

I recommend studying the eight factors (*aṭṭhaṅgika magga*); these are the syllabus. More rapid progress is likely if one makes a resolve to simultaneously strive to meet these qualities, although those at the beginning of the path will find the early qualities both easier to satisfy and understand.

Towards the end of the path, the meaning of each part deepens, and the focus is more on the latter qualities, as the former qualities are satisfied relatively easily.

The eight factors are like guiding principles that lead one to the first and subsequent *path* consciousnesses. These are the four consciousnesses or moments of realisation that mark each stage of the path (*magga-phala*).

Right Intention (Sammā-saṅkappa)

This is the first and necessary factor that sets the scene for the challenge we face. The commitment must be complete. Often the degree of commitment will compete with other duties and responsibilities, which is why it is recommended to leave and join a monastery.

However, whatever the degree of commitment, the most important thing is tenacity, at least in the beginning. Until one opens the *dharma eye*, one is looking for a door in the dark that one isn't sure actually exists. This is why *faith* (*saddhā*) is necessary; one cannot know if the path is really there.

Don't worry if you cannot find the faith for the goal; instead, find faith in the Eightfold Noble Path. Irrespective of any miraculous breakthrough, it offers wisdom in how one progresses through life.

Right View, therefore, is a kind of faith but can be as little as establishing a degree of trust and respect towards the process.

Right Speech (Sammā-vācā)

We have two ways of expressing ourselves: either verbally (including written forms) or physically. Both actions create *karma*.

Generally, we think that verbal expression is less harmful than physical, yet this is erroneous. If we lie, gossip and swear, we are habitually creating *karma*, which returns to us as *unpleasantness* and disdain with our experiences. Only by resisting the temptations to speak harshly, unnecessarily or untruthfully do we attain the *abstinence*, *right speech*, which is a *beautiful* mental factor that stabilises the *citta* and permits higher awareness.

So it is our habitual use of speech that can continuously disturb our inner tranquillity. Only through effort and ongoing diligence can we overcome habits such as gossiping, swearing and untruthfulness.

Right Action (Sammā-kammanta)

The path of the Alchemist is one of virtue. Only by recognising one's harmful actions in speech and deed can the alchemist take control of habits.

Remember our goal is inner tranquillity. Killing, stealing and sexual misconduct all will keep this tranquillity at bay. Such actions arise through *unwholesome* states of consciousness and so are bound to create unpleasant states of mind. This is additional to any societal repercussions from such acts.

One must learn to resist habits. This must come from within; not taking something because somebody was watching is not reflective of spiritual progress.

Neither must one concern oneself with others' actions. This is a personal quest to explore, understand and master *karma*, and trust me, it's worth the effort.

Killing is born out of hatred, and one must learn to foster both respect and compassion for all living creatures.

When one learns to habitually resist harmful actions, one is developing another abstinence called right action.

Right Livelihood (Sammā-ājīva)

The commitment is absolute, and our immediate goal is to develop a skilful use of *karma*. There is no point being personally kind and truthful whilst working in a slaughterhouse or selling arms to kill others. *Karma* does not differentiate between what was and wasn't on *work-time*.

Remember the focus is avoiding creating *unwholesome karma*, and eventually all *karma*. One cannot work in occupations that involve lying, killing, stealing or activities that disrupt inner calmness.

The last abstinence is the mental factor that is present when one develops the aversion to wrong livelihood, *right livelihood*.

Right Effort (Sammā-vāyāma)

This is an ongoing resolve to reach tranquillity by avoiding *unwholesome* states marked by delusion (*moha*), greed (*lobha*) and hatred (*dosa*). One must learn to foster a *wholesome* approach and develop states of mind that lead to tranquillity and peace. Whilst the cutting of the gross fetters strengthens one's ability to react benevolently, one must work diligently to develop these skills before this happens.

The effort must be continuous, without relapse, as this risks losing all the progress thus gained. The effort is analogous to the heat applied to the *retort*, which contains the raw material of *Subjective Reality*.

Right Mindfulness (Sammā-sati)

Mindfulness is paying attention to what is happening here and now. Mindfulness develops initially from reflective wisdom that reviews and seeks the truth *after-the-event* to the presence of a detached viewpoint that seems to always be there, even during sleep.

Mindfulness isn't always a *wholesome* factor; one can become mindful at acquiring wealth or plotting revenge. So this mindfulness must be *right*, i.e. applies to the practice of deepening one's understanding of the dharma. Mindfulness develops into insight (*vipassanā*) as one progresses.

Right Concentration (Sammā-samādhi)

Concentration here means the necessary mental tranquillity and focus that allows the development of refined states of consciousness called *jhāna*. Whilst it is traditionally recognised that it is beneficial to have skill in the *jhānas* for progress, it is not essential. If the wisdom faculty is strong enough, transcendental breakthrough is possible through what is called dry insight. The Zen method, or Chan in China, are examples of this approach.

Right View (Sammā-diṭṭhi)

Here view means something like perspective as well as attitude towards the work. If the first factor is necessary to bring the disciple to the path, this is the factor that allows the disciple to complete it. Ultimately it pertains to personal sacrifice. Following the path means that one will sacrifice the normality a normal perspective grants. Once you make any progression, it is irreversible. This is rarely an issue, yet one must be aware this path is neither easy nor particularly safe.

Study Guide: The Eightfold Noble Path

This chapter examines the Buddhist Noble Eightfold Path as a systematic approach to spiritual awakening, focusing on transforming fundamental ignorance into enlightened awareness while connecting Buddhist principles with alchemical transformation.

Core Concepts

- *Mental withdrawal from sensory distractions for transcendental awareness*
- *Progressive development through the Eightfold Path components*
- *Integration of Buddhist wisdom with alchemical transformation*
- *Importance of commitment and continuous practice*

New Terminology

Aṭṭhaṅgika magga: *The eight factors of the Noble Path*

Dharma Eye: *Spiritual vision that sees reality's true nature*

Magga-phala: *Four consciousnesses marking path stages*

Pañcandriya: *The five senses*

Saddhā: *Faith*

Sammā: *Right or skilful way*

Sammā-ājīva: *Right Livelihood*

Sammā-diṭṭhi: *Right View*

Sammā-kammanta: *Right Action*

Sammā-saṅkappa: *Right Intention*

Sammā-sati: *Right Mindfulness*

Sammā-samādhi: *Right Concentration*

Sammā-vācā: *Right Speech*

Sammā-vāyāma: *Right Effort*

Threefold Training: *Ethics meditation and wisdom*

Main Themes

1. *Nature of Spiritual Blindness*
- *Identification with materiality*
- *Mental withdrawal techniques*
- *Sensory distraction*
- *Transcendental breakthrough*

2. **Path Components**
- *Interrelation of factors*
- *Progressive development*
- *Role of commitment*
- *Transformative practice*

3. *Karma Management*
- *Development of virtues*
- *Mental withdrawal techniques*
- *Preparation for transformation*
- *Transcendental awareness*

Integration Points

- *Links to The Shadow (Chapter 10)*
- *Foundation for Enlightenment (Chapter 6)*
- *Preparation for Dark Night (Chapter 11)*
- *Relationship to Nirvāṇa (Chapter 12)*

Common Misconceptions

- *Verbal expression impact versus physical action*
- *Role of faith in practice*
- *Nature of mindfulness*
- *Necessity of jhāna states*

Reflection

- *Daily integration of Right Action*
- *Experience with Right Concentration*
- *Integration of path components*
- *Practice of Right Mindfulness*
- *Right Effort in spiritual development*
- *Right Intention application*

Dharma

- *Right Livelihood alignment*
- *Right Speech awareness*
- *Understanding of Right View*
- *Working of eight factors together*

Progress Indicators

- *Development of abstinences*
- *Growth in mindfulness*
- *Karma management skills*
- *Mental withdrawal capacity*
- *Transcendental awareness moments*

*"You should not chase after the past nor place expectations on the future.
What is past is left behind.
The future is as yet unreached.
Whatever quality is present you clearly see right there, right there.
Not taken in, unshaken, that is how you develop the heart."*

- *(MN 131, Bhikkhu Ñāṇamoli & Bhikkhu Bodhi,
Middle Length Discourses of the Buddha, Wisdom Publications, 1995)*

Part Three
OBJECT

The Object section of Nigredo delves into the practical mechanics of spiritual transformation, examining the technical aspects of how consciousness evolves through distinct stages of awakening. Here we move beyond theory and symbolism to explore the actual processes that lead to enlightenment, providing a detailed roadmap for those committed to the Great Work of inner alchemy.

This section represents the heart of alchemical practice, where abstract concepts crystallise into tangible methods. We'll examine the precise stages of consciousness development, from the initial breakthrough moments of path consciousness through to the final liberation of full enlightenment. Through understanding these stages, we gain both technical precision and practical guidance for navigating the challenging terrain of spiritual transformation.

The chapters in this section systematically explore the four grades of realisation, the nature of different realms of consciousness, and the specific fetters that must be dissolved for progress to occur. We'll investigate how jhanic states of meditation relate to alchemical transformation, examine the distinct characteristics of each stage of awakening, and provide clear markers for gauging one's progress along the path.

While the technical detail may seem daunting at first, remember that this precision serves a practical purpose — offering clear navigational guidance for those journeying through darkness. Like an astronomer's star chart or a sailor's compass, these teachings offer reliable orientation for those venturing into the unknown territories of consciousness. The Object section bridges theory and practice, transforming abstract understanding into direct experience through systematic development of wisdom.

NIGREDO

The Great Work

Aspect	Manifestation	Transformation
Path	Personal journey	Progressive realisation
Practice	Meditation/insight	Consciousness development
Breakthrough	Path moments	Fetter dissolution
Result	Enlightenment	Liberation from suffering

Grades of Enlightenment

Stage of Stone	Buddhist Grade	Magical Grade	Fetters Realised
Prima Materia	Novice	Student Grades	0
VEIL OF APPARENT REALITY			
Nigredo	Sotāpanna	Adeptus Minor	3
	Sakadāgāmī	Adeptus Major	3
		Adeptus Exemptus	3*
THE ABYSS			
Albedo	Anāgāmī	Majister Templi	5
Citrinitas	Arahant	Magus	10
VEIL OF ISIS			
Rubedo	Bodhissatva (8th Bhumi) Buddha	Ipsissimus	10**

* Three fetters are realised and two weakened.

**All fetters are realised along with the clearing of the residues of the skandhas.

OBJECT

25. The Great Work

*"The Great Work is, before all things,
the creation of man by himself, that is to say,
the full and entire conquest of his faculties and his future;
it is especially the perfect emancipation of his will."* [34]

The Great Work represents the core transformative process of spiritual alchemy — the creation and purification of the philosopher's stone. This chapter explores how this profound inner transformation unfolds through distinct stages, examining both traditional alchemical frameworks and their Buddhist parallels. We investigate the technical aspects of consciousness transformation while providing practical guidance for those beginning this challenging but rewarding journey.

The *Great Work* of the Alchemist is the creation and purification of a magical substance called the *Stone of the Philosophers*. This *stone* is the fundamental ground of being of an enlightened one. The work is personal and takes time. It can take the best part of a decade if one is dedicated and given space to work. Or, it can take several lifetimes, or most of a lifetime, if one is less focused due to all manner of external distraction.

---

[34] *Éliphas Lévi. Transcendental Magic: Its Doctrine and Ritual, translated by A.E. Waite, part 1, p. 58*

There are a number of different approaches towards enlightenment, each a system with its own definitions and viewpoints. Nevertheless, they all point towards the same thing, a path, or backdoor in reality that ultimately can lead one out of it.

Finding this path is not easy. Not that it is really hidden, it is just rather easily overlooked. Take, for example, one of your corneas — the clear bit in the middle of the eye that allows light through. Every time you see something, there is also this clear layer present, and in fact, it's the closest thing the eye sees. Yet, the eye, or in truth the mind, habitually looks beyond this, and so never sees it.

Committing to alchemy, or enlightenment is particularly difficult as one cannot actually understand what one seeks when one begins. Often, it is either deep fantasy or deep suspicion (about reality) that drives one's curiosity.

One cannot be led. Later on, when we explore the *jhānic* consciousnesses you will learn these can only be spontaneously *wholesome*. This means the desire for change has to come from within; nobody can prompt these changes in you.

That said, another can try to *point*, metaphorically, towards where you should be putting your attention. One can with some commitment learn the basic laws of *karma* (Sanskrit: *karma*, Pāli: *kamma*) and consider whether karmic-less action might be possible. As one progresses one's understanding deepens and what seemed vague or even fantasy settles into plausible possibility.

With one's first experience of the transcendental everything changes. The experience reinvigorates one's commitment and faith towards the process.

Yet, reaching this point is not easy. The mind has to have been settled, focused deeply on its goal for the breakthrough to occur.

In this part of *Nigredo* I will, as best as I can, outline what this *Great Work* looks like, from the position of a novice. My purpose is to offer some structure, which almost certainly will look vague towards the end, until one has the knowledge and understanding to see clearly.

In order to avoid confusion I will offer the Buddhist model of *path* as this, I feel, is the most accessible *mystery system* available to the English-speaking student.

In occult theory there are a number of *spiritual paths.* Those systems that incorporate Kabbalah use the model of a *Tree of Consciousness,* in a variety of different configurations as a template for several different paths or ways. Some spiritual paths are purely devotional and lack any need for logic or thought. Here we have the musicians, artists and some degree of mysticism. Other paths are based in pure intellect and might include the Buddhist Path of Dry Insight (*sukkha-vipassanā*), as well as the Magical Grades.

Buddhism, which is both mystical and alchemic, recommends a balanced approach, which, on the *Tree,* follows a central or middle path. Aptly, for alchemists, this is called the *Golden Path.*

The Golden Middle Way.

This path follows what is called the narrow middle way, or the path of the Camel. The Camel relates both to the Hebrew letter ascribed to this part of the *Tree.* Here, the mind is kept focused and tranquil yet also agitated by a kind of dissecting insight. This, in mathematical terms causes the consciousness to *tend towards,* but never reach, the transcendental. Through progressive practice the disciple focuses in on the point between *the intent to think* and the *arising of thought.* Once the disciple *situates themselves* at this point — both the intent to think and subsequent thought cease and subjective/objective reality collapses.

The initial goal of the budding alchemist is to *find* the path. Our eyes for this task is simply faith. Faith isn't required to magically invoke the path—it's not like that. Faith is necessary to adhere to the sacrifices made in following the noble eightfold path (*Ariya Aṭṭhaṅgika Magga*). One needs tenacity. If one keeps digging, and one keeps checking one is digging in the right place, one is sure to find it. If it remains elusive then it is likely one is deluding oneself about how well one is following the eightfold path.

If, like somebody who really doesn't want to look for something, we dismiss it as false at our first failure then the path really isn't for you. In the last part of *Nigredo* we will explore the subjective experience and it can be really hard work. To have any success one must believe there is a path.

To help you, I have endeavoured to, somewhat logically explain what this is. It is technical, this is because I only really have to convince the thinkers, those with faith never really know what to do with *evidence*.

In the last part, we explored the 121 types of *citta* (consciousness). 40 of these moments of awareness are related to transcendental awareness. We will explore these before we finish this part.

Remember, the *citta* is a moment of point awareness. We experience thousands of these every moment, yet each has a single mental or sense object as its focus.

Whole chains of differing *citta* make up an active cognitive moment. This is not a thought, but the part of a thought we remember. And why do we remember it, because on some level, we made a choice.

When the alchemist makes the first breakthrough into transcendental awareness they experience what is called the first path consciousness (*sotāpatti-magga*). This happens only for a single moment, and can never occur in that individual again. Why? Because this was the moment that the first three fetters (*saṃyojana*) were realised. Once the mind *sees* through these delusions it never mistakes them again.

Immediately after this realisation there are either two or three (depending on the innate wisdom of the practitioner) resultant *citta*, called *fruit consciousnesses* (*phala-citta*), which are still transcendental. The easiest way to understand these are they are the ramifications of the realisation from the cutting of the fetters. After these two or three fruit consciousnesses the mind returns to a resting state.

There are four stages to this transmutation of self. Each is marked by moment of *path* consciousness which can never be repeated, and then two or three *fruit* consciousnesses.

If the disciple has little or no meditative practice and has achieved the breakthrough on knowledge and insights alone, then they achieve this at what is equivalent to first *jhāna*. The *jhānas* are special states of consciousness that are developed with meditation where the mind becomes fixed on its meditative object.

If the disciple is an established meditator then they will experience their *path* and *fruit* consciousness at the deepest level of *jhāna* they have mastered.

This means we have five levels of *jhānic* depth for each *path* and *fruit* consciousness, of which there are eight.

Is this important? Yes, if you are more a thinker than meditator.

Whilst the Buddha recommends a degree of meditative mastery, this might be relatively more challenging to a modern practitioner and they might struggle with intrusive thinking.

Is meditation necessary? Yes, but what isn't necessary is *samatha*, or tranquillity meditation, although it helps. Meditation can also be an active kind with a dissective analysis of subjective experience called insight or *vipassanā* meditation.

Note, whilst any single disciple can only ever experience each path moment once, they can, with meditation bring to mind and *dwell* within the most recent *fruit* moment.

These four stages of Buddhist enlightenment seem to correlate to the four stages of the stone, which we know, can part way through produce a magical white, or silver creating substance. At the end of the *Great Work* this substance is red, and creates gold. Again, if we take these as symbolic, the silver pertains to the moon, and the restoration of natural cycles. This arises when the stone has reached the whitening, or *Albedo* stage.

This correlates with the third stage of enlightenment (*Anāgāmi*), where the Buddhist disciple cuts off *sensory desire* and *ill-will*, and largely ceases from creating *unwholesome karma*. This has a healing effect on any interactions, as the lack of ill-will and tendency towards kindness and compassion can calm and soothe. This is our silver making substance which through a relative mastery of *karma* restores natural cycles and heals (lunar influence).

Whilst there are four grades of enlightenment you might have spotted the correlation isn't exact. Both alchemy and the Buddhist path have *preliminary stages*. Both are marked by a degree of struggle in overcoming one's habits in order to reveal the path.

The first path moment occurs at the darkest moment of *Nigredo*. Then for a while things are a bit weird and the practitioner realises how lost they have been. It can take some time to adjust, and some never adjust.

Albedo starts with the second path moment (*Sakadāgāmi*), which represents a commitment to the path as one's faith deepens. At this stage, though, one is still in *Nigredo* it's almost like with this path moment one finds the light and then knows which way to go. But this light is still some way off.

Albedo peaks at the third path moment, where the first *five (gross) fetters* are cut. Here the disciple has cut off *ill-will* and *sensual desire*. This means, that within the sensory sphere, i.e. normal existence, they act relatively karmic-less. This gives them a peaceful and harmonious demeanour, because they don't propagate *karma*. This is our silver substance that heals by restoring (lunar) cycles.

At the third path moment the disciple still has not seen through the five remaining subtle fetters. The moment all five are seen by the mind as illusory, the final path moment occurs and then become fully enlightened.

This is the yellowing or *Citrinitas* of the stone. I think this refers to a subjective glow that manifests around material objects with full enlightenment. The fully enlightened being is holy. They are fully a-karmic. They have no regard for a self and naturally develop some psychic ability.

But what of the reddening, or *Rubedo*. This is our capstone of alchemic progress. What is the equivalent in Buddhism?

Both *Buddhas* (*Buddha* is title and name of a kind of being) and *Arahants* are fully enlightened. Everything an *Arahant* is and can do, so can a *Buddha*.

The difference is the *Buddha* is without residues, whilst the *Arahant* achieves *Nirvāṇa* with residues.

Once one reaches full enlightenment one still looks the same. One will have the same mannerisms if these are not harmful. One, when one thinks, will still think the same way. The most fundamental change is a total lack of reference to self, other than what is necessary for normal interactions. As the mind of the *Arahant* fails to look *inside* there is no differentiation between inside or outside. Thoughts, feelings and ideas are seen to come and go no differently than falling rain drops. Without an inner self, these are just as beautiful yet meaningless.

The *residues* are the experiences (now with no attachment to them), physicality and that karmic debt that occurred prior to realisation. With the physical death of the

Arahant these remaining residues break up — and I like to think that they are responsible for rainbows seen over dying saints.

A *Buddha* is an *Arahant* who finds a way to experience *Nirvāṇa* without residues. Theoretically, this is more akin to the resurrected body of Christ, and interestingly this *process* seems to take three days. Here, if we are to assume that their physicality is largely the same, it seems to involve the permissive *death* of the *Arahant* then a subsequent *possession* by a being-less being!

Here, I think we have our *Rubedo*. A state of being that is without any doubt divine.

Now, it is quite possible that *Arahants* develop psychic power and might, in the right conditions *glow*. But these powers need to be developed. Without any shadow of self, the Buddha has no need to learn or develop anything. They are raw, unconditioned mind with the physical shell of the being that died to welcome them into existence. Hence the deliberate Pāli wordplay on the word *Tathāgata*, that means thus arrived one AND thus gone one.

This being would naturally involve awe, fear, but almost certain faith. This is the red substance that produces gold. Gold is a metaphor for the sun, which symbolically is eternal unity.

Study Guide: The Great Work

The chapter explores the Great Work's transformative process, examining alchemical and Buddhist frameworks for spiritual enlightenment, detailing consciousness transformation and practical requirements for progress.

Core Concepts
- *The Great Work as personal transformation requiring dedication*
- *Golden Middle Way methodology balancing tranquility and insight*
- *Path and Fruit Consciousness stages*

- *Technical framework of consciousness transformation*
- *Integration of Buddhist and alchemical systems*

New Terminology
Active Cognition: *Process of conscious awareness and choice*
Arahant: *Fully enlightened being in Buddhism*
Citta: *Individual moments of consciousness*
Fruit Consciousness: *Resultant states following breakthrough moments*

NIGREDO

Golden Path: Balanced middle way between extremes in spiritual practice

Jhāna: Meditative absorption states

Path Consciousness: Breakthrough moments in spiritual development

Phala-citta: Fruit consciousness; resultant states following path consciousness

Saṃyojana: Fetters binding beings to cyclic existence

Sotāpatti-magga: First path consciousness in Buddhist enlightenment

Store Consciousness: Fundamental layer containing all potentialities

Tathāgata: Title for Buddha meaning "thus gone one" or "thus come one"

Transcendental Awareness: Awareness beyond ordinary experience

MAIN THEMES

1. Transformation Process
- Personal journey requiring dedication
- Multiple approaches to enlightenment
- Progressive stages of realisation

2. Path Structure
- Golden Middle Way methodology
- Balance of faith and practice
- Integration of meditation and insight

3. Consciousness Development
- Technical framework of awareness
- Breakthrough stages
- Role of meditation practice

INTEGRATION POINTS
- Connection to enlightenment concepts
- Relationship to symbolic understanding
- Links to adult developmental stages

COMMON MISCONCEPTIONS
- Path accessibility and recognition
- Role of meditation versus insight
- Nature of transcendental experience

REFLECTION QUESTIONS
- How do personal experiences of suffering relate to alchemical transformation?
- What role does faith play in your spiritual journey?
- How do you understand the relationship between meditation and insight?
- What obstacles have you encountered in recognising the path?

PROGRESS INDICATORS
- Breakthrough experiences
- Development of transcendental awareness
- Dissolution of fetters
- Integration of insights

OBJECT

The Ten Sephirot and Their Attributes

Sephirah	Function	Manifestation
Keter	Crown — Pure Will	Divine Awareness
Chokhmah	Wisdom — Raw Insight	Abstract wisdom, masculine force
Binah	Understanding — Analysis	Form and structure
Da'at	Knowledge — Integration	Union of wisdom and understanding
Chesed	Mercy — Loving—kindness	Harmonious love, Christ-like qualities
Gevurah	Severity — Discipline	Discrimination, division
Tiferet	Beauty — Harmony	Central self, balance
Netzach	Victory — Drive	Instinctive forces
Hod	Glory — Rationalisation	Mental constructions
Malkhut	Kingdom — Physical Reality	Material manifestation

NIGREDO

A three dimensional representation of the Kabbalistic Tree Of Life

OBJECT

26. The Trees of Consciousness

"The Sephiroth are the Ten Sacred Numbers of the universe, through which creation manifests." [35]

The Tree Of Life provides a sophisticated map for understanding how consciousness manifests from its most subtle to its densest forms. This chapter explores consciousness as a layered phenomenon, examining how awareness develops from singular moments of perception into complex spiritual and psychological structures. Through understanding these layers, we gain insight into both the nature of mind and the path of transformation. The Tree model reveals how consciousness evolves through innocent, fallen, and perfected states, offering practical insights for the aspiring alchemist.

Consciousness, we have learned, is represented on the atomic level by the *citta*, a point-awareness of a single object. On the organism level there are thousands of *cittas* experienced sequentially, that seem to occur in a single moment. This gives the illusion that awareness is more like a cloud, rather than many individual occurrences.

A good analogy is the flame of a candle.

Here, the *flame* appears to be a relatively stable thing. Until extinguished, or it runs out of candle, the flame appears to have a degree of permanence.

Yet, there is no *flame*—just many tiny chemical reactions, each which liberates a tiny amount of light. In some regions of this *flame* the reactions are more intense, so the

---

[35] *Fortune, Dion. The Mystical Qabalah*

light appears brighter, even a different colour. Other regions have less perfect conditions for these reactions, or a greater concentration of soot, which alters the appearance at that part.

The *flame* is a mental construction for a pattern that appears. This pattern has no higher *substance*, it is just a pattern. Yet, the mind creates a *thing* called a flame which we assume is a real thing. Yet, if it were a real thing, where does it go when a candle is extinguished? And, if I light a new candle off an already burning one, is this the same flame or a new one?

Most paradoxes of observational science are eliminated once we are aware that *things* are entirely mental, and nothing more than the name of a semi-permanent pattern within subjective experience.

Anyway, back to consciousness.

Consciousness is neither singular nor a thing. It is a pattern that occurs within our sensory experience that has meaning. We give it meaning through learning. We learn by making note of what sensory patterns yield *sukha* (pleasant feelings), versus those that give us *dukkha* (unpleasant feelings).

What begins as a simple awareness, becomes complicated by the fact that consciousness can take itself as an object. This leads from a very rudimentary awareness associated with single cell organisms to developing into a complexity that might be a human being who has a phobia of cotton wool.

The take-home message here is that whilst subjective experience seems to be a completely singular thing, it is, in fact, more like a *hive* mind of many, many smaller awarenesses. When we see a blue cup, our retinal awareness is purely focused on the blue shape. It doesn't know *blue* nor *cup*. All this part knows is to be delighted with blue. Unless one meditates or takes hallucinogenic agents this is not apparent to the average adult, but is to children who can delight in just colour.

Yet, we don't generally experience distracting pleasure from most senses. Why? Because our world has dangers, and those who are distracted are more vulnerable.

Again, rather than reinvent the wheel, I will use established models of a map of the different consciousnesses that make up our human experience. Here we will use the Gnostic/Kabbalistic model called the *Tree Of Life*. For a more modern audience I will deviate slightly in some of the terminology, but established students of the Kabbalah should have no problems identifying these changes.

Object

The *Tree of Consciousness* is a map with ten main principles of human consciousness. These ten aspects are concentric, with the first principle *emanating* or radiating the second, the second emanating the third, etc. I think of this as a light with nine concentric lampshades. The light itself is brightest without any covering, and as each covering is applied, it is dimmer than previously, but brighter than the next.

The *Tree* can exist in three basic forms: an *innocent* form, a *fallen* form, and the *perfected* form. Each form represents a different configuration of consciousness which has dramatic effects on subjective awareness.

There are nine aspects of consciousness in innocent form, twenty or more aspects of consciousness in the fallen form and ten aspects in the perfected form, although one might argue that this is really a *near-perfected* form, as *Nirvāṇa* escapes most attempts to define. On the *Tree* these consciousnesses are numbered and called *Sephirot* —which means number.

Layers of Consciousness

Layer	Function	Manifestation
1st	Primal awareness	Pure knowing
2nd	Pattern recognition	Love/attraction
3rd	Object formation	Self/other divide
4th	Harmonious love	Christ consciousness
5th	Discrimination	Analysis/division
6th	Central self	Identity formation
7th	Drives/emotions	Karmic patterns
8th	Rationalisation	Mental control
9th	Dream consciousness	Fantasy/play
10th	Material awareness	Physical reality

Nigredo

The first nine *Sephirot*.

Alan Watts gave a great talk. He said, what if you could choose who you wanted to be? You could wake up each morning and be somebody else. And maybe you are an eternal being and you have a lot of time to kill. So, you get to be anybody and everybody. But, it gets boring, because deep down, you know you are eternal, so nothing really is a challenge. Not a challenge like us poor mortals. So, So, for the sake of curiosity, you decide to forget who you really are. And you can, because you are all-powerful.

The first awareness arises through primal pure mind acquiring primal delusion (*avidya*). This delusion manifests as light within awareness and is radiantly beautiful. This delusion is a forgetting and through this forgetting a point of singular awareness manifests.

So, this point of knowing comes into existence, but cannot remember what it is or why it is here. This is our first point of consciousness. This is like a light that is turned on for the first time in a world that has only known darkness. The consciousness cannot know that the light with which it sees emanates from itself.

This first awareness isn't aware where it came from. It isn't aware that the light it emanates arises through a desire to know perspective, it is only aware of the beautiful patterns that arise and fall within the chaos. At this level, there are no things. Only raw experience, which is chaotic, but out of which patterns emerge.

Remember that consciousness can take *itself* as an object. This creates a new layer of object-subject separation, and therefore a subconsciousness. Here, I mean a new consciousness is created in the former. This new consciousness needs objective reality, which although formed of the consciousness above, becomes dull and not-knowing.

So each layer of consciousness divides into an objective part, which becomes perceptions and a subjective part which becomes the consciousness of that level.

The original, first consciousness takes the layer's consciousness as its object and forgetting itself takes the perceptions of this level as its own perceptions.

The second layer is therefore created out of the first, primal awareness. This second layer is called the *pleroma*. This is the stuff that the mind uses to make things and beings. It is also what the mind uses to make negative concepts and things.

Each successive layer of consciousness is therefore created from the former, which splits into a *lesser* awareness and dull, mental stuff, that becomes objects of this awareness. The thing to remember is that at all times, all is mind, just that a portion of it adopts dullness and non-sentience to act as objects of the consciousness at that level.

The first awareness is called the demiurge, although it cannot know this until it has fallen to the third layer of awareness, for this is where concepts arise and things, and beings are created. This first awareness is just really a single point of awareness, made possible by omniscience, leaving itself. The residue collapses to a single point of awareness, like an *I/eye*.

But this *eye* cannot know. So it must look. And what it sees is the layer of awareness outside of itself. This is the second layer.

As the *eye* watches the second layer it cannot know that what it sees are patterns, patterns that only make sense because they resonate with it. They resonate because they are expressions of this eye, but it cannot know this, because it wanted to forget.

This *eye* has no reference point in its own layer, it becomes absorbed in the patterns of the second layer. It becomes hypnotised by them. The consciousness of the second layer is therefore akin to love. It is pure and undivided delight in life.

Once the consciousness finds delight in these patterns it develops attraction which is the introduction of linearity. Patterns are favoured over chaos and love develops.

A certain stability is observed in patterns and through this the mind creates the next layer of consciousness.

The third layer is divided into *objective* things and beings and a space appears called self, which is the consciousness that knows the *objects* of this layer. Remember though, that even though these *objects* and *beings* seem to be objective, in truth they are made of the *substance* of the layer of consciousness above, the *pleroma*.

These first three layers represent the most fundamental aspect of consciousness, and generally, unless one is an occultist or meditator an explicit understanding (experience of) is unnecessary.

These first three layers are represented as a triangle on the *Tree Of Life* diagrams, which can confuse some seekers. Rather, the structure is more akin to the *Tetractys* which emphasises the inclusiveness of these consciousnesses.

Remember, every *division* is illusory, a divide in pure knowing into dullness and a lesser awareness.

With the creation of these three consciousness there is the creation of inner and outer, through this inner subjectiveness created in the third layer, that we later call self.

Once the consciousness regards itself as a being, this changes how it interacts. There are now five layers that arise as this being comes to know itself. These five layers represent instinctual aspects as well as those *taught*.

Remember, the tone of the second layer is a pure love and attraction for patterns in sensory experience we call love. Well, the fourth layer represents a love that this *being* has towards other beings and things. At this stage the mind is pure and can only delight in these objects of its own unknown creation.

So, the awareness that manifests in the fourth layer is a kind of parental love, that delights and fosters the beings and things of the fourth layer. It is a kind of harmonious love and related to the Christ-like qualities of forgiveness.

Each subsequent consciousness can only arise through the propagation of fundamental ignorance. Yet, because of this ignorance the mind delights in taking the objects of its own creation, and through this, spawns layers of subsequently diminished awareness.

It is in the fifth layer that the seeds of evil appear. The consciousness delights in the objects and beings of its own creation but now regards *itself*. Self, arises as the subjective awareness of the third layer, and is largely distracted by the joy of the fourth layer, yet, at some stage it gets around to wondering what it actually is.

If the being is happy and safe, the problem of self isn't particularly necessary. A child who never needs to think for themselves will never grow up.

If the being is unhappy however, there is an increasing drive to regard to a self, that is unhappy. It is from this sense of division between inner self and external reality that other divisions occur.

This consciousness therefore is a divisive one, that separates unity into divisions or groups. This consciousness is our discriminative mind, that analyses, and divides phenomena.

Through this discrimination self and other are formalised, and now that inner space of subjectivity has a name and manifests in the layer below as *self*.

The sixth layer pertains to the central viewpoint of an inner self. This *sephirot* occupies a position in the very centre of the *Tree*. This is the stage where the organism clearly differentiates between the parts of subjective experience that are self from those that are other.

The fourth and fifth layers are like polarities of self. The former a tendency toward unity and harmony, the latter a drive towards individuality. The dynamics of each layer manifest in qualities that the individual takes as a balance between selfless existence and selfish existence.

The seventh layer is the layer of drives and emotions. These are both the drives towards selfishness and selflessness, as both manifest through *needs* of the self. This layer represents currents that arise through constant generation of *karma* towards selfish and selfless goals.

The eighth layer is a refinement of the blunt and raw power of the seventh layer. Here mental constructions act to tame and control the emotions of the layer above. Here the function is rationalisation. Note that this rationalisation is retrospective, an observance with a later inference.

The seventh and eighth layers are the *polarities* of the ninth layer. Here we have the instinctive drives and wants (the *Id*) versus a logical idea (*Superego*). These seventh and eighth layers, along with the concept of self create the ninth layer, which is the layer of dreams and fate.

The ninth layer is the last layer that is pure mind. Subsequent layers arise through a mixing of mind and matter. In fact, one could argue the ninth is a dream layer that becomes the tenth when *waking consciousness* mixes the dream-world with materiality creating what we take as *normal experience*.

The ninth layer is therefore the final expression of the innocent mind. Until a child *incarnates*, which is when they first, habitually start to regard themselves as a physical being with vulnerabilities, they live in a world of pure consciousness. This is why a child plays. They live in a world of dreams and fantasy, and lacking any real control, for them *life* is as bizarre as any adult dream. It is only when they feel vulnerable and need to take control of their own physical wellbeing does a need to incarnate manifest.

So, the human *Tree of Consciousness* is a progression of a single awareness, that develops into the complex concept of being in a stepwise process. Certain problems that manifest as personality disorder are often problems of a pre-incarnated being who never really took responsibility.

Incarnation is the point where a being turns their back on fantasy and 'takes' life seriously. Once incarnation has occurred then the *fantasy* consciousness of the ninth layer becomes the dream consciousness, and then a tenth layer is created.

This tenth layer is what we regard as normal, waking consciousness. Here, the dull part of the tenth mixes with material phenomena and lets us recognise that a cup is a cup, rather than just a pattern of colour. It becomes what we habitually called perception, i.e. the knowing that we have experienced this before. The subjective part of the tenth consciousness blends with our five senses and inner sense of being. So when this tenth consciousness feels pain in its leg, it identifies with the leg.

It is important to appreciate that this *Tree* of different, but related awarenesses, is in a kind of dynamic balance. The *Tree* can shift from the pure consciousnesses of the nine *sephirot* to the ten consciousnesses layout, with a tenth awareness emerging that is mixed with materiality. But what is toxic to this innocent structure is lying.

Untruths manifest as a division in the sixth *sephirot*, so that it splits into an outer (lying) side and an inner (truth) side. Remember we are dealing with a *Tree* constructed of awareness. Telling lies beyond the reflexive mistruth of a child, requires deviancy. And this deviancy splits the central consciousness of self into two. Telling lies requires that we create another, fictitious sense of being.

The *sephirot* are holographic—a change in one is reflected throughout the *Tree*, and each *sephirot* now becomes dual. Choice arises, in every layer of awareness, a choice that habitually asks *what's in it for me?*

Each layer now can be visualised to have an other, or outer side. This side represents personal temptation that has arisen, and now we have lost our innocence. These additional *sephirot* are called the *Qlippoth*, as they are like shells or rinds of consciousness that introduce a darkness into the *Tree*.

The Tree of Duality.

This is the *Tree* of *Cain*, who, having slain his brother is banished to a life of hard reality. It is what we take to be normal adult awareness. We might want to believe in *demons* and angels yet it is the taxman or landlord that is a more realistic threat. It arises through the necessity of selfishness because of the needs of physical survival.

The way consciousness can take an object, and then forget itself, means there really is no limit to how dark and confused the mind can get. Selfish behaviour can become an obsession in itself, as can hostility. One's measures of success might include victory and vanquishing of foes that arise purely in mind, yet manifest in great harm to others. And organisms caught up in cycles of violence and greed through delusion in the lower layers of consciousness cannot escape the mental consequences of their actions as deeper awareness are never not aware, but relatively impotent to intercede in a mind that is constantly restless.

There is a tendency for desire and fear to drive the consciousness towards an animalistic ferocity that is tempered by the quality of societal education. Qualities such as respect, fairness, compassion and kindness need to be developed *against* a tendency towards selfishness. This tendency manifests as temptation towards sin in those who have been partially educated about *right and wrong*.

The adult (fallen) *Tree of Consciousness* is established in *becoming*. It habitually regards to a self, and fears for the future of this self. Disease, poverty, failure and death all plague this state of awareness.

The Alchemist learns that neither they are this awareness, nor its structure. Yet, its structure can, through wisdom, be transformed into a form where suffering is minimised or even transcended.

During the preparation stage, and then until the peak of *Nigredo* the alchemist will be troubled by the inclusion of self within the *Tree*. At peak *Nigredo*, where the very first light of *Albedo* manifests, the alchemist is given a direction towards which to progress. This direction is towards selflessness and eventually the eradication of the duality within the central, sixth *sephirot*.

The most popular version of this *Tree* is this *perfected* version, or semi-perfected, one which is more accurately what represents a peak *Albedo* stage *Tree* where duality has been eradicated and the ten *sephirot* are in optimal balance.

Well, that was a fairly long, and complicated introduction to the *Trees*. In our course, the *Trees* are really additional flavour that helps connect our atomic *Abhidhamma* study with normal experience.

> "The Tree Of Life is more than a symbol. It is an actual map of the Universe and the psyche, the Great Chain of Being ranging from the highest spiritual world to the physical world." [36]

---

[36] Regardie, Israel. *The Middle Pillar*

Nigredo

Study Guide: The Trees of Consciousness

This chapter explores consciousness through the Tree Of Life model, examining its manifestation from atomic moments to complex spiritual structures, focusing on psychological and spiritual development through different states of awareness.

Core Concepts
- Consciousness as layered phenomenon
- Tree Of Life as consciousness map
- Evolution through innocent, fallen, and perfected states
- Relationship between awareness levels

New Terminology
Avidya: Primal ignorance or delusion
Demiurge: Creator deity in Gnostic/Platonic tradition
Kundalini: Rising spiritual energy
Pleroma: Gnostic concept of totality
Qlippoth: Shadow aspects of Sephirot
Sephirot: Kabbalistic spheres representing consciousness aspects

Main Themes
1. Nature of Consciousness
- Atomic awareness
- Sequential experience
- Pattern recognition
- Evolution of awareness

2. Tree Structure
- Three manifestation forms
- Ten fundamental principles
- Developmental layers
- Symbolic relationships

3. Consciousness Evolution
- Movement through states
- Self-awareness role
- Layer integration
- Transformational aspects

Technical Framework
- First Layer: Primal awareness/Pure knowing
- Second Layer: Pattern recognition/Love
- Third Layer: Object formation/Self-other divide
- Fourth Layer: Harmonious love/Christ consciousness
- Fifth Layer: Discrimination/Analysis
- Sixth Layer: Central self/Identity
- Seventh Layer: Drives/Emotions
- Eighth Layer: Rationalisation/Control
- Ninth Layer: Dream consciousness
- Tenth Layer: Material awareness

Practical Applications
- Understanding consciousness layers
- Recognising awareness patterns
- Integrating spiritual practice
- Transforming consciousness states

Integration Points
- Links to Evolution of Adulthood
- Connections to Symbols and Meanings
- Relationship to Enlightenment concepts

Common Misconceptions
- Nature of consciousness unity
- Role of self-awareness
- Purpose of consciousness layers

Reflection Questions
- Daily consciousness layer experience
- Thought and perception arising
- Self-relation to consciousness levels
- Awareness changes through practice

Progress Indicators
- Development through layers
- Integration of awareness
- Transformation signs
- Spiritual growth markers

OBJECT

27. The Golden Middle Path

"The Middle Path discovered by the Tathāgata avoids both extremes, giving vision, giving knowledge, and leads to peace, to direct knowledge, to enlightenment, to Nirvāṇa." [37]

The Golden Middle Path represents the delicate balance between extremes that the alchemist must navigate to achieve transformation. This chapter explores how consciousness creates our experience of reality through multiple layers, and reveals the path beyond conceptual extremes. We examine the relationship between the Trees of consciousness, the role of duality in spiritual development, and the ultimate transcendence of all conceptual boundaries. Through understanding these principles, we discover how the alchemist moves beyond both attachment and aversion to find true liberation.

Whilst the *Trees of Consciousness* are fascinating, our work doesn't take place at the macroscopic level. Remember the *Trees* are Holographic, which means we need only focus on part of the *Tree*, and through transforming the right parts, the whole will transform.

I suspect only those with prior knowledge of Gnosticism or Kabbalah will have understood much of the prior talk; nevertheless, we will continue for this talk with the *Trees*.

---

[37] *The Buddha, Dhammacakkappavattana Sutta*

I will summarise the salient points before we continue, just in case I lost some of you.

Our subjective experience is, in the absence of illness, intoxication or mental illness, clean. What I mean by this is we don't notice the mechanisms of our mind. They are invisible and allow you, the subjective centre of being, to fully concentrate on *reality*.

Yet, the truth is both disturbing and mind-blowing.

All is mind. Both your own physicality AND everything you sense. There are ten subjective viewpoints, but they all stack into what appears as 'I'. This 'I' starts off as a very primitive, but godlike awareness, but it descends, drawn on by objects of its own creation, and forgetting itself. By the time this 'I' has descended to *normal* awareness it has forgotten itself, and fully identifies with the objects of its own creation. This is the sleeping *Brahma* (creator God) that dreams the life we think we lead.

Each of the ten layers of consciousness is divided into two, an inner empty part that is aware, and a periphery of objects that this consciousness takes as objective reality.

Until one is skilled, comprehending the higher layers is impossible, although they are experienced daily, the untrained mind cannot remember them.

The first three layers are very abstract and the topic for a later talk. They make up the '*Godhead*' or inner mind.

The last seven layers make up the character of the individual, as well as *creating* the mental arena in which the individual lives (*The Matrix*).

When somebody meditates or takes strong hallucinogenics the *cleanness* of reality breaks down. One can move from a central position of being, and identify with the awareness that is normally perception, hence objects seem to enliven and open up.

Our sense fields are *made* of *resultant consciousnesses*. When we see a blue cup, there is initially a layer of blue resultant awareness in the pattern of a cup. Another layer of awareness lies over this, and is aware of cup. So, when we, subjectively look out, we don't even see the cup, just *know* of its presence.

OBJECT

The alchemist, one way or another, learns to manipulate consciousness (*mercury*) through changing how one responds subjectively. Consciousness, we have learned, exists in *unwholesome* and *wholesome* states. These are determined by whatever mental factors arise with the *citta*. The mental factors here are kind of our *sulphur*, they are intertwined with *citta* and therefore arise due to karmic habit.

The Biblical story of *Genesis* warns us not to eat from the third, maternal *Tree*, the *Tree of Duality*. This warning however is almost always in vain; in fact, some texts explain that "*everybody has to fall*" — a reference *Matrix* fans will understand. We need to create a self that we worry about, otherwise the temptation towards selfishness cannot arise. The mind needs the temptation because in fighting this temptation, it conditions it towards the goal. This temptation is the effort, the fire the disciple must provide in order to process the raw material.

Once our *Tree* becomes *dual* we are bound to suffer. We face a constant dilemma between what is right and what we want. If we fail to resist this, we create *unwholesome karma* and suffer. If we sacrifice our own needs for others, it is initially really difficult, but then as resultant *karma* arises our lives improve. But they only improve as long as we sacrifice our own needs. So, although suffering is minimal, we still suffer even when we gain the heavens.

The Alchemist ponders this dilemma. *Damned if I do, damned if I don't*—that is the conclusion. And this is the paradox, there is nothing you can do, and nothing you cannot do to escape the *Matrix*. Even the act of doing nothing is a choice.

The puzzle of the *Matrix* requires more than logic to transcend.

The truth can only be experienced, it cannot be described.

But, the path towards this experience can be described, which is the substance of all mystery religions.

The Alchemist, like all magicians, begins in Hell.

We will come to the various realms within the sensual. There are several versions of Hell, and one of them is here on Earth. Individuals all have different experiences of reality, and these experiences are directly related to the quality of their *resultant consciousness*. Those who are forgiving and manage any unskilled karmic reactions experience life much more pleasantly than those who are troubled by excesses of greed or anger.

The *sin* of the magician or any thinker is the eating of the fruit. Basically, the more you think you know, the more this creates a rift between sensual experience and mental (subjective) isolation.

A child might see some pink ice cream, and these perceptions of firstly *pink* and then *ice-cream* are the only thoughts that interrupt the experience of taste. This is why they go crazy! An adult with an eating disorder who is binging on ice cream can hardly taste it, as they are experiencing simultaneous guilt, anger and remorse as they try to get good feelings from it.

Those that fill their mind with facts can, if they are not careful, suffer indescribable loneliness and isolation as their subjective self is cut off from bodily feelings by uncontrollable and relentless thoughts. This makes them prone to both depression and addiction.

One way or another the Alchemist finds themselves in Hell. Yet, they are more curious about its torments or tormentors than other poor denizens. They want to know why overthinking leads to torment. Why are innocence and ignorance associated with a happier outlook? So, they decide to study the stuff of the Hellish Subjective Experience and at first they don't like what they find.

Nigredo is the part of realisation of the true cause of our suffering, ourselves. We might be pretty helpless to do anything about it, but experience changes us, and these changes accumulate and make life tiring. All of the bad parts of experience are relived and not let go of, so we habitually torment ourselves.

If we are treated badly we think it is acceptable to return this or repeat it to others. We don't realise every act of anger, greed or delusion directly affects how we perceive things in the future.

Not recognising nor having any ability to stop it, these mental defilements accumulate until we are tired of this existence and left only to fantasise a new, better life.

OBJECT

Life is conditioned until we gain the wisdom and insights to change this. Our direction is inwards and downwards into the mess and tangle of our current ground of being.

One cannot begin the work until one has amassed the ingredients for the *retort*. One must learn to own one's own Hellish parts. One must learn to be truthful with oneself and others. At this stage our being is divided, literally Angel and *Demon*, one geared towards selflessness the other, selfishness. These are also called the two thieves, the good and bad thief that flanked Christ at his crucifixion. *Why thieves?* Because they steal your time. You waste time trying to be good or trying to be evil. One must learn not to surf *karma*, one must learn to break it apart.

One needs to learn to sit with one's faults. And I mean sit. Reacting to guilt and shame with action or deed just turns the wheel. Only when one recognises that the most evil aspect of the universe still has to come from within one's own mind are you getting close.

Contemplating one's *Nigredo* without thoughtless reactions develops four mental factors, also called the *Brahmaviharas* or Divine Abodes. *Brahma* is the sleeping God that dreams the life we experience. These four qualities will, when developed *lift* consciousness out of its current hellish experience, and are called the four *illimitables*. This means they have no upper limit to how much one can develop them.

Note in our previous categorisation of the 52 *cetasikas*, mental factors, only two are in the group *illimitable*— *muditā* (appreciative joy, sharing the joy of another) and *karuṇā* (compassion). This is because *mettā* (loving-kindness) is represented as non-hate and *upekkhā* (equanimity) is already a *wholesome* factor.

Non-hate is kindness, and is a desire not to injure or hurt. Equanimity is fairness and a recognition of the value of all life. Compassion is a desire that others don't suffer and appreciative joy arises as one masters jealousy.

As one progressively learns to use skilled karmic approaches to life, the concept of self diminishes, and it becomes easier. Although this method cannot eliminate the sense of self, and even though relatively empty it remains and can become infected with what are called *Skandha demons* which cause mania.

Nigredo

The alchemist *ascends* the *Tree of Duality* towards a place called *Daʿat*. This is a special *gate* between the two *trees* that acts as a kind of test for the Magician. In both *Trees* is an Abyss that separates the second and third consciousness which is contiguous between them.

The Alchemist therefore establishes themselves on the *Tree of Duality*, and recognising their duality and helplessness gives up on previous understanding. This allows them to relinquish attachment to the known, and when the mental faculty of 'I will know the unknown' is mature, through the development of faith, the mind makes the transcendental leap and the first path moment is experienced.

This *path* moment is the first experience of the transcendental, and creates two or three resultant, *fruit* consciousnesses. The *fruit* consciousness now act as the new ground of being, and the individual is called a stream-winner or *Sotāpanna*.

Now, the relationship to the *Tree* changes. One no longer identifies fully with any of it. One has managed to find a perspective outside of *Conditional Reality* , even though it was a single moment of mind. One's connection to reality is fractured, and now it will never be the same. This is akin to a *red pill* moment, revealing the true nature of *Conditional Reality*.

One now fully recognises the *prison* of conditional experience. At first, one is confused, especially if this break was unplanned or unexpected. One can languish in addiction and mental health thinking one is broken, yet, in truth, one has become *unhinged*.

However, there reaches a second point where realisation occurs and a direction arises. This is the start of *Albedo*, which appears some time after the *Dark Night of the Soul.*

With the arising of the second *path* consciousness, and its subsequent two or three resultant *citta*, faith is invigorated and one finds commitment easier.

It is like the Alchemist is still in Hell, but now it is on the alchemist's terms. Sensory attachments are lessened, as is ill-will, and as one accepts one's duality kindness and compassion develop.

OBJECT

There will reach a point where this benevolence peaks in sacrifice of the self. Here one abandons any future goals, dreams and desires as pointless. Once one has fully sacrificed all future desires, they can cross through the Abyss. With the expunging of self from the *Tree of Duality*, it reverts to the *Tree Of Life*.

The *Subjective Reality* of the alchemist at this stage is one of a natural healer. This is *Albedo*, the white lunar stone. Allegorically, this stone produces silver, which is the metal of the moon. The moon symbolises natural cycles. The Alchemist, either deliberately or through the process is no longer reacting naturally. Their forgiveness, kindness, patience, compassion and detachment has a harmonising and restorative effect.

At this stage, they still have an empty residue of self, and the five subtle fetters. Yet, they have no sensory attachments and only reactive anger, and so will appear almost holy in comparison to the norm.

With ongoing work the alchemist starts to work with what is called the *Veil of Isis*. This veil arises when we are first *cut off* from our mother after birth and is the last of the veils of consciousness that subtly blanket experience. This is the veil that separates our sense of *inner world* and *outside* or *normal* reality.

Once the veil is lifted the alchemist perceives not only the subjective experience but also the atomic experiences of the consciousnesses that make up objective reality. Their mind now penetrates almost completely into reality, they can see the programming as well as the program.

The *Veil of Isis* separates the third and fourth consciousnesses. Remember, the first three consciousness layers make up our inner sense of being, the last seven our sense of personality and experience.

Daʿat is located at the border of this Veil and it is here that the alchemist works.

This work at *Daʿat* represents the final stage of the alchemical transformation, where the practitioner begins to perceive reality in its true nature — as both empty and full, both form and formless. The distinction between subject and object dissolves, and the artificial boundaries created by the mind begin to fade.

Nigredo

In this culminating phase, the alchemist realises that the Trees of Life and Duality were never truly separate, but rather different perspectives of the same ultimate reality. The Golden Middle Path is not a compromise between extremes but rather a transcendence of dualistic thinking, leading to the complete liberation of consciousness from self-imposed limitations.

Study Guide: The Golden Middle Path

This chapter explores consciousness, duality, and transformation through alchemical metaphor, examining how mind creates experience while revealing the path beyond conceptual extremes, culminating in the transcendence of dualistic thinking.

CORE CONCEPTS

- *The layered structure of consciousness*
- *The relationship between Trees of Life and Duality*
- *The transformative process from Hell to transcendence*
- *The role of Daʿat in spiritual transformation*

NEW TERMINOLOGY

Daʿat: *Hidden sphere on Tree Of Life representing knowledge*

Four Illimitables: *Buddhist virtues of kindness, equanimity, compassion and appreciative joy*

Matrix of Conditioned Existence: *Network of habitual patterns and perceptions*

Mercury: *Alchemical principle representing consciousness*

Prima Materia: *The first matter in alchemy*

Skandhas: *Aggregates or heaps of phenomena in Buddhism*

Sulphur: *Alchemical principle representing active force*

Tree of Duality: *Symbolic representation of separated consciousness*

Veil of Isis: *Metaphysical barrier between subjective experience and direct perception*

MAIN THEMES

1. Nature of consciousness

- *Clean subjective experience versus fragmented reality*
- *Ten layers of viewpoint creating illusion of I*
- *Relationship between awareness and perceived objects*
- *Links to Trees of Consciousness*

2. The transformative process

- *Movement from Hell to transcendence*
- *Development of Four Illimitables*
- *Role of sacrifice and surrender*
- *Connection to Dark Night of Soul*

3. Integration and transcendence

- *Working with Trees*
- *Significance of Daʿat*
- *Dissolution of subject-object duality*
- *Links to Realms of Existence*

PRACTICAL APPLICATIONS

- *Understanding layers of consciousness*
- *Working with mental factors*

OBJECT

- Developing Four Illimitables
- Transcending dualistic thinking

INTEGRATION POINTS
- Connection to Trees of Consciousness
- Relationship to Dark Night of Soul
- Links to Realms of Existence

COMMON MISCONCEPTIONS
- Trees are not separate but different perspectives of same reality
- Middle Path is not a compromise but a transcendence
- Transformation requires both understanding and practice

REFLECTION QUESTIONS
- How do you currently navigate between extremes in your spiritual practice
- What is your experience of balancing effort and surrender
- How do you understand relationship between duality and non-duality in your practice
- What role does wisdom play in finding your own middle way

PROGRESS INDICATORS
- Development of Four Illimitables
- Reduction in sensory attachments
- Increased awareness of consciousness layers
- Dissolution of subject-object duality

NIGREDO

"I am a poisonous dragon, present everywhere and to be had for nothing. My water and my fire dissolve and compound. Out of my body thou shalt draw the Green and the Red Lion; but if thou dost not exactly know me thou wilt—with my fire—destroy thy five senses. A most pernicious, quick poison comes out of my nostrils which hath been the destruction of many. Separate therefore the thick from the thin artificially, unless thou dost delight in extreme poverty. I give thee faculties both male and female and the powers both of heaven and earth.

The mysteries of my art are to be performed magnanimously and with great courage if thou wouldst have me overcome the violence of the fire, in which attempt many have lost both their labour and their substance. I am the egg of Nature known only to the wise, such as are pious and modest, who make of me a little world. Ordained I was by the Almighty God for men, but—though many desire me—I am given only to few that they may relieve the poor with my treasures and not set their minds on gold that perisheth. I am called of the philosophers Mercury: my husband is gold philosophical. I am the old dragon that is present everywhere on the face of the earth.

I am father and mother, youthful and ancient, weak and yet most strong, life and death, visible and invisible, hard and soft, descending to the earth and ascending to the heavens, most high and most low, light and heavy. In me the order of Nature is oftentimes inverted— in colour, number, weight, and measure. I have in me the light of Nature; I am dark and bright; I spring from the earth and I come out of heaven; I am well known and yet a mere nothing; all colours shine in me and all metals by the beams of the sun. I am the Carbuncle of the Sun, a most noble, clarified earth, by which thou mayst turn copper, iron, tin, and lead into most pure gold." [38]

---

[38] Vaughan, Thomas. *Magia Adamica: or the Antiquitie of Magic, and the Descent Thereof from Adam Downwards, Proved. Whereunto is Added, A Perfect and Full Discoverie of the True Coelum Terrae, or The Magician's Heavenly Chaos, and First Matter of All Things.* London: Printed by T.W. for H. Blunden, 1650.

OBJECT

28. The Four Grades of Realisation

"Without a foundation in the conventional truth,
The significance of the ultimate cannot be taught.
Without understanding the significance of the ultimate,
Liberation is not achieved" [39]

In this pivotal chapter, we explore how the alchemist navigates between extremes to find the transcendent middle way. While the Trees of Consciousness provide a grand map of inner reality, our practical work focuses on specific transformative points within this holographic system. Through understanding how consciousness creates our experience of reality and learning to work with rather than against our dual nature, we discover the golden path that leads beyond all conceptual extremes. This chapter bridges theoretical understanding with practical application, revealing how apparent opposites can be unified through skilled spiritual practice.

There are four *path* moments of consciousness, and four resultant *fruit* consciousnesses, which act as sequential *ground of being* of the disciple.

In order to understand how the breakthrough occurs, one must understand that some *citta* have roots, and others are rootless. *Roots* give a *citta* stability and influence over other *citta*. Those *citta* that lack roots are often merely functional *citta*, i.e., they perform a function rather than take an active part in cognition.

---

[39] verses 24:10 in Nāgārjuna's Mūlamadhyamakakārikā

There are three *unwholesome roots*, the presence of which create *unwholesome karma* (*akusala*). These *roots* are greed (*lobha*), ill-will (*dosa*) and delusion (*moha*). All *unwholesome* states of mind will have delusion as a root, either by itself in states of restlessness or torpor, or accompanied with either greed or ill-will. Note, greed cannot be present if ill-will is also present as they are opposites, one is the *citta* grasping and clinging, the other the *citta* strikes out at the object.

There are likewise three *wholesome roots* (*kusala*). The consciousness that acts as an anchor of being, the *life continuum* (*bhavaṅga*) is *made* of either two *rooted* or three *rooted* consciousness in a newborn human. These roots are non-greed (*alobha*, meaning generosity), non-hatred (*adosa*, meaning loving-kindness), and non-delusion (*amoha*, meaning wisdom).

The force which *propels* one moment of awareness into creating the next is *karma*. *Karma* is either skilful, and *resultant consciousness* is pleasant and associated with joy or it is unskilful and future *resultant consciousness* will be unpleasant.

Our key to breaking loose of conditionality is the fact that consciousness can take itself as its own object. One can learn to slow and settle the mind through discipline, gently but persistently drawing one's attention to a simple object of focus.

With persistence the harsh barrier of subjectivity/objectivity breaks apart and one becomes aware of the more subtle consciousnesses out of which this object is formed. With persistence one can, momentarily forget where one is, and fully become absorbed within these more subtle consciousnesses. This is called *jhāna*, and effectively short-circuits experience.

Now, it is easy to become sidetracked with *jhāna*. It can be both a great shelter place and a way to develop psychic power (*abhiñña*). Yet, for the truth seeker, these lands of fantasy and wonder are both dangerous and time wasting. One is encouraged, if it's one's inclination to develop *jhāna*, but be wary of both its beguiling nature and the fact that *karma* is still functioning, and once a disciple develops psychic powers, their ability to create adverse *karma* is multiplied.

The true alchemist will recognise these risks, and seek to master the skilful use of *karma* not for heavenly or material gain, but simply for a peaceful life. The alchemist seeks the tranquility of a *citta* that is neither good, nor bad. A *citta* that lacks greed, hate, delusion and has the qualities of non-greed, non-hate and non-delusion with one important caveat, they act this way without any purpose.

Object

Such a *citta* cannot move in its normal way, and collapses in a way that creates *space* (transcendental awareness) in the normal chain of awareness. It is from this single moment of being outside of conditioned reality, that is taken as an object in the resultant *citta* that the realisations arise that see through, or weaken the respective fetters (*saṃyojana*) at each stage of the process.

There is a lovely analogy for these four moments.

The first, is like a lost traveller in a dangerous place who catches sight of a cottage that looks warm and beckoning. Once seen, this occupies all of the traveller's mind and they make a direct path towards the cottage, which is like the second. The third is like when the traveller arrives at the cottage, and confirms it is warm and safe and the fourth is like when the traveller has entered the cottage and is sat warm, safe and comfortable inside.

For the alchemist, the first stage is the most difficult and elusive. Once gained, one's progress is inevitable, but this will be explored in due course.

Thus, the path of realisation unfolds as a gradual process of awakening, where each stage represents a deeper understanding of reality and a progressive liberation from the bonds of suffering. This journey, whether culminating in Arahantship or Buddhahood, leads to the ultimate freedom from the cycle of birth and death, where the practitioner finally realises the true nature of existence and experiences the ineffable peace of *Nirvāṇa*.

Study Guide: The Four Grades Of Realisation

This chapter examines consciousness transformation through Buddhist psychology, exploring how different types of consciousness interact to create spiritual breakthrough.

Core Concepts
- *Consciousness mechanics and karmic relationships*
- *Progressive stages of enlightenment*
- *Interaction between wholesome and unwholesome states*
- *Transcendence through meditative practice*

New Terminology
Adosa: Non-hatred
Akusala: Unwholesome states
Alobha: Non-greed
Amoha: Non-delusion
Dosa: Ill-will
Kiriya: Functional consciousness
Kusala: Wholesome states
Lobha: Greed
Moha: Delusion

NIGREDO

Main Themes

1. Consciousness Nature
- *Root consciousness types and interactions*
- *Wholesome and unwholesome mental states*
- *Karma and consciousness relationship*
- *Enlightenment connections*

2. Path Mechanics
- *Subject-object barrier breakthrough*
- *Absorption states development*
- *Meditative attainment considerations*
- *Shadow work integration*

3. Realisation Stages
- *Mental fetters weakening*
- *Four enlightenment grades*
- *Insight and liberation relationship*
- *Path consciousness connection*

Technical Framework
- *Consciousness root types and their effects*
- *Progressive stages of enlightenment*
- *Correlation between Buddhist and magical grades*

Practical Applications
- *Meditation practice*
- *Karma management techniques*
- *Consciousness transformation methods*
- *Fetter dissolution practices*

Integration Points
- *Connection to Subtle Fetters*
- *Path Consciousness foundation*
- *Arahant preparation*
- *Different Worlds relationship*

Common Misconceptions
- *Jhāna states are not the final goal*
- *Greed and ill-will mutual exclusivity*
- *Liberation versus supernatural powers*
- *Non-linear progress nature*

Progress Indicators
- *Mental fetter weakening*
- *Consciousness state shifts*
- *Meditative attainment depth*
- *Insight development stages*

Reflection Questions
- *Relationship to progressive spiritual development*
- *Reality understanding changes through practice*
- *Insight and transformation connection*
- *Personal progress recognition*

OBJECT

Stages of Enlightenment

Worldling *(puthujjana)*	Non-enlightened beings cannot perceive actual form, this is perceived unconsciously by the sense consciousness. Instead, the 'Shadow' and 'reflection' of phenomena are perceived and all experience is referenced to the self. All ten fetters remain and are unperceived. The being therefore dwells in Apparent Reality and is under the influence of desire, ill-will and ignorance.
Sotāpanna	Upon achieving Stream Winner the disciple is increasingly aware of the biases of perception that will remain until Arahantship — one is not automatically beguiled. The fetters of personality view, attachment to rites and rituals, and skeptical doubt are realised. The remaining seven remain.
Sakadāgāmī	The Once-returner weakens sensual desire and ill-will through deeper insight into impermanence. The fourth and fifth fetters are weakened with the resolve to pursue spiritual wisdom. They still remain with the subtle fetters.
Anāgāmī	The Non-returner experiences complete freedom from sensual desire and ill-will. All five gross fetters are realised and the disciple is largely freed from sensory realm rebirth. The inner, subtle fetters remain.
Arahant	With the total elimination of mental clinging the reflection of phenomena ceases. Phenomena now have no reference to self and are seen as empty. All ten fetters are realised and mental clinging ceases. The skandhas remain but now, without clinging Saṃsāra becomes Nirvāṇa. The Arahant experiences Nirvāṇa with residual stains from their remaining skandhas which dissolve with physical death.
Bodhisattva 8th Bhumi	The disciple who cannot 'abandon' humanity progresses through lifetimes of selfless compassion and when the eighth bhumi is reached, all discursive cognition ceases. All phenomena now are seen as translucent and dreamlike with an inner luminosity. The Bodhisattva realises the ten fetters yet is bound by their vow to return for the benefit of all living beings. This precludes the Arahant's state of abandonment and will condition rebirths until full Buddhahood is achieved.
Tathāgata *(Buddha)*	Buddhic perception is a state of awareness that is so subtle that it requires no active cognition. Knowing is no longer dual; it is continuous, omnipresent, and without limits, transcending all conceptual distinctions. All fetters are realised. Access to limitless and perfect dharma. The eight consciousnesses are transformed into the three kayas—three manifestations of perfect unity.

Nigredo

The Realms of Six Classes of Being

Formless Realm
Pure consciousness, beyond form

B — **Brahma Gods** — **F**
L   *Refined perception,*   **O**
I   *subtler reality*   **R**
S   **M**
S
F **Devas** **R**
U *Pleasure, bliss, but still* **E**
L *impermanent* **A**
R   **L**
E   **M**
A **Human Realm** **S**
L *Potential for awakening,* **E**
M *moral agency* **N**
         S
W **Animal Realm** **O**
O *Instinct-driven, survival,* **R**
E *limited awareness* **Y**
F
U **Hungry Ghosts** **R**
L **(Pretas)** **E**
R *Endless craving,* **A**
E *dissatisfaction, hunger* **L**
A
L **Hell Realm** **M**
M *Intense suffering, punishment,*
       torment

The six classes of Being—Demons, Ghosts, Animals, (The Woeful Realm), Humans, Deva and Brahma Gods (The Blissful Realm) and the Formless, where there are 'beings' that are pure mind—i.e., they lack any sensory consciousness. Hate, ignorance and craving binds beings to the lower realms. Kindness, generosity and wisdom causes rebirth in highly, heavenly realms.

OBJECT

29. Realms of Existence

"The first step to the knowledge of the wonder and mystery of life is the recognition of the monstrous nature of the earthly human realm as well as its glory." [40]

This chapter explores the intricate relationship between consciousness, karma, and the various realms of existence. Through understanding how the life-continuum (bhavaṅga) shapes our experiential reality, we gain insight into the nature of human suffering and the potential for transformation. We examine how different types of consciousness influence our perception and capacity for spiritual growth, while exploring the relationship between mind, body, and the various planes of existence. This knowledge provides both a theoretical framework and practical implications for those seeking to understand their current state of being and possibilities for transcendence.

Consciousness is either karmically creative, i.e. *wholesome* (*kusala*) or *unwholesome* (*akusala*) which creates the respective *karma*; functional (*kiriya*), where it performs merely a function with negligible *karma* or, resultant (*vipāka*). Understanding *resultant consciousness* (*vipāka*) is essential for progress in spiritual development. *Resultant consciousness* is that awareness that arises as a result of a previous decision that had karmic weight. Now, we are not just talking about big mistakes but every moment of awareness when a decision is made. It could be as basic as the first time we identified what others mean by *blue*. Once, most of us, decided what *blue* was, this *karma* creates a response that generally will last our

---

[40] Campbell, J. (1949). *The Hero with a Thousand Faces*. Pantheon Books, p. 121.

lifetime. We will hardly notice it most times, yet, whenever *blue* is detected our resultant consciousness mixes with it, and should our attention need it, instantly we know this quality. This explains traumatic projection where once a perception of danger is made, it is very hard then to stop making it, and folk suffer inappropriate fear. Trauma itself doesn't necessarily complicate things, but the meanings we attach to it often obscure the truth, making resolution difficult. Furthermore, trauma brutalises us, it allows us to justify the development of our own anger and delusions.

The Life Continuum.

At the heart of our being is the *life continuum* (*bhavaṅga*). This is neither physical, nor strictly a thing, but can be likened to a light that pulses every moment of existence. This pulsating light serves as both the *structure* and *gate* of the mind, relying on electromagnetic (*eddy*) currents centred in the heart, which result from the circulation of iron in haemoglobin. The circulating blood sets up currents within the nerve cells, on which the mind is based.

This *life continuum* is in truth a series of *citta*, point moments of awareness, that arise, are present and then cease. Each one conditions the next *citta*. Each *citta* can take previous *citta* as an object, meaning that although a *citta* exists only once, the mind can *look back* through this chain of occurrences. These *citta* are identical and of one of nineteen types. They are resultant *citta* — they are the result of the last cognitive process in the previous existence. A being's last moment of awareness takes a specific object or experience that karmically *sums up* one's life experience.

So, the *life continuum* is the resultant consciousness from our last cognitive moment in our previous existence. This is particularly important in near-death experience, even in those where somebody genuinely thought they were going to die but didn't. In these individuals they might literally die, but then, when they don't physically die, their new *life continuum* (new existence) starts based on the *karma* of their last life. This is obviously confusing and manifests as a complete change in personality.

Furthermore, I believe that individuals suffering from severe mental illness, psychological trauma, or addiction can experience a metaphysical death without a physical one. Here, the *life continuum* can change to that of a Hell being or animal, which results in protracted misery as the person is now literally experiencing Hell. For many unfortunate individuals, Hell is almost certainly experienced here on

Earth. There may also be a metaphysical Hell—one in which weighty *karma* within sensory or mental consciousness complicates and delays the natural disintegration of the mind.

Life-continuum (Bhavanga) of different beings

Type of Being	Life-continuum — (resultant consciousness)
Hell Being or Ghost	Rootless Investigating Consciousness associated with displeasure.
Animal	Rootless Investigating Consciousness associated with neutral feeling.
Human	Double Rooted (kindness, non-greed) with pleasant feeling (two kinds)
Human	Double Rooted (kindness, non-greed) with neutral feeling (two kinds)
Human	Triple Rooted (kindness, non-greed, wisdom) with pleasant feeling (two kinds)
Human	Triple Rooted (kindness, non-greed, wisdom) with neutral feeling (two kinds)
Angel or Brahmic Being	Jhanic Form-sphere Resultant Consciousness of five grades, depending on degree of skill in mastery.
Formless Being	Jhanic Formless Sphere Resultant Consciousness of four types, each pertaining to a different realm of the formless.

In the *Abhidhamma* we learn that the *life continuum* is of nineteen different types of consciousness. Nine of these types of consciousness are associated with *jhanic* consciousness and heavenly beings, which we will explore in the next talk.

Of the remaining ten, eight are associated with human rebirth. One is associated with animal rebirth and one with Hellish rebirth. Now, the eight types of human *life continuum* are rooted, and as we have learned, this gives stability to the *citta*. These eight rooted consciousnesses are all *wholesome* resultant consciousnesses, meaning they represent satisfactory conclusions. Upon evaluation of the previous life, a *wholesome rooted resultant* arises. Four of these consciousness are triple *rooted*, which we know gives an individual aptitude towards the *dharma*. Note that these individuals experience three *fruit* moments after a *path* moment. The other four *wholesome citta* are double rooted, having non-greed (*alobha*) and non-hate (*adosa*) as *roots*.

We can only really be reborn as humans if we have two or three rooted resultant consciousness. If, when summing up our lives, we have absolutely nothing to show, then our rebirth consciousness is unrooted—essentially *meh*—and we end up as an animal. Those who have psychologically died, either through genuine belief in inevitable demise, or a near-death experience, or through trauma and addiction, can, in addition to *human* rebirth experience the more challenging, hellish rebirth.

The thing to grasp here is that it is the quality of one's *life continuum* that dictates what sort of experience we have. If the *life continuum* is one of the *jhanic* consciousnesses this permits heavenly rebirth. If it is rooted it leads to human rebirth. And if it is a resultant consciousness that is essentially indifferent, one's experience is hellish.

The *life continuum* is like the structure of the mind. If one has a three rooted awareness then these three *roots* resonate with the kindness, generosity and wisdom of any experience. Yet, for a Hell being none of these qualities are recognised, and so responses are limited to only those of self-importance.

Hell beings can be of two types, *Demons* and *Ghosts*. *Demons* are the more spiritually blind and see the world as hostile and deserving of plunder. *Ghosts* are evolved *Demons* troubled by shame, guilt, and remorse, which they attempt to escape through addiction.

Once, however, the alchemist makes the first breakthrough, their *life continuum* changes, they go through a partial death of self. Their *life continuum* is likely triple rooted, and these *roots* being kindness, generosity and wisdom means from this point onwards they will always be aware of these attributes in every subsequent experience.

This doesn't mean the individual at this level can't act in *unwholesome* ways, more that they will always be aware of the moral implications of every act. Therefore, once the alchemist reaches the first path moment, their *life continuum* becomes triple rooted. Furthermore, this is not like the normal triple-rooted human *life continuum*. Here, the *roots* seem fused into a single element that simultaneously embodies kindness, generosity, and wisdom as persisting factors.

The *life continuum* therefore dictates the realm of subjective experience of the being. Lower *quality* life continuum yields a mind that fails to notice benevolent qualities leaving the individual almost completely self-focused. I cannot imagine how important an understanding of this is in the management of PTSD and severe psychological trauma, as well as addiction. This *life continuum* can be changed, but only through a near-death experience or dedicated spiritual training. I think the latter point should offer great hope to those who find themselves in a literal hell.

Understanding the nature of consciousness and its various manifestations through the *life continuum* offers profound insights into human experience and suffering. This knowledge, rooted in ancient Buddhist wisdom yet relevant to modern psychological understanding, provides a framework for transformation and healing. Through conscious cultivation of *wholesome* states and spiritual practice, we can elevate our *life continuum*, moving from states of suffering towards increasingly refined levels of awareness and peace. This journey of transformation, while challenging, remains accessible to all who seek it, offering hope for those trapped in lower realms of consciousness and pointing the way towards liberation.

Roots of Consciousness

Consciousness Type	Characteristics	Experience
Triple-rooted	Wisdom, non-greed, non-hate	Spiritual human potential
Double-rooted	Non-greed, non-hate	Nornal human awareness
Unrooted	Basic awareness	Animal/hellish experience
Jhanic	Meditative absorption	Heavenly realms

Nigredo

Study Guide: Realms Of Existence

This chapter examines the relationship between consciousness, karma, and realms of existence, with a particular focus on how the life-continuum (bhavaṅga) shapes experiential reality and influences spiritual transformation.

CORE CONCEPTS
- Quality of consciousness determines experience
- Transformation is always achievable through spiritual practice.
- Understanding karma affects spiritual progress
- Mind and body are interconnected
- Consciousness operates in predictable patterns

NEW TERMINOLOGY

Arūpa-loka: Formless realm
Bhavaṅga: Life-continuum consciousness
Deva-loka: Heavenly realms
Double-rooted consciousness: Consciousness containing non-greed and non-hate
Functional consciousness: Basic mental operations without karmic weight
Kāmāvacara: Sense-sphere consciousness
Karmically creative consciousness: Mental states generating new karma
Rūpa-loka: Form realm
Triple-rooted consciousness: Consciousness containing wisdom, non-greed, and non-hate
Vipāka: Resultant consciousness

MAIN THEMES
1. Nature of consciousness
- Types of karmic influence
- Role of life-continuum
- Relationship between mind and physical body

2. Realms of existence
- Human consciousness types
- Hellish and animal realms
- Heavenly states

3. Transformative processes
- Near-death experiences
- Spiritual development
- Psychological healing

TECHNICAL FRAMEWORK

Life-continuum manifestations:

1. Physical basis
- Heart-centred electromagnetic field
- Relationship to blood circulation
- Neural network interactions

2. Psychological aspects
- Moment-to-moment awareness
- Memory and perception
- Karmic imprinting

3. Spiritual dimensions
- Potential for transformation
- Role in enlightenment
- Connection to death process

PRACTICAL APPLICATIONS
- Growing awareness of moral implications
- Reduced self-focus
- Natural expression of wisdom
- Integration of spiritual insights
- Development of triple-rooted consciousness

INTEGRATION POINTS
- Links to Shadow Work (Chapter 10)

Object

- Connection to Enlightenment (Chapter 6)
- Links to Dark Night (Chapter 11)
- Connection to Raw Substance (Chapter 4)
- Links to Fisher-King Wound (Chapter 8)
- Relationship to Rebis (Chapter 9)

COMMON MISCONCEPTIONS

- Understanding trauma and its relationship to consciousness
- Clarification of life-continuum nature
- Distinction between different types of consciousness

REFLECTION QUESTIONS

- How do you understand the relationship between consciousness and karma?
- What is your experience of different states of mind and their effects?
- How do you relate to the concept of rebirth in your practice?
- What role does ethical behaviour play in your spiritual development?

PROGRESS INDICATORS

- Growing awareness of moral implications
- Reduced self-focus
- Natural expression of wisdom
- Integration of spiritual insights
- Development of triple-rooted consciousness

Formless Realm (Arupa Loka)

Level	Realm	Jhāna State	Key Characteristics
31	Neither-perception-nor-non-perception	Fourth formless jhāna	Beings entirely of mind, unable to perceive the Dhamma
30	Nothingness	Third formless jhāna	State of complete void
29	Infinite Consciousness	Second formless jhāna	Realm of boundless consciousness
28	Infinite Space	First formless jhāna	Realm of limitless space

Form Realm (Rupa Loka)

Level	Realm	Jhāna State	Key Characteristics
27-23	Pure Abodes (Suddhavasa)—Peerless devas to Untroubled devas	Fourth jhāna	Accessible only to non-returners and Arahants
22	Unconscious beings		Only body present, no mind

21-20	Very Fruitful devas & Refulgent Glory	Third jhāna	Experience jhanic bliss
19-18	Unbounded & Limited Glory	Third jhāna	Varying degrees of jhanic bliss
17-15	Streaming, Unbounded & Limited Radiance	Second jhāna	Radiant existence
14-12	Great Brahmas, Ministers & Retinue	First jhāna	Home to Great Brahma

Sensual Realm (Kama Loka)

BLISSFUL REALMS			
LEVEL	REALM	REQUIREMENTS	KEY CHARACTERISTICS
11-6	Various Deva Realms	Ten wholesome actions	Including realms of creation and power
5	Human Realm	Virtue and wisdom	Rare and precious birth opportunity
WOEFUL REALMS			
4	Asuras	Unwholesome actions	Realm of constant conflict
3	Hungry Ghosts	Wrong views, lack of virtue	Perpetual unfulfilled desires
2	Animals	Unwholesome actions, animal-like behaviour	Visible non-human beings
1	Hell	Severe unwholesome actions	Temporary realm of intense suffering

OBJECT

30. Different Worlds and Jhāna

*"The jhānas are stages of mental unification and are not,
in themselves, paths to insight or enlightenment.
Without insight,
they can lead only to rebirth in a corresponding realm of existence."*[41]

In this chapter, we explore the fascinating realm of consciousness beyond ordinary physical reality, examining how the mind can achieve extraordinary states of awareness through meditative absorption (jhāna). We will explore how consciousness can take itself as an object, forming self-sustaining states that serve as the foundation for profound meditative experiences and what traditional teachings describe as heavenly realms. Although these states mark significant achievements in mental development, we will also examine their role within the broader path of spiritual transformation.

This next bit is fascinating, and I will attempt to keep it relevant. Whether you believe any of the following rests on whether you can accept that there are certain ways a *citta* (consciousness) can take a *citta* as an object that results in a kind of temporary stability of the *citta*. What I am suggesting is consciousness finds a way of being self-sustaining without the need for a heart base, which is required for all sensory sphere sense awareness.

---

[41] Bodhi, B. (2006). *The Noble Eightfold Path: Way to the End of Suffering.* Buddhist Publication Society, p. 89.

If this seems possible, then it suggests the existence of the heavenly realms (*deva-loka*). This is the only requirement for their possibility.

Our normal *sense-sphere* (*kāmāvacara*) awareness needs circulating blood with a certain amount of iron to create electromagnetic currents. These currents support the mind, which is, if it is *anything*, electromagnetic. The instant our blood stops flowing, sense-sphere awareness is cut off.

However, some have experienced awareness beyond the sensory plane. This is *jhanic* awareness (*dhyāna* consciousness), but can only arise in those who have experienced this prior to this point. This isn't too uncommon, as most experience *jhāna* in childhood, and any habitual thinker thinks in the *jhanic* plane.

The *jhanic* awareness is different, as there are no odours, tastes or bodily feeling. There are only three real consciousnesses: visual, sound and mind.

Normal awareness depends on the presence of the mind, which is based on, or arrived at through the *life continuum* (*bhavaṅga*). This is a stream of identical resultant *citta*.

Heavenly awareness, and therefore the entire being, also has a *life continuum* made of resultant *citta*. These, however, are like little knots of self-sustaining *jhanic* consciousness. This is when awareness has been bent so far into noticing itself it collapses into a self-sustaining *seed*. These self-sustaining seeds form the foundation of heavenly existence.

Now, we don't know that all heavenly beings have this mechanism of stability onto which they can build existence, although this is the likely mechanism on which angels (*devas*), but not gods arise. Why? Because both Angels and *Jhanic* consciousness cannot tolerate ill-will (*vyāpāda*) as a mental factor. If *ill-will* is present, it destabilises the *citta*, it blows it apart. Ill-will is a hindrance to forming *jhāna*, which is when consciousness identifies with its own object, as well as being almost instantly lethal to angels!

So, what exactly is *jhanic* consciousness?

We have all experienced *jhanic* consciousness; we just tend to experience it momentarily without any control. Meditators, profound abstract thinkers, artists,

Object

sportspeople and musicians become naturally more adept at cultivating and accessing it. Occultists and meditators, however, attain a greater range of *jhāna* through the careful selection of appropriate meditative objects.

In normal awareness, consciousness seems to dart after its object. In normal experience, consciousness is more akin to a swarm of many point awarenesses called *citta*.

Certain forms of *citta* have a stabilising effect. A right balance of karmic forces causes a propagation of resultant awareness that consciousness can then take as an object. By turning awareness in on itself, one's awareness reaches the point and *merges* with this object.

It's possible, through practice and mastery, to learn to create these self-sustaining chains of awareness and then focus deeper into the actual components of each *citta*.

Each time the mind makes a new distinction in the *citta*, it creates a new perception with its resultant consciousness. The meditator can then progress into deeper and more subtle worlds of awareness. Until this distinction is made, the mind of the meditator lacks the subtle perception to even notice this experience.

Jhāna arises when the practitioner's mind fully merges with its meditative object. At that moment, the mind *forgets* conditioned existence and completely switches off. This puts the physical body into the equivalent of deep, restful sleep as all adrenaline and background sympathetic tone (anxiety) is cut off.

Initially, this can be distracting, as increased blood flow to the pelvic and abdominal organs is felt. In reality, the sensation of *kundalini* is simply conscious awareness of progressive sympathetic tone relaxation.

Jhanic awareness requires a *life continuum*, composed of one of nine types of *jhanic wholesome resultant consciousness*. At this level, without any distraction of things or beings, the only functioning level of consciousness (from the *Tree*) is the second, which is love (*mettā*).

This means the *citta*, being twisted upon itself, is looking into the very structure of self. Self and thing cannot occur at this level, only love, which manifests as rapture (*pīti*) and fascination.

And so this is what the *citta* experiences. Initially, the experience is marked with bodily zest and feelings of energy as the sympathetic nervous system relaxes. Later, the meditator gets closer and closer to the experience of the first layer of the *Tree Of Life*. Prior to this, however, they experience degrees of overwhelming heavenly love and bliss (*sukha*).

There are two classes of *jhanic* experience: the *fine-material* or *form jhānas* (*rūpa-jhāna*) and the *formless jhānas* (*arūpa-jhāna*). The first are perfect mental worlds not too dissimilar to our own, but the latter are abstract and alien.

Jhanic consciousness can be both a help and a hindrance. While it can act as a refuge for a being, its fantastic and *addictive* nature can easily sidetrack a seeker from their main goal.

Still, it is helpful if one is so inclined, as it creates a tranquility of mind that at its zenith is the closest mundane *citta* get to the transcendental *citta*.

Jhāna has five levels in the *fine-material (form) realm* and four levels in the *formless* realm. If a practitioner has established mastery in *jhāna* and maintained mastery, then on physical death, the rebirth linking consciousness can be *jhanic* rather than normal, and their next existence will be in the highest realm they achieved mastery in.

Those that achieve mastery in the *formless realms* can be reborn in these strange solipsistic places. Here, there is only mind. No vision nor hearing. There are no concepts that rely on materiality; space and extent only apply to the first realm, and here it is empty space. Even *being* only applies to the first realm; beyond this mind is not limited by being, all beings are one and none. Beyond the second *formless realm*, descriptive language loses meaning. The third realm is that of *nothingness*, while the most abstract is known only as *neither perception nor non-perception*.

There is even a realm where awareness enters temporal stasis and consciousness is frozen for mind-blowing periods of real time. Those who master seeking true oblivion get the best *Conditional Reality* can offer and can suspend themselves beyond the extinction of this universe only to return to *Saṃsāra* in some new and distant universe.

OBJECT

If developed, *jhāna* can bestow certain psychic or magical abilities (*abhiññā*). However, this is generally not recommended, as it often leads to disastrous *karma*.

Jhāna is still a *normal* awareness, even if it a highly developed one. It can be developed without regard to moral training and can offer a shelter to a mind that might be rightly troubled because of shoddy behaviour. It can lead to powers and abilities that can be used unwisely but is, thankfully, remarkably difficult to develop to any degree of mastery.

In *jhanic* awareness, the *citta* remains the same type; however, it *takes* a part of itself as an object, thereby breaking its normal function and behaviour.

It is said that the *citta* that becomes transcendental (path and fruit *citta*) take Nirvāṇa as their objects. These *cittas* operates with three *roots* functioning as a single unit: non-hatred (*adosa*), non-greed (*aloha*), and non-delusion (*amoha*), which enable the leap into transcendental awareness.

And what is transcendental awareness? This is an awareness that lacks any inner regard towards a permanent and lasting self. With this, all anxiety, fear, guilt, shame, worry, hate, jealousy, lust, envy and delusion is eradicated, and the sympathetic tone collapses, the heart rate slows, and the skin takes on a reddish/blue colour.

In a *Buddha*, there is only really this type of awareness, unless they are speaking, then they will use *functional citta*. An *Arahant* experiences this as a single moment and as resultant fruition moments, but they still have *residues* which differentiates them from a *Buddha*.

Jhanic experience is helpful, but advanced development is not essential to the path, so don't stress if you find tranquility meditation difficult.

In conclusion, the journey through *jhanic* states represents a profound exploration of consciousness itself. While these states offer extraordinary experiences and insights, they are ultimately tools on the path to awakening rather than the destination itself. The true goal remains the liberation from suffering through the realisation of the ultimate truth, whether achieved through *jhanic* mastery or other means of practice.

Study Guide: Different Worlds And Jhāna

This chapter explores consciousness beyond physical reality, examining jhanic states and their relationship to spiritual development. It focuses on how consciousness can become self-sustaining, forming the basis for meditative experiences and heavenly realms.

CORE CONCEPTS

- *Consciousness beyond physical form*
- *Nature of jhanic states and consciousness*
- *Relationship between meditation and heavenly realms*
- *Progressive development through practice*
- *Self-sustaining awareness patterns*

NEW TERMINOLOGY

Abhiññā: *Higher psychic powers*

Bhavaṅga: *Life continuum maintaining mental continuity*

Fine Material Realms: *First five jhanic states with form-based experiences*

Formless Realms: *Four highest jhanic states transcending material form*

Kundalini: *Spiritual energy at spine base*

Pīti: *Rapture*

Sobhana cetasikas: *Beautiful mental factors*

Sukha: *Bliss*

Vyāpāda: *Ill-will*

MAIN THEMES

1. Consciousness Beyond Physical Form

- *Self-sustaining awareness patterns*
- *Relationship to heavenly realms*
- *Nature of consciousness beyond ordinary reality*

2. Jhanic Consciousness

- *Visual, sound, and mind consciousness types*
- *Natural occurrence in daily activities*
- *Progressive development through practice*

3. Realm Categories

- *Fine material realms (5 levels)*
- *Formless realms (4 levels)*
- *Relationship to spiritual development*

PRACTICAL APPLICATIONS

- *Meditation practice development*
- *Relationship to spiritual growth*
- *Role in moral development*
- *Integration with daily activities*

INTEGRATION POINTS

- *Connection to enlightenment understanding*
- *Foundation for path consciousness*
- *Relationship to subtle fetters*
- *Links to realms of existence*

COMMON MISCONCEPTIONS

- *Jhāna as end goal rather than tool*
- *Necessity of advanced development in jhāna*
- *Role of physical manifestations*

REFLECTION QUESTIONS

OBJECT

- What is your experience with meditative absorption?
- How do you understand the relationship between concentration and insight?
- How do you relate to transcendent states?
- What role does tranquility play in your practice?

PROGRESS INDICATORS

- Development of concentration abilities
- Increased awareness of subtle mental states
- Growing stability in meditation
- Natural occurrence of jhanic states in daily life

Jhanic Realms

Realm Type	Levels	Key Features
Fine Material (Form)	5	Form-based experiences
Formless	4	Beyond material form

Nigredo

"In order to understand, I destroyed myself."

- *The Book of Disquiet*, Fernando Pessoa.

OBJECT

31. Path Consciousness

"The secret of alchemy is this: there is a way of manipulating matter and energy so as to produce what modern scientists call a 'field of force'. This field acts on the observer and puts him in a privileged position vis-à-vis the universe." [42]

Path consciousness represents a pivotal moment in spiritual awakening where the mind directly experiences nibbāna. This chapter explores the nature of these transformative states of consciousness, examining how they arise, their relationship to the stages of enlightenment, and the conditions necessary for their emergence. We'll investigate the different types of consciousness involved in spiritual breakthrough and understand why these experiences cannot be forced but must arise naturally through proper cultivation of mind.

In truth, when we say path consciousness, we mean a type of *citta* (consciousness or mind-state) that has taken *nibbāna* as its object. For one situated in *nibbāna*, awareness transcends *consciousness*, and whilst *cittas* still arise in the *Arahant* (fully enlightened being), they lack any karmic potential and are simply part of the enlightened awareness.

The *citta* that *takes nibbāna* must be a triple-*rooted wholesome* consciousness with all of the beautiful mental factors (*sobhana cetasikas*) and wisdom (*paññā*). One cannot expect to deliberately cultivate path consciousness if one's mind is fixed on gain or profit. Indeed, the sacrifices one makes to find and walk the path must be without condition.

---

[42] Fulcanelli, as quoted in Jacques Bergier's *Morning of the Magicians* (1963)

For the *Sotāpanna*, or stream-enterer, just prior to realisation they experience a *citta* called *change of lineage* (*gotrabhū*). This is the point they let go of worldly concepts about self and make a commitment towards the unknown. This is not something one decides, but often manifests as a profound and frequently unrecognised inner conflict that can bring great despair and hopelessness.

As we know, there are four path moments, each followed by two fruition moments in two-rooted individuals or three path moments in those with three *roots*.

The path moment (*magga-citta*) is when the fetters (*saṃyojana*) are broken. For the first three fetters, this might be the last of the three, meaning there might have been growing doubt before this point. The first three fetters are broken with the first path moment. The next two fetters are weakened but not broken by the second path moment. At the third path moment, the fourth and fifth fetters are broken, which means for the *Anāgāmī* (non-returner), they have cut the first five fetters and eliminated sensuous plane rebirth.

The fourth and final path moment is the point where all fetters, the first five gross fetters and the last five subtle fetters, are broken.

Each path moment is therefore an *aha* moment of increasing fundamental depth.

The *cittas* that follow this *aha* moment embody the implications of this new perspective. These implications invariably liberate the individual from attachments that cause suffering. These fruit moments (*phala-citta*) are therefore deeply calming and can be relived by the disciple at will with minimal training.

The fruit *cittas* are *resultant consciousnesses* that act as new grounds of being for the disciple. This is the lowest reference point of any self. As each offers liberating wisdom, it tends to soothe and calm the disciple.

There are, as we have learned, four path *cittas* and four fruit *cittas*.

These *cittas* are still mundane, but are classed as *jhāna* due to their self-sustaining nature; each *citta* is triple-*rooted* and *wholesome*.

Even a disciple with modest skill in *jhāna* is considered to have experienced an equivalent state if they attain path consciousness.

Object

Those who have established *jhanic* practice might, if their mastery is sufficient, experience path moments at deeper levels of *jhāna*, second through to fifth.

This means there are forty types of these *cittas* that all take *nibbāna* as their object. Four stages each with a path and fruit consciousness—eight types, each of five levels of possible *jhāna*.

The most important aspect in developing the conditions is the cultivation of the beautiful mental factors and wisdom, which provides the *citta* with the conditions necessary to take *nibbāna* as its object.

You cannot force enlightenment, only create the conditions for its arising.

In conclusion, the path to enlightenment unfolds naturally when the right conditions are present. Like a lotus flower emerging from muddy waters, the mind gradually purifies itself through understanding and letting go. The journey through the various stages of enlightenment is not a matter of willpower but of allowing wisdom to arise through the cultivation of *wholesome* states and the gradual dissolution of the fetters that bind us to suffering.

Study Guide: Path Consciousness

Path consciousness represents a transformative state where mind directly experiences nibbāna, marking crucial moments in spiritual awakening.

CORE CONCEPTS

- Path consciousness as transcendent awareness taking nibbāna as object
- Breaking of fetters through insight
- Role of beautiful mental factors
- Natural progression of awakening

NEW TERMINOLOGY

Citta: Point of consciousness or mind-state

Dvihetuka-puggala: Person with double-rooted consciousness

Gotrabhū-citta: Change of lineage consciousness

Magga-citta: Path consciousness that takes nibbāna as its object

Nibbāna: The ultimate goal of Buddhist practice; complete liberation

Paññā: Wisdom

Phala-citta: Fruition consciousness following path moments

Saṃyojana: The ten fetters binding beings to saṃsāra

Sobhana cetasikas: Beautiful mental factors

Tihetuka-puggala: Person with triple-rooted consciousness

Nigredo

Main Themes

1. Nature of Path Consciousness
- Definition and characteristics of magga-citta
- Relationship to nibbāna
- Role of beautiful mental factors
- Connection to enlightenment

2. Stages of Transformation
- Change of lineage consciousness
- Path and fruition moments
- Breaking of fetters
- Links to Shadow work

3. Conditions for Awakening
- Triple-rooted consciousness
- Beautiful mental factors
- Role of wisdom
- Connection to symbols and meanings

Integration Points
- Links to Sotāpanna
- Foundation for Sakadāgāmī
- Preparation for Anāgāmī
- Connection to Arahant

Common Misconceptions
- Forcing enlightenment through willpower
- Confusing mundane jhāna with path consciousness
- Expecting immediate results
- Overlooking importance of beautiful mental factors
- Seeking experiences rather than understanding

Reflection Questions
- How do you understand the relationship between ordinary and transcendent consciousness?
- What conditions support spiritual breakthrough in your experience?
- How do you relate to the concept of irreversible transformation?
- What role does preparation play in spiritual development?

Progress Indicators
- Observable signs of development through path moments
- Breaking of fetters at different stages
- Development of beautiful mental factors
- Natural unfolding of wisdom

Key Passages
- The path requires unconditional sacrifice
- Enlightenment cannot be forced; one can only cultivate the necessary conditions.
- Like a lotus emerging from muddy waters, the mind naturally purifies

OBJECT

The Rebis

THE SHADOW
The unseen, repressed self. That which is denied does not disappear—it waits in darkness. The shadow is the hidden fears, the buried desires, the unintegrated parts of the self. To reject it is to remain ruled by it.

THE REBIS (THE ALCHEMIST)
The integrated being—the union of all opposites. The alchemist stands at the centre, embodying balance, wholeness, and self-mastery. No longer bound by division, they hold within them all aspects of the self, neither rejecting nor clinging.

THE INFANT
The beginning of self-awareness. Innocence, curiosity, and unshaped potential. The child sees the world without filters, yet they do not understand themselves. They hold the mirror of perception, but the reflection is not yet clear.

THE SHEPHERD
The guardian of the natural order. Care, connection, and harmony. The shepherd represents guidance and protection, but without strength, they risk becoming passive, unable to hold boundaries.

THE OLD MAN
The wisdom of experience. Knowledge, reflection, and foresight. The old man sees beyond the moment, but wisdom alone is not enough—without action, knowing becomes stagnation.

THE WARRIOR
The disciplined force of will. Strength, aggression, and survival. The warrior represents the ability to act, to fight, and to endure. Without wisdom, they become violent. Without strength, they become powerless.

THE KING (EGOTIC FANTASY)
The illusion of control. Power, status, and the seduction of the self-image. The king is authority and dominion, yet they are bound by their own reflection—mistaking their persona for their being.

The alchemist is not a single self but a synthesis of many. To awaken is not to reject, but to integrate—to take up all that has been cast aside and see it for what it is. The self is not one, nor many, but the reconciliation of all that has ever been.

Nigredo

The Sotāpanna or Stream-Enterer

"Bhikkhus, suppose that this great ocean were to become utterly full of corpses so that there would be no room for the fish and turtles, for the crocodiles and porpoises, for the sharks and other creatures that live in the water. What do you think, bhikkhus, would that great ocean be disturbed because of that?"

"Yes, venerable sir."

"So too, bhikkhus, when a noble disciple has abandoned the three fetters, he has cut off the lower fetters, has ended up in the plane of misery, the bad destinations, the lower realms, in hell. He is incapable of committing the six great wrongs. He is incapable of taking life; he is incapable of taking what is not given; he is incapable of sexual misconduct; he is incapable of false speech; he is incapable of malicious speech; he is incapable of harsh speech."

— *Saṃyutta Nikāya* 12.68

OBJECT

32. Sotāpanna

"The path of spiritual evolution is a progressive unlearning of fear and the acceptance of love." [43]

The Sotāpanna represents a crucial milestone on the spiritual path — the first taste of genuine enlightenment. This chapter explores how breaking through three fundamental illusions (fetters) leads to an irreversible transformation in consciousness. We'll examine the different paths through which this realisation occurs, its documented effects, and what it means both practically and spiritually for the aspiring alchemist. Understanding this stage is essential, as it marks the point where theoretical knowledge transforms into direct experiential wisdom. The Sotāpanna is the name of the being who experiences the first stage of enlightenment.

D o not be put off by how vague *enlightenment* may seem. It is not only very real but documented to the exact mind moment it happens in Buddhism, and I am not kidding. There are many systems that have evolved to explain this phenomenon. Most are somewhat obscured by devotional themes, which can complicate its message.

Enlightenment is a process where the mind realises a number of fundamental truths.

---

[43] Williamson, M. (1992). *A Return to Love: Reflections on the Principles of "A Course in Miracles"*. HarperCollins, p. 24.

These *truths* are so fundamental that once realised, they are so obviously true that one's entire perspective changes relative to those who have yet to realise these truths.

These *truths* are obscured by what are called *fetters* (saṃyojana in Pāli).

A fetter is an illusion. An illusion is something that *fools* the mind or senses. Often, we can only see the illusion with a change of perspective. It is abrupt changes of perspective, say in sudden mental trauma or Zen Buddhism, that can give one the opportunity to see these fetters.

Once you have seen something is an illusion, you now know it's illusory. So, once you realise or *cut* the fetters it cannot be undone — enlightenment is a one-way trip!

One becomes a *Sotāpanna* when one cuts (realises) the first three of ten fetters. It is said one is drawn towards either *anicca* (impermanence), *śūnyatā* (emptiness) or *dukkha* (suffering) as a focal point, and this quality is examined until it causes a *loosening* of mental ideology.

So, the individual who is to become *Sotāpanna* notices either emptiness, impermanence or suffering as a fundamental truth, and through this conviction can see the first three fetters that bind one to eternal incarnations.

For example, the first fetter is called *personality view* (sakkāya-diṭṭhi).

One type of *Sotāpanna* might have seen that there is nothing that is distinctly personal in one's self-identity; we are utterly relational beings and thus notices emptiness of self in things.

Another might recognise that nothing is stable in life; definitions can only operate out of a past and not a present. Here one recognises the fundamental quality of impermanence.

The last might recognise the universality of suffering. Often this path might involve considerable despair and hopelessness. But once suffering is truly seen as universal, it loses contrast as *all* becomes suffering.

Sotāpanna means stream winner or stream enterer.

One *enters* the stream of consciousness when one learns to detach one's identity from it. One recognises the delusional idea that a *self* dwells within; any self is simply a perspective of the now. One sees one's behaviours, attitudes, reactions, ideals and everything as merely conditions of circumstance and lacking anything that uniquely identifies a *me*.

I suspect there are those who realise the first two fetters of *personality view* and *attachment to rites and rituals* (*sīlabbataparāmāsa*) — addiction or even destitution might be enough, but without realising the third fetter they remain kind of lost — halfway between 'normality' and enlightenment. I suspect a sizeable fraction of mental illness might be accountable to this phenomenon.

The *Sotāpanna* has realised the first three fetters, and the moment this happens they undergo what is called a *change of lineage* (*gotrabhū*). Now, part of me wants to play this down, rationalise it, yet, in truth it is a remarkable moment.

From this point on, the individual has cut away part of what binds them to *saṃsāra* (cycles of rebirth). Such is the transformation and weakening of the fetters through achieving *Sotāpanna* that the individual can no longer suffer unfortunate rebirth, and in no more than seven rebirths they will achieve full enlightenment. Now whilst this sounds improbable, I will show you in time that the *maths* indeed work out. The problem is we need to cover quite a bit of work until you can understand *how* this can be true.

You cannot not notice the moment when this change of lineage happens, although you could easily equate it with a stroke or particularly mind-blowing drug experience. In fact, I think both *jhāna* (meditative absorption) and transcendental breakthroughs might well occur during psychedelic drug use, leaving confused and seemingly broken people afterwards if not recognised.

The term *Sotāpanna* is from the Buddhist scriptures, and I think it is important to mention here I feel that the third fetter, *vicikicchā* (sceptical doubt), which is essentially the loss of doubt in the scripture, can pertain to any effective method of enlightenment — i.e. here, this is the point of our leap of faith — but this faith need not be in Buddhism, but rather in the existence of a path, regardless of who described it.

There is a distinct process that takes one from normal consciousness towards the transcendental. The *Sotāpanna* makes the break towards and tastes for a single mind moment a milder version of transcendental consciousness. Although at this stage it is the weakest, its effect is profound, and for two or three moments of awareness one experiences the resultant awareness of these insights.

Change of lineage pertains to the lineages of a normal and enlightened person.

The lineage of a normal person is bound by *fate*. They believe they are a conditioned thing in a world of conditionality. In insisting that they exercise *free will*, they become bound by it. Again, whilst these comments may sound glib and farcical, the maths really does check out, and I hope you stay with me long enough for me to try to prove it!

Once one *becomes Sotāpanna* one has loosened one's ties with fate (*karma*), although generally you wouldn't know this at the time.

The single experience of a mild transcendental awareness and its resultant awareness acts as a refuge for future experience. This provides a detached perspective that was previously absent. This detachment cuts one's ties with things that previously might have been important.

Clearly, you can appreciate how confusing this might be if it happens almost accidentally through drug use or mental illness. One has metaphorically died toward one's old life, and this can be both distressing and confusing.

The weakening of attachment allows one to notice acts of greed or hatred and these become increasingly intolerable. There is a natural inclination to reducing one's *unwholesome karma* through a distinct awareness of consequence.

For some, the moment of realisation comes after a particularly difficult period called the *Dark Night of the Soul*. Here, doubt in conditioned reality plagues the individual, who lacking faith is often in a tussle between mind and heart.

This is a course about alchemy. I can write about my understanding and bring in concepts already largely developed. This means that whilst the *Sotāpanna* might mean the first grade of Buddhist enlightenment, it describes a real phenomenon that is independent of whatever system describes it.

So, in alchemy, on achieving *Sotāpanna* the alchemist has merely identified the raw substance which now will need processing. To get to this stage requires faith and the development of what is called the *faculty of I will know the unknown*.

With the dissolution of *personality view*, the alchemist who achieves *Sotāpanna* has found that all within is dark, unworked and unsatisfactory. It can be a dark time as one recognises one's part in one's own suffering, and the utter helplessness of this situation is largely that which gives the *Dark Night* its bite.

Now the alchemist must work with this raw material — eventually reducing subjective experience to categories or *skandhas* (heaps) of phenomena. This involves developing understanding of *karma* through a new perspective, which now develops as the *mind* or *dharma eye*.

A certain shift in orientation occurs, and towards the end of *Sotāpanna*, a choice emerges. This will be explored in the next chapter.

The journey of the *Sotāpanna* is thus both profound and challenging, marking the beginning of an irreversible transformation. Like an alchemist who has discovered the *prima materia* (the alchemical first matter), the *Sotāpanna* has found the essential substance needed for the *Great Work*. This discovery, though initially unsettling, opens the door to deeper understanding and eventual liberation. The path ahead requires patience, wisdom, and unwavering dedication as one continues to dissolve the remaining fetters that bind consciousness to the wheel of existence.

Citta involved in Enlightenment

Type of Consciousness	Characteristics	Function
Path (magga-citta)	Takes nibbāna as object	Breaks the fetters binding consciousness.
Fruit (phala-citta)	Resultant consciousness	Establishes new ground of being
Change of lineage	Transitional state	Shifts worldly to transcendent

Enlightenment by Fetters

Stage	Fetters Realised	Path Moments	Fruit Moments
Stream-entry	The first three gross fetters	1	2-3
Once-returner	Remaining 2 gross weakened	1	2-3
Non-returner	All 5 gross	1	2-3
Arahant	All	1	2-3

NIGREDO

First Three Gross Fetters

Fetter	Nature	Effect of breaking the fetter
Personality view	Self-identity illusion	Recognition of emptiness
Ritual attachment	Dependence on forms	Freedom from rigid patterns
Skeptical doubt	Uncertainty about path	Confidence in practice

Study Guide: Sotāpanna

This chapter explores the first stage of enlightenment, examining how breaking three fundamental fetters leads to an irreversible transformation in consciousness. It details the paths through which this realisation occurs and its implications for spiritual development.

CORE CONCEPTS
- *Reality of enlightenment as documented process*
- *Breaking of first three fetters*
- *Change of lineage experience*
- *Stream entry phenomenon*
- *Dark Night experience*

NEW TERMINOLOGY

Anicca: *Impermanence*

Dukkha: *Suffering*

Gotrabhū: *Change of lineage (moment of transition in consciousness)*

Sakkāya-diṭṭhi: *Personality view fetter*

Saṃyojana: *Fetters binding beings to saṃsāra*

Sīlabbataparāmāsa: *Attachment to rites and rituals*

Śūnyatā: *Emptiness*

Vicikicchā: *Skeptical doubt*

MAIN THEMES

1. Nature of Enlightenment
- *Reality of enlightenment*
- *Role of fundamental truths*
- *Connection to fetter system*

2. Three Paths
- *Impermanence recognition*
- *Emptiness realisation*
- *Suffering understanding*

3. Transformation Process
- *Breaking of first three fetters*
- *Change of lineage experience*
- *Stream entry phenomenon*

TECHNICAL FRAMEWORK
- *Consciousness transformation*
- *Recognition of stream entry*
- *Shift in perspective*
- *Natural ethical development*

PRACTICAL APPLICATIONS

OBJECT

- *Regular meditation focusing on impermanence*
- *Self-observation of attachment patterns*
- *Mindful awareness of daily activities*
- *Study of Buddhist texts*
- *Regular reflection on three fundamental paths*

INTEGRATION POINTS

- *Connection to Dark Night of the Soul*
- *Links to Shadow Work*
- *Relationship to Symbols and Meanings*
- *Connection to Fable of Alchemy*

COMMON MISCONCEPTIONS

- *Distinguishing genuine insight from intellectual understanding*
- *Managing Dark Night experience*
- *Integrating new perspectives*

- *Maintaining practice momentum*
- *Balancing spiritual practice with worldly responsibilities*

REFLECTION QUESTIONS

- *How do you understand stream-entry?*
- *What is your experience with seeing through fundamental illusions?*
- *How do you relate to the three fetters described?*
- *What role does doubt play in your spiritual practice?*

PROGRESS INDICATORS

- *Detachment from self-view*
- *Natural moral inclination*
- *Reduced doubt in practice*
- *Enhanced awareness*
- *Karmic skill development*

Nigredo

The Sakadāgāmi or Once-Returner

A Sakadāgāmi has not only eradicated the first three fetters but has also significantly weakened the fetters of sensual desire and ill will. Such a person is destined to return to the human realm at most one more time before attaining enlightenment.

"With the fading away of passion and aversion, he enters and dwells in the second jhāna... If he is one who returns once, he makes an end of suffering on returning once more to this world."

– Saṃyutta Nikāya 12.70

OBJECT

33. Sakadāgāmī

"The way of the sage is to act but not to compete." [44]

The journey from initial spiritual awakening to deeper realisation is marked by distinct stages of transformation. This chapter explores Sakadāgāmī, the second stage of enlightenment, where the practitioner becomes a "once-returner" — one who will achieve full enlightenment in no more than one more lifetime. We examine how the initial insights of the Sotāpanna mature into a profound commitment to the spiritual path, resulting in naturally diminished sensual desire and ill-will. Through understanding this stage, we gain insight into how spiritual realisation progressively deepens and transforms the individual's relationship with conditioned existence.

Sakadāgāmī is the name of a being who has achieved the second stage of enlightenment in the Theravāda Buddhist tradition. This stage follows the attainment of *Sotāpanna* (Stream-Enterer) and arises after a deliberate choice or decision, rooted in an increasing awareness of the law of *karma* (cause and effect).

The *Sotāpanna* has awakened to three fundamental truths, which are:

> 1. There is no enduring self or *personality*; instead, there is only behaviour that is conditioned and reflexive (*anicca*).

---

[44] Lao Tzu, Tao Te Ching, Chapter 81. Translation by D.C. Lau (1963). Penguin Classics.

2. Moral virtue cannot be achieved through mere actions; one must embody intrinsic goodness (*sīla*).

3. There exists a path out of the cycle of conditionality and suffering (*dukkha*), which requires a leap of faith in the teachings of the Buddha (*saddhā*).

With the breakthrough to *Sotāpanna*, a new perspective emerges, often referred to as the *mind's eye* or *dharma eye* (*dhammacakkhu*). This perspective is based on a single moment of mild transcendental awareness, followed by two or three moments of *resultant consciousness*. Although this experience occurs in a fraction of a second, it plants a seed in the mind that, even if neglected, gradually broadens moral perspective and makes spontaneous acts of hatred impossible.

It is important to note that while the term *Sotāpanna* is rooted in Buddhist teachings, the state it describes is an actual existential transformation. Many individuals may undergo such an awakening without fully understanding what has occurred, leading to confusion and a sense of isolation.

Although the process of enlightenment is said to culminate within seven lifetimes for a *Sotāpanna*, the initial years can be challenging. This transformation is akin to a metaphorical death and rebirth. The values and attachments of the unenlightened state are drastically altered, which can lead to confusion and depression. Attempts at *recovery*, implying a return to the previous state, are often futile, as the entire direction of the being has shifted. This vulnerability can make individuals susceptible to excessive religiosity or exploitation.

The *Sotāpanna* experiences an increasing divide between their former self and their emerging enlightened state. This manifests as a choice: to either return to and embrace *normality* or to follow their heart and delve deeper into the spiritual journey. This pivotal decision, reminiscent of the *red and blue pill metaphor*, leads to the next breakthrough.

Those *Sotāpanna* who are deeply conflicted between *normality* and the unknown often endure what is termed the *Dark Night of the Spirit*. This phase begins with the choice and culminates in the next stage, known as *The Crucifixion*. It is a period marked by depressive symptoms intertwined with spiritual themes.

Object

Sakadāgāmī, meaning *once-returner*, signifies a being who will achieve full enlightenment in this life or, at most, one more earthly existence. The term *returner* refers to re-entering the plane of sensual consciousness, i.e., normal human existence. This stage represents a significant increase in spiritual resolve and commitment. Once the *Sotāpanna* decides that pursuing enlightenment is the paramount goal of their existence, they move toward the realisation that defines the *Sakadāgāmī*.

Before this commitment, the *Sotāpanna* still grapples with sensual desire, anger, ill-will, and delusion. While they have eliminated the first three fetters (*personality*, *doubt*, and *attachment to rites and rituals*), they remain bound by the others. Upon making this commitment, they become acutely aware of the unsatisfactoriness of anger and greed. Although they are still tempted, these tendencies are significantly diminished compared to their pre-commitment state.

This commitment enables them to focus entirely on overcoming the spiritual obstacles of attachment, ill-will, and delusion. Consequently, the fourth and fifth fetters —*sensory desire* and *ill-will*—are weakened, though not entirely eradicated. A genuine inner resolve to elevate one's moral conduct facilitates this weakening.

While the commitment itself cannot guarantee enlightenment, it sets the individual on a trajectory toward realisation. This realisation often arises from a profound insight into the emptiness (*suññatā*), impermanence (*anicca*), and suffering (*dukkha*) inherent in conditioned reality. Such an insight validates one's spiritual inclinations, reinvigorating and deepening their dedication to the path. In alchemical terms, this is akin to gradually *turning up the heat*.

The *Sakadāgāmī* is imbued with resolve, marking the point where the darkness of *Nigredo* (a term borrowed from alchemy symbolising the initial stage of transformation) begins to lighten. With growing detachment, the *Sakadāgāmī* becomes increasingly aware of the intricate workings of *karma* and naturally adopts *wholesome* actions. They disdain violence but may still wrestle with personal feelings of reactive ill-will and greed.

This gradual and intuitive understanding of *karma* trains the individual to act as a dampener of karmic consequences. They become increasingly peaceful, promoting harmony in their interactions. As the metaphorical stone lightens and transitions from *Nigredo* to *Albedo* (symbolising purification), they begin to emerge as natural healers.

This transformative journey will be further explored in the next chapter.

The journey of the *Sakadāgāmī* is a testament to the transformative power of spiritual commitment and insight. It is a path marked by challenges and profound realisations, where each step forward brings greater clarity and peace. As the *Sakadāgāmī* continues to weaken the fetters that bind them to the cycle of suffering, they inspire others through their growing wisdom and compassion. This stage of enlightenment is not merely an individual achievement but a beacon of hope, illustrating the potential for all beings to transcend the limitations of conditioned existence and move closer to ultimate liberation.

The Three Marks of Existence

Path	Focus	Realisation
Anicca	Impermanence	Nothing stable exists
Śūnyatā	Emptiness	No inherent self
Dukkha	Suffering	Universal unsatisfactoriness

Study Guide: Sakadagāmī

The second stage of Buddhist enlightenment (Sakadāgāmī) represents the progression from initial awakening to deeper spiritual transformation, marked by weakened mental fetters and enhanced karmic understanding.

Core Concepts

- *Three fundamental realisations of Sotāpanna: no-self, true virtue, liberation possibility*
- *Development of dharma eye and commitment deepening*

OBJECT

- Progressive weakening of sensual desire and ill-will
- Enhanced understanding of karma and natural virtue

NEW TERMINOLOGY

Dhammacakkhu: The eye of dharma, representing spiritual insight

Saddhā: Faith or confidence in Buddha's teachings

Suññatā: Emptiness or voidness in Buddhist philosophy

MAIN THEMES

1. Nature of Transformation
- Progression from Sotāpanna realisation
- Development of dharma eye
- Transition through Dark Night
- Connection to Dark Night of the Soul

2. Characteristics of Attainment
- Weakening of sensual desire and ill-will
- Natural development of virtue
- Enhanced karmic understanding
- Links to The Shadow

3. Practical Implications
- Reduced reactivity to stimuli
- Natural healing presence
- Community influence
- Connection to Call to Adventure

4. Stages of Transformation
- Dark Night period
- Initial breakthrough
- Sakadāgāmī realisation

PRACTICAL APPLICATIONS
- Sequential study approach
- Daily life observation
- Journal keeping
- Group discussion
- Regular reflection

INTEGRATION POINTS
- Connection to Dark Night of the Soul
- Links to The Shadow concept
- Relationship to Call to Adventure
- Progression toward Anāgāmī stage

COMMON MISCONCEPTIONS
- Recovery means returning to previous state
- Commitment guarantees enlightenment
- Transformation happens instantly
- Process requires religious framework

REFLECTION QUESTIONS
- Understanding of weakening sensual desire and ill-will
- Changes in relationship to sense pleasures
- Evolution of path commitment
- Role of ethics in practice

PROGRESS INDICATORS
- Reduced reactivity to sensual stimuli
- Decreased anger and aversion
- Natural inclination toward wholesome action
- Enhanced community impact

NIGREDO

The Anāgāmi or Non-Returner

An Anāgāmi has completely eradicated the first five fetters, including sensual desire and ill will. After death, an Anāgāmi is reborn in the Pure Abodes, where they attain final Nibbāna without returning to the human realm.
"With the abandoning of pleasure and pain... he enters and dwells in the fourth jhāna... If he is one who does not return, he makes an end of suffering in that very state."

– Saṃyutta Nikāya 12.70

OBJECT

34. Anāgāmī

*"When you make the two one,
and when you make the inner as the outer and the outer as the inner...
then shall you enter the Kingdom."* [45]

The Anāgāmī represents a profound milestone on the spiritual path — the third grade of enlightenment where sensory attachments and ill-will are completely transcended. This chapter explores how this state manifests as natural healing abilities and karmic mastery, while examining its parallels to the alchemical Albedo phase. We'll investigate how the Anāgāmī's consciousness transforms from individual seeker to universal healer, and why this stage represents a critical choice point between contentment and further spiritual development.

The *Anāgāmī* is the name of a being who has realised the third grade of enlightenment. While this is a Buddhist term, one assumes they describe a real phenomenon through the lens of Buddhism. The *Anāgāmī* is the equivalent stage of *Albedo* or the whitening of the stone in alchemical tradition. The *stone* represents the *Subjective Reality* of the alchemist, which has deviated from normal fate and now has *mastered* sensory-based *karma*.

Anāgāmī means *non-returner* — what does this mean? The mind of the *Anāgāmī* no longer clings to sensory experience, nor will ill-will arise spontaneously. With the breakthrough into the third level of transcendental experience (known as the third

---

[45] *The Gospel of Thomas, Saying 22.* In Meyer, M. (2007). *The Nag Hammadi Scriptures.* HarperOne.

stage of enlightenment or *Sakadāgāmī*), the mind completely liberates itself from all of the gross (first five) fetters. At a fundamental level, the mind of the *Anāgāmī* will never cling enough to sensory-based desire (or ill will) to permit rebirth in the sensory realm. They have cut away the gross fetters which bind them to this part of *saṃsāra* and will never return to the earthly realm.

The *Anāgāmī* realises that attachment to sensory phenomena and ill-will are tiresome distractions and, having made a resolve to work on refraining from such mental states, tends to become both benevolent and healing. No longer operating out of a sense of selfness and eager to settle the troubled minds of others, they become natural healers. They do this through restoring balance, by acting to dampen karmic forces. They tend to absorb *unwholesome karma* directed at them through wisdom, compassion and understanding, whilst themselves being natural beacons of wisdom and calmness.

In alchemy, we learn that at the state of whiteness, the stone is capable of turning base metals into *silver*. We are halfway there, and now the stone displays magical, transformative properties. *Silver*, in alchemy, is a reference to the moon. The moon creates cycles, evident both astrologically and biologically. It is the lesser light of the firmament.

So, the stone, or *Subjective Reality* of the alchemist at *Albedo*, is one that restores harmony and balance. It heals, not through any positive influence, but more through an elimination of what causes imbalance. Through wisdom, insight and earthly detachment, the *Anāgāmī* is able to naturally heal and restore balance.

For many, this is the ceiling of their earthly journey. There really is no need to seek further unless one is driven by a greater goal. The *Anāgāmī* will, upon earthly death, be reborn in a fairly exclusive region of the mental heavens, where they will achieve full realisation.

However, if they wish to pursue the path, this is when the real *inner* work is set to begin. Generally, at this stage, the material life of the *Anāgāmī* is approximating their spiritual life. Things make sense, and their understanding of *karma* tends to create relative success and fortune. Some are more than content supporting a family or community with their wisdom and providence.

Object

In alchemy, this is the stage of multiplication — an integration between the personal, often solitary existence of the once hermit with their social environment. Such an individual has found deep peace and will find genuine enjoyment in helping others face the challenges of life.

There might arise at some later time, maybe even shortly before the physical death of the *Anāgāmī*, a certain restlessness with the status quo, and once again they might look deeper into conditioned reality.

This journey of the *Anāgāmī* represents a profound transformation in consciousness, where the boundaries between the spiritual and material worlds begin to dissolve. Like the alchemical process of turning base metals to silver, the *Anāgāmī's* presence transmutes the suffering of others into wisdom and peace. Their path illuminates the possibility of transcending earthly attachments while remaining deeply engaged in the healing of the world, much like the moon's gentle light that guides travellers through darkness.

Study Guide: Anāgāmī

The third stage of enlightenment (Anāgāmī) represents transcendence of sensory attachments and ill-will, paralleling the alchemical Albedo phase and manifesting as healing abilities and karmic mastery.

Core Concepts

- Complete liberation from sensory attachments and gross fetters
- Natural development of healing capacity through karmic dampening
- Alchemical transformation symbolised by base metals to silver
- Integration of spiritual and material existence
- Choice between contentment and further spiritual progress

New Terminology

Albedo: *Alchemical whitening phase corresponding to Anāgāmī state*

Anāgāmī: *Third grade of enlightenment, meaning "non-returner"*

Gross fetters: *First five fetters binding to sensory realm*

Karmic dampening: *Process of absorbing and neutralising unwholesome karma*

Multiplication: *Integration stage between personal and social existence*

Main Themes

- Transcendence and Liberation
- Healing and Restoration
- Alchemical Transformation
- Material—Spiritual Integration

NIGREDO

- Karmic Mastery

PRACTICAL APPLICATIONS

- Natural healing through wisdom and compassion
- Restoration of balance in communities
- Integration of spiritual wisdom in daily life
- Service to others through karmic understanding
- Transformation of suffering into wisdom

INTEGRATION POINTS

- Connection to Sakadāgāmī (Chapter 33)
- Foundation for Arahant (Chapter 36)
- Relationship to Path Consciousness (Chapter 31)
- Links to Subtle Fetters (Chapter 35)
- Connection to Symbols and Meanings (Chapter 4)

COMMON MISCONCEPTIONS

- Need for further progress beyond Anāgāmī state
- Nature of healing abilities
- Relationship between spiritual and material life
- Role of sensory detachment
- Purpose of karmic dampening

REFLECTION QUESTIONS

- How does sensory detachment manifest in daily life?
- What is the role of healing in Anāgāmī's interactions?
- How does detachment influence worldly responsibilities?
- What is the significance of the base metals to silver metaphor?
- What factors influence further spiritual development choices?

PROGRESS INDICATORS

- Absence of sensory attachments
- Natural healing abilities
- Karmic mastery
- Integration of spiritual-material existence
- Service to community

OBJECT

35. The Subtle Fetters

> *"Only by discovering alchemy have I clearly understood that the Unconscious is a process and that ego's rapport with the Unconscious and its contents initiate an evolution, more precisely, a real metamorphosis of the psyche."* [46]

The subtle fetters represent the final and most refined obstacles on the path to complete enlightenment. While an Anāgāmī (non returner) has overcome the gross fetters related to sensory existence, these five subtle fetters continue to bind consciousness to existence in increasingly subtle ways. This chapter explores how these deep-seated patterns of attachment manifest and the methods for their transcendence, marking the transition from the white stone (Albedo) to the red stone (Rubedo) in alchemical terms.

The *ten fetters* (*saṃyojana*) are divided into two groups of five, those that pertain to *externally* orientated awareness, the *gross fetters*, and those that pertain to *internal* experience, the *subtle fetters*.

An individual who has realised the *gross fetters* will have no attachment to sensory phenomena and is called an *Anāgāmī* (non-returner). The *subtle fetters*, the remaining five, are still present in the *Anāgāmī*, so there will be rebirth, but only a heavenly rebirth is possible.

---

[46] Jung, C.G. (1968). *Psychology and Alchemy (Collected Works Vol. 12)*. Princeton University Press, p. 478.

Another way to understand this is that the mind has lost all desire of existing as a sensual being but hasn't eradicated the clinging towards some kind of existence.

The *subtle fetters* are attachments to increasingly subtle phenomena that arise *inside* as opposed to attachment towards the sensory phenomena *outside*.

The work of the disciple until they reach *Anāgāmī* is largely to do with the skilful use of *karma*. This promotes tranquillity and harmony, and eventually the disciple might well re-establish themselves within a community. This, as hinted at before, is part of multiplication, the eleventh of the twelve stages of spiritual alchemy.

The stone at this stage is *Albedo*, the *white stone* which transmutes base metals into *silver* — we recognise that *silver* pertains to the moon, and the moon is about natural cycles. So the stone, the *Subjective Reality* of the alchemist, performs what appears to be *healing* when in truth this is nothing more than a return to balance through the skilled use of *karma*.

The *work* of the alchemist might well be over for most at this stage. The stone is only *half* done, but its results even at this stage are effective and the alchemist at this stage will have subtle taints of holiness. Even without any further work, upon physical death this being can only be reborn in a heavenly realm (*brahma-loka*), where they are bound to achieve full liberation as an *Arahant*.

There are five types of *Anāgāmī* — ranging from those who progress slowly to those who will continue to realise the *fetters* and achieve Arahantship in the same life. *Sariputta*, one of the Buddha's chief disciples, achieved all four grades in a single night — he was one of the keenest students but just couldn't achieve stream-entry (*Sotāpanna*), probably because he tried so hard. Once he achieved Arahantship he is said to have proven this to his doubters by flying into the audience hall, although in truth, this only proves psychic power (*iddhi*) and not Arahantship.

The Fetter of Becoming

The first *subtle fetter* is the mind's attachment to being (*bhava-raga*). It doesn't matter what you are *being*, we subtly crave existence and this manifests in future desires and goals. The *Anāgāmī* who is aware of the *fetters*, as well as their possible future, might look forward to the idea of a heavenly rebirth. Habitually we all look towards a future and consider what we might like or not like. Unless this *fetter* is realised, the subtle clinging of the mind when one is close to physical death will create a *rebirth linking consciousness* that will then be the basis of the next existence.

So the *Anāgāmī* has a puzzle. They must examine deeply their attachment to becoming, and any sort of future existence. Only once they have truly seen where the attachment arises can they develop the necessary insights to eradicate this viewpoint.

The Fetter of Annihilation

The second *subtle fetter* is the inverse of the first. The first is the mind's attachment to becoming, the second, its desire for unbecoming (*vibhava-raga*). Folk who have got this far through intense suffering might find the first *subtle fetter* deceptively easy as they already cling to annihilation. Those that suffer can cling to the idea that everything just stops, ceases.

The second puzzle therefore for the *Anāgāmī* is to find where their mind clings to ceasing or annihilation. The idea that things can stop, be empty, cease is pretty confusing to the mind. In order to *cease*, one must mentally create it and then mentally hide its existence. This is how we get the illusion that our mind might be calm when in truth it is just appearing to empty itself. This emptying is an active process — so a mind imagining to cease and stop has to actively work at it.

It is possible through disciplined meditation to *turn* the mind inwards in such a way that all perception, and therefore consciousness *ceases*. Again, this is an illusion of ceasing as one in truth is short-circuiting the mind and keeping it short-circuiting by mental discipline. Individuals who practice this sort of meditation can, on death, be born into the realm of the non-percipient beings (*asaññasatta*), a place of fine matter that creates motionless beings like statues frozen in time. This is a mental and abstract realm, still real, that houses these beings for vast periods of time — greater than the duration of the lifespan of a universe. Eventually the mental forces that sustain this short-circuit weaken and these beings *die* and are reborn in the sensual realms.

Again, the disciple must carefully identify their attachment to ideas of ceasing, stopping, ending or annihilation.

The Fetter of Conceit

Conceit (*mana*) is not just about thinking you are *better* than another. It is attempting to compare yourself in any way. See, in comparison, no matter how you do it, you need a concept of self.

Conceit is going to be a challenge for the *Anāgāmī*. They are starting to feel very different from most people. They are no longer bound by habit (fate) and might enjoy considerable success, authority and recognition.

They cannot either just try to *stay humble*. It gets pretty tricky at this level; even humility operates out of a respect for a sense of self.

The *Anāgāmī* might well recognise that this is their last earthly life. This kind of makes the fearful side of life evaporate. Life almost becomes like you are a tourist and with little earthly attachment one no longer worries about death, disease or poverty.

It is paradoxical yet once this *fetter* is realised, it liberates the individual to act purely without any consideration to how this might look. Without *conceit* the disciple now acts in ways that are unpredictable — generally we habitually consider how somebody might typically react — yet, in an individual who has realised this *fetter* they will no longer have any degree of predictability.

The Fetters of Restlessness and Primal Delusion

The last two *fetters* are *restlessness* (*uddhacca*) and *primal delusion* (*avijjā*). The *fetters* are like layers of an onion. We have progressed through the gross fetters which deal with the *outside world*. The subtle layers are our inner world and where the mind becomes attached to the illusory concept of self. Attachment to being, annihilation and *conceit* (relational being) are all somewhat easy to explain. The last two *subtle fetters* are so deep that they are features of the process of consciousness itself.

Restlessness arises as a function of *primal delusion*, which both creates conditioned reality and prevents the mind from settling. Only in *jhāna* (meditative absorption) and full enlightenment does the mind still — in *jhāna* this stillness is both relative and transient. Only with full enlightenment does the mind 'find itself' and become still.

Restlessness is always present in all *unwholesome citta* (consciousness). It manifests externally as agitation, commonly seen in anger, greed, and delusion.

Object

It is *primal delusion* which is seated deeply within the *citta* that keeps it in eternal motion, *citta*, creating through this delusion, karmic forces that eternally will cause subsequent *citta* to arise in this life and through the rebirth linking consciousness, future existence.

At this stage (*Nigredo*) I am simply trying to outline the path the alchemist takes, in the later parts we will explore primal delusion more closely.

The *work* that faces the *Anāgāmī* who is moving *actively* (rather than the inevitable, passive route) is intensive. Often it requires mastery of *jhanic* meditation to settle the mind enough where primal delusion is observable. Meditative mastery, whilst advisable, is not, however, essential. Insight (*Vipassanā*) meditation is associated with a continuous mental enquiry centred on one of the three fundamental truths — i.e. emptiness (*suññata*), impermanence (*anicca*) or suffering (*dukkha*). This approach is like an an ongoing challenge related to sensory and mental phenomena arising from sudden insight.

The passive move towards Arahantship is inevitable and it is said that once one becomes an *Arahant* one either physically dies within a week, or, enters a monastery and operates as such. This is probably more a recognition of the inevitable progress which manifests Arahantship as one is progressing towards physical death, which, from its new perspective, allows for the realisation of the *subtle fetters*.

Those *Anāgāmī* that are actively working on these *fetters*, would likely therefore be in still relatively good physical health and on Arahantship enter a monastic order if they were not already present.

We will start to cover what Arahantship means in the next chapter, but remember at this level our understanding of the higher grades will be limited by comprehension.

The journey through the *subtle fetters* represents the final refinement of consciousness, where the practitioner must confront and transcend the most fundamental aspects of existence itself. This process, analogous to the final stages of spiritual alchemy, transforms the *white stone* into the *red stone* — the ultimate realisation of enlightenment. It is a path that requires both profound wisdom and unwavering dedication, leading to the complete liberation from all forms of suffering and the cycle of existence.

Nigredo

Study Guide: The Subtle Fetters

The chapter examines the five subtle fetters binding consciousness after Anāgāmī status, connecting Buddhist understanding to alchemical stages, particularly the Albedo phase.

Core Concepts
- Gross versus subtle fetters distinction
- Five subtle fetters and their nature
- Relationship between Anāgāmī state and alchemical transformation

New Terminology
Arūpa-raga: Attachment to formlessness
Avijjā: Ignorance/primal delusion
Bhava-raga: Subtle attachment to existence
Brahma-loka: Heavenly realms for Anāgāmī rebirth
Mana: Conceit
Rūpa-raga: Attachment to form
Uddhacca: Mental restlessness
Vibhava-raga: Desire for non-existence

Main Themes
1. Nature of subtle fetters
- Division between gross and subtle attachments
- Relationship to consciousness and rebirth
- Role in spiritual transformation
- Connection to Albedo phase

2. The five subtle fetters
- Attachment to being
- Desire for non-existence
- Conceit
- Restlessness
- Primal delusion

3. Paths of transformation
- Active versus passive progress
- Role of meditation and insight
- Connection to multiplication stage
- Links to enlightenment

Practical Applications
- Meditation practice development
- Insight cultivation techniques
- Observation of mental patterns
- Work with subtle attachments

Integration Points
- Links to Arahant
- Foundation for Path Consciousness
- Preparation for Different Worlds
- Connection to Realms of Existence

Common Misconceptions
- Confusing psychic phenomena with enlightenment
- Mistaking temporary spiritual states for permanent attainment
- Assuming all progress requires active practice
- Overlooking subtle fetters importance
- Misunderstanding conceit's role

Progress Indicators
- Diminishing future existence concern
- Natural dissolution of comparative thinking
- Deepening meditative stability
- Growing emptiness insight
- Spontaneous action development

Reflection Questions
- How does attachment to existence manifest subtly?
- What is the relationship between existence and non-existence desire?

OBJECT

- *How might spiritual accomplishment strengthen conceit?*
- *Why is restlessness fundamental to consciousness?*
- *How does primal delusion maintain becoming?*
- *What are practical challenges in observing subtle mental patterns?*

The Subtle Fetters

Fetter	Manifestation	Liberation Path
Being	Future planning	Seeing attachment to existence
Non-being	Desire for non-existence	Understanding active emptiness
Conceit	Comparison with others	Transcending self-reference
Restlessness	Mental agitation	Deep meditation practice
Delusion	Root ignorance	Direct insight

NIGREDO

The Arahant

An Arahant is one who has eradicated all ten fetters, leading to the cessation of rebirth and the attainment of Nibbāna. This is the final stage of enlightenment in Theravāda Buddhism.
"He understands: 'Birth is destroyed, the holy life has been lived, what had to be done has been done, there is no more coming into any state of being.'"

– Saṃyutta Nikāya 22.59

OBJECT

36. Arahant

"The Arahant has done what had to be done, laid down the burden, attained the true goal, destroyed the fetters of being, and is completely liberated through final knowledge." [47]

The Arahant represents the pinnacle of spiritual transformation — a being who has achieved complete enlightenment and dwells in Nirvāṇa. This chapter explores the unique characteristics of Arahant consciousness, examining how these fully enlightened beings operate beyond conventional reality while still engaging with the world. We'll investigate the different types of enlightenment, the nature of functional consciousness, and draw important parallels between Buddhist understanding and alchemical stages of transformation.

The *Arahant* is the name of a being who has achieved full enlightenment. Rather than *holy*, which they can be, they are more alien than familiar, and it can be difficult to both spot and certify an *Arahant*. The *Arahant* dwells in *Nirvāṇa* (*nibbāna* in Pāli). They have transcended all *ten fetters* (*saṃyojana*) and found the necessary distinction between mind and primal delusion (*avijjā*). Now, all phenomena are just phenomena — they arise in the mind of the *Arahant* but the

---

[47] The Dhammapada, verse 423. Translation by Acharya Buddharakkhita (1985). Buddhist Publication Society.

Arahant doesn't identify with them. Whilst they are capable of transient discomfort or pain, they no longer identify with it; there is no sufferer.

Liberated from fear, greed and illusion, they exist without choice or volition, for there is no perspective of 'I', which is necessary for evaluating choice. Without any 'I' in mentation, thoughts cannot get caught up with perception and 'thinking' largely ceases, being replaced by *jhanic* calm and bliss. The *Arahant* is indifferent to this *bliss* — yet the prevailing calmness will tend to reverse any disease caused by stress.

Arahants are unpredictable and masters of *going with the flow*. This means, when they want, they tend to blend in. Whether they still operate out of some sense of self-purpose or they become agents of the universe cannot be known.

Some *Arahants* will have developed psychic powers (*siddhis*), but all will have advanced social powers, simply from being *detached*.

Once Arahantship is achieved, without volition, *karma* largely ceases. The consciousnesses of the *Arahant* are no longer classified as *wholesome* or *unwholesome* as this pertains to *karmic* outcome. Instead, the *Arahant* (and *Buddha*) uses *functional consciousness* — i.e. it acts merely as a function rather than acting with a karmic intensity to create future *resultant consciousnesses*. Externally, most actions will be either benevolent and kind or completely incomprehensible.

In the *Abhidhamma* therefore, several classes of *citta* are exclusively for *Arahants* or *Buddhas*. Additionally, there is a unique form of functional consciousness called the Arahant's smiling consciousness. This is a strange consciousness that arises through deep insight into the futility of effort. It replaces previous disappointment or judgement of perhaps unwise action with an increased acceptance as one recognises the *dance* of life.

Whilst the *Arahant* has achieved full enlightenment, this can be subdivided into two types.

When full enlightenment is realised, the *Arahant* still has the material body, perceptions, thoughts and experiences of their prior existence. These are called *residues* (*upādisesa*) and remain with the *Arahant*, normally until physical death, when they dissolve.

Object

Rarely, the *Arahant* will become a *Buddha*. However, before this can occur the individual must have mastered the *pāramīs*, which means *perfections*. The mastery of the *pāramīs* can take many, many lifetimes. So, for a *Buddha* to arise these need perfecting before enlightenment. Why? Because, once one becomes a *Sotāpanna* (stream-enterer) the ties to *saṃsāra* weaken and one then has only seven lifetimes to perfect them.

So, for a *Buddha* to arise, the individual must spend many lifetimes perfecting these ten *qualities* but refrain from full enlightenment. An individual who follows this path is called a *Bodhisattva*, who will then often go through all four stages in the lifetime prior to Buddhahood.

Such an individual will therefore achieve Arahantship with residues, and then, through a number of different ways, transform the residues, clearing them.

The second type of full enlightenment is therefore called *nibbāna* without residue (*anupādisesa-nibbāna*) and is that of the experience of a *Buddha*.

Arahants don't experience the death consciousness and therefore have no rebirth linking consciousness. The *Arahant* has already established themselves in *nibbāna*; death is more the transition to Buddhahood, albeit somewhat posthumously!

This, I hope the keen alchemists may have noticed, is our deathlessness or immortality attributed to the stone.

The stage of the stone which correlates to Arahantship is *Citrinitas*, or yellowing. This probably pertains to a change of perception once the mind is freed from primal delusion. Primal delusion to the mind is like a beguiling light, and once the mind frees itself, material objects, being correctly seen as made of consciousness, glow.

Rubedo, the final stage of the stone, I feel equates to Buddhahood. Only a *Buddha* has direct control over phenomena, and whilst *Arahants* can develop psychic powers, the power of a *Buddha* is incomparable. The red stone, we know, can transmute base metals to gold, and gold in alchemy pertains to the sun.

The sun represents the eternal radiance of divinity. Unlike the white stone, which restores balance, the red stone brings forth divinity directly in ways that are miraculous. Its power is to transform individuals into divine beings through a direct demonstration of magical power. To a *Buddha*, it is not *magic*—just a natural state.

Well, that's the end of part Three of *Nigredo*. I trust you are still following. My intent is to describe the work that faces the alchemist and explicitly outline what *it* is.

In the last part, I hope to describe the journey, what challenges we face. The most dangerous and taxing part of alchemy is the first part. So, even when the going gets tough, remember this.

As we conclude this exploration of the *Arahant* state and its alchemical parallels, we see that the journey of spiritual transformation mirrors the *Great Work* of the alchemists. Just as base metals are purified into gold, *The consciousness* is refined through stages of enlightenment until it reaches the ultimate state of liberation. The path may be challenging, but the transformation it promises is nothing less than the complete transmutation of the ordinary into the divine.

Study Guide: Arahant

The chapter explores the Arahant state as the pinnacle of spiritual transformation, examining consciousness beyond conventional reality and drawing parallels with alchemical traditions.

CORE CONCEPTS

- *Transcendence of all ten fetters and liberation from fear, greed, and delusion*
- *Operation through functional consciousness without generating karma*
- *Parallel between Buddhist enlightenment and alchemical transformation stages*
- *Distinction between enlightenment with residues and complete liberation*

NEW TERMINOLOGY

Anupādisesa-nibbāna: Enlightenment without residue, complete liberation

Arahant: Fully enlightened being

Asava: Mental effluents/taints

Citrinitas: The yellowing phase in alchemy corresponding to advanced spiritual realisation

Kiriya citta: Functional consciousness that operates without generating karma

Parinibbāna: Final liberation at death

Skandhas: Aggregates of experience

Tathāgata: Thus-gone one — epithet of the Buddha

Upādisesa: Enlightenment with residues, maintaining physical form

Object

Main Themes
- Arahant Consciousness
- Functional consciousness operation
- Freedom from karmic generation
- Transcendence of self-identity

States of Enlightenment
- Enlightenment with residues
- Enlightenment without residue
- Path to Buddhahood
- Alchemical correlations

Technical Framework
- Nature of functional consciousness
- Relationship between enlightenment types
- Progressive stages of transformation

Practical Applications
- Study of enlightenment stages
- Understanding transcendent consciousness
- Exploration of wisdom and spontaneous action

Integration Points
- Connection to Different Worlds and Jhāna
- Foundation for Path Consciousness
- Preparation for The Subtle Fetters
- Links to The Great Work

Common Misconceptions
- Distinction between Arahant and Buddha paths
- Nature of residual conditioning
- Role of functional consciousness

Reflection Questions
- How does the cessation of ego-formation affect daily functioning?
- What distinguishes functional from karmically active consciousness
- How do residues influence Arahant experience
- What is the significance of Arahant's smiling consciousness
- How does Citrinitas metaphor illuminate Arahant perception
- What distinguishes Arahant enlightenment from Buddha's liberation

Progress Indicators
- Transcendence of fetters
- Development of functional consciousness
- Manifestation of spontaneous wisdom
- Integration of alchemical transformations

"We do not 'come into' this world; we come out of it, as leaves from a tree. As the ocean 'waves,' the universe 'peoples.' Every individual is an expression of the whole realm of nature, a unique action of the total universe,"

- Alan Watts, The Book: On the Taboo Against Knowing Who You Are.

Part Four
SUBJECT

The final section of Nigredo explores the deeply personal dimensions of spiritual transformation through direct experience. While the previous sections laid out the theoretical framework, historical context, and practical methods, here we delve into the lived reality of the spiritual journey — examining how these teachings manifest in the crucible of individual consciousness.

Each seeker's path is unique, yet certain patterns emerge that transcend personal circumstances. Through sharing one practitioner's journey from conventional life through crisis to awakening, we gain valuable insights into how the alchemical process unfolds in real time. This section examines the challenges, setbacks, and breakthroughs that characterise the path while acknowledging both the deeply personal nature of spiritual work and the universal patterns that emerge across different traditions.

The chapters that follow trace a journey from initial seeking through profound disorientation to eventual reorientation toward truth. We explore how early curiosity and professional development often interweave with personal crisis to create the conditions for awakening. Through examining specific experiences of "the Fall," exile, wandering, and commitment, we gain practical insight into how theoretical understanding transforms into direct realisation.

Remember that while these accounts may resonate with your own experience, each person's path is ultimately unique. The purpose of sharing these personal narratives is not to create a template to follow, but rather to provide reassurance and orientation for those navigating similar territory. Like ancient maps that marked both safe harbours and dangerous shoals, these stories serve as guides while acknowledging that each seeker must find their own way through the darkness of transformation.

NIGREDO

"The cave wherein the dragon sleeps is the very cave that must be entered. At the darkest point of the hero's journey, there lies the greatest treasure."

— Joseph Campbell, *The Hero with a Thousand Faces* (1949)

SUBJECT

Introduction to Subject

The one who seeks, should not cease seeking, until they find.
And when they find, they will be dismayed.
And when they are dismayed they will be astonished,
and they will be king over the all. [48]

The final section of Nigredo explores the personal dimensions of spiritual transformation through direct experience. While each seeker's journey is unique, understanding how others have navigated similar territory can provide valuable orientation and reassurance. This section examines the challenges, setbacks, and breakthroughs that characterise the path, while acknowledging both the deeply personal nature of spiritual work and the universal patterns that emerge across different traditions.

While *my* path is truly irrelevant, perhaps even distracting, the subjective experience of the path might prove useful. This part of *Nigredo*, and the corresponding final part of each stage in this *course*, will therefore approach the *dharma* from a subjective viewpoint. Often, we face the hurdles of enlightenment without understanding; yet, some understanding allows an *orientation* to the *dharma*, which can be reassuring if nothing else.

In truth, I cannot definitively say whether mental illness might manifest as spiritual symptoms, and there would be inherent danger in assuming this correlation. What I can share is my personal belief that the symptoms of my mental illness were likely

---

[48] *Meyer, M. (2007). The Nag Hammadi Scriptures, Gospel of Thomas. HarperOne, Saying 2.*

manifestations of spiritual awakening. I share my story not as an authority on either enlightenment or mental illness, but simply as a traveller's tale which, being no less fantastic than any medieval sailor's stories, should be taken as such.

Don't feel you need to traverse the challenging aspects of this path alone — although you might well prefer solitude. Nevertheless, seeking support and medication, if needed, poses no *harm* to the enlightenment process. The Buddhist concept of *upāya* (skilful means) teaches us that various methods can lead to awakening. Accept that this path spans years and decades, remain humble in your practice of *sīla* (ethical conduct), and persist in your journey.

Remember that the path to enlightenment, or what the Buddha termed *bodhi* (awakening), is deeply personal yet universal. Like the ancient alchemists working through the stages of the *Great Work*, beginning with *Nigredo* (the blackening), we each must face our own *Shadows* while recognising our fundamental interconnectedness. May your journey, whether walked alone or alongside others, lead you toward deeper understanding and lasting peace.

SUBJECT

37. What Went Before

"The longest journey is the journey inward."[49]

The path of spiritual transformation often begins long before we recognise it as such. This chapter explores how early curiosity, professional development, and personal crisis can interweave to create the conditions for spiritual awakening. Through examining one seeker's journey from conventional medical practice to mystical understanding, we gain insight into how apparent obstacles and suffering often serve as catalysts for deeper transformation.

The very curiosity that started me on this quest has been with me from my earliest memories. Looking back, the path this took me on is now obvious, yet only in retrospect.

I took to science easily and might have done to religion, yet I was raised in an atheist/agnostic family. So, rather than have a religious system to love or hate, I was already outside of any church or temple, and remained simply curious.

Despite as much access to information as one could reasonably expect of those times, I remained unsatisfied and unquenched with just facts. I was only 11 when I ordered and purchased Aleister Crowley's Magick, much to the concern of a possibly Christian bookseller. This book, along with a meagre handful of esoteric texts sat on a single shelf underneath a significant array of more mainstream books and although I read it avidly several times, lacking any Hebrew, Greek or Latin

---

[49] *Hammarskjöld, D. (1964). Markings. Faber & Faber, p. 58*

knowledge, and scant religious or mystical experience it remained an enigma for about twenty years.

I was shy and naturally academic. Well, in truth I have a kind of eidetic memory, I can remember most things I hear. This gave me an edge academically as I could often recall the moment I was taught, and would even dream that I was 'teaching' what I had learned that day.

My strength in sciences helped me gain a place at medical school. I was pretty average, working apparently just what I needed to do to get through exams. Any *esoteric* curiosity would have to wait as I learned a more practical set of skills. Perhaps my attempt to study Chinese Medicine and Acupuncture in my final year, which wasn't authorised, might have suggested my desire to know what is both unconventional and somewhat obscure.

My medical career took me to many new places and countries. Initially I enjoyed the challenge of Emergency Medicine but then found anaesthesia, which, for obvious reasons, fascinated me. Anaesthesia is a pretty challenging speciality where academic skill meets a need for precise physical precision. However, once I had gained fellowship of the anaesthetic college and passed the necessary exams it no longer really interested me, and was in many ways, just a job.

My interest in the mind remained from my childhood, and in addition to my formal medical training, I trained in hypnotherapy and the emerging field of neurolinguistic programming. Hypnotherapy fascinated me, but also frustrated me. There was a lot of babble and folk who might achieve results, but never really knew how, beyond *the unconscious mind is powerful*.

I suffered a wanderlust that took me from hospital to hospital, learning new skills but still remaining empty and unsatisfied inside. The more I approached *the end* of the medical career ladder, the more this uncertainty took me. I moved from anaesthesia and thought psychiatry would offer the satisfactory answers, yet, it only offered more questions.

So, in my mid-thirties I stalled and developed a depressive illness. Work, in many senses was rewarding, both financially and status-wise, yet these didn't seem ideal things to settle on.

Subject

Fighting my depression, I took myself to a new country and trained in general practice. I enjoyed the challenges again whilst learning but found the prospect of a career again daunting. I distracted myself by building a practice that involved my enhanced skills and offered regular hypnotherapy to some of my patients.

I guess it was working with psychiatric patients who responded 'too well' to my hypnotherapy that persuaded me to look outside of what I was comfortable with. I remember working as a new *locum (temporary doctor)* at a practice where I had such a beneficially unnerving effect that I resigned after a single day, so concerned I was that I was deluding myself and even risking harm to my patients.

Now, it is clear that for all my life I have been seeking something I couldn't describe or even know, yet there was deep confusion and alienation for most of the journey — what Buddhists might call *dukkha*, or existential suffering.

I had been a diligent and keen doctor, certainly was no angel, yet I cared deeply for my patients and practice. But my depression had deepened and I had doubts about the true authenticity of modern practice and the motto 'do no harm' has never left my physician's psyche.

At this stage I was breaking apart and disturbed by increasingly unexpected effects with my hypnotherapy I could no longer practice within comfortable and conventional parameters. It is a requirement that any doctor notify their health registration boards if they doubt the integrity of their practice, and, somewhat innocent of the subsequent fallout, I reported myself over my seemingly enhanced hypnotic skills.

The next chapter is about my *fall*—and there is no point *contaminating* this essential spiritual phase with mundane *facts*. Still, it has relevance as it cranked up my suffering into possibly necessary levels of angst, so I will briefly discuss it here.

After reporting myself, I was allowed to return to practice *supervised*. This was a disaster, and my mental health deteriorated. I returned to my family home pretty broken and unsure what to do with my life. Unfortunately, the medical board in my own country now took it upon itself to *investigate* me—which was probably fair and diligent, yet I was mentally breaking down, and was expected to go through tribunals and psychiatric assessments, despite at no time trying to return to practice.

Nigredo

Now, I am not really that interested in how I think I should or should not have been treated, but I think it is important that I suffered. The spiritual path by all means doesn't have to be hard, we make it hard. But it is important to recognise despair, desolation and hopelessness are valid spiritual symptoms—what mystics might call *The Dark Night of the Soul.* This doesn't mean that one shouldn't seek modern psychiatric help, more a way of understanding both the serious nature and challenges a seeker may face.

Remember that no path is the same, and it is doubtful that anyone can give you the answer you seek, this you must find yourself. These are just tales from a fellow traveller, which are predominantly to reassure, and maybe offer an orientation to where you may be heading.

In the end, this journey of seeking—whether through science, medicine, or esoteric practices—led me to understand that what I was searching for was not external knowledge or achievement, but rather an inner awakening. The very obstacles and suffering that seemed to impede my path were, in fact, integral to my spiritual development. Like the Buddha's journey from prince to ascetic to enlightened being, sometimes we must lose everything we think we are to discover who we truly are.

Study Guide: What Went Before

A personal journey from medical practice to spiritual awakening, demonstrating how professional expertise, personal crisis, and inner seeking interweave to catalyse spiritual transformation.

CORE CONCEPTS

- Scientific training and mystical understanding integration
- Role of personal crisis in spiritual transformation
- Journey from conventional medicine to spiritual awakening
- Professional expertise relationship to spiritual seeking
- Dark Night experiences as transformative catalysts

NEW TERMINOLOGY

Bodhi: *Awakening or enlightenment in Buddhism*

Dukkha: *Existential suffering or dissatisfaction*

Eidetic memory: *Ability to recall images, sounds, or objects with high precision*

Sīla: *Ethical conduct or moral discipline*

SUBJECT

Upāya: Buddhist concept of skilful means or expedient methods

MAIN THEMES

1. Origins of Seeking
- Early spiritual curiosity despite secular background
- Natural academic ability and scientific inclination
- Connection between medical training and mystical interests

2. Professional Development
- Evolution through medical specialties
- Integration of conventional and alternative practices
- Crisis of confidence and ethical concerns
- Professional consequences of awakening

3. Spiritual Crisis and Transformation
- Development of depression and doubt
- Dark Night experiences
- Loss of identity leading to deeper understanding
- Integration of scientific and mystical worldviews

PRACTICAL APPLICATIONS
- Self-reflection on personal seeking journey
- Integration of professional expertise with spiritual development
- Recognition of crisis as transformation catalyst
- Balance of conventional practice with spiritual understanding

INTEGRATION POINTS
- Connection to The Shadow concept
- Foundation for understanding Enlightenment
- Preparation for working with The Rebis
- Links to Dark Night of the Soul experiences

COMMON MISCONCEPTIONS
- Spiritual path must always be difficult
- Professional success conflicts with spiritual development
- Crisis indicates failure rather than potential transformation
- Scientific understanding opposes mystical insight

REFLECTION QUESTIONS
- How has your own journey of seeking manifested throughout your life?
- What role has professional or academic achievement played in your spiritual development?
- In what ways have personal crises served as catalysts for deeper questioning?
- How do you integrate conventional knowledge with spiritual understanding?

PROGRESS INDICATORS

Recognition of dukkha in daily life

Integration of professional and spiritual aspects

Acceptance of personal crisis as growth opportunity

Development of balanced perspective between scientific and mystical understanding

KEY QUOTES
- The one who seeks, should not cease seeking, until they find
- Accept that this 'path' spans years and decades, remain humble in your practice of sīla

NIGREDO

What Went Before

Phase	Manifestation	Transformation
Early Life	Academic success	Foundation for seeking
Medical Career	Professional mastery	Growing dissatisfaction
Crisis	Depression/doubt	Spiritual awakening
Integration	Loss of identity	Deeper understanding

The Fall

State	Characteristics	Transformation
Pre-Fall	Inherited paradigms, External authority	Natural development
The Fall	Rebellion, Pride, Self-determination	Necessary transition
Post-Fall	Personal responsibility, Authentic seeking	Spiritual awakening

SUBJECT

38. The Fall

"The fall of man in Paradise is the fall into consciousness." [50]

The concept of "the Fall" represents a critical transition in spiritual development — the moment when we reject inherited beliefs and begin forging our own understanding of reality. While often viewed negatively in religious traditions, this chapter explores how this departure from innocence serves as an essential step toward authentic spiritual awakening. Through examining both personal and universal aspects of this transition, we'll investigate how this process of breaking down old paradigms creates the foundation for genuine transformation.

Our division of a *path* into stages is entirely artificial. Concepts such as *the fall* or *incarnation* are just this, and generally these stages are somewhat blurred. In my experience, these stages are marked by very specific dream experiences. You cannot control these stages, although diligent work might bring them closer. Furthermore, these stories are just stories and not your story. Nevertheless, despite it being strangely uncomfortable discussing a concept of self I no longer believe in, perhaps offering a more subjective analysis complements the objective attitude in the rest of this work.

I do not condone the use of intoxicants, nor do I condemn them. They have their costs and risks, and both the *Bhagavad Gita* and the Buddha warn us that at best they

---

[50] Jung, C.G. (1968). *Psychology and Alchemy (Collected Works Vol. 12).* Princeton University Press, p. 122.

provide a *false* viewpoint (a practitioner can only achieve the false realms). Nevertheless, my path was initially alchemical, and I suspect that medieval and contemporary spiritual alchemists either deliberately or accidentally poisoned themselves. Mercury and most heavy metals and their compounds are toxic, particularly to nerves. Alcohol — probably distilled — was certainly available to monastic alchemists, and many very astute mystical authors suffered from alcoholism as well as other addictions. Cannabis is a sacred plant in *Shaivite Hinduism* and used in dizzying amounts. Opium or laudanum was popular and led to the visionary poems of Samuel Taylor Coleridge as well as Tolkien.

The use of intoxicants, I feel, is a kind of shortcut to developing disciplined meditative practice. It can give the user enough experience of something mystical and otherworldly which gives confidence in doubting the solidity and realness of subjective experience.

It seems quite possible that a misunderstood *jhanic* experience, however fleeting and unstable, might be the real reason behind all addiction. The intoxicant providing a low-grade but still sufficient environment for *jhāna* to occur, which manifests as *pīti* (rapture), *sukha* (happiness) and *upekkhā* (equanimity). However, because the only way the addict has of accessing this *jhāna* is through substance use, this develops *taṇhā* (craving), which is attached to the drug. Furthermore, most substance use is morally frowned upon, and individuals in addiction tend to morally decline, which acts as an increasingly difficult barrier to achieving *jhāna*, and probably explains tolerance.

My advice is to avoid all intoxicants — *jhāna* isn't that difficult once one learns to settle the mind and it's free. Spiritual progress is clearly possible but only to a certain point with intoxicants, and then one must address the addiction before starting to develop meditative practice.

What is the Biblical Fall?

The *Fall* itself has nothing to do with intoxicants but represents a turning away from the paradigm of a conditioned reality we inherit from our upbringing and culture. It is in many ways a stage of maturity, and whilst it most commonly occurs during our *rebellious* teenage years it can be delayed or brought on early.

The *Fall* is about selfhood. It can be imagined as a hardening of the sense of self we build up in childhood, but now one that is self-conceptualised to the degree it believes it can make its own decisions. Prior to this, we didn't make any big decisions and if we did we deferred responsibility for outcome or blame to some authority figure. But only once we go through the fall do we carefully consider the personal outcome for any decisions. Note, these can still be very selfish, yet in these, we always regard *what's in it for me?*

The *Tree Of Life* described a balanced and idealistic map of early childhood awareness. Yet, as concepts of self creep into our understanding, our whole cognition becomes bent around our personal needs and wants. The more we succumb to selfish ideology the more we habitually think and act selfishly.

As we habitually consider *what's in it for me*, we impose a duality on experience, an inner sense of self, and external *objective* reality we call *other*. This division increases the more we have to maintain a distinct inner experience, such as when we lie. Unabated, these inner aspects of self take on *demonic* qualities and we can react to them, creating further acts of selfishness.

So, the *Fall* is both natural and essential. One must *dismiss* the paradigms we have been taught, which is an act of rebellion and pride. However, if we embellish this rebellion and pride we are moving towards an identity that is really an adversary, and should we react to these seeds of selfishness that appear in awareness, through *karma*, we hurt ourselves and others. Note, it is pride and rebelliousness that deludes us into justifying selfish expressions of self. Astute readers will notice who I am talking about and why he is the king of the *demons*. The *cause* of such pride is terrifyingly simple and it's due to being named!

The nature of an individual's *fall* will always have a combination of pride and another quality, such as lust, greed or anger. It happens when they justify such acts by rejecting their old paradigm. It could be drug use, as with myself, or through an act of final rebellion such as *coming out* with regards to sexuality, or even science. Or it could be taking responsibility for one's own finances, possessions, or whatever. What I am trying to emphasise is that whilst *the fall* sounds bad, it isn't. It is simply the process of taking control of one's own life, and an act which is rebellious and involves the rejection of the previous paradigm and construction of a new, self-orientated one.

My Fall

It is almost two decades later that I can explain my experiences. When they happen, you cannot know, and it is confusing and often distressing. The rebelliousness of the *Fall* is empowering and can allow the achievement of great material goals. Yet, it is also the darkness of *Nigredo* that will, at some stage, need to be transmuted through understanding.

Until *my fall* my attitude to intoxicants was largely *it's not for me*, with the exception of alcohol, which is almost promoted in my culture. Furthermore, it didn't happen the moment I tried any intoxicant. It happened when my paradigm shifted to accommodate a personal appreciation of intoxicants and a justification in their future use.

Whilst I was unaware of this process when I was going through it, there was a moment that was strangely symbolic and specific. During a vivid dream I scaled a spiral staircase up a tower made of an invisible substance, I could really see was a set of floating steps forming the ascending spiral staircase. Suddenly, all these stones fell, and me along with them.

The *Fall* is associated with the *Tarot* card — *The Tower* — and I cannot say to what degree any prior knowledge of this might have influenced the symbology of my dream.

Only when one is utterly responsible for oneself is change possible. Pride and our ideas of what self-determination means influence our actions at this stage. Often, we might wander moralistically as we explore and test new boundaries. Sometimes our pride can take us deeply into dark lands and strand us there, yet, alchemy has to start when one is in Hell, which is often the case.

In the end, the *Fall* represents not just a departure from innocence, but a necessary step towards genuine spiritual awakening. Like the alchemical process of *solve et coagula* — dissolution and recombination — we must first break down our inherited paradigms before we can reconstruct a more authentic understanding of reality. This process, though often painful and confusing, ultimately leads to the possibility of true transformation and the potential for higher consciousness. The key lies not in avoiding the *Fall*, but in recognising it as an essential part of our spiritual journey, and learning to transmute its darker aspects into wisdom and understanding.

SUBJECT

Study Guide: The Fall

The Fall represents a critical transition in spiritual development, marking the rejection of inherited beliefs and paradigms in favour of self-determined consciousness.

CORE CONCEPTS

- transformative vessel as container for personal responsibility
- relationship between consciousness and altered states
- integration process through recognition and transformation

NEW TERMINOLOGY

Jhāna: Meditative absorption states

Pīti: Rapture or joy in meditation

Saṃsāra: Cycle of rebirth and conditioned existence

Sukha: Happiness or pleasure in meditative states

Taṇhā: Craving or thirst

Upekkhā: Equanimity or mental balance

MAIN THEMES

1. Nature of spiritual transition
- artificial division of spiritual path into stages
- role of dream experiences in marking transitions
- connection between intoxicants and spiritual seeking
- links to Dark Night of the Soul

2. Understanding the Fall
- rejection of inherited paradigms
- development of self-determined reality
- role of pride and rebellion
- connection to Fisher-King Wound

3. Transformative process
- breaking down of conditioned reality
- development of personal responsibility
- integration of Shadow aspects
- links to Shadow Work

PRACTICAL APPLICATIONS

- daily meditation practice
- journaling of spiritual experiences
- mindful observation of mental patterns
- integration of insights into daily life
- recognition of transformative moments

INTEGRATION POINTS

- connection to Enlightenment concepts
- links to Trees of Consciousness
- relationship to Nigredo process

COMMON MISCONCEPTIONS

- intoxicants as spiritual shortcuts
- fall as purely negative experience
- rebellion as inherently destructive

REFLECTION QUESTIONS

- What paradigms or belief systems have you rejected on your spiritual journey?
- How has your understanding of pride and self-determination evolved?
- What role has rebellion played in your spiritual development?

PROGRESS INDICATORS

- growing comfort with personal authority
- recognition of inherited versus authentic understanding
- development of disciplined practice
- integration of Shadow aspects
- natural unfoldment of spiritual insight

NIGREDO
The Transformation of Subjective Awareness

1. The Crow (Nigredo - The Beginning of the Path)

Reality is perceived as unsatisfactory, suffering inevitable, and all things impermanent. The alchemist recognises the emptiness of external existence and the futility of attachment to self-identity, social status, and rituals. With the breakthrough of Sotapanna, one of the three marks of existence is penetrated, and the first fetters fall away. The path is now seen, but suffering remains.

2. The Dove (Sakadagami - Faith & Compassion Develop)

The perception of reality shifts—though suffering is real, it is conditional, arising from mental constructs rather than external forces. Most sentient beings remain deluded, yet faith, forgiveness, compassion, and fairness begin to develop. The mind is now tempered by wisdom, though attachment to the self persists.

3. The Pelican (Albedo - The Bodhisattva Path Begins)

Desire and anger are sacrificed, refining the heart-mind. The Anagami stage arises, free from attachment to the sensory world. The alchemist now moves beyond self-liberation, engaging more deeply with the world through Bodhicitta—the commitment to aid all beings in their own awakening. The Bodhisattva path begins.

4. The Peacock (Citrinitas - The Purification of Mind)

Reality is now the path itself. The alchemist ceases to perceive suffering as external—recognising that all things arise only within the mind. Adversity is no longer resisted, but embraced as a means of purification. Through willing sacrifice, the remaining attachments to self dissolve. The final subtle fetters are realised, and Arahantship becomes possible.

5. The Red Stone (Bodhissatva 8th Bhumi - The Final Transcendence)

The last obscurations—both afflictive and cognitive—are cleared. Conceptual reality dissolves, and all mental movement ceases. The alchemist no longer perceives separation between self and world. The luminous mind, free from all conditioning, stands at the threshold of Buddhahood. The transformation is complete.

The alchemic path is not a search for knowledge but a refinement of perception. To walk it is to strip away illusion—not by force, but through understanding. As the mind clears, suffering is seen for what it is—self-arising, self-resolving. What remains, beyond all concepts, is the luminous mind, free and unobscured.

SUBJECT

39. Exile

*Now Cain said to his brother Abel, "Let's go out to the field."
And while they were in the field, Cain attacked his brother Abel and killed him.
Then the LORD said to Cain, "Where is your brother Abel?"
"I don't know," he replied. "Am I my brother's keeper?"
The LORD said, "What have you done? Listen!
Your brother's blood cries out to me from the ground.
Now you are under a curse and driven from the ground,
which opened its mouth to receive your brother's blood from your hand.
When you work the ground, it will no longer yield its crops for you.
You will be a restless wanderer on the earth."[51]*

In this chapter, we explore the profound psychological and spiritual meaning behind the Biblical story of Cain and Abel, revealing how this ancient narrative illuminates the universal human experience of exile from innocence. Through careful examination of these archetypal figures, we discover how consciousness evolves from pure awareness through stages of rebellion, materialism, and eventual integration. This journey of exile represents a necessary phase in spiritual development, where we must confront our own capacity for both creation and destruction.

With the arising of Pride, we cut ourselves free from childish ideas and move to a self-orientated paradigm of reality. We grow up — or at least think we do.

---

[51] *The Bible, Genesis 4:8—12, King James Version.*

Nigredo

Remember our *holy books* are alchemical — *what does this mean?*

They outline the development of being and offer guidance on how we might develop into fully realised beings.

For example, in the Bible, the first human being is *Adam*. Now we know this cannot be the literal first hominid organism, and taking this meaning simply doesn't make sense. However, if we consider *Adam* as the name of the first stage of being human, it makes much more sense.

Adam, in Hebrew, means *red earth.* This is our first sense of awareness as a living being, i.e. the awareness of a young child. This awareness is pure, heart consciousness that initially is naturally open and receptive, without judgement or bias.

We learn that from this heart awareness a second awareness develops that is lateralised, i.e. from one side. *Eve* is the name of this awareness, and she represents the mental reflection of being. Initially, *Eve* lacks conditionality, and she reflects her partner's consciousness without imperfection or error.

Yet *Eve* desires to know, and once tempted to eat from the *Tree Of The Knowledge Of Good and Evil*, she starts to learn about things like death, disease, poverty and suffering.

Once she persuades *Adam* to consider these things, his blissful existence is shattered, and they are both ejected from the *Garden of Innocence.*

Now, these events happen to us all. We start off life with a period of blissful innocence which lasts until we realise that life is *dukkha* — inherently unsatisfactory and filled with suffering. We start with an open and unbiased awareness but gradually descend into the world of the mind, and 'grow up'.

Once you understand the characters in *Genesis* are aspects or stages of awareness that we all go through, things make much more sense.

Once exiled, the story moves to the sons of *Adam* and *Eve*: *Cain, Abel* and eventually *Seth.*

SUBJECT

Cain, which means *worker*, represents our emerging dominant consciousness that will eventually reject the samsaric illusions of childhood, including belief in an invisible, divine authority. *Cain* slays *Abel*, and with this, takes his autonomy as the highest authority. He turns his back on what his parents taught him and enters the world of the purely material. Thus, the lineage of *Cain* involves a descent from the Spiritual into the Material, with the whole lineage of *demons* as well as Tribal kings included.

Seth, who means *the appointed*, represents those who find a way to resist the fall or return after falling and eventually unite spirituality with materiality. The lineage of *Seth* includes the prophets such as *Noah* and so forth.

Between *Seth* and *Cain*, we have the slain *Abel*. *Abel* can only be a ghostly figure of moral guidance as he is a slain consciousness. *Abel* remains as our conscience, a ghostly presence that remains to guide us from descending into pure materiality. As *Cain* continues to pursue materiality, the ghostly *Abel* tries to warn us. If we listen to these warnings, we become ghostly ourselves, dissociated from the enjoyment of life, and we suffer inner turmoil.

If we successfully pursue a spiritual path and gain wisdom and mastery over material temptation, we can return to our divinity and find ourselves *appointed*, but only when the *Cain* and *Abel* within us have settled their differences.

With *my* path, the moment I rejected all that I had been taught was my *Cain* moment. Now, one is truly in the wilderness, and one's highest moral authority is the self. Recognising the world as dangerous and hostile, it becomes easier to act out of purely self-interest, and life then becomes a wrestle between the temptation to act selfishly and the ghostly conscience that seems to insist we suffer for such acts.

It is kind of liberating initially, for shame only reappears when one starts to doubt oneself as the ultimate authority, and there is power in shamelessness. Being our own ultimate authority, it is relatively easy to justify all manner of shoddy behaviour, and it is only with the despair and hopelessness of the *Dark Night* that this paradigm of selfness shatters.

Nevertheless, rebellion is as necessary as any other stage, and we kind of rebel just as much as we need to, even if this results in death or banishment. The battle between *Cain* and *Abel* continues however, and slowly a global disenchantment arises manifesting in what we recognise as depression. If we are fortunate to have the time to reflect, we might find the truth, like a blackened diamond in a sack of coal, but for many their life ebbs away, and they slowly dement and crumble.

In this eternal dance between our material and spiritual natures, we must ultimately find the *Middle Way* — the path of balance that the Buddha taught. Just as the mythological *Seth* represents the synthesis of opposing forces, our journey through life's trials leads us towards integration rather than rejection. The key lies not in suppressing either our *Cain*—like materialism or our *Abel*-like spirituality, but in transcending their apparent opposition to discover a higher unity, where both aspects of our nature can coexist in harmony. This is the true meaning of enlightenment — not an escape from the world, but a profound reconciliation with all aspects of existence.

Symbology of Genesis

State of Being	Representation	Significance
Pure Awareness	Adam	Original awareness
Reflective Mind	Eve	Development of thought
Material Nature	Cain	Worldly engagement
Spiritual Nature	Abel	Moral conscience
Integration	Seth	Transcendent unity

Study Guide: Exile

The chapter examines the alchemical interpretation of Cain and Abel, revealing how

Biblical narratives encode guidance for psychological development and spiritual transformation.

SUBJECT

CORE CONCEPTS
- Consciousness development from pure awareness to conditioned mind
- Inner conflict between material and spiritual natures
- Integration path through transcendence of duality

NEW TERMINOLOGY

Brahmacarya: *Noble conduct of life*

Dominant Consciousness: *Primary way of processing and interpreting reality*

Dukkha: *Buddhist term for unsatisfactory nature of existence and suffering*

Garden State: *Metaphor for original consciousness before conceptual thinking*

Ghostly Presence: *Symbolic representation of persistent moral awareness*

Mokṣa: *Spiritual liberation*

Skandha Māras: *Demons or temptations of the five aggregates*

MAIN THEMES

1. Biblical allegory as alchemical instruction
- Holy texts as maps of consciousness evolution
- Symbolic interpretation of Genesis
- Connection to stages of spiritual development

2. Stages of consciousness
- Adam as primary awareness
- Eve as reflective consciousness
- Cain as material mind
- Abel as spiritual conscience
- Seth as integrated being

3. The process of exile
- Loss of innocence
- Development of self-authority
- Conflict between material and spiritual

PRACTICAL APPLICATIONS
- Recognition of symbolic meaning in spiritual texts
- Understanding consciousness evolution
- Appreciation of necessary rebellion
- Movement toward integration
- Development of balanced perspective

INTEGRATION POINTS
- Links to Shadow Work
- Connection to Fisher-King Wound
- Links to Dark Night of the Soul
- Connection to Rebis

COMMON MISCONCEPTIONS
- Holy texts are merely historical records
- Enlightenment means escape from the world
- Rebellion is purely destructive

REFLECTION QUESTIONS
- How do you relate to spiritual exile in your own life
- What aspects of former identity have you left behind
- How has your relationship with conventional reality changed through spiritual practice

PROGRESS INDICATORS
- Recognition of symbolic meaning in spiritual texts
- Understanding of consciousness evolution
- Appreciation of necessary rebellion
- Movement toward integration
- Development of balanced perspective

Nigredo

"I have had to experience so much stupidity, so many vices, so much error, so much nausea, disillusionment, and sorrow, just in order to become a child again and begin anew."
– Hermann Hesse, Siddhartha (1922)

SUBJECT

40. Wandering

"Not all those who wander are lost." [52]

The wandering phase represents a critical period where the spiritual seeker navigates between conventional life and deeper meaning. This chapter explores how the aspiring alchemist often achieves conventional success while harbouring an inexplicable dissatisfaction that eventually leads to transformation. Through examining this tension between worldly achievement and spiritual yearning, we discover how the wandering phase, though potentially distressing, serves as essential preparation for deeper alchemical work.

I guess the difference between the seeker and everybody else is a subtle distrust of *settling-down* into normal life. Often, the seeker refuses to let go of the magic and wisdom of childhood and settle for normal, habitual existence.

However, we must start somewhere and once we believe ourselves to be our own highest authority we face a choice — do we let go of our childish fantasies and *grow-up* or do we reject convention and follow our hearts?

In truth, we do a bit of both. Yet, at this stage, we lack wisdom and faith, and so we might try *normal* life whilst harbouring our fantasies in our hobbies or interests. If we are lucky, we might be able to balance things, yet, fortune really doesn't build an alchemist. Strife, conflict and suffering build alchemists. After all, progress is dependent on understanding and eventually rejecting all we think we know.

---

[52] *Tolkien, J.R.R. (1954). The Fellowship of the Ring, from the poem "All that is gold does not glitter."*

One must have a certain degree of academic astuteness for the alchemic path — perhaps if one has a master to explain, this is less important. Yet, for most of us, it involves a lot of reading.

So, it was certainly in my case that I *enjoyed* a certain material success along with what appeared to be more than satisfactory existence. Yet, deeply held *fantasies* of *goodness* would constantly conflict any real sense of enjoying this success, and as I moved from junior to more senior medical ranks, the frank unfairness of life, even if not necessarily to myself, prohibited any true satisfaction. I enjoyed *making a difference* yet became too absorbed in the humanitarian dilemmas of healthcare and began to silently despair at the narrow and selfish ideologies of apparent success.

Saṃsāra, the cycle of birth, death, and rebirth driven by *karma* and desire, and *Nirvāṇa*, the cessation of this cycle and ultimate liberation, are very similar in their essence. In fact, it is not that *Nirvāṇa* is distant or obtuse, it is the fact that it is right in front of our faces that makes it so elusive. Our minds are simply restless in *Saṃsāra* whereas in *Nirvāṇa* there is no restlessness and we are perfectly satisfied in *being*.

For many, *Saṃsāra* is enough. Lacking the necessary insights, the mind can be perfectly satisfied chasing material goals and facing *normal* challenges. Yet, for those who become seekers, *success* in *Saṃsāra* is empty, hollow and increasingly meaningless.

Whilst one has goals the mind can be satisfied. However, upon achieving these goals one remains disappointed and empty. It's like in childhood where one can lay awake at night fantasising about a Christmas present or holiday. Once achieved, even if it fully lives up to expectation, and joy, is limited, and eventually fades.

In Buddhism, suffering is referred to as *dukkha*, a central concept that underscores the unsatisfactory nature of existence. There are three primary types of *dukkha*:

1. **Dukkha-dukkha**: This is the most apparent form of suffering, encompassing physical pain, mental anguish, and the inevitable hardships of life.

2. **Vipariṇāma-dukkha**: This is the suffering associated with change, highlighting the transient nature of joy and happiness. Even in moments of bliss, the awareness that they are fleeting can bring discomfort.

3. **Saṅkhāra-dukkha**: This is the most profound form of suffering, rooted in the very fabric of conditioned existence. It arises from the impermanent and interdependent nature of all phenomena.

Subject

The danger of succeeding is that once one has achieved one's dreams, they are often not quite what one expected. Unfortunately there are plenty of *successful* people who fail to recognise this, and will be deeply unhappy with what they have worked for.

I can remember a certain confusion in my failure to be satisfied with this success, particularly as I was more than well read in most areas of understanding. I thought I understood *the mind* and yet, I had no answers.

Until one has the *breakthrough* in awareness one can only understand phenomena from the aspect of self. The answers we need might be right in front of us, yet, we simply don't see them. Our minds can only recognise what we think we want, or fear, with anything that is between these polarities becoming effectively invisible.

Depression slowly creeps into one's existence as this subtle dissatisfaction becomes pervasive. It worsens because we cannot recognise nor understand it, and it is prolonged as we naturally strive to fight it. Motivation and engagement in a life we no longer can fully experience becomes an effort rather than joy, and we might simply seek oblivion.

The Seeker is increasingly dissatisfied and suspicious of *Saṃsāra* which plunges them into a living Hell. They can become dark as *demonic* reflections of the *Qlippoth*, a concept from Kabbalistic mysticism representing the shadow side of the *Tree Of Life*. Addiction, rejection, and isolation exacerbate the situation, increasing the sense of hopelessness and despair.

Eventually we must reach the point where we are happy to reject our concepts of who we are and what our world is, but it is like shedding a particularly adherent layer of skin. It can take time, involve great distress and has risks of great harm to ourselves or others. This means we often take ourselves away from those that loved us, and seek a solitary existence.

We cannot proceed with the vehicle of self we developed from childhood. This must give way, but it is rarely a smooth process. It often involves great mental distresses as we must let go of all previous concepts of being, and one often must work this out by oneself.

All wander, to a degree; some of us, however, cannot help but become bewitched by the darkness and inevitably, we must wander into the night.

Yet, it is in this wandering, through the darkness and despair, that the seeker begins to uncover the light within. The journey is not about reaching a destination but about embracing the process of transformation. Through surrendering the self and its illusions, we find a deeper connection to the essence of being, where the boundaries of *Saṃsāra* and *Nirvāṇa* dissolve, and we come to rest in the eternal present. It is here, in this profound stillness, that the seeker finally becomes the alchemist, transmuting suffering into wisdom and darkness into light.

Wandering

STATE	CHARACTERISTICS	OUTCOME
Initial Success	Material achievement, intellectual growth	Growing dissatisfaction
Questioning	Recognition of life's unfairness, spiritual yearning	Development of doubt
Crisis	Depression, isolation, addiction potential	Breakdown of false self
Transformation	Rejection of conventional identity, solitary path	Spiritual awakening

Types of Suffering

TYPE OF DUKKHA	MANIFESTATION
Dukkha-dukkha	Direct suffering
Vipariṇāma-dukkha	Suffering from change
Saṅkhāra-dukkha	Existential suffering

SUBJECT

Study Guide: Wandering

The chapter explores the seeker's journey through conventional life and spiritual awakening, examining how initial success and subsequent dissatisfaction lead to transformation, investigating the relationship between material achievement and spiritual development, while highlighting how suffering catalyses alchemical transformation.

CORE CONCEPTS

- *Retention of childhood wisdom*
- *Balance between material and spiritual pursuits*
- *Role of intellectual capacity in spiritual development*
- *Understanding of Saṃsāra and Nirvāṇa as interconnected states*
- *Transformative power of suffering*

NEW TERMINOLOGY

Dukkha-dukkha: *Direct suffering from physical and mental pain*

Qlippoth: *Shadow side/dark forces in Kabbalah*

Saṅkhāra-dukkha: *Existential suffering inherent in conditioned existence*

Vipariṇāma-dukkha: *Suffering caused by impermanence and change*

MAIN THEMES

- *The seeker's fundamental resistance to conventional life*
- *Material achievement as temporary satisfaction*
- *Growing awareness of life's unfairness*
- *Development of spiritual yearning*
- *Three types of Buddhist dukkha*
- *Role of dissatisfaction in transformation*
- *Development of the alchemical perspective*

TECHNICAL FRAMEWORK

Initial Success: *Material achievement, intellectual growth*

Questioning: *Recognition of life's unfairness, spiritual yearning*

Crisis: *Depression, isolation, addiction potential*

Transformation: *Rejection of conventional identity, solitary path*

PRACTICAL APPLICATIONS

- *Recognition of dissatisfaction as transformative catalyst*
- *Development of spiritual perspective*
- *Breakdown of conventional identity*
- *Navigation between worldly responsibilities and spiritual aspirations*

INTEGRATION POINTS

- *Connection to Fisher-King Wound (Chapter 8)*
- *Links to Dark Night of the Soul (Chapter 11)*
- *Connection to Shadow Work (Chapter 10)*
- *Links to The Rebis (Chapter 9)*

COMMON MISCONCEPTIONS

- *Success guarantees satisfaction*
- *Spiritual development requires abandoning material life*
- *Suffering is purely negative*
- *Nirvāṇa is distant from everyday experience*

NIGREDO

REFLECTION QUESTIONS

- *What forms of dissatisfaction have led you to deeper spiritual seeking?*
- *How do you navigate between worldly responsibilities and spiritual aspirations?*
- *What role does suffering play in your spiritual development?*
- *Examine your relationship with conventional success*
- *Consider your personal Dark Night experiences*

PROGRESS INDICATORS

- *Growing awareness of life's deeper meaning*
- *Ability to recognise different forms of suffering*
- *Development of spiritual perspective*
- *Capacity to embrace transformation*
- *Integration of material and spiritual aspects of life*

SUBJECT

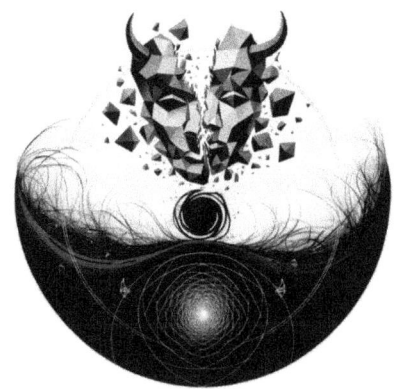

41. The Night

*"The Dark Night of the Soul comes just before revelation.
When everything is lost,
and all seems darkness,
then comes the new life and all that is needed."* [53]

The descent into spiritual darkness represents a crucial phase of the alchemical journey where the aspirant must confront their inner divisions and Shadow aspects. This chapter explores how our consciousness fragments into multiple aspects, the nature of our inner "demons," and the process of integration that leads to breakthrough. Through understanding the difference between what exists and what manifests, we learn to navigate the territories of our own darkness and emerge transformed.

In all accounts of Spiritual Progress, one must start by going inwards and downwards. Fortunately, this almost seems a natural tendency for most of us; we are naturally inclined towards that which is spiritually harmful. Some of us question this tendency rather than accepting it, and our decline fascinates us as much as it hurts us.

Our sense of being arises seemingly singularly, yet at some stage it becomes apparent that we are intrinsically divided. Freud classified these divisions into an instinctive and animalistic *Id*, an idealistic and elevated *Super-Ego* and a poor,

---

[53] *Campbell, J. (1988). The Power of Myth*

divided *ego* mitigating a path between these. In the Kabbalah, these are called the *nefesh* (animal soul), *ruach* (intellectual soul), and *neshamah* (spiritual soul).

Initially, we can use our rational mind to build a satisfactory model of existence, which functions adequately up to a point. Our rational mind cannot answer some questions. These become problematic to it and are often dismissed with vigour and disdain. Our rational mind cannot initially understand that the suffering it is trying to comprehend arises through and is compounded by its attempts to understand it.

We create a concept of self based on dualistic qualities that are essentially meaningless, and we try to extract self-worth from this sorry mess. The more we struggle with who we are, the more we become divided.

The Alchemist must turn and face this inner mess of memories and unpick their very constituents of being. One must become fearless, achieved through overarching curiosity and a genuine dislike for self. Often the most challenging times are when we refuse to accept an aspect of self because we fear losing it.

The Night begins when one realises that at the heart of one's suffering is oneself. It is a tedious process of unremitting inner strife where one's only focus is *to understand*.

Life might be exceptionally difficult, and it is hard not to blame others and feel victimised. One can then oscillate between anger and victimhood whilst enjoying the self-destructive qualities of both. Once one realises that the only goal seems to be to *tear oneself apart*, it can help, albeit darkly.

Frustration can bring back infantile consciousness, and we can find ourselves in rage and tantrum, despising others and fostering dark hatreds. These hatreds can progress into numbing doubts and paralysis, and even psychosis.

Now, gentle reader, before we move on to the *creatures of this night*, let us briefly consider the difference between *existent* and *manifest*. A mountain that looks like an elephant might exist. It is real, at least from a conventional point of view. Yet, its shape reminds us of an *elephant*, but is there an existent elephant?

No. There is no real elephant, just a pattern or shape that *reminds* us of an elephant. The Elephant is *manifest* but not real.

How do we define a *creature*? In occult terms, a creature manifests—appears to exist—as a product of the *pleroma*, whose feature is differentiation—*go forth and multiply*. In simpler terms, a creature is the label we give to a being whom we expect has a degree of autonomy or even sentience.

We only are aware of the creatures we can perceive. Thankfully, those creatures of immediate relevance tend to be easily perceived, especially if they are of similar size, and are either seeing us as food, or we see them as food. Yet, many more creatures remain hidden, either because they are much smaller than us, or neither of us has any use for the other. In a single tree or shovelful of earth, there are whole kingdoms of hidden and perhaps irrelevant creatures that have always existed but remain hidden.

The idea of *demons* is strangely repulsive to many, and even some of our clergy are hesitant in discussing them. Maybe it's more coincidental rather than strange as our world suffers from moral ignorance; we are blind to what might be instruments of its propagation.

So, what exactly are *demons*?

Remember how we have this tendency to lump our experiences together into a sense of self? This is a process or habit that eventually, as alchemists, we must learn to stop. Yet, it is a deep and habitual process of the unenlightened mind. And those experiences which we have forgotten or deny will lump themselves together into sub-personalities of increasing manifest reality.

Depending on just how we break, we fall apart into subgroups of self that we accept, our dominant personality, and subgroups of self we reject, our subconscious or *Shadow* personality. These rejected or lost sub-personalities become the *demonic* forces that confuse us. They are *manifest*, i.e., can appear as urges, thoughts, perceptions, but in truth, they don't exist. This might be hard to get your head around initially; the best way is to try to accept that they are both real AND not real!

If we refuse to accept we have problems with lust, then we find we get the lusty *demons*; the same applies with anger, pride, gluttony, etc. We can pretend that we don't suffer with this problem, yet it will remain until we face and address it. Until this, we remain tormented and could do great harm by giving in.

Unless you are particularly interested in *demons*, and there is a pretty difficult path called the path of the dragon (or serpent) that shares the same goal as the other paths, an in-depth knowledge of the *Qlippoth* and its *demons* is probably unnecessary. It is, however, fascinating.

For the alchemist, one must learn to recognise one's own *demons* and through love and curiosity wish them to become integrated. We are not interested in cherishing and supporting their individuality, neither do we look for gifts. We must recognise the toddler within us and when it wants to tantrum. We must embrace our jealousy, rage and pride, not to embellish, but to contemplate.

We probably start off small, recognising our deceitful speech or actions, before moving to *deeper* issues such as lust, envy and finally treachery. Only when one recognises the most terrible being in our mental schemata has to be, and always had been ourself, can we fully identify with our own inner darkness.

It's both terrifying and dreadful to approach and embrace this inner darkness, yet bringing this all together heals all. One instantly accepts both the worst and the best, and unified, we find ourselves at the lowest state of being. We recognise our most terrible sin, which is the betrayal of being, which arises when the false and empty simulacrum takes residence in the mind through the act of naming.

Yet, at the peak of the *Dark Night*, we recognise this simulacrum to be utterly empty. Just a composite of the complete range of duality, which fuses into a single moment of empty unity. This brief sense of empty unity, which cannot have either a centre or edge, is the breakthrough moment, where all hope is lost, and letting go, transcendental awareness manifests.

Whilst this moment might be obvious, one's suffering doesn't suddenly abate. Yet, there seems to be one moment where, upon awakening, the rays of the dawning sun suddenly bring the hope one so longed for.

In this final transformation, akin to the Buddhist concept of satori or the alchemical opus magnum, we discover that the darkness we feared was merely the *Shadow* cast by our own light. The journey through the night, though harrowing, reveals itself as the necessary path to wholeness. As the dawn breaks, we understand that the *demons* we fought were aspects of ourselves seeking integration, and the darkness we traversed was the very ground of our awakening. This is the paradox of the spiritual journey: that which we most feared becomes the gateway to our liberation.

> "These pains you feel are messengers. Listen to them." [54]

Study Guide: The Night

The chapter explores psychological descent into darkness as a transformative spiritual stage, examining consciousness division, inner conflict, and breakthrough through Shadow integration.

---

[54] *The Essential Rumi (translated by Coleman Barks)*

Subject

Core Concepts
- Divided consciousness
- Multiple aspects of self
- Breakthrough experience

New Terminology

Nefesh: Animal soul (Kabbalah)

Neshamah: Spiritual soul (Kabbalah)

Opus Magnum: The Great Work of spiritual transformation

Pleroma: Fullness/totality in Gnostic thought

Ruach: Intellectual soul (Kabbalah)

Satori: Sudden enlightenment in Zen Buddhism

Simulacrum: An image or representation of something

Main Themes

1. The Divided Self
- Nature of psychological fragmentation
- Role of rational mind in understanding
- Development of self-concept
- Links to Shadow Work

2. The Descent Process
- Recognition of inner division
- Confrontation with Shadow aspects
- Role of curiosity in transformation
- Connection to Dark Night

3. Integration Mechanics
- Understanding manifestation versus existence
- Working with demonic aspects
- Path to breakthrough
- Links to Fisher-King Wound

Technical Framework
- Division and Integration Process
- Multiple selves and unification through acceptance
- Shadow aspects and conscious integration
- Rejected qualities and loving curiosity
- Empty wholeness and transcendental breakthrough

Practical Applications
- Self-reflection and introspection
- Shadow work and integration
- Acceptance of psychological complexity
- Recognition of limiting patterns
- Integration of divided aspects of self

Integration Points
- Connection to Rebis
- Links to Shadow Work
- Connection to Enlightenment
- Links to Fisher-King Wound

Progress Indicators
- Growing comfort with inner darkness
- Reduced fear of Shadow aspects
- Natural integration of rejected parts
- Development of unified awareness
- Recognition of empty nature of self

Reflection Questions
- How do you understand and work with your own inner divisions?
- What aspects of yourself have you found most challenging to face?
- How do you distinguish between genuine insight and spiritual materialism?

The Long Dark Night of the Soul

Aspect	Manifestation	Integration Path
Division	Multiple selves	Unification through acceptance
Darkness	Shadow aspects	Conscious integration
Demons	Rejected qualities	Loving curiosity
Unity	Empty wholeness	Transcendental breakthrough

Confusion

Aspect	Before Breakthrough	After Breakthrough
Awareness	Limited, personal	Expanded, inclusive
Decision-making	Normal functioning	Difficult, paralysed
Motivation	Conventional goals	Undefined seeking
Self-concept	Stable, defined	Empty, dissolving

SUBJECT

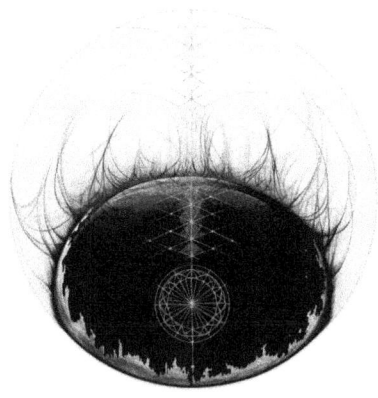

42. Confusion

"In my beginning is my end... In my end is my beginning." [55]

The breakthrough moment of stream-entry (sotāpatti) marks a profound and irreversible shift in consciousness that fundamentally alters one's relationship with reality. This chapter explores both the immediate experience of this spiritual breakthrough and the challenging period of integration that follows. Through examining the nature of this transformation, we gain insight into how such experiences reshape our understanding of self, reality, and the spiritual path. While potentially destabilising, this phase represents a crucial step in the alchemical transformation of consciousness.

I suspect that only those who are in established religious orders can have any idea what that breakthrough moment was. It is unexpected and extraordinarily difficult to describe subjectively. It is almost like suddenly becoming uncaught, and awareness expands to include everything within one's sensory fields. If a perspective could be gained, it falls through phenomena—knowing it—as it falls through chains of causality and conditionality. And whilst one seems to know that this would happen if a perspective is chosen, no perspective arises, so it's simply an undifferentiated awareness pregnant with knowing.

It is timeless and utterly impossible to define. The scope is vast, which makes us think it has to occupy a significant amount of time, yet, it is a single moment. I now have learned that this single moment is followed by two or three reactionary

---

[55] *Eliot, T.S. (1943). Four Quartets, "East Coker". Harcourt.*

moments, called *phala citta* or *resultant consciousness* in Buddhist terminology. In truth, I cannot recall any particular experience other than wonder and delight. The whole process settled within half an hour, yet, it divided my life into that which was before, and that which came after, a kind of veil that, passing through, changed everything.

I recognised *something* had happened, but couldn't describe it then. I had been looking, seeking something, but understood very little then. It was only when I had studied the *Abhidhamma* many years later that I found descriptions matching my experience — what the Buddhist texts refer to as *stream-entry* or *sotāpatti*.

Whilst the experience is unmissable, and the process naturally orientates one towards the path, and subsequent realisations, it can be quite confusing to one who is unguided. One must achieve the second *grade* of awakening, *Sakadāgāmī*, until one develops certainty, confidence and commitment.

One can find oneself in a kind of twilight zone, particularly if one is atheist or agnostic. I suspect many might think this experience is a mental illness, physical illness or even divine intervention, but lacking any context one might easily miss its significance. This is relevant because following the experience, one is no longer interested in previous goals and dreams. This manifests as a subtle but pervasive disinterest in participating in the challenges of everyday life. This can, of course, be destructive and causes great confusion and hurt to oneself and one's loved ones.

Fortunately, despite suffering this confusion and abrupt change of motivational outlook, I had some understanding, however limited. It was very confusing but at least I suspected that this was something to do with Spiritual Enlightenment, even if, at that stage, I still didn't believe in *it*.

Generally however, whilst there are realisations these arise in conflict with previous ideas, and whilst one is certain that one is *different* (from beforehand), without explicit knowledge of the process, one cannot quantify or qualify this, and there is a period of confusion that might well last until the second grade. At this stage all one can say is that one's suspicions about conditioned reality deepen.

Functionally, it was crippling, as any desire to *return* to my old way of being evaporated and I found decisions almost impossible. If asked what *I* wanted, or didn't want, it kind of glitched my mind, and the only answer was a dark void. It was frustrating and increasingly destructive to *normal* life. I could act with full effort and energy towards anything that didn't involve myself.

A kind of listless emptiness replaces one's sense of self that is utterly unexplainable. Thoughts that try to involve self-concept just get caught up in this emptiness and cease, without objection or reflection, like a soft, dark, black hole, absorbing light without process.

I suspect that, in truth, one continues an *inner* progress that is invisible to the *being* slowly evaporating. While recognising only a strange paralysis, this feels frustrating and confusing. I would even say that initially it was distressing, but only because this inner paralysis worried others. One feels alien and is only interested in something one really cannot define or conceptualise, yet it is only challenging when one tries to *return* to one's previous outlook and being.

It lasted about five years until I experienced the second breakthrough moment, after which things became easier. It was during these five years that I formally explored *jhāna*, the meditative absorptions described in Buddhist practice.

This journey through the stages of awakening reveals the profound nature of the Buddhist path. The initial breakthrough, while destabilising, serves as a catalyst for deeper understanding. The subsequent period of adjustment, though challenging, ultimately leads to a more authentic way of being. The experience demonstrates that what we often consider *normal* consciousness is merely one mode of perception, and that there exists a deeper level of awareness waiting to be discovered through dedicated practice and patience.

Study Guide: Confusion

A detailed exploration of stream-entry (sotāpatti) experience and its aftermath, focusing on the breakthrough moment and integration challenges that transform consciousness and self-perception.

CORE CONCEPTS
- *Breakthrough experience and immediate aftermath*
- *Integration period and its challenges*
- *Transformation process and resolution pathway*

NIGREDO

- Role of formal practice and guidance

NEW TERMINOLOGY

phala citta: resultant consciousness following breakthrough

sakadāgāmī: second grade of awakening

sotāpatti: stream-entry, initial spiritual breakthrough

MAIN THEMES

1. Nature of breakthrough
- Immediate experience of expanded awareness
- Timeless quality of the moment
- Role of resultant consciousness
- Connection to enlightenment

2. Integration challenges
- Loss of previous motivations
- Difficulty with decision-making
- Changes in self-concept
- Links to Dark Night experiences

3. Transformation process
- Development of inner emptiness
- Role of meditation practice
- Timeline of adjustment
- Connection to deeper stages

PRACTICAL APPLICATIONS

- Engagement with local Buddhist centres
- Working with experienced meditation teachers
- Participation in Dharma groups
- Integration with meditation communities

INTEGRATION POINTS

- Connection to enlightenment concepts
- Links to establishing spiritual practice
- Foundation for understanding no-self
- Relationship to Dark Night experiences

COMMON MISCONCEPTIONS

- Breakthrough versus gradual development
- Nature of integration challenges
- Role of formal practice
- Importance of guidance

REFLECTION QUESTIONS

- How to handle spiritual uncertainty
- Changes in identity after insights
- Maintaining balance during transformation
- Role of community support
- Balance of theory versus experience

PROGRESS INDICATORS

- Development of understanding
- Shift in awareness and perception
- Changes in decision-making capacity
- Evolution of self-concept
- Movement toward second breakthrough

TECHNICAL FRAMEWORK

- Expanded awareness development
- Integration process stages
- Resolution pathways
- Practice methodology

SUBJECT

43. Commitment

"In alchemy, one becomes what one is: there is no transformation of something into something else but rather a revelation of what was always already there." [56]

This chapter explores the delicate balance required when navigating the path between initial spiritual breakthrough and full enlightenment. We examine how the aspirant must maintain ordinary life while experiencing profound inner transformation, and discuss practical approaches for handling the psychological challenges that arise during this critical period. The text offers guidance on managing unusual phenomena and maintaining stability while progressing naturally toward enlightenment.

Outside of established religious organisations, enlightenment, at least initially, is very confusing. The spiritual path has its dangers, which in Buddhist tradition are called '*The skandha-māra*'—representing the five aggregates of clinging that manifest as temptations of identity one might attach to while becoming increasingly selfless.

From the point of first experiencing *Unconditional Reality*, one changes, but these changes occur at a deeper level than identity and shake its very roots. Subjectively, this is awful and manifests as mental handicaps and suffering. Habits run deeply and, despite being cut away from their moorings, continue to half-function, creating a general listlessness and disinterest that might be called spiritual depression or *Dark Night of the Soul*.

---

[56] *Hillman, J. (2009). Alchemical Psychology*

In truth, one is no more *empty* than one has ever been, yet, now one is painfully aware and cannot understand what is happening.

There is a Zen kōan, a paradoxical statement that points towards enlightenment, that I think offers deep wisdom for when we are in these strange periods: *Before enlightenment, chop wood, carry water. After enlightenment, chop wood, carry water.*

This reminds us whilst we are in this vulnerable state to maintain those habits that are necessary. Despite tasting the bliss of the unconditioned state *Nirvāṇa*, it is still some way off, even if guaranteed. Until we have a deeper understanding, we cannot simply give up on *normal* life. We must push on through the tedium of existence and foster those habits that promote a healthy and simple life.

Despite this, these five years were exhausting. Suddenly one has opened one's mind and can experience all manner of unbelievable experiences, yet, to everybody else, one has gone insane. This clearly is also a worry to oneself, and one must remember the mystical wisdom in silence, and, as much as possible, keeping the inner and outer worlds separate.

One becomes mystically energised, and this can cause all sorts of strange phenomena. I had to stop wearing mechanical watches, as they would simply stop. One's intuition can be terrifying and disturbing to both oneself and others. It is very easy to become unbalanced, and the need for identity creates grandiose ideas that beg to become delusions.

I had some truly amazing experiences, yet deep down must have known to be wary to read anything into them. Perhaps my rational medical side, who was avidly taking notes, offered me the stability to realise that this was a process, not a destination.

One cannot look for, or bring on enlightenment; it doesn't work that way. One can only work towards providing the conditions for its arising, and focus so much on this work that one truly forgets *why* one is doing it.

In the end, the path to enlightenment is both profound and ordinary. Like water flowing downhill, enlightenment follows its natural course once obstacles are removed. The key lies not in the extraordinary experiences or phenomena but in the simple dedication to practice, the willingness to face whatever arises, and the courage to keep chopping wood and carrying water, even when the ground beneath our feet seems to disappear.

Commitment

Aspect	Before Commitment	After Commitment
Desire	Strong attachment	Weakened grip
Anger	Reactive	Diminished
Virtue	Practiced	Natural
Understanding	Intellectual	Intuitive

Study Guide: Commitment

The chapter examines the period following spiritual breakthrough, focusing on maintaining balance between inner transformation and daily life while managing psychological challenges.

CORE CONCEPTS

- Awakening as a natural process requiring patience
- Balance between mystical experiences and mundane life
- Importance of maintaining stability during transformation
- Role of silence and mindful discretion in spiritual development

NEW TERMINOLOGY

Kōan: *Paradoxical statement used in Zen practice to provoke enlightenment*

Skandha Māras: *Five aggregates of clinging manifesting as temptations*

MAIN THEMES

1. Nature of Commitment
- Maintaining practice despite confusion
- Balance between mystical and mundane
- Role of silence and discretion
- Connection to Dark Night

2. Psychological Challenges
- Manifestation of Skandha Māras
- Management of unusual phenomena
- Risk of grandiose delusions
- Links to Shadow Work

3. Integration Process
- Balancing inner and outer worlds
- Maintaining necessary habits

Nigredo

- Role of rational observation
- Connection to Enlightenment

PRACTICAL APPLICATIONS

- Maintaining daily functions
- Navigating unusual experiences with stability
- Importance of stability
- Focus on practice fundamentals

INTEGRATION POINTS

- Connection to Dark Night Chapter 11
- Links to Shadow Work Chapter 10
- Connection to Enlightenment Chapter 6
- Links to Great Work Chapter 25

COMMON MISCONCEPTIONS

- Enlightenment eliminates the need for ordinary activities
- Spiritual awakening can be forced or sought directly
- Unusual phenomena indicate spiritual progress

REFLECTION QUESTIONS

- What helps maintain spiritual practice during challenging times
- How to handle unusual experiences or phenomena
- What role does silence play in the spiritual journey

PROGRESS INDICATORS

- Ability to maintain normal function
- Balance between experience and expression
- Natural rather than forced progress
- Growing stability amid transformation

SUBJECT

44. Spiritual Orientation

"The most fundamental aggression to ourselves, the most fundamental harm we can do to ourselves, is to remain ignorant by not having the courage and the respect to look at ourselves honestly and gently." [57]

The spiritual path reaches critical momentum when the practitioner experiences deeper insights into the nature of reality. This chapter explores how initial breakthroughs in understanding manifest and evolve, particularly focusing on the transition between early stages of enlightenment. We examine how meditative absorption, ethical conduct, and personal insight interweave to create profound shifts in consciousness, while acknowledging that each person's journey unfolds in its own unique way.

There reaches a point in the evolving confusion of the *Sotāpanna* (one who has attained the first stage of enlightenment) where one's commitment to the path increases significantly. It is said that with each stage of enlightenment, the actual moment arises through an insight into either:

- **emptiness** — a lack of intrinsic substance (*śūnyatā*);
- **impermanence** — a lack of stable permanence (*anicca*);
- or **suffering** — a recognition of the dissatisfactory nature of *Conditional Reality* (*dukkha*).

---

[57] Chödrön, P. *When Things Fall Apart*

For me, this was the sudden and absolutely certain feeling that I couldn't possibly exist (emptiness). The thoughts that led me to this absolute conclusion were trivial in comparison to what seemed paradoxical, and for two or three moments, the conviction was overwhelming. I delighted in what seemed to be paradoxical, that *I realised* that this 'I' couldn't possibly exist.

It was much simpler and less wonderful than the first stage — there wasn't any surreal or fantastic experience, just utter certainty that I couldn't possibly exist — in any way that I conventionally understood.

The *Sakadāgāmī* (once-returner) is the name of the state of being of the second stage. There are no *fetters* that are *gained*, but there is a significant *weakening* of the remaining two *gross fetters* — those of *sensory desire* (*kāma-rāga*) and *ill-will* (*vyāpāda*). This manifests as an increase in spiritual resolve, and movement towards the Spiritual Path.

It is not necessary to experience *jhāna* (meditative absorption) to achieve these breakthroughs, but it certainly helps. *Jhāna* focuses the mind onto a simple object, allowing it to become fully absorbed in the object, for a period of time. It is not essential that one gains *jhāna* prior to enlightenment, for there is a path called the *path of bare insight* (*sukkha vipassanā*) — but I suspect we all experience first *jhāna* a lot more often than we recognise.

First *jhāna* is simply when through becoming fixated on a sensory object, we *forget* to think about ourselves for a few moments, and we experience joy (*pīti*). This 'touching' of *jhāna* is neither stable nor really under any control, and very different to the sustained *jhāna* achieved through focusing, say, on a meditative *kasina* disk, but it is still *jhāna*. We can achieve this through listening to music, or becoming absorbed in other dynamic phenomena such as watching a show or reading a book.

For me, being absorbed in my studies, and reflecting whilst listening to music seemed to be sufficient. This might be at odds with what established meditators tell us about *jhāna* — they are talking about controlled and masterful control over this phenomenon, whereas I contend that even fleeting and poorly controlled *jhāna* is sufficient for the breakthrough.

I experienced much deeper forms of *jhāna* at different stages of my journey, yet, the message I am trying to impart is that while refined meditative states have value, they are not always essential and can sometimes distract one from the path.

When I experienced this breakthrough I had yet to study Buddhism with any degree of sincerity or seriousness, but I was aware of the need for morality — I think my paradigm at this stage was focused on the 42 moral statements of Maat! Nevertheless, one must either instinctively or through guidance be following a moral framework, analogous to the noble eightfold path (*Ariya aṭṭhaṅgika magga*) for progress to be possible. One must have a deep suspicion of temptation and a desire to resist it.

Following this breakthrough there was a recognition of my confusion and uncertainty and this resulted in a stabilisation of my manic and fraught overthinking. I would slowly withdraw for a period and eventually let go of my preceding goals and motivations with increasing ease. It took time, for it was another six years before I experienced the next breakthrough, during which time I had written my first six books and spent significant down time. Only with this breakthrough did my concepts of being on a path really solidify.

The journey of spiritual awakening is deeply personal yet universal in its fundamental truths. Whether through sustained practice or spontaneous insight, the path unfolds uniquely for each seeker. The key lies not in rigid adherence to specific methods but in maintaining sincere inquiry, ethical conduct, and openness to truth in whatever form it manifests. As you continue your own journey, remember that enlightenment often comes not through forcing progress, but through allowing understanding to arise naturally.

Keep on learning and practising and you will get there.

Nigredo

Study Guide: Spiritual Orientation

This chapter examines the progression through early Buddhist enlightenment stages, focusing on breakthroughs, meditative absorption, and ethical conduct in spiritual development.

CORE CONCEPTS

- Relationship between meditation and enlightenment
- Role of ethical conduct in spiritual progress
- Integration of spiritual insights
- Nature of enlightenment experiences
- Progression through stages of awakening

NEW TERMINOLOGY

Anicca: Impermanence

Dukkha: Suffering, unsatisfactoriness

Kāma-rāga: Sensual desire or lust

Kasina: Visual meditation object

Maat: Ancient Egyptian concept of truth, balance, and moral order

Sukkha *vipassanā*: Dry insight meditation without jhanic attainment

Śūnyatā: Emptiness, lack of intrinsic substance

Upāya: Skilful means

Vyāpāda: Ill-will or aversion

MAIN THEMES

- Nature of enlightenment experience
- Meditative development
- Path progression
- Integration of breakthroughs
- Ethical foundation

- Role of spontaneous realisation

PRACTICAL APPLICATIONS

- Development of ethical conduct
- Practice of meditation and absorption
- Integration of insights into daily life
- Cultivation of spiritual resolve

INTEGRATION POINTS

- Connection to Chapter 3 (Evolution of Adulthood)
- Links to Chapter 6 (Enlightenment)
- Links to Chapter 7 (The Call to Adventure)

COMMON MISCONCEPTIONS

- Formal jhāna is required for enlightenment
- Progress must be forced through rigid practice
- Enlightenment comes only through formal meditation

REFLECTION QUESTIONS

- How has your understanding of the path evolved through practice?
- What role does ethical conduct play in your spiritual development?
- How do you maintain balance between effort and allowing in practice?

PROGRESS INDICATORS

- Increased commitment to spiritual practice
- Weakening of fetters
- Stabilisation of mind
- Clear direction in practice
- Integration of insights into daily life

Subject

Insight	Recognition of emptiness	Breakthrough experience
Absorption	Natural jhanic states	Concentration development
Ethics	Moral framework	Path foundation
Integration	Personal understanding	Universal truth

Progression

Aspect	Challenge	Solution
Physical	Disruption of normal function	Maintain basic routines
Mental	Confusion and instability	Rational observation
Social	Isolation and misunderstanding	Selective silence
Spiritual	Grandiose delusions	Focus on practice

Progress Indicators

Stage	Characteristics	Changes
Initial breakthrough	Insight into emptiness	Certainty of non-self
Integration period	Confusion and withdrawal	Stabilisation of mind
Further development	Increased commitment	Weakening of fetters
Path solidification	Clear direction	Established practice

Nigredo

"*This body is not mine, I am not this body, this body is not my self.*"
— *Anattalakkhana Sutta (SN 22.59)*

SUBJECT

45. No Self

"What we call 'I' is just a swinging door which moves when we inhale and when we exhale." [58]

In this chapter, we explore the profound implications of realising non-self (anatta) at the Sakadāgāmī stage of enlightenment. We examine how this understanding gradually transforms one's experience, the challenges that arise during this phase, and practical approaches for navigating the dissolution of self-identity. The text addresses both traditional Buddhist methods and alternative paths particularly relevant for Western practitioners, while offering guidance on avoiding common pitfalls of spiritual materialism.

With the realisation of *Sakadāgāmī*, the second stage of enlightenment, one gains mainly resolve and spiritual direction. It took many years, despite this profound insight, for thoughts and feelings to comfortably settle on the fact that the self is entirely conceptual.

I recognise that *my path* was hardly the conventional path of the Buddhist disciple, yet, it seems this is hardly necessary and might, in some ways, bring its own issues. Being a solitary student of the *dharma* one is left fully to explore its meaning without any corruption from even a well-meaning, but still deluded *superior*. Within religious institutions, merit (within the community) can arise through simple persistence, and many can become incredibly familiar with the *dharma* yet still lack the necessary breakthroughs.

---

[58] *Suzuki, S. (1970). Zen Mind, Beginner's Mind*

My studies at this stage were largely mystical, and a mixture of gnostic and Eastern philosophies. It would be only as I approached what I take as the third stage, *Anāgāmī*, did my focus fully settle on the Buddhist scriptures.

The *ideal* path is one of discipline and largely *samatha* (tranquility) meditation until one develops the faculties of insight. Yet, it is reported that the *Western* intellect finds tranquility meditation particularly difficult and often *vipassanā* (insight meditation) is well established in the seeker before the need and resolve to practice tranquility is manifest.

Samatha meditation is not necessary, and for those who find sitting meditation difficult but have the overthinking, that might manifest as *mental illness*, don't stress too much if this is a challenge. The main benefit is that tranquility meditation offers a *shelter* where one can enjoy peace and even *jhanic* bliss as an escape from the stresses of normal life — during which deeper insights may arise.

However, it is the insights that arise through a near constant examination of *Subjective Reality* that do all the heavy lifting, and it is likely that the modern spiritual seeker is already *troubled* by this.

Recognising this overthinking as *vipassanā* helps–but probably not much, as it tends to be exhausting to oneself and others at first.

I recommend that one learns to *feed* this curious beast with quality content, which means dragging one's attention from the fantastic to the more mundane, practical learnings of your favourite system.

Writing helped me, almost as a *completion activity*, where I summarised my own understanding of old paradigms. One must almost *put to bed* old concepts of self in order to fully move on to new pastures of experience.

One notices that this fundamental idea that *there cannot be a self* slowly detoxifies one's *Subjective Reality*. The mind is hesitant to pursue egoistic defences and one withdraws from arguments to defend this concept of self. Unlike the more painful and confusing experience of *Sotāpanna* (stream-entry), once one achieves *Sakadāgāmī* one is more focused and less attached to the disappointments of conditioned existence. This is, however, quite subtle and one remains participant in life, but increasingly *aloof* and without any particular conceit.

With a decreasing sense of self it can be quite easy to grasp onto grandiose or fantastical ideas of identity. These are known as the *skandha demons*, and can be particularly problematic if one has access to *jhanic* experiences, which can easily be misinterpreted as divine messages or beings. It is unlikely, in truth, that these are actual entities, demonic or otherwise. Instead they represent fragments of self that *take shelter* within otherworldly concepts.

Sometimes it is unavoidable to identify as such, and probably harmless, in the big picture. Yet, it is from these delusions that cults are created, so one must always retain a sober and cautious attitude and actively dismiss any ideas that arise. At best, one feels slightly foolish; at worst, one might face psychiatric institutionalisation.

The journey beyond the concept of self is both liberating and challenging. As one progresses through the stages of enlightenment, the dissolution of self-identity becomes more pronounced, yet more natural. The key is to maintain awareness of the process while avoiding the pitfalls of spiritual materialism and the temptation to create new, more sophisticated forms of self-identification. Through continued practice and vigilance, the path unfolds naturally, leading towards ever-greater freedom from the bonds of self-conception.

"The ego exists as a series of defensive reactions to death anxiety." [59]

Study Guide: No Self

This chapter explores the Sakadāgāmī stage of enlightenment, focusing on non-self understanding and providing guidance for both traditional Buddhist and Western practitioners in navigating self-concept dissolution.

CORE CONCEPTS
- Understanding non-self (anatta)
- Progressive dissolution of self-identity
- Balance of insight and tranquility practices

[59] Becker, E. (1973). The Denial of Death

NIGREDO

- Integration of Western intellectual approaches
- Management of spiritual materialism

NEW TERMINOLOGY

Anatta *(Non-self, absence of permanent self)*
Karuṇā *(Compassion)*
Kshanti *(Patience)*
Mettā *(Loving-kindness)*
Mokṣa *(Liberation)*
Saṃsāra *(Cycle of rebirth, conditioned existence)*
Tathāgatagarbha *(Buddha-nature)*

MAIN THEMES

1. Nature of Self-Dissolution
- Progressive weakening of self-concept
- Relationship between insight and tranquility
- Role of intellectual understanding
- Connection to enlightenment

2. Meditation Approaches
- Western challenges with traditional methods
- Integration of overthinking as practice
- Balance of samatha and vipassanā
- Links to evolution of adulthood

3. Working with Delusion
- Recognition of skandha demons
- Management of spiritual materialism
- Processing through writing
- Connection to Shadow work

COMMON MISCONCEPTIONS

- Mistaking jhanic experiences for divine messages
- Developing new forms of spiritual identity
- Becoming attached to spiritual experiences
- Neglecting practical aspects of practice
- Over-emphasis on intellectual understanding

INTEGRATION POINTS

- Regular journaling of insights and experiences
- Balanced meditation practice
- Ongoing study of Buddhist texts
- Regular reality-checking of experiences
- Maintaining connection with daily life

REFLECTION QUESTIONS

- How has your understanding of self changed through practice?
- What challenges have you faced in letting go of self-identity?
- How do you work with spiritual experiences without becoming attached?

PROGRESS INDICATORS

- Decreased attachment to self-concept
- Reduced defensive reactions
- Greater equanimity in daily life
- Natural unfolding of practice
- Integration of insights into daily experience

SUBJECT

46. First Steps

"The journey of a thousand miles begins with a single step." [60]

In this chapter, we explore the delicate period following an initial glimpse of enlightenment, examining how the spiritual seeker navigates the challenging transition from profound insight back to ordinary life. Like ice gradually thawing, this phase marks the subtle beginning of deep transformation, where external changes may be imperceptible while internal reconstruction occurs. We'll investigate how to integrate spiritual awakening with daily existence while maintaining the delicate balance between mundane responsibilities and the pull toward liberation.

Enlightenment bestows a glimpse of something beyond description, which proves both unhelpful and tends to alienate and confuse. Yet, when this confusion settles, one is left with a beacon — subtle, but ever-present — towards which one inevitably gravitates.

Suspicions are confirmed that there exists something profoundly wrong with the world; through that transcendental experience, we recognise ourselves as prisoners of our own mind (*saṃsāra*). Eventually, one commits to finding this hidden and perilous path towards liberation (*mokṣa*).

The process resembles *thawing*.

---

[60] *Traditional translation of Tao Te Ching, Chapter 64 by Lao Tzu,*

Nigredo

For a time, nothing appears to change. All movement at this stage is mental, a reconstruction of being with new goals and ideals. This is our embryonic *Buddha-nature* (*Tathāgatagarbha*), developing as we quietly gestate an entirely new form of consciousness.

Months may pass before we feel sufficiently courageous to return to conventional life. We begin gradually, remembering the ancient Zen koan:

> *Before Enlightenment, chop wood, fetch water.*
> *After Enlightenment, chop wood, fetch water.* [61]

We must attend to our daily needs and gradually rebuild our capacity to maintain material existence.

Like ice melting, there might be sudden fractures and whole segments might fall away. This is natural, and one must cultivate patience (*kshanti*), compassion (*karuṇā*) and loving-kindness (*mettā*) towards friends and family who might struggle to understand our sudden transformation of character.

It will be the most challenging, relentless and painful work you have ever undertaken. Yet, paradoxically, it is also easier than anything previously attempted. Why?

Now you possess spiritual direction. Every thought turns towards *Nirvāṇa* and liberation from conditioned existence (*saṃsāra*). Though ultimate success is inevitable, can you sustain the wait? The initial steps are almost imperceptible, mere subtle nudges that establish one on the path before awareness of treading it arises. For a time, there are no rewards, and one advances through sheer faith alone, like wading through mud.

Eventually, one reaches what could be viewed as a midpoint between the alchemical stages of *Nigredo* (the blackening) and *Albedo* (the whitening), where one finally emerges from the subterranean cave of being to feel the first weak rays of sunshine on one's face — as if for the first time.

---

[61] *Traditional Zen saying. Layman P'ang (740—808)*

Subject

At this point, confidence soars as not only has direction been established, but now one journeys in sunlight until the path's end.

This emergence marks not an end but a beginning — the dawn of true practice. As the light grows stronger, the path becomes clearer, yet paradoxically more subtle. The journey continues through increasingly refined states of consciousness, each step revealing new depths of understanding and fresh challenges to overcome. Yet now, bathed in the light of awareness, every obstacle serves as a teacher, every setback an opportunity for growth, as we progress inexorably towards complete awakening.

> "I felt my energy revive, and said to myself, In spite of everything
> I shall rise again: I will take up my pencil,
> which I have forsaken in my great discouragement,
> and I will go on with my drawing.
> From that moment everything has seemed transformed for me." [62]

Study Guide: First Steps

This chapter examines the initial post-enlightenment phase, focusing on the transition from spiritual insight to daily life integration, using the metaphor of thawing ice to illustrate subtle yet profound internal transformation.

CORE CONCEPTS

- Recognition of conditioned existence
- Internal reconstruction while maintaining external stability
- Gradual integration of spiritual insights with daily life
- Development of patience and compassion
- Movement from darkness to light

NEW TERMINOLOGY

Buddha-nature (Tathāgatagarbha): Embryonic development of new consciousness
Karuṇā: Compassion
Kshanti: Patience
Mettā: Loving-kindness
Mokṣa: Liberation
Nirvāṇa: State of enlightenment
Saṃsāra: Conditioned existence

MAIN THEMES

---

[62] Letter #136 in "The Letters of Vincent Van Gogh," edited by Vincent van Gogh and published by Constable & Robinson Ltd, New York, 2011. This moment marked a significant turning point in Van Gogh's life, as he recommitted himself to his artistic endeavours despite previous setbacks.

NIGREDO

1. Nature of Awakening
- Initial glimpse and resulting confusion
- Recognition of conditioned existence
- Development of Buddha-nature

2. Process of Transformation
- Mental reconstruction phase
- Gradual integration with daily life
- Role of patience and compassion
- Thawing process metaphor

3. Path Progression
- Movement from darkness to light
- Faith-based initial practice
- Emergence of confidence
- Transition from Nigredo to Albedo

PRACTICAL APPLICATIONS
- Balance of spiritual and mundane activities
- Integration of practice with daily life
- Cultivation of patience and compassion
- Maintenance of daily responsibilities

INTEGRATION POINTS
- Connection to Enlightenment
- Links to Shadow Work
- Relationship to Symbols
- Connection to Call to Adventure

PROGRESS INDICATORS
- Recognition of conditioned existence
- Development of patience
- Integration of practice with daily life
- Growing spiritual confidence
- Natural emergence of compassion
- Sustained practice despite challenges
- Clear sense of direction

REFLECTION QUESTIONS
- How do you maintain daily responsibilities while undergoing spiritual transformation
- What helps you stay grounded during periods of profound change
- How do you balance solitude and engagement with others

SUBJECT

47. Establishing the Way

"In Zen practice we want to harmonise our inner world with the outer world. When these are in harmony, we are one with our surroundings, and this is enlightenment." [63]

In this chapter, we explore the subtle yet profound changes that occur after initial enlightenment experiences. As the spiritual path becomes established, confusion gives way to natural direction, though not through intellectual understanding. We examine how transcendental consciousness transforms everyday awareness, leading to spontaneous virtue and authentic service. The journey through this stage reveals how genuine spiritual progress manifests not through striving, but through the natural unfolding of wisdom and compassion.

Although metaphorical, attaining the second stage of enlightenment appears to provide direction. While confusing at first, and incomprehensible on an intellectual level for years to come, one develops an instinct that gradually matures.

Buddhist teaching explains that a key distinction between the *citta* (consciousness) of an unenlightened person and that of a *Sotāpanna* (stream-enterer) lies in how the mental *roots* operate. In the unrealised mind, only one root functions at any given moment — either greed, hatred, or delusion. Even in *wholesome* states, only one positive root—non-greed (generosity), non-hatred (loving-kindness), or non-delusion (wisdom) — can manifest in a single thought-moment.

---

[63] *Suzuki, S. (1970). Zen Mind, Beginner's Mind*

Upon realisation, the *Sotāpanna* gains access to the *phala* (fruition) consciousness following the *magga* (path) moment. This transcendental consciousness can seemingly accommodate all three *wholesome roots* simultaneously, though this may be difficult to comprehend from our mundane perspective. The *unwholesome roots* remain forever unstable.

The *phala cittas*, typically two or three *resultant consciousness* moments arising immediately after attaining the path, likely replace the *bhavaṅga* (life-continuum) consciousness of the practitioner, representing the deepest aspect of being. These become an internal sanctuary, providing solace even amid life's fiercest storms.

Initially, the Buddhist teaching that a *Sotāpanna* would have at most seven more lifetimes seemed incredible. Buddhism's precise nature challenges belief yet becomes awe-inspiring with understanding. The transformations through Arahantship appear incomprehensible, but only to the non-persistent scholar — reminiscent of that line from *The Matrix*: "The Answers are coming."

Looking back nearly a decade, while there was clearly direction and purpose to my progress, the experience itself was purely instinctual and challenging. Bereft of purpose or goals, I was practically blind and distressed. I found solace in what might be called therapeutic play — immersing myself in clearly defined projects, primarily writing.

For approximately four months, I maintained a daily routine — breakfast, several hours of writing, followed by a lengthy, brisk walk. In retrospect, this might be classified as mania, though it was unusually contained and lacked many typical negative features. During this period, I wrote, attempted to edit, and published six books exploring mental illness and spirituality.

This project helped restore some semblance of routine, and though I wouldn't write again for couple of years, it initiated my gradual return to a more conventional, less hermetic existence.

The trauma and confusion from my treatment by medical boards and the loss of my career persisted, but affected me only when directly contemplated. I engaged with life where possible. Though I missed financial security, reflecting on the stress required to return to medicine made it seem worthless.

Subject

Being *good* isn't straightforward. Internal critics challenge our efforts, while others may perceive us as weak or naive. This creates much of our suffering — we aspire to goodness and righteousness but fear ridicule or exploitation.

This perhaps explains why the selfless Buddhist finds goodness natural, while the pious Christian might experience torment. Striving to be *The Good* requires constant maintenance, whereas with selflessness, no alternative exists. Consider a well-lit empty room — darkness absent until the smallest dust mote creates shadow.

The eleventh alchemical stage, multiplication, depicts domesticated life — the *Return of the Hero* or divine descent into materiality. Despite feeling broken, empty, and professionally rejected, I gradually reintegrated into life. Finding myself purposeless, I created purpose through helping others.

When nameless, utterly silent emptiness replaces self-concept, *wholesome karma* flows naturally. Complete inner joylessness allows appreciation of others' happiness without attachment or envy.

While I now recognise this as a process, it felt bleak then. My entire being felt raw and sensitive. Despite anxiety, detachment, and confusion, I accepted gradual return to *normal* existence, suspecting its benefit, though everything felt intensified. I progressed uncertainly, but in the right direction.

During difficult periods, I contemplated retreating to my former hermetic simplicity. This gravitational pull persists temporarily. Challenges seem endless and thankless, but difficulty stems from unrecognised attachments to an illusory past. Release brings sudden lightness of being.

The alchemist naturally emerges from *Nigredo* once direction establishes. Brief transcendental experience provides perspective on thoughts, feelings, and consciousness without complete identification. This awareness teaches karmic consequences, gradually reducing hatred, greed, and ignorance.

Without masterful guidance, the process remains unconscious, yet despondency gradually yields to wonder. Daily realisations of deep truths emerge through continuous contemplative mindfulness — *vipassanā*.

Nigredo

Eventually, one must acknowledge positive progression. Beyond this comes realisation of ultimate control. The alchemist, viewing from transcendental perspective, observes their karmic interactions, naturally developing *wholesome* responses based on non-greed, non-hatred, and non-delusion. These create positive *karma*, improving welfare. Interactions become restorative, transforming unwholesome *karma* into *wholesome* responses.

Approaching *Albedo*, this represents the stone's *silver transmuting* property. *Silver* symbolises the moon and natural cycles. The Alchemist habitually absorbing *unwholesome karma* and reflecting *wholesome* responses restores natural environmental balance, manifesting as subtle healing — first mentally, then physically. Though unnoticed by the unrealised, this process is neither miraculous nor mysterious.

This realisation brings danger if one attaches to identity, commonly manifesting as fantasies of becoming a great healer or prophet. Vigilance against mundane fantasy is essential. This *skandha-māra* (*demon* of aggregates) can cause great harm if embellished. Cult temptations inevitably diminish beneficial powers, leading to coercion, secrecy, and eventual downfall. When such fantasies arise, one must laugh at oneself and the beautiful demon's enchantment.

Confidence grows as life's workings become clear. We realise that while still inhabiting a challenging world, we've become mere observers rather than permanent residents.

Keep seeking.

As the journey continues, the path becomes increasingly subtle yet profound. The initial confusion gives way to clarity, not through intellectual understanding but through lived experience. The transformation continues, each step revealing new depths of wisdom and compassion, while the ultimate truth remains both intimately close and infinitely vast. In this eternal dance of awakening, we find our true nature not in the extraordinary, but in the simple act of being present to whatever arises.

SUBJECT

Study Guide: Establishing the Way

This chapter examines post-enlightenment transformations, focusing on how spiritual direction naturally emerges and consciousness transforms, leading to spontaneous virtue and authentic service.

CORE CONCEPTS

- *Consciousness transformation through phala replacing bhavaṅga*
- *Natural emergence of virtue without striving*
- *Alchemical multiplication stage and silver transmutation*
- *Integration of wholesome mental roots*
- *Transcendental perspective development*

NEW TERMINOLOGY

Bhavaṅga-citta: *Background consciousness maintaining mental continuity between active thoughts*

Magga-phala: *Combined path and fruition consciousness moments*

Phala consciousness: *Transcendental consciousness following enlightenment*

Skandha-māra: *Demon of aggregates representing attachment to spiritual identity*

Sotāpanna: *Stream-enterer stage of enlightenment*

MAIN THEMES

1. Transformed Consciousness

- *Transcendental insight integration*
- *Wholesome mental roots development*
- *Enlightened versus ordinary awareness*
- *Relationship to everyday wisdom*

2. Path Integration

- *Return to conventional existence*
- *Creative expression as healing*
- *Development of natural routine*
- *Balance between transcendental and mundane*

3. Spiritual Maturity

- *Natural emergence of virtue*
- *Release of spiritual identity*
- *Service without attachment*
- *Transformation of unwholesome karma*

PRACTICAL APPLICATIONS

- *Mindful observation of karmic interactions*
- *Development of wholesome responses*
- *Integration of transcendental perspective*
- *Healing through natural balance restoration*

NIGREDO

INTEGRATION POINTS

- *Connection to enlightenment processes*
- *Relationship to Shadow work*
- *Links to symbolic understanding*
- *Evolution of adult consciousness*

COMMON MISCONCEPTIONS

- *Attachment to healer identity*
- *Necessity of conscious striving*
- *Separation of spiritual and conventional life*
- *Nature of true spiritual progress*

REFLECTION QUESTIONS

- *How has your relationship with virtue evolved naturally through practice?*
- *What role does service play in your spiritual development?*
- *How do you maintain authenticity in conventional reality?*
- *How do you balance transcendental insight with everyday wisdom?*
- *What is your relationship to spiritual identity?*

PROGRESS INDICATORS

- *Natural emergence of wholesome action*
- *Release of striving and spiritual materialism*
- *Integration of transcendental perspective*
- *Development of healing capacity*
- *Authentic service without attachment*

SUBJECT

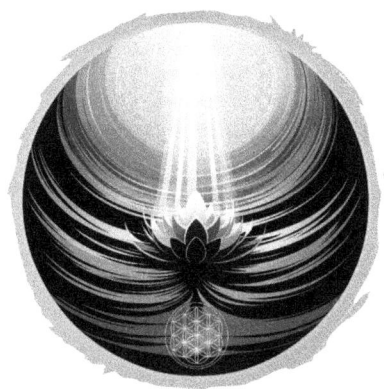

48. The Key to the Gate

"Man Stands in His Own Shadow and Wonders Why It's Dark." [64]

The Key to the Gate marks the culmination of the Nigredo phase, where the initial darkness of spiritual transformation begins to yield to the first rays of genuine wisdom. This chapter explores how authentic spiritual understanding emerges gradually yet inexorably, independent of external conditions. We examine the transition from spiritual desolation to renewed faith, while acknowledging the psychological challenges that accompany this profound transformation.

Spiritual liberation (*mokṣa*) or emancipation, is almost impossible to understand whilst one is trapped in material reality. *What is the point of Church?* one might ask, and through ignorance, one might assume a handful of mundane reasons.

It seems one's faith, in something better than *this*, really does go out, like an extinguished candle. To find it, it needs to be ignited by another, who might not always be human.

We lost hope during the *Dark Night of the Soul*, a profound period of spiritual desolation and transformation and for a while have been pushing on, blind, weary and uncertain. Yet, with an increasing and natural understanding of *karma*, we are undoing past mistakes and slowly improving our environment.

---

[64] ~ *Zen Proverb*

Nigredo

There reaches a point where the gloom of existence starts to lift and we experience, like rays of sunlight reaching the deepest and darkest part of an ancient forest, glimmers of hope.

Now, whilst this process is very slow, painfully slow, it does have qualities that set it aside from everything else. This, recovery of self, will be completely independent of anything else. It is step wise, gradual and completely impervious to conditioned existence. It is the gradual dawning of wisdom, the blossoming of which is inevitable.

When things are dark from now on, they can never get so dark as to extinguish this radiant wisdom. At this stage one still suffers *confusion* — yet, this confusion under the radiance of wisdom is shown to be simply old habits that are retained for sentimentality.

There will be more challenges and dangers to face, but now one has an inner sun that grants one fortitude and renewed vigour in treading a path which is suddenly adorned with fragrant flowers and the healing essence of the chalice.

Once one realises one is on the right path, through a rising crescendo of evidence, Joy returns and can be quite overwhelming. This can be rapturous as relief is manifested and one enters *jhāna* (meditative absorption) spontaneously. Meditation on the Brahmacarya (the noble conduct of life), the *Brahmā's Chariot* of the four illimitable qualities, kindness, compassion, appreciative joy and equanimity becomes second nature and one can naturally excel in these meditations.

The mental ramifications are significant and can be problematic. It is clearly very easy to identify with or idolise previous saints or divine aspects. Furthermore, one recognises there is a truth to something that was unbelievable. This can seriously mess with one's head until one overcomes the ninth *fetter*, which is restlessness (*uddhacca*), on the path to enlightenment.

We must at all times remember we are merely students studying the most fantastic syllabus in existence. It all eventually makes sense, and we are *hacking* our sense of being—bound to be a few distracting glitches.

We must remember we are on a path, and this is the first half of the process. Each path is more fantastic than the rest, and yes, we are approaching the level of *saint*, which is mind-blowing.

Subject

Yet, we have hardly scratched the surface.

Reminds me of *The Matrix*.

> *Buckle your seatbelt Dorothy,*
>
> *because Kansas is going bye-bye*

Thus ends *Nigredo*, the alchemical stage of blackening, symbolising the initial phase of spiritual transformation.

As we continue this journey, we must embrace the unfolding mystery with humility and courage. Each step forward reveals new dimensions of existence, challenging our perceptions and expanding our understanding. The path is not without its trials, but it is through these very challenges that we grow stronger and more attuned to the profound truths that lie ahead. Let us walk this path with unwavering faith, knowing that the light within us will guide us through even the darkest of times.

Study Guide: The Key To The Gate

The chapter examines the transition from Nigredo phase to spiritual awakening, focusing on the emergence of wisdom from darkness and the psychological challenges of transformation.

CORE CONCEPTS

- *Awakening process as gradual transformation*
- *Role of karmic understanding in spiritual development*
- *Psychological integration of altered states*
- *Systematic path progression*
- *Management of spiritual experiences*

NEW TERMINOLOGY

Mokṣa: *spiritual liberation in Indian religions*

Brahmacarya: *noble conduct of life following spiritual principles*

Uddhacca: *mental restlessness, ninth fetter in Buddhist psychology*

MAIN THEMES

1. *Nature of spiritual liberation*
- *Impossibility of understanding mokṣa in material reality*
- *External ignition of faith requirement*
- *Emergence from Dark Night*
- *Connection to enlightenment*

2. *Process of transformation*
- *Development of wisdom*
- *Independence from external conditions*
- *Natural understanding of karma*
- *Relationship to Dark Night of the Soul*

3. *Psychological integration*

NIGREDO

- Management of spontaneous jhanic states
- Development of divine qualities
- Identification challenges with saints
- Shadow work integration

INTEGRATION POINTS
- Connection to Chapter 6 Enlightenment
- Connection to Chapter 10 The Shadow
- Connection to Chapter 11 Dark Night of the Soul
- Connection to Chapter 47 Establishing the Way

PRACTICAL APPLICATIONS
- Meditation on Brahmacarya
- Development of four divine qualities
- Management of altered states
- Balancing humility with insight

PROGRESS INDICATORS
- Natural understanding of karma
- Spontaneous jhanic states
- Development of inner wisdom
- Independence from external conditions

REFLECTION QUESTIONS
- Understanding of spiritual liberation evolution
- Role of faith in current practice
- Maintaining perspective during intense spiritual experiences

COMMON MISCONCEPTIONS
- Enlightenment as instant versus gradual process
- Independence from external conditions meaning
- Relationship between psychological and spiritual growth

Subject

"Like the moon, come out from behind the clouds! Shine."

- often attributed to Gautama Buddha.
This phrase appears in Thomas Byrom's poetic rendering of the Dhammapada,
a collection of sayings of the Buddha.

"...and we emerged to see once more the stars."

– *Dante Alighieri, Inferno, Canto XXXIV*

APPENDIX

Glossary & Index

Alchemic Terms

AIR —*Primary element of movement and intellect*
Associated: thought, expansion;
Class: Primary elements

ALBEDO [al—BAY—doh]— *Second whitening phase of alchemical transformation representing purification and illumination*
Associated: lunar consciousness, purification;
Class: Alchemical stages

ALEMBIC [ah—LEM—bik]— *Transformation vessel used for spiritual distillation and refinement*
Associated: containment, transformation;
Class: Alchemical equipment

BATH OF MARY—*Gentle heating vessel symbolising gradual spiritual transformation* Associated: gentle change, nurturing;
Class: Alchemical equipment

BLACK CROW—*Symbol representing initial darkness and decomposition of Nigredo*
Associated: darkness, beginning;
Class: Alchemical symbols

BLACK SUN—*Symbol representing illumination found in darkness*
Associated: darkness, enlightenment;
Class: Alchemical symbols

CADUCEUS [kah—DOO—see—us]—*Two serpents intertwined around a staff representing balanced opposing forces*
Associated: duality, healing;
Class: Alchemical symbols

CALCINATION —*First operation breaking down ego through intense heat*
Associated: purification, burning;
Class: Alchemical operations

CITRINITAS [sih—TREE—nih—tahs]—*Third yellowing phase developing wisdom*
Associated: solar consciousness, maturation;
Class: Alchemical stages

COAGULATION—*Final stage of spiritual completion*
Associated: manifestation, wholeness; Class: Alchemical stages

CONJUNCTION—*Union of purified elements into new whole*
Associated: integration, harmony;
Class: Alchemical operations

COPPER (VENUS ♀)
- *Metal associated with harmony and integration*
Associated: Balance, relationships, artistic expression
Class: Alchemical symbol
Related Terms: Venus, Metals, Planetary correspondences
Etymology: Latin cuprum, from Cyprus, source of copper in ancient times

CRUCIBLE —*Container for intense transformation*
Associated: testing, purification;
Class: Alchemical equipment

DISSOLUTION—*Stage of dissolving illusions and facing subconscious*
Associated: fluidity, revelation;
Class: Alchemical operations;

DISTILLATION—*Further purification of the spirit*
Associated: refinement, clarity;
Class: Alchemical operations

EARTH—*Primary element of manifestation and form*
Associated: stability, grounding;
Class: Primary elements

FERMENTATION—*Death and rebirth process in two parts*
Associated: transformation, renewal;
Class: Alchemical operations

FIRE—*Primary element of transformation*
Associated: energy, passion;
Class: Primary elements

GOLD (SUN ☉)—*Metal symbolising spiritual perfection and enlightened consciousness*
Associated: Illumination, divine wisdom, highest attainment
Class: Alchemical symbol
Related Terms: Sun, Rubedo, Philosopher's Stone
Etymology: Old English gold, from Proto—Germanic *gulþą

GREEN LION—*Symbol representing the raw spiritual seeker*
Associated: beginning stage, hunger;
Class: Alchemical symbols

Appendix

Hermetic Vessel—*Sealed container representing focused consciousness*
Associated: containment, transformation;
Class: Alchemical equipment

Iron (Mars ♂)
- *Metal representing willpower and determination*
Associated: Strength, courage, martial qualities
Class: Alchemical symbol
Related Terms: Mars, Metals, Planetary correspondences
Etymology: Old English īsern, from Proto—Germanic *īsarną

Lead (Saturn ♄)—*Metal symbolising base matter and limitation*
Associated: Foundation, discipline, structure
Class: Alchemical symbol
Related Terms: Saturn, Prima Materia, Nigredo
Etymology: Old English lēad, from Proto—Germanic *laudą

Mercury (☿)—*Element symbolising fluidity and transformation*
Associated: Adaptability, communication, alchemical processes
Class: Alchemical symbol
Related Terms: Quicksilver, Hermetic principle, Caduceus
Etymology: Latin Mercurius, Roman god of commerce

Nigredo [ni—GRAY—doh]—*First blackening phase representing darkness and decomposition*
Associated: Shadow work, purification;
Class: Alchemical stages

Opus Magnum [OH—pus MAG—num]—*The complete alchemical work of spiritual transformation*
Associated: Great Work, stages;
Class: Alchemical processes

Ouroboros [oo—ROH—bor—os]—*Serpent eating its tail representing cyclical nature*
Associated: cycles, unity;
Class: Alchemical symbols

Pelican—*Symbol of self—sacrifice and nurturing transformation*
Associated: sacrifice, nurturing;
Class: Alchemical symbols

Philosopher's Stone—*Ultimate achievement representing spiritual perfection*
Associated: enlightenment, completion;
Class: Alchemical symbols

Prima Materia [PREE—mah mah—TAIR—ee—ah]—*The original substance or starting point*
Associated: potential, beginning;
Class: Alchemical substances

Quintessence [kwin—TESS—uns]—*The fifth element representing spirit*
Associated: integration, transcendence;
Class: Primary elements

Rebis [RAY—bis]—*Symbol of unified duality and balance of opposites*
Associated: integration, wholeness;
Class: Alchemical symbols

Red Lion—*Symbol of mastered spiritual energy*
Associated: mastery, completion;
Class: Alchemical symbols

Retort [ri—TORT]—*Sealed vessel for transformation*
Associated: containment, focus;
Class: Alchemical equipment

Rubedo [roo—BAY—doh]—*Final reddening phase representing completion*
Associated: perfection, integration;
Class: Alchemical stages

Salt—*Represents physical form and manifestation*
Associated: stability, grounding;
Class: Alchemical principles

Secret Fire—*Transformative power of spiritual awareness in alchemy*
Associated: Inner transformation, spiritual catalyst, hidden wisdom
Class: Alchemical concept
Related Terms: Kundalini, Dragon's breath, Alchemical heat
Etymology: English secret (hidden) + fire (transformative element)

Separation—*Alchemical process of discerning true from false elements*
Associated: Discrimination, purification, analysis
Class: Alchemical operation
Related Terms: Solve et coagula, Distillation, Calcination
Etymology: Latin separatio, act of separating

Serpents—*Dual serpents representing fixed and volatile aspects of transformation*
Associated: Duality, integration, cycles of nature
Class: Alchemical symbol
Related Terms: Ouroboros, Caduceus, Kundalini
Etymology: Latin serpens, from serpere (to creep)

Silver (Moon ☽)—*Metal symbolising intuition and receptive consciousness*
Associated: Reflection, emotions, subconscious mind
Class: Alchemical symbol
Related Terms: Moon, Albedo, Lunar consciousness
Etymology: Old English seolfor, from Proto—Germanic *silubrā

SOLVE ET COAGULA [SOL—vay et koh—AG—yoo—lah]—Principle of breaking down and recombining
Associated: analysis, synthesis;
Class: Alchemical processes

SQUARED CIRCLE—Symbol representing integration of heaven and earth
Associated: unity, balance;
Class: Alchemical symbols

SULPHUR [SUL—fur]—Represents consciousness and active principle
Associated: spirit, animation;
Class: Alchemical principles

TIN (JUPITER ♃)—Metal associated with expansion and wisdom
Associated: Growth, abundance, benevolence
Class: Alchemical symbol
Related Terms: Jupiter, Metals, Planetary correspondences

Etymology: Old English tin, from Proto—Germanic *tiną

WATER—Primary element representing emotion and dissolution
Associated: feeling, purification;
Class: Primary elements

Buddhist Terms

ABHIDHAMMA [ah—bee—DAH—mah]—Advanced Buddhist psychological and philosophical teachings analysing consciousness, mental factors, and matter
Associated: Buddhist theory, consciousness studies
Class: Buddhist scripture
Related Terms: Dharma, Sutta, Vinaya
Etymology: Pāli, abhi (higher/special) + dhamma (teachings)

ABHIÑÑA [ah—BING—yah]—Supernatural powers or higher knowledge developed through advanced meditation
Associated: Clairvoyance, meditation, spiritual development
Class: Meditative attainment
Related Terms: Jhāna, Samadhi, Siddhi
Etymology: Pāli, abhi (higher) + ñña (knowledge)

ADOSA [ah—DOH—sah]—Mental factor of non-hatred or loving-kindness
Associated: Goodwill, wholesome mental states
Class: Beautiful mental factor

Related Terms: Mettā, Alobha, Amoha
Etymology: Pāli, a (non) + dosa (hatred)

AKUSALA [ah—KOO—sah—lah]—Unwholesome or unskillful actions, speech or thoughts that lead to suffering
Associated: Karma, ethics
Class: Ethical quality
Related Terms: Kusala, Karma, Cetana
Etymology: Pāli, a (non) + kusala (wholesome)

ĀLAYA [ah—LIE—yah]—Ground or store consciousness that contains karmic seeds and potentials
Associated: Consciousness theory, Yogacara
Class: Type of consciousness
Related Terms: Vijnana, Citta, Manas
Etymology: Sanskrit, Ālaya (dwelling place)

ALOBHA [ah—LOH—bah]—Mental factor of non-greed or generosity

Associated: Wholesome mental states
Class: Beautiful mental factor
Related Terms: Dana, Adosa, Amoha
Etymology: Pāli, a (non) + lobha (greed)

AMOHA [ah—MOH—hah]—Mental factor of non—delusion or wisdom
Associated: Insight, wholesome mental states
Class: Beautiful mental factor
Related Terms: Panna, Vijja, Adosa
Etymology: Pāli, a (non) + moha (delusion)

ANĀGĀMĪ [ah—nah—GAH—mee]—Non-returner, third stage of enlightenment
Associated: Stages of enlightenment
Class: Noble person
Related Terms: Sotāpanna, Sakadāgāmī, Arahant
Etymology: Pāli, an (non) + agami (returning)

ANICCA [ah—NEE—chah]—Impermanence, the constant

APPENDIX

change of all conditioned phenomena
Associated: Three characteristics
Class: Universal characteristic
Related Terms: Dukkha, Anatta
Etymology: Pāli, a (non) + nicca (permanent)

ARAHANT [AH—rah—hant]—Fully enlightened being who has eliminated all mental defilements
Associated: Enlightenment, Nirvāṇa
Class: Noble person
Related Terms: Buddha, Bodhisattva, Anāgāmī
Etymology: Pāli, Arahant (worthy one)

ARIYA AṬṬHAṄGIKA MAGGA [ah—ree—yah ah—THAN—gee—kah MAG—gah]—Noble Eightfold Path leading to liberation
Associated: Buddhist practice
Class: Path of practice
Related Terms: Four Noble Truths, Middle Way
Etymology: Pāli, ariya (noble) + aṭṭha (eight) + aṅga (factors) + magga (path)

AVIDYA [ah—VEED—yah]—Fundamental ignorance or delusion about the nature of reality
Associated: Mental defilements
Class: Root defilement
Related Terms: Moha, Kilesa, Asava
Etymology: Sanskrit, a (non) + vidya (knowledge)

BHAVAṄGA [bah—VAHN—gah]—Continuous flow of consciousness that maintains individual existence between active cognitive processes
Associated: Buddhist psychology, consciousness studies
Class: Mental process
Related Terms: Citta, Cetasika, Consciousness

Etymology: Pāli, bhava (existence) + anga (factor)

BODHI [BOH—dee]—Complete awakening or enlightenment that ends the cycle of rebirth
Associated: Buddhist soteriology, enlightenment
Class: Spiritual attainment
Related Terms: Buddha, Nirvāṇa, Enlightenment
Etymology: Pāli/Sanskrit, budh (to awaken)

BRAHMACARYA [brah—mah—CHAR—yah]—Noble or holy life focused on spiritual development
Associated: Buddhist ethics, spiritual practice
Class: Ethical conduct
Related Terms: Sīla, Noble Eightfold Path, Right Action
Etymology: Sanskrit, brahma (divine) + carya (conduct)

BUDDHA/BUDDHAS [BUD—dah]—Fully enlightened being who has discovered and taught the path to liberation
Associated: Buddhist history, enlightened beings
Class: Spiritual attainment
Related Terms: Bodhi, Dharma, Nirvāṇa
Etymology: Sanskrit/Pāli, budh (to awaken)

CETASIKA [cheh—TAH—see—kah]—Mental factors that arise with consciousness and condition its quality
Associated: Buddhist psychology, mental states
Class: Mental phenomena
Related Terms: Citta, Consciousness, Mental Factors
Etymology: Pāli, ceta (mind) + sika (associated with)

CITTA [CHIT—tah]—Momentary instance of consciousness that knows or experiences an object
Associated: Buddhist psychology, consciousness studies

Class: Mental phenomena
Related Terms: Cetasika, Consciousness, Mind
Etymology: Pāli/Sanskrit, cit (to know)

DHAMMA [DAH—mah]—The teachings of the Buddha and ultimate truth about reality
Associated: Buddhist doctrine, truth
Class: Buddhist teachings
Related Terms: Buddha, Dharma, Truth
Etymology: Pāli form of Sanskrit dharma

DHARMA [DAR—mah]—Sanskrit term for the Buddha's teachings and ultimate truth about reality
Associated: Buddhist doctrine, truth
Class: Buddhist teachings
Related Terms: Buddha, Dhamma, Truth
Etymology: Sanskrit form of Pāli dhamma

DOSA [DOH—sah]—Hatred or ill will that creates unwholesome mental states
Associated: Buddhist psychology, unwholesome states
Class: Mental defilement
Related Terms: Kilesa, Akusala, Unwholesome
Etymology: Pāli, dus (to become corrupted)

DUKKHA [DUK—kah]—Universal unsatisfactoriness and suffering inherent in conditioned existence
Associated: Buddhist philosophy, Four Noble Truths
Class: Fundamental truth
Related Terms: Four Noble Truths, Suffering, Saṃsāra
Etymology: Pāli, du (bad) + kha (space)

DUKKHA-DUKKHA [DUK—kah DUK—kah]—Obvious physical

NIGREDO

and mental suffering like pain and distress
Associated: Buddhist philosophy, types of suffering
Class: Category of suffering
Related Terms: Dukkha, Suffering, Pain
Etymology: Pāli, duplication of dukkha for emphasis

GOTRABHŪ [go—trah—BOO]—Transformative moment of consciousness preceding enlightenment
Associated: Spiritual transformation, enlightenment process
Class: Mental state
Related Terms: Magga, Phala, Nibbāna
Etymology: Pāli, gotra (lineage) + bhū (becoming)

JHĀNA [JAH—nah]—State of meditative absorption characterised by intense concentration and bliss
Associated: Meditation, concentration, altered states
Class: Meditative attainment
Related Terms: Samadhi, Samatha, Vipassanā
Etymology: Pāli/Sanskrit, from jhāyati (to meditate)

KAMA-RAGA [KAH—mah RAH—gah]—Sensual desire and attachment to pleasurable experiences
Associated: Mental defilements, craving
Class: Mental factor
Related Terms: Taṇhā, Lobha, Kilesa
Etymology: Pāli, kama (sensual) + raga (lust)

KAMMA [KAH—mah]—Intentional action and its corresponding results
Associated: Causality, ethics, rebirth
Class: Universal law

Related Terms: Vipāka, Cetana, Saṅkhāra
Etymology: Pāli form of Sanskrit karma (action)

KARUṆĀ [kah—ROO—nah]—Compassion and desire to remove suffering
Associated: Divine abodes, spiritual qualities
Class: Mental factor
Related Terms: Mettā, Muditā, Upekkhā
Etymology: Pāli/Sanskrit (compassion)

KSHANTI [KSHAN—tee]—Patient endurance and acceptance
Associated: Spiritual virtues, mental cultivation
Class: Perfection
Related Terms: Viriya, Adhitthana, Nekkhamma
Etymology: Sanskrit (patience)

KUSALA [KOO—sah—lah]—Wholesome or skillful mental states and actions
Associated: Ethics, mental development
Class: Mental quality
Related Terms: Akusala, Punna, Sila
Etymology: Pāli (wholesome/skillful)

LOBHA [LOH—bah]—Greed or attachment
Associated: Mental defilements, unwholesome states
Class: Mental factor
Related Terms: Dosa, Moha, Kilesa
Etymology: Pāli (greed)

MAGGA—CITTA [MAH—gah CHIT—tah]—Path consciousness arising at enlightenment
Associated: Enlightenment process, consciousness
Class: Mental state
Related Terms: Magga, Phala-citta, Lokuttara

Etymology: Pāli, magga (path) + citta (consciousness)

MAGGA-PHALA [MAH—gah PAH—lah]—Path and fruition moments of enlightenment
Associated: Enlightenment stages, spiritual attainment
Class: Mental states
Related Terms: Magga, Phala, Nibbāna
Etymology: Pāli, magga (path) + phala (fruit)

MAJJHIMĀ PAṬIPADĀ [MAJ—jee—mah pah—tee—PAH—dah]—Middle way between extremes
Associated: Buddhist practice, spiritual path
Class: Philosophical principle
Related Terms: Noble Eightfold Path, Four Noble Truths
Etymology: Pāli (middle way)

METTĀ [MET—tah]—Loving—kindness and universal goodwill
Associated: Divine abodes, spiritual qualities
Class: Mental factor
Related Terms: Karuṇā, Muditā, Upekkhā
Etymology: Pāli (loving—kindness)

MOHA [MOH—hah]—Delusion or ignorance
Associated: Mental defilements, unwholesome states
Class: Mental factor
Related Terms: Lobha, Dosa, Avijjā
Etymology: Pāli (delusion)

MOKṢA [MOHK—shah]—Liberation from cyclic existence
Associated: Spiritual liberation, enlightenment
Class: Spiritual attainment
Related Terms: Nibbāna, Vimutti, Nirodha
Etymology: Sanskrit (liberation)

Appendix

MUDITĀ [MOO—dee—tah]—Sympathetic or appreciative joy
Associated: Divine abodes, spiritual qualities
Class: Mental factor
Related Terms: Mettā, Karuṇā, Upekkhā
Etymology: Pāli/Sanskrit (sympathetic joy)

NĀMA [NAH—mah]—The mental or non—physical aspects of existence including consciousness and mental factors
Associated: Mind, consciousness, mental phenomena
Class: Buddhist concept
Related Terms: Rūpa, Citta, Cetasika
Etymology: Pāli, nāma (name/mind)

NIBBĀNA/NIRVĀṆA [nir—VAH—nah]—The unconditioned state of complete liberation from suffering and the cycle of rebirth
Associated: Enlightenment, liberation, awakening
Class: Buddhist goal
Related Terms: Saṃsāra, Arahant, Four Noble Truths
Etymology: Sanskrit, nir (out) + vana (blowing)

OJA [OH—jah]—The material quality of nutrition that sustains physical life and growth
Associated: Material qualities, nutrition
Class: Buddhist concept
Related Terms: Rūpa, Four Great Elements
Etymology: Pāli, oja (essence/nutriment)

PAÑÑĀ [PAN—yah]—Transcendent wisdom or insight that sees reality as it truly is
Associated: Wisdom, understanding, insight
Class: Buddhist concept
Related Terms: Vipassanā, Three Trainings
Etymology: Pāli, paññā (wisdom)

PAPANCA [pah—PAN—cha]—Mental proliferation or conceptual elaboration that creates complexity from simple experience
Associated: Mental processes, conceptual thinking
Class: Buddhist concept
Related Terms: Saṅkhāra, Avijjā
Etymology: Pāli, papañca (proliferation)

PAṬICCASAMUPPĀDA [pah—tee—cha—sum—UP—pah—dah]—The law of dependent origination explaining how suffering and existence arise
Associated: Causality, conditionality
Class: Buddhist doctrine
Related Terms: Four Noble Truths, Saṃsāra
Etymology: Pāli, paticca (dependent) + samuppada (arising)

PHALA—CITTA [PAH—lah CHIT—tah]—The consciousness that immediately follows path consciousness, experiencing Nirvāṇa
Associated: States of consciousness, enlightenment
Class: Buddhist concept
Related Terms: Magga—citta, Nirvāṇa
Etymology: Pāli, phala (fruit) + citta (consciousness)

PĪTI [PEE—tee]—Rapture or joy arising from meditation and spiritual development
Associated: Meditative states, jhāna factors
Class: Buddhist concept
Related Terms: Sukha, Jhāna
Etymology: Pāli, pīti (joy)

PRĀṆA [PRAH—nah]—The vital life force or energy that animates living beings
Associated: Life force, vitality
Class: Buddhist/Hindu concept
Related Terms: Life Faculty, Jivitindriya
Etymology: Sanskrit, prāṇa (breath/life—force)

RŪPA [ROO—pah]—Physical matter or material form subject to change and impermanence
Associated: Materiality, physical phenomena
Class: Buddhist concept
Related Terms: Nāma, Four Great Elements
Etymology: Pāli, rūpa (form)

SAKADĀGĀMĪ [sah—kah—DAH—gah—mee]—Once-returner, second stage of enlightenment requiring one more human rebirth
Associated: Stages of enlightenment
Class: Buddhist attainment
Related Terms: Sotāpanna, Anāgāmī, Arahant
Etymology: Pāli, sakad (once) + agami (returning)

SAKKAYA-DITTHI [sah—KYE—ah DIT—tee]—Personality view or belief in a permanent self or soul
Associated: Wrong views, delusion
Class: Buddhist concept
Related Terms: Anatta, Ten Fetters
Etymology: Pāli, sakkaya (personality) + ditthi (view)

SAMATHA [SAH—mah—tah]—Meditation focused on developing mental tranquility and concentration
Associated: Meditation practices
Class: Buddhist practice
Related Terms: Vipassanā, Jhāna
Etymology: Pāli, samatha (tranquility)

SAṂSĀRA [sum—SAH—rah]—The cycle of repeated birth, death and rebirth driven by ignorance and craving
Associated: Cyclic existence, rebirth
Class: Buddhist concept
Related Terms: Nirvāṇa, Karma, Three Marks

NIGREDO

Etymology: Sanskrit, sam (together) + sara (flowing)

SAMSKĀRA [sum—SKAH—rah]—Mental formations or volitional activities that create karma
Associated: Mental factors, karma
Class: Buddhist concept
Related Terms: Cetasika, Karma
Etymology: Sanskrit, sam (together) + kara (making)

SAMYOJANA [sum—yo—JAH—nah]—The ten fetters binding beings to cyclic existence
Associated: Mental bonds, defilements
Class: Buddhist concept
Related Terms: Kilesa, Four Paths
Etymology: Pāli, sam (together) + yojana (binding)

SAṄKHĀRA-DUKKHA [Suhn—KHA—ra—DOO—kha]—The inherent unsatisfactoriness present in all conditioned phenomena
Associated: Buddhist philosophy, suffering, impermanence
Class: Buddhist concept
Related Terms: Dukkha, Anicca, Anatta
Etymology: Pāli, saṅkhāra (formations) + dukkha (suffering)

SATIPAṬṬHĀNA [sa—tee—pat—THA—na]—The four foundations of mindfulness: body, feelings, mind, and mental phenomena
Associated: Buddhist meditation, mindfulness practice
Class: Buddhist practice
Related Terms: Mindfulness, Vipassanā, Samatha
Etymology: Pāli, sati (mindfulness) + patthana (foundation)

SĪLA [SEE—la]—Ethical conduct and moral discipline forming the foundation of Buddhist practice
Associated: Buddhist ethics, moral training
Class: Buddhist practice
Related Terms: Precepts, Right Action, Right Speech
Etymology: Pāli, meaning virtue or moral conduct

SĪLABBATAPARĀMĀSA [see—LAH—buh—tuh pah—RAH—mah—suh]—Attachment to rites and rituals, one of the ten fetters binding beings to saṃsāra
Associated: Buddhist psychology, mental hindrances
Class: Buddhist concept
Related Terms: Fetters, Attachment, Delusion
Etymology: Pāli, silabbata (rites and rituals) + paramasa (attachment)

SKANDHA-MĀRA [SKAN—dha MA—ra]—Demons or obstacles, arising from the five aggregates of existence
Associated: Buddhist psychology, spiritual obstacles
Class: Buddhist concept
Related Terms: Mara, Aggregates, Hindrances
Etymology: Sanskrit, skandha (aggregate) + mara (demon)

SKANDHAS [SKAN—dhas]—The five aggregates comprising human experience: form, feeling, perception, mental formations, and consciousness
Associated: Buddhist psychology, theory of mind
Class: Buddhist concept
Related Terms: Form, Consciousness, Perception
Etymology: Sanskrit, meaning heaps or aggregates

SOBHANA CETASIKAS [so—BHA—na che—TA—si—kas]—Beautiful or wholesome mental factors that contribute to positive states of mind
Associated: Buddhist psychology, mental states
Class: Buddhist concept
Related Terms: Cetasikas, Mental Factors, Consciousness
Etymology: Pāli, sobhana (beautiful) + cetasika (mental factor)

SOTĀPANNA [so—ta—PAN—na]—Stream—enterer; one who has achieved the first stage of enlightenment
Associated: Buddhist soteriology, stages of enlightenment
Class: Buddhist attainment
Related Terms: Nirvāṇa, Path, Fruit
Etymology: Pāli, sota (stream) + apanna (entered)

SUKHA [SOO—kha]—Pleasant feeling or happiness—both physical and mental
Associated: Buddhist psychology, positive states
Class: Buddhist concept
Related Terms: Vedana, Pleasure, Joy
Etymology: Pāli, meaning happiness or ease

SUKKHA-VIPASSANĀ [SOO—kha vi—PAS—sa—na]—Dry insight meditation practiced without first developing deep concentration
Associated: Buddhist meditation, insight practice
Class: Buddhist practice
Related Terms: Vipassanā, Samatha, Jhāna
Etymology: Pāli, sukkha (dry) + vipassanā (insight)

ŚŪNYATĀ [SHOON—ya—ta]—Emptiness or voidness, the lack of inherent existence in all phenomena
Associated: Buddhist philosophy, ultimate reality
Class: Buddhist concept
Related Terms: Anatta, Anicca, Middle Way
Etymology: Sanskrit, from sunya (empty)

SŪTRA [SOO—tra]—Discourses of the Buddha containing teachings and dialogues

APPENDIX

Associated: Buddhist scripture, teachings
Class: Buddhist text
Related Terms: Dharma, Abhidhamma, Vinaya
Etymology: Sanskrit, meaning thread or discourse

TAṆHĀ *[TAHN—ha]—The mental factor of craving or thirst that drives cyclic existence*
Associated: Attachment, desire, clinging
Class: Mental factor
Related Terms: Dukkha, Upadana, Bhava
Etymology: Pāli, lit. thirst

TATHĀGATA *[ta—TAH—ga—ta]—An epithet for the Buddha meaning one who has gone to or come from thusness*
Associated: Buddha titles, enlightened beings
Class: Buddhist terminology
Related Terms: Buddha, Arhat, Bodhisattva
Etymology: Sanskrit/Pāli, tatha (thus) + gata (gone)

TATHĀGATAGARBHA *[ta—TAH—ga—ta—GAR—ba]—The inherent potential for enlightenment present in all beings*
Associated: Buddha nature, enlightenment potential
Class: Mahayana doctrine
Related Terms: Buddha Nature, Dharmakaya, Śūnyatā
Etymology: Sanskrit, Tathāgata (thus gone) + garbha (womb/essence)

UPEKKHĀ *[oo—PEK—kha]—Mental factor of equanimity and balanced engagement with experience*
Associated: Brahmaviharas, meditation states
Class: Mental factor
Related Terms: Mettā, Karuṇā, Muditā
Etymology: Pāli, upa (near) + ikkha (to see/look)

UPĀYA *[oo—PAH—ya]—Skillful methods used to guide beings toward enlightenment*
Associated: Teaching methods, compassion
Class: Buddhist practice
Related Terms: Bodhicitta, Paramita, Dharma
Etymology: Sanskrit, literally, skilful means

VICIKICCHĀ *[vi—chi—KI—cha]—Skeptical doubt that hinders spiritual progress*
Associated: Mental hindrances, defilements
Class: Mental factor
Related Terms: Nivarana, Kilesa, Samadhi
Etymology: Pāli, vi (divided) + cikiccha (thinking)

VIPARINAMA—DUKKHA *[vi—pa—ri—NA—ma—DUK—kha]—The suffering caused by impermanence and change*
Associated: Types of suffering, impermanence
Class: Buddhist doctrine

Related Terms: Dukkha, Anicca, Saṅkhāra
Etymology: Pāli, viparinama (change) + dukkha (suffering)

VIPĀKA *[vi—PAH—ka]—Consciousness that arises as the result of past karma*
Associated: Karma, consciousness types
Class: Mental factor
Related Terms: Karma, Citta, Cetasika
Etymology: Pāli, vi (special) + paka (ripening)

VIPASSANĀ *[vi—PAH—sa—na]—Meditation practice developing insight into the true nature of reality*
Associated: Buddhist meditation, wisdom practices
Class: Meditation technique
Related Terms: Samatha, Sati, Paññā
Etymology: Pāli, vi (special) + passana (seeing)

VYĀPĀDA *[vya—PAH—da]—Mental factor of ill—will or malevolence toward others*
Associated: Mental defilements, unwholesome states
Class: Mental factor
Related Terms: Dosa, Kilesa, Akusala
Etymology: Pāli, lit. ill—will

NIGREDO

States of Consciousness

Meditative States

FORM-SPHERE—Refined level of consciousness accessed through deep meditation where awareness transcends ordinary sensory experience
Associated: Meditation, mental development
Class: Plane of consciousness
Related Terms: Jhāna, Fine—material realm
Etymology: Pāli rūpaloka

FRUIT CONSCIOUSNESS—Result of Path Consciousness that follows immediately after breakthrough
Associated: Enlightenment, spiritual attainment
Class: Transcendental state
Related Terms: Path Consciousness, Nirvāṇa
Etymology: Pāli phala citta

JHANIC CONSCIOUSNESS [JAH—nik]—Advanced meditative state characterised by deep concentration and absorption
Associated: Meditation, altered states
Class: Mental state
Related Terms: Samatha, Form—sphere, Formless—sphere
Etymology: Pāli, jhāna (meditation)

PATH CONSCIOUSNESS—Momentary transcendental awareness that occurs at each stage of enlightenment
Associated: Enlightenment, spiritual development
Class: Transcendental state
Related Terms: Fruit Consciousness, Nirvāṇa
Etymology: Pāli magga citta

ROOTLESS CONSCIOUSNESS—Basic awareness lacking wholesome or unwholesome roots
Associated: Mental states, consciousness types
Class: Type of consciousness
Related Terms: Consciousness, Mental factors
Etymology: Pāli ahetuka citta

SENSE-SPHERE PLANE—Ordinary level of consciousness dominated by the five physical senses and mind
Associated: Ordinary experience, sensory awareness
Class: Plane of consciousness
Related Terms: Consciousness, Mental factors
Etymology: Pāli kamaloka

Experiential States

APPARENT REALITY-Conventional experience of the world as consisting of solid objects and beings
Associated: Conventional experience, ordinary perception
Class: Mode of experience
Related Terms: Conditional Reality, Ultimate Reality
Etymology: Latin, apparens + realis

CONDITIONAL REALITY—Experience governed by cause and effect relationships
Associated: Buddhist metaphysics, dependent origination
Class: Mode of experience
Related Terms: Apparent Reality, Unconditioned Reality
Etymology: Latin, condicionalis + realis

PRE-VERBAL—State of pure sensory awareness before language acquisition
Associated: Child development, pure perception
Class: Developmental state
Related Terms: Garden of Eden, Pure awareness
Etymology: English, pre (before) + verbal (relating to words)

OBJECTIVE REALITY — Consensual understanding of reality based on mutual agreement
Associated: Shared experience, conventional truth
Class: Mode of experience
Related Terms: Subjective Reality, Apparent Reality
Etymology: Latin, obiectivus + realis

SUBJECTIVE REALITY—Personal experience of existence unique to each individual
Associated: Personal experience, consciousness
Class: Mode of experience
Related Terms: Objective Reality, Apparent Reality
Etymology: Latin, subiectivus + realis

UNCONDITIONED REALITY—Nirvāṇa; reality free from causes and conditions -
Associated: Enlightenment, liberation
Class: Ultimate reality
Related Terms: Nirvāṇa, Conditional Reality
Etymology: Latin, prefix un + condicionalis + realis

APPENDIX

Metaphors

GARDEN OF EDEN—Metaphor for pre—verbal consciousness before conceptual thinking
Associated: Childhood development, pure awareness
Class: Alchemical metaphor
Related Terms: Tree of Knowledge, Pure Experience, Pre—verbal State
Etymology: Biblical reference, Genesis

FISHER-KING WOUND—Metaphor for psychological or spiritual trauma that initiates the alchemical journey
Associated: Spiritual awakening, psychological transformation
Class: Mythological metaphor
Related Terms: Dark Night of Soul, Nigredo
Etymology: Arthurian legend, Grail mythology

TREE OF DUALITY—Symbol representing the division of experience into subject and object
Associated: Knowledge acquisition, conceptual thinking
Class: Alchemical metaphor
Related Terms: Garden of Eden, Tree of Knowledge, Perception
Etymology: Buddhist and Biblical synthesis

WHITE RABBIT—Symbol for the elusive nature of pure consciousness and spiritual awakening
Associated: Spiritual seeking, awakening
Class: Literary metaphor
Related Terms: Matrix, Pure Consciousness
Etymology: Lewis Carroll's Alice in Wonderland, later The Matrix

Psychological Concepts

LOST CHILD—Archetypal pattern representing abandoned or neglected aspects of early development
Associated: Inner child work, trauma healing
Class: Psychological concept
Related Terms: Shadow, PTSD, Inner Child
Etymology: Modern psychological term

MATRIX—Underlying structure or framework that shapes conscious experience and reality
Associated: Reality frameworks, consciousness studies
Class: Philosophical concept
Related Terms: Perception, Consciousness
Etymology: Latin matrix (womb, source)

OEDIPAL—Relating to unconscious attraction to the parent of opposite sex and rivalry with same sex parent
Associated: Psychoanalysis, developmental psychology
Class: Psychological concept
Related Terms: Projection, Shadow
Etymology: From Greek myth of Oedipus

PERCEPTION—Mental process of recognising and interpreting sensory information
Associated: Cognitive psychology, consciousness studies
Class: Psychological concept
Related Terms: Matrix, Consciousness
Etymology: Latin perceptio (gathering, receiving)

PTSD—Post—traumatic stress disorder characterised by persistent mental and emotional stress
Associated: Trauma, anxiety disorders
Class: Clinical diagnosis
Related Terms: Trauma, Lost Child
Etymology: Modern medical term, post (after) + trauma + stress + disorder

PROJECTION—Psychological defence mechanism where one attributes unwanted qualities of self onto others
Associated: Defence mechanisms, Shadow work
Class: Psychological concept
Related Terms: Shadow, Perception
Etymology: Latin proicere (to throw forth)

SHADOW—Deep unconscious aspects of personality containing repressed or denied elements
Associated: Depth psychology, unconscious mind
Class: Psychological concept
Related Terms: Projection, Lost Child, Persona
Etymology: From Jungian psychology, derived from Latin umbra (Shadow)

Kabbalistic Terms

BINAH (Hebrew: בינה)
[bee-NAH]
The third Sephirah on the Tree Of Life, representing divine understanding, analytical intelligence, and structure.
Associated: Higher mind, comprehension
Class: Sephirah
Related Terms: Chokhmah, Da'at, Tree Of Life
Etymology: Hebrew binah (understanding, discernment)

CHESED (Hebrew: חֶסֶד)
[KHEH-sed]
The fourth Sephirah, symbolising mercy, grace, and expansive loving-kindness.
Associated: Compassion, expansion
Class: Sephirah
Related Terms: Gevurah, Tiferet, Tree Of Life
Etymology: Hebrew chesed (kindness, mercy)

CHOKHMAH (Hebrew: חָכְמָה)
[khokh-MAH]
The second Sephirah, representing divine wisdom, insight, and the creative spark.
Associated: Wisdom, intuitive knowing
Class: Sephirah
Related Terms: Binah, Keter, Tree Of Life
Etymology: Hebrew chokhmah (wisdom)

DA'AT (Hebrew: דַּעַת)
[DAH-aht]
The "hidden" or unenumerated Sephirah that emerges in the balance of Chokhmah and Binah, representing knowledge, unification, and conscious awareness.
Associated: Knowledge, integration
Class: Hidden Sephirah
Related Terms: Chokhmah, Binah, Tree Of Life
Etymology: Hebrew da'at (knowledge)

GEVURAH (Hebrew: גְּבוּרָה)
[geh-voo-RAH]
The fifth Sephirah, representing strength, discipline, and divine judgment or restriction.
Associated: Severity, boundaries
Class: Sephirah
Related Terms: Chesed, Tiferet, Tree Of Life
Etymology: Hebrew gevurah (power, might, severity)

HOD (Hebrew: הוֹד)
[HOHD]
The eighth Sephirah, representing splendour, form, ritual, and the intellectual process of refinement.
Associated: Logic, clarity, surrender
Class: Sephirah
Related Terms: Netzach, Yesod, Tree Of Life
Etymology: Hebrew hod (majesty, splendour)

KETER (Hebrew: כֶּתֶר)
[KEH-ter]
The first and highest Sephirah, symbolising the divine crown, will, and the origin of consciousness.
Associated: Supreme consciousness, unity
Class: Sephirah
Related Terms: Ain Soph, Chokhmah, Tree Of Life
Etymology: Hebrew keter (crown)

MALKHUT (Hebrew: מַלְכוּת)
[mal-KHOOT]
The tenth and final Sephirah, representing manifestation, physical reality, and the vessel of divine presence.
Associated: Earth, sovereignty
Class: Sephirah
Related Terms: Yesod, Tree Of Life
Etymology: Hebrew malkhut (kingdom)

NETZACH (Hebrew: נֵצַח)
[NEH-tsakh]
The seventh Sephirah, representing victory, endurance, and active energy in manifestation.
Associated: Will, eternity
Class: Sephirah
Related Terms: Hod, Tree Of Life
Etymology: Hebrew netzach (victory, eternity)

QLIPPOTH / QLIPOT (Hebrew: קְלִיפּוֹת)
[klee-POHT / KLEE-pot]
The "husks" or unbalanced forces in Kabbalah that oppose or distort the divine order of the Sephirot.
Associated: Shadow, spiritual imbalance
Class: Kabbalistic concept
Related Terms: Tree of Death, Sitri Achra, Sephirot
Etymology: Hebrew qlippah (peel, husk); qlippoth is plural

SEPHIROT (Hebrew: סְפִירוֹת)
[seh-fee-ROHT]
The ten divine emanations through which the Infinite reveals itself and creates the world.
Associated: Divine structure, Tree Of Life
Class: Core Kabbalistic doctrine
Related Terms: Tree Of Life, Qlippoth
Etymology: Hebrew s'firah (counting, emanation); plural sephirot

TIFERET (Hebrew: תִּפְאֶרֶת)
[tif-EH-ret]
The sixth Sephirah, symbolising beauty, balance, compassion, and the harmonious blending of Chesed and Gevurah.
Associated: Integration, heart
Class: Sephirah
Related Terms: Chesed, Gevurah, Tree Of Life
Etymology: Hebrew tiferet (beauty, glory)

YESOD (Hebrew: יְסוֹד)
[yeh-SOHD]
The ninth Sephirah, representing foundation, subconscious structure, and transmission of divine energy into the material world.
Associated: Psyche, energetic flow
Class: Sephirah
Related Terms: Malkhut, Hod, Netzach
Etymology: Hebrew yesod (foundation)

Appendix

Practices & Techniques

Meditation & Transformative Methods

Gentling—Gradual process of softening rigid mental patterns through mindful awareness
Associated: Psychological healing, mindfulness
Class: Therapeutic approach
Related Terms: Mindfulness, Healing, Integration
Etymology: English, gentle (kind/soft)

Jhāna practice [JAH—nah]—Advanced meditation states characterised by intense concentration and mental absorption
Associated: Deep meditation, altered consciousness
Class: Meditative attainment
Related Terms: Samatha, Concentration, Absorption
Etymology: Pāli, jhāna (meditation/contemplation)

Kasina [KAH—see—nah]—Meditation objects used to develop concentration, such as coloured disks or elements
Associated: Concentration practices, visualisation
Class: Meditation aid
Related Terms: Samatha, Jhāna, Meditation objects
Etymology: Pāli, kasina (whole/complete)

Kenosis [ken—OH—sis]—Practice of emptying or letting go of self—centred thinking
Associated: Spiritual emptying, ego dissolution
Class: Transformative method
Related Terms: Emptiness, Non—self, Liberation
Etymology: Greek, kenosis (emptying)

Samatha [sah—MAH—tah]—Meditative practice focused on developing mental tranquility and concentration
Associated: Buddhist meditation, mental cultivation
Class: Meditation technique
Related Terms: Jhāna, Vipassanā, Concentration
Etymology: Pāli, samatha (calmness/tranquility)

Solve et Coagula [SOL—vay et ko—AG—you—lah]—Alchemical process of dissolution and recombination of consciousness
Associated: Spiritual transformation, psychological integration
Class: Transformative method
Related Terms: Alchemy, Transformation, Integration
Etymology: Latin, solve (dissolve) + et (and) + coagula (coagulate)

Vipassanā [vee—PAH—sah—nah]—Insight meditation practice aimed at understanding the true nature of reality
Associated: Buddhist meditation, wisdom development
Class: Meditation technique
Related Terms: Samatha, Mindfulness, Wisdom
Etymology. Pāli, vi (special) + passana (seeing/insight)

States & Attainments

Buddhist Attainments & Mystical States

ANĀGĀMĪ [ah—NAH—gah—mee]— Third stage of Buddhist enlightenment meaning "non-returner"
Associated: Buddhist enlightenment, spiritual realization
Class: Buddhist attainment
Related Terms: Sotāpanna, Sakadāgāmī, Arahant
Etymology: Pāli, an (non) + agami (returning)

ARAHANT [AH—rah—hant]— Fourth and final stage of Buddhist enlightenment meaning "worthy one"
Associated: Buddhist enlightenment, complete liberation
Class: Buddhist attainment
Related Terms: Sotāpanna, Sakadāgāmī, Anāgāmī
Etymology: Pāli, Arahant (worthy, noble)

BODHI [BOH—dee]—Complete and perfect enlightenment or awakening
Associated: Buddhist enlightenment, supreme wisdom
Class: Buddhist concept
Related Terms: Nirvāṇa, Enlightenment
Etymology: Sanskrit/Pāli, budh (to awaken)

CHRIST CONSCIOUSNESS—State of divine awareness associated with Jesus Christ
Associated: Christian mysticism, spiritual awakening
Class: Mystical state
Related Terms: Gnosis, Enlightenment
Etymology: English, Christ + consciousness

DARK NIGHT—Period of spiritual crisis and profound difficulty in contemplative practice
Associated: Mysticism, spiritual development
Class: Mystical state
Related Terms: Nigredo, Spiritual Crisis
Etymology: English, dark + night

GNOSIS [NOH—sis]—Direct spiritual knowledge or insight into ultimate reality
Associated: Mysticism, esoteric wisdom
Class: Mystical state
Related Terms: Enlightenment, Christ Consciousness
Etymology: Greek, gnosis (knowledge)

SAKADĀGĀMĪ [sah—kah—DAH—gah—mee]—Second stage of Buddhist enlightenment meaning "once-returner"
Associated: Buddhist enlightenment, spiritual development
Class: Buddhist attainment
Related Terms: Sotāpanna, Anāgāmī, Arahant
Etymology: Pāli, sakad (once) + agami (returning)

SATORI [sah—TOH—ree]— Sudden flash of insight or enlightenment in Zen Buddhism
Associated: Zen Buddhism, enlightenment experiences
Class: Buddhist state
Related Terms: Kensho, Enlightenment
Etymology: Japanese, satori (understanding)

SOTĀPANNA [soh—tah—PAN—nah]—First stage of Buddhist enlightenment meaning "stream-enterer"
Associated: Buddhist enlightenment, spiritual awakening
Class: Buddhist attainment
Related Terms: Sakadāgāmī, Anāgāmī, Arahant
Etymology: Pāli, sota (stream) + apanna (entered)

APPENDIX

Index

Abhidhamma: 12, 138

Adosa: 157, 260, 268, 277, 391

Air: 15, 166

Akusala: 144, 156, 260, 261, 265, 392, 393

Ālaya: 127, 128, 138, 391

Albedo: 12, 255, 409

Alobha: 260, 268, 277, 391

Amoha: 260, 277, 391

Anāgāmī: 8, 302, 407

Anicca: 288, 297, 309, 361, 395, 396

Apparent Reality: 23, 122

Arahant: 8, 263, 313

Ariya aṭṭhaṅgika magga: 363

Avidya: 242

Bhavaṅga: 15, 270

Binah: 238, 400

Bodhi: 41, 42, 44, 143, 273, 322, 392

Brahmacarya: 382, 384

Buddha: 16, 235

Cetasika: 129, 150-161

Chesed: 95, 237, 238, 400

Chokhmah: 238, 400

Citta: 10, 139-141, 215, 407

Da'at: 237, 253-256, 400

Dark night: 7, 109-117, 408

Dependent origination: 10, 196-200, 206-208

Dhamma: 271, 391, 392

Dharma: 14, 268

Dissolution: 5, 236, 405

Dosa: 156, 214, 222, 260, 261, 391, 393, 396

Dukkha: 191, 336

Earth: 4, 172

Ego: 22, 347, 368-369, 409

Fetters: 8, 263, 211-218

Fruit consciousness: 45, 235, 281-282

Gevurah: 400

Gnosis: 69, 402

Gold: 6, 235, 38

Great Work: 8, 219, 228-229, 235-236, 405

Hod: 238, 400

Integration: 14, 317, 405

Iron: 43, 97, 106, 133, 168, 258, 266, 274

Jhāna: 16, 275, 282, 407

Kamma: 144, 178-181, 230, 306

Karma: 15, 178-181, 225, 407

Karuṇā: 253, 370, 372, 374, 393, 394, 396

Kshanti: 370, 372, 374

Kusala: 144, 260, 261, 265, 391

Lead: 6, 227, 388-389, 409

Lobha: 156, 214, 222, 260, 391, 393

Lost child: 106, 107, 399

Magga: 196, 284

Matrix: 8, 124-125, 129, 135, 397
Mindfulness: 28, 196
Moha: 156, 214, 222, 260, 391, 392, 393
Mokṣa: 372, 381, 384
Muditā: 253, 393, 396
Nāma: 15, 128, 129, 132, 134, 394
Nibbāna: 42, 134, 281, 282, 283, 284, 291, 393
Nigredo: 5, 217, 405
Nirvāṇa: 16, 235, 393, 396
Objective reality: 53, 121-123, 183
Oja: 134, 394
Papanca: 127, 394
Path consciousness: 8, 236, 281-283
Perception: 6, 153, 202-203, 409
Phala: 202, 281-283, 354
Philosopher's stone: 77, 85, 123, 213, 216, 389
Pīti: 330, 333, 362, 394
Prāṇa: 133, 169, 394
Projection: 104-107, 131, 134, 266, 399, 406
Rebis: 7, 100-102

Retort: 58, 69, 71, 74, 222, 253
Rūpa: 10, 134
Sakadāgāmī: 8, 294-299
Samatha: 16, 367, 370, 399
Saṃsāra: , 188-192, 284, 393, 405
Saṃyojana: 15, 282
Self: 5, 243-244, 367, 409
Separation: 29, 36, 45, 59, 69, 90, 204, 242, 380
Sephirot: 10, 95, 237, 241, 244, 246, 247, 248, 400
Shadow: 6, 100-107, 284, 350, 397
Sīla: 28, 196, 322, 326, 327, 392, 393
Silver: 147, 303, 389
Skandhas: 212, 217, 228, 256, 263, 291, 317
Sobhana cetasikas: 278, 282
Sotāpanna: 8, 287-292, 394
Sukha: 240, 276, 278, 330, 333, 394
Śūnyatā: 45, 288, 292, 298, 361, 364, 396

Sūtra: 16, 16, 101, 102, 126, 127, 165, 171, 394
Taṇhā: 330, 393, 396
Tathāgata: 249, 263, 264, 317, 396
Tathāgatagarbha: 370, 372, 374, 396
Tin: 258, 391, 389
Transcendence: 16, 257, 390
Transmutation: 6, 84, 76, 394
Upāya: 322, 326, 364, 394
Upekkhā: 253, 330, 333, 393, 394
Vicikicchā: 289, 292, 394
Vipāka: 144, 393, 395
Vipassanā: 16, 367-368, 370, 394, 399
Vyāpāda: 362, 395
Water: 81, 165-173

APPENDIX

Part Two — Albedo

A COURSE IN MODERN ALCHEMY

The Second Stage of the Great Work

*A*lbedo follows *Nigredo* as the whitening phase of the alchemical process. If *Nigredo* was dissolution and disillusionment, *Albedo* is purification and integration. The alchemist now begins to stabilise perception, master *karma*, and refine awareness. This is a phase of clarifying the mind, recognising conditioning, and preparing for deeper transformation.

Where *Nigredo* forced the alchemist to confront suffering, *Albedo* is where awareness begins to lift from blind reactivity to precise perception. The trials now are more subtle—misinterpretations of insight, the temptation of spiritual certainty, and the early emergence of deeper wisdom.

Mythos
Framing Albedo through Symbol and Story

The Seven Deadly Sins
This chapter examines the seven deadly sins not as moral failings, but as habitual distortions of perception. The alchemist learns how pride, wrath, greed, desire, and sloth keep the mind bound to conditioned existence. Recognising how these forces operate allows the seeker to interrupt their influence rather than repress them.

The Cosmos
This chapter provides a structured model of reality, explaining different planes of consciousness and their relationship to conditioned experience. The alchemist begins to see how *karma* and perception shape the experience of reality and why human birth is uniquely suited for liberation.

Rebirth and *Saṃsāra*
Saṃsāra is not a linear journey but a conditioned cycle. The alchemist learns how habitual tendencies and karmic formations drive repeated patterns of being, keeping the mind bound to suffering.

Hell and Hell Beings
Hell is not an external place but a state of mind, created by unwholesome *karma* and unresolved delusions. The alchemist sees how resentment, anger, and denial create self-sustaining suffering, both in life and beyond.

Angels and Gods
Higher realms exist, but they are not liberation. The alchemist learns that even pleasure and peace can be traps if clung to as final states. The heavens are not freedom but pleasant distractions for those who have not yet recognised the deeper nature of existence.

Nigredo

The Alchemist
What does it mean to be an alchemist? This chapter examines the mindset, discipline, and qualities necessary to engage in the Great Work. The alchemist learns to balance faith with insight, curiosity with discipline, and progress with humility.

The Moon
The Moon is a symbol of reflection and illusion. The alchemist begins to see how perception is like the Moon—bright but empty, beautiful but deceptive, illuminating but incomplete. This marks a turning point in recognising the limitations of conditioned reality.

The White Stone
The alchemist's awareness is transmuted from raw suffering into refined perception. Here, the alchemist stabilises their ability to transform unwholesome states into clarity, purifying *karma* through insight rather than suppression.

Grace and the Healing of Shame
Shame is the root of many distortions—it creates self-rejection, projection, and avoidance. Grace is the process of reintegrating all rejected aspects of self, healing the wounds of identity, and transforming guilt into wisdom.

A New Kind of Demon
Temptation now shifts—rather than crude desires or anger, the alchemist faces more refined distortions of perception. Spiritual pride, certainty, and the belief in special status emerge as new traps on the path.

The Holy Guardian Angel
Conscience is no longer resisted but recognised as guidance. The alchemist begins to sense an inner compass that directs their choices, no longer acting out of blind reaction but from refined understanding.

The Master of the Temple
A new paradigm emerges—the alchemist is no longer bound by conditioned perspectives. Reality is seen as it is, not as it was assumed to be. This is not final enlightenment, but the first stable glimpse of freedom.

Dharma
Understanding the Mechanics of Reality

The Crystal Universe
Reality is not solid or fixed—it is a dynamic interplay of conditioned factors. The alchemist begins to see how causality, *karma*, and perception interact, forming a vast but intelligible network of interwoven relationships.

Fate and Determinism
Is everything predetermined? No—but habitual reactions give the illusion of fate. The alchemist learns how volition and awareness create space for choice, allowing them to step outside the cycle of conditioned response.

Different Types of Consciousness
Consciousness is not a single entity—it arises in layers and modes, shifting based on object, conditioning, and habitual momentum. This chapter explores how awareness can be refined, expanded, and purified.

Volition and *Karma*
Karma is not punishment or reward but the natural consequence of mental, verbal, and physical actions. Here, the alchemist learns to consciously create wholesome *karma* and purify past tendencies.

APPENDIX

Resultant Consciousness
Perception is not passive—it is shaped by past *karma*. The alchemist sees how thoughts and reactions arise from previous conditioning, and how insight allows them to break free from automatic responses.

The Life Continuum
Consciousness flows in an ongoing stream, moment to moment, lifetime to lifetime. Understanding this stream allows the alchemist to influence future states of being.

Unwholesome *Karma*
All suffering arises from twelve types of unwholesome *citta* (mind-states). This chapter examines each one in detail, allowing the alchemist to systematically eliminate their influence.

Wholesome *Karma*
Just as suffering has mechanics, so does liberation. By understanding wholesome mind-states, the alchemist begins to stabilise joy, clarity, and non-reactivity.

The Cognitive Series
Perception follows predictable patterns. This chapter explores how awareness shifts from stimulus to response, showing how the mind habitually constructs experience.

Types of *Karma*
Different karmic actions create different results. The alchemist learns to recognise which actions lead to suffering, which to stability, and which to liberation.

Transcendental Consciousness
There is a consciousness beyond conditioned experience. This chapter introduces the supramundane path-moments that arise as a direct break from samsaric perception.

The Anāgāmī (Non-Returner)
At this stage, sensory attachment and ill-will are completely abandoned. The alchemist is now no longer bound to worldly existence, preparing for Citrinitas, the golden stage of perception.

OBJECT
The Mechanics of Alchemical Transformation

Hollowness
The disciple begins to recognise that everything they once believed about themselves is dross—raw material for transformation. Despite a newfound faith in the path, they are left feeling empty and directionless. The world feels increasingly meaningless, and decision-making becomes paralysing as attachment to old paradigms dissolves. The disciple becomes a hollow vessel, an unsettling but necessary state for new insights to arise.

The Beast
The disciple must now confront the Beast, a representation of the egoic self entangled in illusion and instinct. The Beast must be sacrificed, but this is no simple process—anger, desire, and self-protection resist the surrender. Biblical and alchemical imagery of dragons and the sacrificial lamb depict the struggle of this stage.

The Watcher of the Abyss
Here, the disciple faces Choronzon, the demon of fragmented self-identity. This is the threshold of the Abyss, where all remaining illusions about self and reality must be shattered. Madness or delusion arises for those who fail to relinquish their conceptual identity, while those who cross the Abyss do so by letting go of all mental constructs.

Nigredo

Brahma's Chariot
A deepening understanding of jhanic states begins here. The disciple learns that jhāna is not just a meditative achievement but a means of stabilising awareness in the higher realms. This chapter outlines the different stages of meditative absorption and how they correlate with spiritual awakening.

Mara
The final remnants of desire arise as Mara, the tempter. Mara is not an external being but the remaining Shadows of craving and attachment. The disciple must learn to recognise Mara's subtle tricks—egoic pride, complacency, the illusion of spiritual superiority—and let them go.

The Dark Night of the Spirit
The disciple enters a final purification phase, experiencing profound despair and detachment from previous sources of meaning. This is not a punishment but a stripping away of all that remains of egoic identity. Faith in the process is essential, as the disciple feels utterly abandoned.

The Crucifixion
The old self is completely dissolved. Using Crucifixion imagery, this chapter explores the final death of ego—a state of absolute surrender where even spiritual aspirations must be sacrificed. It is not a choice but an inevitability, marking the point of no return.

The Death of the Self
Following the Crucifixion, the ego is fully dismantled. This is true *Albedo*, the whitening of perception. No longer bound by habitual thought patterns, the disciple experiences a new kind of clarity and detachment, no longer identified with their old fears, desires, or self-narratives.

Chop Wood, Carry Water
Despite the transformation, life continues. The disciple must reintegrate into the world, now engaging with daily responsibilities from a place of detachment. This chapter explores how ordinary life is no longer a burden but a simple unfolding of events, free from personal drama.

Thaumaturgy
Here, the disciple discovers that miracles are simply natural outcomes of correct perception. The extraordinary arises not from power or effort but from a complete lack of resistance to reality. True thaumaturgy is effortless interaction with the world.

The Appointed
Having dissolved their self-identity, the disciple now functions as an instrument of the path. There is no personal goal, only a deep, wordless understanding that everything unfolds exactly as it should.

Tourist
This final chapter warns against complacency. Many seekers mistake partial insight for completion, becoming spiritual tourists who collect experiences rather than fully surrendering to the path. The disciple must remain vigilant against subtle egoic reintegration.

SUBJECT
How the Realised Alchemist Moves Through the World

Experiment
Even after deep realisation, the process never truly ends. The disciple must now test their insights in real-world situations, learning how enlightenment expresses itself through action.

APPENDIX

Metanoia
A radical shift in perception occurs. What once seemed real now appears illusory, and vice versa. This chapter explores how the disciple adapts to this new way of seeing.

Cycles of Learning
Spiritual progression is not linear. Old insights must be revisited from new levels of awareness. What was once difficult to understand now appears obvious, yet new subtleties emerge.

Inner Worlds
Perception itself is a construct, arising from mental conditioning. This chapter examines how states of consciousness create the experience of reality.

Cultivating the Way
Enlightenment is not an end point but a way of being. The disciple must continue deepening their wisdom and refining their actions, ensuring they remain aligned with the path.

Dreams of Destiny
A discussion of intuition, synchronicity, and the sense of being guided. The disciple experiences a flow of events that seem orchestrated by a deeper intelligence.

The Way In, The Way Out
Different traditions describe the same process in different metaphors. This chapter explores commonalities between mystical traditions, showing how all roads lead to the same realisation.

Alien
Having seen through the illusion of the world, the disciple now struggles to relate to ordinary people. They feel like an alien in their own society.

Dojo
A reflection on the importance of spiritual training grounds. The disciple recognises that life itself is the real dojo, where training never ends.

Two Roads
A decision arises: should the realised one retreat from society or engage with the world? This chapter explores the two possible paths after awakening.

A New Kind of Confidence
True confidence arises not from ego but from deep understanding. The realised practitioner moves through the world with certainty but without arrogance.

The Prodigal Self
The journey comes full circle. The disciple, having seen through all illusion, returns to the world—not as a seeker, but as one who simply is.

Albedo **is purification, but not completion. The next stage,** *Citrinitas*, **represents the maturation of wisdom—where perception moves beyond conditioned consciousness entirely. The work is not yet finished—but the way forward is clear.**

Nigredo

Black Cloak

APPENDIX

Black Cloak

I've fallen out of favour.
I don't know what to do.
My overlords of high esteem.
Have left me all a-blue.

I tried my best, I really did.
Despite the vague instruction.
I manned the trench, whilst others fell.
And witnessed their destruction.

"Healer-priest thy role is set,
To push beyond mundanity."
Yet when I rose to face the dark.
They feared my new profanity.

Now my tools are grief and loss,
I side with all that's bleak.
My trials are over, the damage done.
A purpose must I seek.

I have no edge, no cut nor thrust.
My power is extinguished.
Yet here I am, without my light.
Identity relinquished.

What role am I now all is gone?
Abandoned and defenceless.
Yet here I am, without my light.
One who wields the darkness.

www.drsimonrobinson.com

NIGREDO

"Patience is the strength of the stone. Discipline is the fire that shapes it."

— *Hermetic proverb (traditional attribution)*

APPENDIX

ABOUT THE AUTHOR

Simon Robinson has spent a lifetime navigating the space between reason and the unknown. Trained in medicine at the University of Manchester (1994), he built a career spanning anaesthesia, general practice, and medical hypnosis, earning fellowships from the Royal College of Anaesthetists (London, 2003) and the Australian College of General Practitioners (Brisbane, 2011). Yet beneath the structure of professional success, a deeper restlessness stirred—one that no title, career path, or certainty could settle.

That restlessness first lay dormant, tempered by the demands of training and the constant movement through hospitals in Manchester, Cambridge, Chester, Torquay, Crewe, Melbourne, Sydney, Brisbane, and Rockhampton. But when the time came to finally settle, the weight of certainty felt heavier than uncertainty ever had. Depression followed—a rupture that didn't break him, but instead, set him in motion again. The search for something beyond the boundaries of conventional truth became the only path forward.

Now based in Scarborough, UK, Robinson writes with a simple intention: to share the wisdom that dissolves suffering. His work is not about offering answers, but about lighting the way for those who, like him, have searched for something more.

Beyond his personal journey, Simon is a founding and active member of the Wordbotherers—a vibrant collective of authors and poets nestled in rural North Yorkshire. Through this platform, he regularly shares his writings, offering readers a diverse tapestry of stories and reflections. Explore more of his work and the collective's literary endeavours at https://wordbotherers.com.

Nigredo